The African American Religious Experience in America

Recent Titles in
The American Religious Experience
Philip Goff, Series Editor

The Buddhist Experience in America
Diane Morgan

The New Religious Movements Experience in America
Eugene V. Gallagher

The Latter-day Saint Experience in America
Terryl L. Givens

The African American Religious Experience in America

Anthony B. Pinn

The American Religious Experience
Philip Goff, Series Editor

Greenwood Press
Westport, Connecticut • London

Library of Congress Cataloging-in-Publication Data

Pinn, Anthony B.
 The African American religious experience in America / Anthony B. Pinn
    p. cm.—(The American religious experience)
 Includes bibliographical references and index.
 ISBN 0-313-32585-5 (alk. paper)
    1. African Americans—Religion. I. Title. II. Series: American religious
experience (Greenwood Press (Westport, Conn.))
 BL625.2.P56 2006
 200'.89'96073—dc22   2005018674

British Library Cataloguing in Publication Data is available.

This book is included in the *African American Experience*
database from Greenwood Electronic Media. For more
Information, visit www.africanamericanexperience.com.

Library of Congress Catalog Card Number: 2005018674
ISBN: 0-313-32585-5

First published in 2006

Greenwood Press, 88 Post Road West, Westport, CT 06881
An imprint of Greenwood Publishing Group, Inc.
www.greenwood.com

Printed in the United States of America

The paper used in this book complies with the
Permanent Paper Standard issued by the National
Information Standards Organization (Z39.48-1984).

10 9 8 7 6 5 4 3 2 1

To Rev. Anne H. Pinn (1931 — 2005)

Contents

Series Foreword

Philip Goff

Some years ago, Winthrop Hudson, a leading religious historian, began his survey book on religion in America with a description of a London street. "When Americans walk down the street of an English city," he wrote, "they will be reminded of home."[1]

Few would dispute that for many years this was the case. Multiple faith traditions in today's United States trace their roots to English lineage, most notably the Episcopal, Methodist, and Baptist churches. But that sort of literary device would not hold up under the pressure of today's diversity. Lutherans, Presbyterians, and Dutch Reformed adherents would balk at such oversimplification—and those are just a few among only the Protestant Christians. Add the voices of Jews, Eastern Orthodox, Muslims, Buddhists, and Irish, Italian, and Polish Catholics, and we would have a powerful chorus demanding their stories be told. And their stories do not begin on the streets of London.

Of course, Hudson knew that was the case. His point was not that all significant American religions began in England, but that, "with only a few exceptions, the varied religious groups of America have their roots abroad."[2] But clearly the "abroad" Hudson worked with was predominantly European, even if not entirely English. Today's scholarship has broadened that focus to include African, Asian, Central and South American, as well as Canadian and some "home grown" traditions that are on their way to becoming worldwide faiths. If ever scholarship in American religion has reflected the lineage of its people, it is in the recent writings that have moved beyond conventional ideas of faith traditions to include non-Anglo peoples who, while often existing off the radar screen of the establishment, have nonetheless formed much of the marrow of American religious life.

Although our studies of American religion have expanded to include more migrating faith groups from more areas of the world, the basic question that divided historians early in the twentieth century remained: namely, are traditions of American life (religion, politics, economics, etc.) transplants from the Old World, or did something entirely new and unique form in the New World? That is, should we seek to comprehend America's present religious scene by understanding its roots? Or should we try to understand it by looking at its transformations?

Of course, the truth lies somewhere in between. One cannot understand present-day Methodists or Buddhists by knowing their Old World beginnings in England and China or Japan. Nor can one determine the transformations those faith traditions underwent in America without knowing a good deal about their Old World forms. The American experience, then, is one of constancy of tradition from one angle and continual revision from another. The fact that they may look, think, and sound different than their Old World forms does not negate the fact that they are still recognizably Methodist and Buddhist in their new contexts.

This book series is meant to introduce readers to the basic faith traditions that characterize religious life today by employing that continuum of constancy and change. Each volume traces its topic from its Old World beginnings (when they apply) to its present realities. In doing so, readers will see how many of the original beliefs and practices came to be, as well as how they transformed, remained nearly the same, or were complemented by new ones in the American environment. In some cases—African Americans and Mormons most clearly—the Old World proved important either implicitly or imaginatively rather than explicitly and literally. But even in these cases, development within the context of American culture is still central to the story.

To be sure, each author in this series employed various approaches in writing these books. History, sociology, even anthropology all play their parts. Each volume, then, may have its idiosyncrasies, as the authors chose which approaches worked best at which moments for their respective topics. These variations of approach resemble the diversity of the groups themselves, as each interacted in various ways at different stages with American society.

Not only do these volumes introduce us to the roots and development of each faith group, they also provide helpful guides to readers who wish to know more about them. By supplying timelines and glossaries, the books give a deeper sense of beliefs, behaviors, and significant figures and moments in those religions. By offering resources for research—including published primary and secondary sources as well as helpful web sites—the series presents a wealth of helpful information for formal and informal students of religion in America.

Clearly, this is a series conceived and published with the curious reader in mind. It is our hope that it will spur both a deeper understanding of the varieties of religious experience in the United States and better research in the country's many and always changing traditions.

Notes

1. Winthrop Hudson, *Religion in America*, 4th ed. (New York: Macmillan, 1987), 11.

2. Ibid., 11–12.

Acknowledgments

This book has been roughly four years in the making. Over the course of those years, I have received the support and encouragement of numerous friends and colleagues. While I cannot mention them all by name, I must thank my friends and colleagues at Williams College. During the spring of 2004, I was the Sterling Brown Visiting Professor of Religious Studies and, while I was in Williamstown, my colleagues in African American Studies and Religious Studies—particularly Denise Buell—gave me an intellectually and socially comfortable space in which to work. (Fred and Mark, from the car service, provided intriguing commentary and insights during those numerous rides to the airport in Albany. Thanks!) In addition, I was the Lynette S. Autry Visiting Professor of Humanities at Rice University (the institution I now call "home") during the spring of 2003. My colleagues there were kind and generous, and such a welcoming environment made it easy to complete a good deal of work on this project. I extend my gratitude to the folks in the Religious Studies Department as well as colleagues in other divisions of the university: Caroline Levander, Edward Cox, Alexander Byrd, and John Boles.

I am fortunate to have a number of excellent graduate students at Rice University, and I would like to take this opportunity to thank them—Torin Alexander, Paul Easterling, and Derek Hicks—for their challenging questions and comments. I would also like to thank my student and research assistant, Stephen Finley, for the charts and graphs he developed for this project, as well as the other ways in which he helped me complete this work.

Although I no longer teach at Macalester College, I remain in touch with good friends there. They have made my frequent trips back to the Twin Cities enjoyable, encouraging my work and keeping me balanced. My thanks to Calvin Roatzel for his wise counsel. Thanks to Ramón,

Robbie, and John for dinner, pool, and lots of laughs. Other friends, really brothers, away from Minnesota continue to provide strength and counsel. Benjamin and Eli, good "lookin' out"! (By the way, "text messages" boyyyeee!) I am also grateful for assistance received from Claude Jacobs and Bishop William Stokes.

I would like to extend my gratitude to my family, particularly my mother and my wife, CJ, for their encouragement over the years.

Finally, I must thank my friend, Philip Goff, who is the editor of the series through which this book is published, for his challenging comments and insightful suggestions on an early draft of the manuscript. I would also like to thank my editor at Greenwood Press, Kevin Downing, for humor and patience.

Thanks to all! And while these individuals and others helped me complete this volume in numerous ways, I alone am responsible for any errors it contains.

A Note on Language

Readers will note that I use the term African when referring to the black presence in North America prior to the Emancipation Proclamation and the Civil War. After that time, I use African American. I do so because I believe it is only after this war and its sociopolitical ramifications that those of African descent and white Americans are forced to begin thinking about a diverse citizenship, composed of more than the descendants of European colonists. In light of this, it is only as a result of this forced reevaluation of the population of the United States that one can rightly think of Africa's descendants in North America as having an identity marked by both worlds—Africa and North America.

Introduction

For a good number of years I have taught students about the nature and meaning of African American religion: how it develops, what shapes and informs it, and how it is expressed in word and deed. In providing courses that address these dimensions of African American religion and religious experience, I have concerned myself with presenting the material in ways that focus attention on the vibrant and complex nature of both the form of religion and its content. In short, rather quickly, students come to realize that there is no African American *religion*. Instead, it is more accurate to assert the presence of African American *religions*. But what else should one expect to encounter?

Over the course of centuries, African Americans have developed theologies and religious practices that respond to the "big" questions of life: What is the nature of existence? Who am I? Why am I here? What sense can be made of collective pain and suffering? And so on. These religious practices and their supporting theological doctrines come in a variety of forms and respond to the needs of particular segments of the overall African American population. Some of these traditions are theistic—committed to a belief in God or gods—but this type of belief is not the litmus test for religion. For some African Americans, belief in god(s) is not the basis of their religious experience.

The religious landscape of African American communities is "thick," that is, complex and diverse. This being the case, how best does one understand it, explore it, come to understand what frames African American religious experience? In short, how does one describe or present African American religious experience in ways that capture its complexity and diversity?

This book is a response to these basic questions in that it provides important descriptive information concerning various forms of African

American religious experience. While no one book can cover all modes of religious experience within such a diverse community, this text seeks to bring into relief some of the more prominent traditions. Each chapter is arranged in such a way as to provide readers with a snapshot of the origins of the particular tradition, the nature of African American participation, and the general beliefs held by most adherents.

With the structure of each chapter briefly noted, a word should be added concerning how this introductory text is framed. Let me begin by reiterating a basic point: African American communities are diverse, made up of people with competing philosophical, sociopolitical, and economic perspectives and levels of obtainment. Another level of diversity involves the ways in which African Americans express themselves religiously—their religious experience. These complexities only intensify in that the religious landscape of African American communities is thick with a variety of traditions. While African Americans claim them all, none are embraced solely by African Americans. For African Americans, like others involved in the traditions highlighted here, participation is based on the appeal and usefulness of how particular traditions respond to the big questions of life.

Even historically black churches, while predominantly African American in membership, are not strictly African American in composition. Predominantly white denominations also claim a diverse membership, composed of African Americans, Latinos(as), and so on. Furthermore, traditions such as Voodoo and Santería claim adherents from a variety of racial and ethnic groups. In addition, African American communities house members of Eastern traditions such as Buddhism. This is all to say that African Americans share religious traditions with a variety of other groups. Put differently, African American Lutherans or Baptists or practitioners of African-based religions such as Voodoo are not necessarily different from participants from other racial or ethnic groups on the level of doctrine or even style of worship (i.e., the style of dress, the way songs are sung, and so on). African American Lutherans, Presbyterians, Episcopalians, Roman Catholics, and so on are not different from their white counterparts in any doctrinally or ritually significant way. Hence, the ability to claim a tradition, or even the way in which a tradition is expressed in worship, is not what makes unique religious expression in African American communities. Rather, it is often the case that what marks African American participation in Christian denominations and the other religions discussed in this volume is the unique nature of their struggle for inclusion, and the ways in which this struggle for equal footing within a given tradition is shaped by the sociohistorical conditions that have influenced African American communities. Highlighted, then, in this volume is the development of African American participation in various religious faiths based on a struggle against exclusion.

Readers will come to recognize the blending of religious worlds that marks African American religious experience—Europe, Africa, and so on. Beginning with discussions that date back to the early African presence in the Americas and moving forward, attention is given to historical development, along with some information on basic doctrinal and ritual sensibilities that inform the expression of each tradition. Depth is given to historical presentation through a separate section, late in the book, providing biographical sketches of some of key figures, as well as through the primary documents contained in the appendices. A timeline of important events related to particular traditions, a bibliography of selected text for further study, and a glossary round out the book.

I am not so bold as to believe that readers can walk away from this book arguing that they know what it means to be African American and religious. But I do believe the snapshots presented here will give readers a sense of the richness and complexity of African American religious experience. It is my hope that the book will help readers avoid some of the pitfalls, the oversimplifications, marking too many discussions of African American religious traditions and religious experience. If nothing else, readers will finish this text with a basic understanding of and an appreciation for the reality of African American religious expression: African American religion comes in a variety of forms, all of them vital, and religious African Americans share their religious worldviews and practices with communities of believers that extend well beyond the borders of the African American religious landscape.

Not all the traditions discussed in this book are considered to have significant numbers of African American participants. But inclusion in this volume is not limited to traditions with the involvement of large numbers of African Americans. The aim is to present a range of examples, a variety of ways in which African Americans express themselves religiously. In this regard, demonstration of the diversity of practices—some of them obvious and others less often noticed—is more significant than the number of African American participants. In this way, a more textured and detailed "mapping" of the African American religious landscape is possible. The arrangement of the chapters is not at all intended to convey a perception of importance to any of the various traditions. The traditions have equal importance. After general information (the first two chapters), the chapters on the religious communities are in alphabetical order.

While this book will not answer all questions concerning African American religious experience, it is a beginning. If nothing more, I hope it will generate new questions and insights, based on a deeper level of recognition and appreciation.

Chapter 1

Historical Context of the African American Religious Experience

Dark Laborers and the Issue of Religion: Enslaved Africans

Contact between Africans and the English took place long before the development of the slave trade.[1] During the mid-sixteenth century English travelers began trading with Africans and writing descriptions of the people encountered. It is safe to say that the English (and Africans) noted differences in appearance and practice. Physical bodies, as philosopher Cornel West argues, were soon implicated by and attached to the negative connotations of "blackness" and the positive connotations of "whiteness." So for the English, whose idea of beauty depended on paleness, Africans represented a people unattractive and with odd practices. At their worst, differences in appearance, social habits, and cultural production were interpreted by the English in ways that painted Africans as of less human value and fitted for hard labor.

Understanding themselves to be "civilized," colonists reasoned that Africans must be uncivilized and deserving of the poor treatment and little attention to the cultivation of the inner self they received. This is not to say that English colonists conceived of other Europeans as their equals. Africans, however, were distinguishable in ways other Europeans were not, and this made the degrading of Africans relatively easy to justify. Tied to this difference and degradation was often a sense that Africans were religiously "heathenistic" while the Puritans and other colonists possessed the "truth" to the extent that they were Christian (and English).

Africans began to arrive in the North American colonies as a source of labor in 1619. It was not until some years later when England officially entered the slave trade that Africans began to serve for life in extremely large numbers. With time, it became standard that Africans were regarded as property for life and through all generations, not as

Opening to slave holding area at Emina, in Ghana.

human beings of the same order as Europeans. Africans were distinguished in name—Negar or Negro—and by physical appearance.[2]

The presence of *enslaved* Africans in New England is first noted in Boston and is dated to the 1630s.

Although one might speculate that trading in slaves was a practice more likely associated with southern colonies, some in New England began trips to Africa to gain slaves as early as the 1640s. Prior to the eighteenth century, the number of slaves in the Puritan colonies was fairly small, less than ten percent of the total population.

In spite of the slave trade's being a rather dangerous undertaking, Massachusetts merchants took the lead in New England, supplying New Englanders as well as southerners with enslaved Africans. It was not uncommon to read advertisements such as the following in local papers:

To be Sold on reasonable Terms a Negro Man aged about 26 years, and a Negro Boy aged about 14 years, and a Negro Woman aged about 24 years and her child, to be seen at Mr. James Pecher's House in Salem Street Boston.[3]

The financial gain attached to trade—sugar, rum, molasses, and slaves— allowed New England to make up for its inability to produce agricultural goods to the same degree achieved in southern colonies.[4]

Beyond legal rationales and economic need, some provided another rationale for the utilization of slave labor. This theological rationale would gain ground and in some respect be "perfected" by southerners. Yet even among some northerners, the enslavement of Africans was jus-

Gate leading to the boat used to transport enslaved Africans.

tified in that slavery had biblical precedence and divine sanction. Assuming slaves were descendants of the biblical figure Ham, who was the son of Noah, and Ham's son, Canaan, some pointed to the following scriptural story in support of African slavery:

> Noah was the first tiller of the soil. He planted a vineyard; and he drank of the wine, and became drunk, and lay uncovered in his tent. And Ham, the father of Canaan, saw the nakedness of his father, and told his two brothers outside. . . . When Noah awoke from his wine and knew what his youngest son had done to him, he said, "Cursed be Canaan; a slave of slaves shall he be to his brother."[5]

For many slave owners, slaves had no need for religion because they had no soul to save. In this respect, enslaved Africans were considered of no more importance or value than cattle. They were chattel. Some colonists understood themselves to be responsible for spreading the Gospel, yet this did not translate into effective work with enslaved Africans.

Christianization of Slaves in the North

Resistance to the evangelizing of slaves often centered on a fear that such efforts would result in slaves thinking of themselves as equal to their owners and in this way becoming disobedient and dangerous. Others argued that Africans were not intellectually capable of understanding the scriptures and church doctrine. Cut throughout these arguments was a concern that converting slaves could topple the delicate hierarchy and rationale for slavery.

For some colonists, these concerns created a tension but did not destroy completely a concern with the religious needs of Africans. In fact, many saw slavery as an opportunity to bring Africans into a proper understanding of God's word; in this way, they added to the Kingdom of God by converting the lost.[6] Africans, the argument went, were capable of understanding the Gospel if it were presented to them—being essentially the same as Europeans in all the important ways and possessing, more importantly, a soul. However, many who advocated religious instruction for slaves understood that this conversion would not disrupt the system of slavery. In fact, acquaintance with the Christian faith would make for better slaves because they would understand the divine plan and their place within it. Put simply, obedience to God required obedience to human authority. Historian Albert Raboteau provides a glimpse of this inequality within the context of Christian community when saying, "In New England meetinghouses the slaves listened to sermons segregated in galleries, corners, or rear pews. When black Puritans died they were still segregated from whites in graveyards. Black church members were generally not allowed to participate in church government."[7]

For many influential colonists in the North such as Cotton Mather of Massachusetts, God placed Africans under the control of Puritans as part of a providential plan, and this fostered a responsibility that Puritans must accept with all sincerity and seriousness. Because God ultimately controlled the destiny of each human, Christians could not afford to neglect any soul. Again we come to the religious rationale for the Puritan presence in the New World and their contacts with peoples of color in the New World: conversion of sinners. From the perspective of slave-owning Puritans, it was an act of kindness and spiritual sensitivity to enslave the body and free the heathen's soul. In order to accomplish this end, Mather suggested that the children of slave owners or capable white servants teach Africans church doctrine. This system of instruction was impractical in most cases, and in such cases he urged colonists to hire educators. In spite of whatever efforts existed, few Africans received fellowship into Puritan churches.

It is safe to say that some Africans found the style and content of Puritan doctrine less than appealing, and this also may account for the small numbers to some extent. Yet it is also important to remember that the Puritan version of the Christian faith required access to the written word and time for reflection. Slaves were not taught to read, and they had limited leisure time. Another difficulty preventing large-scale participation was the strict regulations concerning church membership—new conduct related to a new relationship with God. Enslaved Africans were not given control over their affairs. From the perspective of slave owners, strong moral and ethical convictions lived out by slaves could harm the system of slavery, when they were not simply irrelevant. It is likely that many slave owners feared the ramifications of Africans being exposed to the "freeing" potential of the scriptures and being encouraged to think, even on religious issues.

Thinking slaves are dangerous slaves, and dangerous slaves will not remain content to provide free labor. Even if the slave system could survive the Christianization of slaves, church services and instruction would result in lost labor time. Even worse, because only "heathens" could be enslaved, conversion of Africans would implicitly require Puritans and other slaveholders to free them because Christians should not hold other Christians in bondage. Puritans and other Christian slaveholders faced a dilemma. Religious instruction might result in economic loss and the destruction of the social fabric that held people in their allotted spaces, but failure to spread the Gospel meant disobedience to God's call for the evangelizing of the lost.

Christianization of Slaves in the South

In southern areas, the Society for the Propagation of the Gospel in Foreign Parts gave notable attention to converting slaves after 1702. This organization, a wing of the Anglican Church, made quite clear the beneficial relationship between Christianizing slaves and the economics of slaveholding. Preachers associated with the Society for the Propagation of the Gospel argued that a proper relationship with God would in fact encourage slaves to accept the existing social order as part of God's ultimate plan for human community. Society preachers were sympathetic to the slave system in their sermons and slave instruction by advocating the benefits of conversion as a tool by which to create more loyal slaves. It was argued that service to God first required good service to earthly authority. Using this theological justification of the slave system, while teaching the catechism through memorization, Society missionaries (the few there were) worked southern plantations. Although mission efforts are marked by what some considered success, in general these early efforts were less than productive. Memorizing the catechism proved difficult, and teaching slaves to read and write was forbidden by law.

The colonies would not experience large-scale conversion, of both Europeans and Africans, until the first Great Awakening.

Beginning in the 1730s, a series of revival meetings and a general ethos of spiritual renewal emerged and gave shape to what we have come to call the Great Awakening. This widespread push toward righteousness gave strong attention to a type of conversion marked by fantastic spiritual breakthrough, expressed in strong emotional terms.

Baptist and Methodist evangelists traveled and preached this return to God, bringing into their various churches both the bound and the free. Beyond the initial impact of the Great Awakening, it is estimated that as many as ten thousand Americans of African descent joined Methodist churches between 1786 and 1790, and Baptist churches claimed roughly twenty thousand members of African descent during this same period.[8] This first Great Awakening was matched by a second wave of religious revivals in the early 1800s, this time focused on the middle portion of the country, or the frontier, as it was known. It is believed that between 1846 and 1861 the African membership of Methodism increased to some two hundred thousand members, and the number of African Baptists increased from two hundred thousand to roughly four hundred thousand.

Why were Methodist and Baptist evangelists so effective in converting enslaved Africans? These traveling preachers displayed an ability to address the geographical and attitudinal demands of the South. Furthermore, and of great importance, their theology and style of religious practice entailed a concern with individual salvation, marked by an expressed relationship with God, as opposed to the more formal attention to church structures and policies promoted by Anglican preachers. This religious individualism of sorts also promoted an understanding of God's working in the human heart that made it possible for anyone to preach the Gospel. The demands of literacy required by Anglicans was superseded by a desire or calling from God to ministry as the requirement for preaching in Methodist and Baptist churches.

The aesthetics of worship within Baptist and Methodist circles may have reminded those of African descent of ritual practices and theological sensibilities associated with Africa. For example, the practice of water baptism in Baptist churches may have held links for enslaved Africans to the water rituals and spirits associated with some West African religious traditions. Related to this, the emotional worship associated with Methodist and Baptist revivals might have been a pleasant connection to the practice of spirit possession also found within many African-based religious traditions. Also of importance is the manner in which the preachers' fiery sermons pricked the conscience of slaveholders who became increasingly concerned with their own salvation and the spiritual welfare of those around them.

Enslaved Africans began to play a role seldom known prior to this period: preaching the Gospel. Preaching the Gospel was not limited to those with formal training, nor was it limited to whites. Throughout the areas touched by the great revivals, and in areas without restrictions concerning black preachers, those of African descent proclaimed the Gospel to both whites and blacks.

Clearly, as a result of revival fervor, some slave owners understood the importance of converting enslaved Africans. This understanding often was enacted in passive ways, however, such as including "house slaves" in church activities and family prayer. This passive approach was not enough. Preachers suggested that enslaved Africans receive more than just Sunday acquaintance with the teachings of Jesus Christ. The Christianization of the enslaved had to reach more extensively into the life of Africans through plantation missions such as those established by Presbyterian minister Charles C. Jones.

Plantation-based missions were particularly important because they afforded an opportunity to worship on a regular basis to those who lived far from existing churches. In addition to making church attendance geographically convenient, Jones also promoted the spreading of the Gospel message through print media. He, like others before him, met with resistance because slaveholders feared mission activities would ultimately enhance the spiritual welfare of slaves and also harm the stability of the slave system through abolitionist "talk." That is to say, preachers might lace their conversation with abolitionist appeals for the end of slavery. As was the case earlier, missionaries made an effort to ease such worries by respecting existing prohibitions against slave literacy and by preaching a theology that maintained the social status quo—obedient slaves, prosperous slaveholders.

Concluding Thoughts: The "Africanization" of American Religion

Implied in this chapter is a tale of limited and paranoid effort to bring opportunity for religious experience to enslaved Africans. Efforts do not take systematic form until the 1700s, and from that time to the Civil War and the end of slavery in 1865, there was energetic debate over the merit of Christianizing enslaved Africans. This ethos of reluctance, combined with the critique offered by slaves of the hypocrisy present in evangelization by slave system–supporting preachers, held strong consequences.

Not all those of African descent, whether free or bound, responded to this Christianizing process in the same way. For some, the hardships of enslavement created an absurd world that could only be responded to by rejecting all traditional forms of religious practice and embracing practices that did not give consideration to the idea of a God or gods. In addition, it is likely that some of the Africans brought to North American colonies were familiar with Christianity based on its long presence in Africa, and the transition to Christian practice in the colonies was fairly easy. Some encountered Christianity for the first time and embraced it, with modifications to meet their particular needs within their unique social context. Others combined Christianity with traditional African practices and developed religious systems that greatly resembled belief systems such as Vodu and Santería. Still others maintained as best they could the Islamic faith they carried from Africa.

Africans in the North American colonies—as was also the case in other areas of the New World—forged a complex and multilayered religious life. Hence, to understand African American religious experience as it has developed over almost four centuries requires attention to a variety of religious practices and sensibilities. In the next chapter, this process of exploration begins with a survey of the varieties of African American religious experience that will be examined in more detail beginning in Chapter 3.

Notes

1. This chapter is an extension of the historical portrait provided in Anthony B. Pinn and Anne H. Pinn, *Fortress Introduction to Black Church History* (Minneapolis: Fortress Press, 2001), introduction. Copyright © 2002 Augsburg Fortress. Used by permission.

2. For information on this see Cornel West, *Prophesy Deliverance! An Afro-American Revolutionary Christianity* (Philadelphia: Westminster Press, 1982), chap. 2.

3. From the *Boston News Letter*, August 25, 1718. Quoted in Lorenzo Johnston Greene, *The Negro in Colonial New England* (New York: Atheneum, 1969), 40.

4. See Greene, *The Negro in Colonial New England*, 15–24.

5. Revised Standard Version (RSV) Genesis 9:20–22; 24–25.

6. Cotton Mather, "The Negro Christianized: An Essay to Excite and Assist That Good Work, the Instruction of Negro-Servants in Christianity" (Boston, 1706), quoted by Alden T. Vaughan, ed., *The Puritan Tradition in America: 1620–1730* (New York: Harper and Row, 1972), 268.

7. Albert Raboteau, *Slave Religion: The "Invisible Institution" in the Antebellum South* (New York: Oxford University Press, 1978), 110.

8. Ibid., 131.

Chapter 2

Development of the African American Religious Experience

The Formation of African American Religions

Africans enslaved and brought to the North American colonies came from culturally rich communities, vibrant with sociopolitical, economic, and religious life.[1] While the angst of the Middle Passage, the voyage from the coast of West Africa to the New World, and the accompanying destruction of cultural groups through the dispersement of slaves to various locations made substantial retention of African cultural practices such as religious ritual difficult, Africans maintained certain practices as distinct and combined others with the religious and social realities encountered.

Drawing from African and European signs, symbols, myths, and rituals, enslaved Africans in North America forged systems of meaning. The content of these systems found expression in many forms including music, decorative arts, folk tales, and religion. It is the last form, religion, that gives us perhaps our best vantage point from which to note the development of blacks in relationship to themselves, others, and the expansive universe. Wrestling with these relationships gave rise over time to religious forms located in and articulated through the black churches, Voodoo, and participation in other modes of religious experience, not all of which initially were developed within the context of black communities.

The Varieties of African American Religious Experience

The Africanization of Christianity

Those who sought to shape the Christian faith in ways that responded to their existential condition and spiritual needs developed what is commonly referred to as the "Invisible Institution." This term is used as a reference to the secret religious meetings held by enslaved Africans, also called hush arbor meetings, during which they worked out religious symbols, myths, and doctrine. Although the secret nature of these meetings explains a lack of detail concerning them, accounts collected through the early twentieth-century Workers Project Administration (WPA) provide some sense of what these meetings entailed.

Slaveholders considered even the most seemingly docile slaves potentially rebellious, and so an effort was made to know their whereabouts and activities at all times. One can imagine the danger involved in participation in these secret religious meetings. Those caught faced punishment, perhaps death, but for the spiritual experience these meetings entailed, many considered attending them worth the risk. One former slave described the happenings in the "prayin' ground down in the hollow." At times, he recounts, "we come out of the field, between 11 and 12 at night, scorchin' and burnin' up with nothin' to eat, and we wants to ask the good Lawd to have mercy. . . . We takes a pine torch . . . and goes down in the hollow to pray. Some gets so joyous they starts to holler loud and we has to stop up they mouth." The joy and excitement associated with this time of prayer away from the gaze of whites might cause some to "get so full of the Lawd and so happy they draps unconscious."[2]

At times the sense of religiosity embraced in the relative privacy of hush arbor meetings required a rejection of worldly activities such as dancing, drinking, and the playing of certain types of music. It was understood that living a Christian life required a denial of secular practices and an embrace of a strict lifestyle. Such a lifestyle required a recognizable conversion experience often entailing a long period of remorse over the sinfulness of one's behavior followed by surrender of old ways and an embrace of a more godly form of conduct.

It was often difficult to develop a sense of community in which such a degree of holiness could be practiced and nurtured. Participation in churches run by slaveholders did not always allow for the spiritual companionship necessary. As historian John Boles rightly notes, however, some churches, particularly evangelical churches such as the Methodists and Baptists, in the southern states allowed whites and blacks to share accountability and responsibility for shaping religious community and life. Boles argues that from their very beginning in the Old South, these churches claimed black members, and in some cases blacks signed (usually with an "X") the charters of these churches.[3] Boles writes:

> Baptists and Methodists welcomed black converts with open arms. Their worship services were integrated, with blacks sitting in the

Churches (though usually in the back pews or in the balcony), Hearing the same sermons, taking communion with whites, Participating in church discipline, even occasionally voting, and Being buried in the same cemeteries. Seeing blacks as souls to convert, The Baptists and Methodists in their openness to slaves as persons stood as an open rebuke to the planter aristocracy.[4]

This attempt at egalitarian community within the context of church life did not entail a sustained critique of slavery or efforts toward emancipation by southern Methodists and Baptists. They reasoned it was far better to have access to converting slaves to the Christian faith than to speak about slaves' physical freedom and forfeit opportunities for religious ministry. Boles provides a sympathetic analysis of this conservative social stance and liberal religious ethos. He does so by saying that, although the South was racist and slavery a troubling reality, blacks had a more liberated existence in churches than anywhere else in southern society. In other words, they were "participating in the church disciplinary procedures, testifying against whites and speaking on their own behalf in the face of white charges, and black testimony was apparently taken at its worth—this at a time when blacks could not testify against whites in the civil courts of the land. Slaves were held by the whites, and by the slaves themselves, to the same moral code as whites. Not only did this reinforce the bondsperson's sense of self-worth, but it provided an arena for moral growth and leadership." Furthermore, "blacks were occasionally appointed deacons, were often allowed to preach to mixed audiences, and were addressed in the church records (letters of admission and dismissal) the same as whites."[5] What Boles describes was far from absolute equality. Yet, what one finds is a strong black Christian community in fellowship, to some degree, with white Christians. Religion, to the degree possible within a racist society, eased social tensions within the context of evangelical churches in which all were God's children seeking "to make heaven their home."

Boles argues that the "Great Revival" of 1800–1805 sparked religious growth in the South in the same manner that the Great Awakening motivated religious commitment and excitement in New England and the Middle Atlantic area. He argues that this turn toward religious involvement evolved from an intense appeal to God for a change, for the "blessing of revival" and the righteousness it would promote.[6] This portrayal of religious life differs drastically from what is commonly thought. In fact, even for Boles, who suspected such developments even on a limited basis, there was a degree of astonishment associated with this discovery. In his words:

> I began reading church minutes from early Baptist churches especially. I was simply astonished to read of slave members, of slaves taking communion with whites, of slaves being admitted either by letter or by confession of faith, of blacks and whites being addressed as brother and sister, of blacks participating in church disciplinary hearings and even giving testimony in cases regarding whites. . . . I realized that the relationship of blacks and whites in the antebellum churches was more complex than I had been led to expect or would have ever imagined.[7]

Boles's point notwithstanding, the continued reluctance on the part of most to include those of African descent in the full workings of the church (and society) made the development of independent black churches more attractive and necessary. This was the case among free and enslaved Africans, north and south.

Clearly the invisible institution grew into visible black churches and gave expression to beliefs, desires, and sacred and secular goals of enslaved Africans and their descendants. Early black churches expressed, in fuller form, the nascent religious sensibilities and ritual structures forged during hush arbor meetings. At times outlawed and more frequently harassed, many of these early, independent churches increased their membership and maintained their autonomy even before the Emancipation Proclamation (1863). It is within these independent and visible church structures that much of what we currently recognize as the "Black Church Tradition" took shape.

What these churches represent is not just Christianity in African communities. They point also to the *africanization* of the Christian faith, by addressing the particular needs of Africans in America. Furthermore, they marked the soft presence of African structures through, for example, the importance of water baptism and spirit possession complete with "dancing in the spirit." Even understandings of conversion as a process or journey harken back to African understandings of initiation and secret societies. In both cases, for Africans in America and in Africa, religious renewal involves a struggle, a movement through time during which the person encounters challenges, until she or he ultimately gains new knowledge and relationship with spiritual forces and human community. In short, conversion in the context of black religion and initiation in the context of Africa both involve symbolic death and rebirth through which the individual releases old ways of being in the world and embraces new understandings of life and how it should be lived.

Baptist Churches

While records of the participation of Africans in white churches dates back to the 1600s, scholars believe the first independent churches, founded and run by Americans of African descent, developed in the 1700s. For example, historical records point to the development of a black Baptist church in the South as of 1750 (according to the church's cornerstone), named Silver Bluff Church (of Silver Bluff, South Carolina). Throughout the South and elsewhere, black Baptist churches developed because the style of worship and the theological commitments of the Baptist framework proved appealing. And numbers would continue to grow after the Emancipation Proclamation, as the "recently freed" exercised their independence in part through the selection of their religious affiliations. With time, these autonomous Baptist churches formed regional and, eventually, national conventions. Today there are numerous conventions bringing together Baptist congregations from across the country. The three largest are the National Baptist Convention, USA, Incorporated; the National Baptist Convention of America; and the Progressive National Baptist Convention. With a combined membership of over 12 million, these conventions claim a significant percentage of all African American Christians, and count among their number internationally known figures such as Reverend Jesse Jackson.

Methodist Churches

Black Baptist churches dominated the South, but in the North an early religious mark was made in black communities through the establishment of independent black Methodist congregations. The first such congregation was the Bethel Church founded by Richard Allen and others who left St. George's Methodist Episcopal Church (Philadelphia, Pennsylvania) in 1787 because of racism. This church was dedicated in 1794, having first taken the form of a Free African Society in 1787. Blacks had for a good number of years embraced Methodism in part because of the access to ministry and worship initiated by Methodist evangelists during the first Great Awakening. Perhaps this taste of religious liberty kept Allen within Methodism, hoping for an even fuller participation in the church. However, with time, subtle forms of discrimination became overt and proved too great a stumbling block to full Christian fellowship.

Once word spread through the region concerning the establishment of Bethel Church, other black Methodists with similar experiences sought to increase fellowship across geographic lines. What resulted was the development of the African Methodist Episcopal Church (AME)—the first black denomination in the country—in 1816. In New York, a similar development took place resulting in the African Methodist Episcopal Church Zion (AMEZ). The AME Church Zion started with the organization of the African Methodist Episcopal Church of the City of New York in 1801. A desire for organizational reach and strength resulted in the formation of a conference in 1821, and "Zion" was added to the name of the organization in 1848. Finally, in the South, in 1870, white Methodists encouraged the formation of an independent denomination composed of southern black Methodists. This new denomination, formed in order to avoid losing blacks to the AME and AMEZ churches, was named the Colored Methodist Episcopal (CME) Church (changed to the Christian Methodist Episcopal Church in the mid-twentieth century).

While there are differences with respect to political sensibilities and practice that separate the Baptist conventions, there are few differences worth noting regarding the Methodist denominations. The major difference concerns the nature and place of origin as opposed to deep doctrinal disagreement. This raises a question: Why three major black Methodist denominations, if they all believe the same thing?

Mindful of the merits of this question, recognition of the benefits of merger is long standing, and efforts to accomplish it date back to 1864 when AMEZ and AME representatives unsuccessfully met at Bethel Church in Philadelphia to consider the possibility of unification. Talks in the early twentieth century between the AMEZ Church and the CME Church seemed promising but were unsuccessful. Serious conversation did not resume until the period of the Civil Rights Movement, but not even the unification sparked by a common quest for racial justice was strong enough to pull these denominations together.

Conversations have historically stalled when representatives from the various Methodist groups could not work out, for example, critical issues such as the authority of bishops within a unified church. In the corporate world, mergers often entail downsizing, but would these churches be willing to reenvision the framework and size of the hierarchy in order to accommodate the merger? How would the resources of these three denominations be reallocated within the context of a new denomination, without some of them feeling as if they had given up more than others? Such questions continue to plague conversations concerning merger.

African American Pentecostals

Some years after the formation of these independent Baptist and Methodist churches, African American Pentecostal churches emerged. These churches developed through a blending of two primary concerns: (1) a deep relationship with God marked by an attempt to live a pure life—referred to as sanctification, and (2) a commitment to a step beyond salvation by which the believer received the Holy Spirit in keeping with scripture.

The theological and ritual differences between African American Pentecostal churches and the other denominations previously mentioned stem in significant ways from scripture. In the Acts of the Apostles, Pentecostals found these words, and used them to frame their understanding of the Holy Spirit's involvement in human life: "Seven weeks had gone by since Jesus' death and resurrection, and the Day of Pentecost had now arrived. As the believers met together that day, suddenly there was a sound like the roaring of a mighty windstorm in the skies above them and it filled the house where they were meeting. Then, what looked like flames or tongues of fire appeared and settled on their heads. And everyone present was filled with the Holy Spirit and began speaking in languages they didn't know, for the Holy Spirit gave them this ability."[8] The largest African American denomination to grow out of this push toward a holy life marked by the presence of the Holy Spirit (with evidence of "speaking in tongues" as on the Day of Pentecost) is the Church of God in Christ. Initially called the Church of God, it was founded, in 1896, by Charles Mason and Charles Jones. Based on what Mason referred to as the leading of the Lord, the name was changed in 1897 to Church of God in Christ.

From its beginnings, this Pentecostal movement produced numerous other denominations and independent Pentecostal churches, accounting for a significant percentage of the total number of African American Christians in the United States. To put it simply, at the end of the twentieth century, the Church of God in Christ had spawned numerous other denominations and claimed some five million members.

While Methodist, Baptist, and Pentecostal churches dominate the African American religious landscape, it must also be noted that many African Americans claim membership in predominantly white denominations. For example, there are better than two million African Americans in the Roman Catholic Church, with a legacy and connection to Roman Catholicism that extends back for a number of centuries. In addition, African Americans in Presbyterian churches such as missionary

Alexander Crummell during the nineteenth century and ethicist Katie G. Cannon in the late twentieth century have labored to reframe the work of that denomination in ways that speak in strong terms to the needs and condition of African American communities. The same holds true for African Americans in Episcopal churches and Lutheran churches.

The Varieties of African American Religious Experience

Blending of Traditions

There is another side to the great revivals, mentioned in Chapter 1, that sparked the development and growth of an Africanized Christianity. The success of fiery services associated with these revivals must not be overestimated. For example, as historian Margaret Washington Creel argues, the effect of these revivals among the Gullah of South Carolina was minimal. The challenge of converting slaves was amplified in areas such as coastal South Carolina, where mission efforts had little steam until the 1830s and faced the challenge of a large and somewhat insular African population. Even when mission work was marked by what some considered success, early efforts to Christianize enslaved Africans were less than productive because oppression of their flesh made status-quo depictions of the Gospel difficult for slaves to embrace. Albeit undeniably important and central to any understanding of African American religious culture in North America, churches do not tell the full story of African American religious experience.

Life in North America forced a certain type of angst through the negation of African humanity. In turn, this negation was confronted through religious experience and expression, a working through religious sensibilities, performance, and aesthetics for the purposes of an African population. In some instances this religious experience took the form of Christian faith and practice. In other cases it entailed a tenacious affirmation of African traditional religious practices.

The hush arbors, the secret meetings of enslaved Africans, which fostered Christianity that took shape in black churches also spawned a host of other religious traditions. If the hush arbor meetings were clandestine, as is the common belief, who can assume that these meetings served only to nurture Africanized Christian thought and practices? One must be mindful of other religious formulations. In other words, various religious practices lived together, some with more open expression than others. As historian Michael Gomez notes, there is substantial evidence suggesting religious practices outside church structures in the colonial and antebellum (prior to the Civil War) South. By the early 1800s, the vast majority of Africans living in the United States were born here rather than having arrived via the Middle Passage, thereby marking the emergence of cultural formations, including religion, which showed a polycultural dimension.

Again, the Middle Passage and the hardships of enslavement ruptured many aspects of life, most notably community and family as understood in West Africa. Yet these hardships did not completely destroy the cultural fabric of the life and worldview brought along in the memories of those sold into slavery. Evidence of this is present with respect to the religious sensibilities of many enslaved Africans. Work within the social sciences on material culture makes it difficult to think about religious practices in narrow ways. The decorative arts, as a case in point, speak to a cultural richness and religious complexity that should push one to think about religious thought and experience in multilayered ways. Too many slave quilts, for example, display signs and symbols that are easily associated with West African religious sensibilities and cosmology. This is certainly a reasonable assertion when one considers current thought on these quilts. As Bill Arnett, an authority on decorative culture, notes, "Every great quilt whether it be a patchwork, applique, or strip quilt is a potential Rosetta stone. Quilts represent one of the most highly evolved systems of writing in the New World. Every combination of colors, every juxtaposition or intersection of line and form, every pattern, traditional or idiosyncratic, contain data that can be imparted in some form or another to anyone." Why would not some of this "data that can be imparted in some form or another to anyone" speak to the religious memories enslaved Africans held that were not related to the Christianity they were reluctantly taught in the New World?[9]

As readers will come to discover, the religious history of enslaved Africans and their descendants is complex, layered, and nuanced. This complexity and "thickness" have been long recognized with respect to the Caribbean and South America, where the predominance of Roman Catholicism (and the cult of the saints) and the large number of Africans provided a religiously insular environment. Although more visible in these areas, the Caribbean and South America, such a complexity must also be acknowledged in North America.

If we are mindful of the fact that religious conversion in large numbers comes late to the North American colonies (the Great Awakenings), should we be satisfied to dismiss the presence of African gods and the practices they require simply because of a less-than-welcoming environment? No, material remains and recorded narratives speak to signs, symbols, and practices associated with West African cultural groups—Yoruba, Fon, Ewe, Dahomey, and others—that represent a grand and complex African religious culture on North American soil. It is likely that the Christian God replaced other representations of the African high God, but that does not mean lesser deities died or were completely consumed in the persons of Jesus Christ and the Holy Spirit.

What is meant here will become clear as readers move through the remaining chapters but, simply put, some Africans maintained religious and theological links to African belief systems through a continuing devotion to deities such as Shango, God of thunder, the ancestors, and lesser spirits associated with natural forces and the land. It was understood that attention to the gods, spirits, and ancestors was necessary to maintain a balanced life. But alterations in practice were necessitated by the differences between the environments (natural and social) of North America and Africa. Nonetheless, a deep reverence for the ancestors is attested to in the elaborate burial practices, which include leaving favored objects to be used by ancestors in the spirit world, as well as markings on gravesites found throughout African communities in America. This attention to the deceased is also associated with a belief in reincarnation and the interconnectedness of the physical and spiritual realms accessible through certain bodies of knowledge and practice prevalent in the belief system of slaves taken from the Akan and Igbo peoples of Africa.

Voodoo and Hoodoo

In areas such as Louisiana, Voodoo was produced through a combining of practices derived from Africa with the area's Catholic ethos. Some practitioners, figures like the priestess Marie Laveau, developed large followings and helped to shape a powerful cultural reality that remains very much alive in the "low country" and beyond. Hoodoo is a version of Voodoo focusing on magical practices that manipulate spiritual forces. It lacks Voodoo's cosmological complexity. Charms, amulets, and other religious materials attest to the thriving religious consciousness represented by Voodoo and Hoodoo. There are clear distinctions between these two. Concisely stated, Voodoo is more closely related to West African devotion to the Vodou or gods and Hoodoo involves a less ritually and theologically complex attention to root work, or conjure. Hoodoo is less formal cosmologically, and it is more concerned with magical manipulation of mundane items for the securing of protection or material gain or the alteration of problematic relationships. For example, concerning use of Hoodoo, one man says the following:

> I was hoodoo by a woman years ago. I was just crazy about her. I could not sleep or do anything for thinking about her. She would come to the house where I stayed and go and see everyone but me, knowing I wanted her to come to see me so bad. I just could not stand it, so one day I told a man about it, and he said, "You throw the hoodoo back on her and make her suffer. You go down the road, and the first bone you see, pick it up and hold it high above your head, and wish your bad luck on her while you are swinging that bone around your head three times." I did. After that I got all right and didn't care for the girl. And she got crazy about me, but I didn't care for her.[10]

In contrast, Voodoo is a complex system that is more concerned with every dimension of human life. Generally, Voodoo does not seek to harm or manipulate others for selfish aims. Rather, Voodoo is more concerned with the production of harmony and balance within the lives of practitioners.

Islam and the Nation of Islam

While it is an important dimension of African American religious life, the story of Voodoo and Hoodoo does not capture fully the richness of the African American religious landscape. For example, Allen Austin, a professor of African American Studies, writes that African Muslims traveled with Spanish explorers while other Muslims arrived as servants in Spanish Florida and Louisiana. There is also evidence to suggest that a good percentage of the Africans brought to the North American colonies were Muslims who maintained various dimensions of their faith. This presence is noted in advertisements for slaves with Islamic names such as "Mamado" (Mamadu).

Although those in North America did not have the religious knowledge necessary to document this Islamic presence in substantive ways, there are accounts of African Muslims such as Job Ben Solomon, a runaway slave, who could write and quote the Qur'an. There is also Bilali from Guinea who lived on Sapelo Island in Georgia. WPA interviews with Bilali's descendants speak about the continuation of Islamic practices by pointing to diet, prayer habits, the witness of faith, use of Arabic language, and the passing down of Islamic names to children. Such efforts to maintain the Islamic faith in the North American environment met with mixed success, at times resulting in a blending of Christianity and Islam through which Jesus, for example, was linked to Muhammad. The development of Islamic sensibilities continued beyond the antebellum period. To understand properly these more recent development, it is helpful to provide some context by placing Islamic teachings within the context of dissatisfaction with Christianity.

The late nineteenth and early twentieth centuries mark a significant migration of African Americans into northern (and southern) cities due to economic difficulties and sociopolitical oppression in the rural South and the promise of opportunity within urban areas. Upon arrival in cities such as Chicago, migrants found themselves economically frustrated and socially isolated. Many naturally turned to African American churches for assistance only to find that many of these churches were more interested in safeguarding their mainstream status than meeting the socioeconomic and spiritual needs of the new arrivals. Large numbers of migrants, complete with their "less refined" religious ways and economic difficulties, caused a strain on established churches. The churches responded to this strain by turning inward. This turn inward, a change in their posture toward the world and its problems, was marked by a preoccupation with individual salvation as opposed to an understanding of the Gospel of Christ as committed to spiritual and mundane betterment. It was not until the Civil Rights Movement that African American denominations gave renewed attention to a fuller range of human needs: spiritual growth, economic opportunity, social flexibility, and political voice.

In spite of these difficulties, some migrants developed a presence in mainline African American Methodist and Baptist denominations, and some moved into white denominations. Still others participated in the Pentecostal movement, or the Holiness churches. The latter differed from Pentecostal churches in that they, unlike their Pentecostal neighbors, did not insist on speaking in tongues as *the* sign of one's having the Holy Spirit. Some migrants found the goals of African American churches at odds with their lower economic and social standing as migrants during the period before and after World War I. They needed, then, a religious orientation or culture that better addressed their socioeconomic, spiritual, and political needs and questions.

Numerous religious opportunities developed. For example, the Moorish Science Temple (1913), founded by Timothy Drew, or Noble Drew Ali, took Christian principles and added an understanding of African Americans as Asiatic or Moors. Under the leadership of Noble Drew Ali, this organization encouraged a familiarity with non-Western thought. In fact, it was argued by members of this group that their teachings included the thought of Muhammad, Confucius, Buddha, and Jesus. The organizational goal was to rethink the position of African Americans based on a reconfigured relationship with the divine.

Other traditions, such as the Nation of Islam, emerged during this period and embraced a similar theological and cultural stance premised upon the divine election of African Americans and the demonic nature of current conditions. An accurate membership count is impossible. Yet, of the two—the Moorish Science Temple and the Nation of Islam—the latter has held a more consistent place in African American communities, in part through the fit between its nationalistic rhetoric and social critique and the growing frustration of African Americans with segregation and discrimination. From 1930, with the first appearance of Master Fard Muhammad, through the ministries of the Honorable Elijah Muhammad and Malcolm X (before Malcolm X left the Nation of Islam in 1964) to the current work by Minister Louis Farrakhan, the Nation of Islam has remained a deeply controversial religious and social force.

Whereas the Nation of Islam's status within the orthodox Islamic world is questionable, the Honorable Elijah Muhammad's son, Imam Warith Deen Muhammad, has worked to establish an "orthodox" African American Islamic community, one engaged in interreligious dialogue with the Roman Catholic Church and other traditions as well. The number of African Americans who have become Sunni Muslims over the past several decades is quite impressive, with estimates typically exceeding 1.5 million. In both cases, the "orthodoxy" of Warith Deen and the Nation of Islam under the leadership of Minister Farrakhan, African Americans participate in a religious ethos as old as the arrival of Islamic slaves such as Job Ben Solomon and Bilali.

Other Twentieth-Century Movements

Marcus Garvey's Universal Negro Improvement Association (UNIA) and its African Orthodox Church during the early twentieth century also provided a religious outlet, one that continued to embrace black pride and cultural nationalism that had marked the nineteenth century. Garvey, like Noble Drew Ali and Elijah Muhammad, argued that there was a profound link between people of African descent and what is best about the universe. Continuing this theme, according to Garvey, God would reestablish the greatness of Africa through the progressive activities of African Americans.

Garvey's movement, the Universal Negro Improvement Association, was the largest mass movement of African Americans in the history of the United States. The preamble to the UNIA's constitution is telling and worth quoting at length for what it says about the organization's philosophical and social orientation:

> The Universal Negro Improvement Association and African Communities League is a social, friendly, humanitarian, charitable, educational, institutional, constructive, and expansive society, and is founded by persons, desiring to the utmost to work for the general uplift of the Negro peoples of the world. And the members pledge themselves to do all in their power to conserve the rights of their noble race and to respect the rights of all mankind, believing always in the Brotherhood of Man and the Fatherhood of God. The motto of the organization is: One God! One Aim! One Destiny! Therefore, let justice be done to all mankind, realizing that if the strong oppress the weak confusion and discontent will ever mark the path of men, but with love, faith and charity toward all the reign of peace and plenty will be heralded in the world and the generation of men shall be called Blessed.[11]

Marcus Garvey's movement played a major role in the shaping of African American life during the twentieth century. Yet, there are other figures who did not achieve the same level of public attention, but who are important nonetheless. For instance, seldom discussed in any detail, the ministry of figures such as Father Hurley and Prophet Jones, within the Black Spiritual Movement, as well as Father Divine (The Peace Mission Movement) and Sweet Daddy Grace (The Universal House of Prayer for All Peoples) must be mentioned in this context. These four developed religious practices and sensibilities that responded to the socioeconomic hardships of the early to mid-twentieth century. Drawing on the Bible, numerology, Eastern traditions, and spiritual guides in some cases, these religious leaders forged connections between religiosity and materiality, spiritual health and physical well life.

While those traditions and practices briefly noted in the preceding text have on many levels maintained their visibility and vibrancy within African American communities, one cannot forget the impact of Buddhism on the religious landscape of African American communities. Like many in the United States during the late twentieth century, some African Americans turned to the East in search of religious experience that would make life in postmodern America bearable. This quest was premised on a simple dissatisfaction with the consumer-driven goals associated with the American Dream: Is there more to life than this? Through the New Age Movement and what has come to be called New

Religious Movements in more general terms, many Americans tapped into traditions such as Buddhism in search of a balanced life through spiritual discipline.

From entertainers such as Tina Turner to executives like Hip Hop mogul Russell Simmons, Eastern practices and sensibilities have proven themselves important structures for some African Americans seeking spiritual fulfillment and religious fitness. Concerning the importance of such practices, Simmons makes a comment that would undoubtedly ring true for those in this country who have found spiritual peace outside traditions typically recognized as a part of African American religious life. Simmons writes in his autobiography, "The practice of yoga changed my life. Over the past six years I've been practicing yoga, and in that time found a spiritual center to my life. My spiritual sense is stronger than ever, so the teachings of all the great religions sound good to me. The yoga practice of quieting the mind through asana practice, as well as meditation, is about clearing the mind of fluctuation so that you can one day know your true self. . . . My experiences with yoga have taught me the practice of finding God everywhere—especially within myself."[12]

Concluding Thoughts

What historian Gayraud Wilmore refers to as the "deradicalization of traditional black churches," the general movement away from social activism, encouraged the further development of alternate religious organizations and movements that drew from the rich religious resources that have marked African American communities for centuries. For example, the Nation of Islam and Pentecostal churches noted earlier developed during the twentieth century in part as a response to the needs of migrants and the reluctance of black churches to adjust their sensibilities and structures in order to address the changing nature of black life. It is also during this period of relative withdrawal from the pressing issues of black life by many black churches that African-based traditions such as Voodoo and Santería increased in visibility and geographic reach. Religious traditions coming from the Caribbean gained wider attention as many African Americans rejected the black church and embraced African-based traditions as a way of connecting themselves spiritually with Africa. An effort has been made through the teachings and practices of African-based traditions in African American communities to forge a strong self-consciousness that pushes African American identity beyond the confines of a slave past to the rich legacy of Africa.

This movement into African-based religious traditions such as Santería involved interaction with Latinas and Latinos who immigrated to the United States, bringing with them ritual and doctrinal expertise. Yet because much of the inner workings of Santería require knowledge of Spanish—if not the language of Santería's progenitor in Nigeria (Yorùbá)—some African Americans have felt discomfort with traditional Santería houses. Furthermore, some have sought to remove the Catholic elements found in Santería and replace them with more "authentic" presentation of the religion of the Yorùbá and other African cultural groups. A prime example of this is Oyotunji Village, in Sheldon, South Carolina, and its tradition of Orisa-Vodou. And while Orisa-Vodou is "dominated by the Yorùbá reality, there was also, however, a Dahomean and Congolese influence. According to Chief Ajamu [Minister of Foreign Relations for the Village], there is no conflict in incorporating these various cultural elements. The task of building a cultural complex that speaks directly to the needs of African Americans (a mixture of various African cultural groups) requires the blending of various cultural realities."[13]

Others explore the intersections between black church structure and the theology of traditions such as Voodoo in the form of black Spiritual churches that also grow in visibility during the final phases of the Great Migration in the mid- and late twentieth century. From northern states such as Michigan to communities in Louisiana, Spiritual churches have provided a means by which many African Americans continue a connection to the spiritual world, and in this way receive supernatural assistance with mundane problems. In both subtle and overt ways, Spiritual churches seek to contour what can be oppressive tendencies within U.S. society, and in this way provide a greater sense of self and a greater range of life options.

While African American religiosity is expressed in diverse ways, it is clear that the various manifestations of African American religion noted in this chapter, at their best, have provided African Americans with ways of forging new life options and relative security. Even the brief overview provided in this chapter points to the complexity and vitality of African American religious experience in the context of the United States. But it is not enough to simply recognize that religious experience comes in various forms and means of expression; it is also important to know something of the history, beliefs, and practices of these various expressions of religious commitment. In the following chapters, attention is given to a more detailed presentation.

Notes

1. This chapter involves a reworking of Anthony B. Pinn, "African American Religions in the US Context," an anchor essay in Gary Laderman and Luis León, eds., *Encyclopedia of Religion and American Culture*, vol. 1 (Santa Barbara, CA: ABC-CLIO, 2004). Excerpts from Anthony B. Pinn, *Religion and American Culture: An Encyclopedia, Volume One* (2003). Reprinted with permission.

2. Ira Berlin et al., *Remembering Slavery* (New York: The New Press, 1998), 197–98.

3. John B. Boles, "Evangelical Protestantism in the Old South: From Religious Dissent to Cultural Dominance," in Charles Reagan Wilson, ed., *Religion in the South* (Jackson: University Press of Mississippi, 1985), 30.

4. Ibid., 28.

5. Ibid., 30–31.

6. Ibid., 20–22.

7. John B. Boles, "Coming of Age in the Bible Belt," in John B. Boles, ed., *Autobiographical Reflections on Southern Religious History* (Athens: University of Georgia Press, 2001), 123.

8. Acts of the Apostles 2:1–4, *The Living Bible* (paraphrased).

9. Cited in Maude Southwell Wahlman, "A Foreword," in Jacqueline L. Tobin and Raymond G. Dobard, *Hidden in Plain View: A Secret Story of Quilts and the Underground Railroad* (New York: Anchor Books, 2000), 8–9. Also, Dobard, "Stitching Ideas into Patterns," in Tobin and Dobard, *Hidden in Plain View*, 30–31. For additional information on quilts, including ties to African sensibilities see: Gladys-Marie Fry, *Stitched from the Soul: Slave Quilts from the Ante-bellum South* (New York: Dutton Studio Books in association with the Museum of American Folk Art, 1990); John Michael Vlach, *The Afro Tradition in Decorative Arts* (Athens: University of Georgia Press/Brown Thrasher Books, 1990); Sharon F. Patton, *African-American Art* (New York: Oxford University Press, 1998).

10. Harry Middleton Hyatt, *Folk-lore from Adams County, Illinois*, 2nd ed. (Hannibal, MO: Western Printing and Lithography Co., 1965), 835.

11. Quoted in Gayraud Wilmore, *Black Religion and Black Radicalism* (Garden City, NY: Doubleday, 1972), 203–204.

12. Russell Simmons, with Nelson George, *Life and Def: Sex, Drugs, Money, + God* (New York: Crown Publishers, 2001), 217–18.

13. Anthony B. Pinn, *Varieties of African American Religious Experience* (Minneapolis: Fortress Press, 1998), 87.

Chapter 3

Black Spiritual Churches

Not all African American churches are the same. There is tremendous diversity, although the edifices housing various congregations appear aesthetically similar on several fronts. There are churches built within the context of old storefronts, grand cathedrals housing churches from various denominations, modest edifices with steeples and other markers of Christian community. It can be difficult to distinguish the religious commitments and theological assumptions by the exterior of the church. Yet, within some of these churches, one finds images of saints, Native Americans, and other elements such as incense and votive candles that point to a blending of traditions—Roman Catholicism, Voodoo, Protestantism—that is unusual in typical manifestations of African American churches. These churches are known as black Spiritual churches.

Origin of Spiritual Churches

Spiritual churches began to develop within African American communities during a rich period of religious expansion and diversification, a period, beginning at the end of the nineteenth century and moving through the mid-twentieth century. The ability to secure needed services and goods through nontraditional means had great appeal during the period of the Spiritual movement's strong growth—around the time of the Great Depression—because African Americans in large numbers were denied full access to the socioeconomic mechanism for individual and communal growth through traditional means.[1]

In large measure composed of African Americans who were new to northern and southern cities as a result of the Great Migration, these congregations were not always noticeable based on the name of the church.

Some, however, made use of the term *spiritual* within the name of the church. Those who used this term argued it was a marker of their desire as a religious body to live in accordance with the scriptural admonition to seek God in spirit and in truth. When asked to explain the use of the term *spiritual*, most point to John 4:24, which says: "God is a Spirit and they that worship Him must worship Him in spirit and in truth."

Whether in the name or not, members of Spiritual congregations have been quick to distinguish their activities and beliefs from those associated with the Spiritualist Movement. Clear markers of difference include the following: Spiritualist churches are primarily white congregations with ties to the Spiritualism Movement of the 1800s, complete with its attention to communication with the deceased. There is a somewhat pragmatic sensibility to both *Spiritualist* churches and *Spiritual* churches in that both advocate the ability to address one's material needs and concerns through spiritual practices. A sense of this connection to a spirit world is also present in some of the other African American churches. However, what serves to distinguish black Spiritual churches from other African American churches, such as Methodist and Baptist churches, is what anthropologist Hans Baer notes as the tendency in black Spiritual churches to emphasize "the manipulation of one's present condition through magico-religious rituals and esoteric knowledge."[2] Most African American churches, regardless of denomination, understand that human life involves interaction between seen and unseen forces. Yet, Spiritual churches address this interaction, seeking to manipulate it, using resources and rituals that would be unacceptable within the context of other African American churches. Even Pentecostal churches with their attention to spiritual influences on human interactions would label many Spiritual church practices "witchcraft" or "Voodoo." Those who suggest that Spiritual churches draw from Voodoo in their activities and beliefs are pointing essentially to the general understanding held in most of these churches that certain activities (e.g., burning candles of a particular color and the use of holy oil and water as well as incense) can be undertaken and certain items secured to achieve particular ends through guarded knowledge.

During services it is not uncommon for scriptural passages recited in a particular way, with the person in a proscribed posture, to be used as a way of adjusting one's financial situation. Some Spiritual churches, in spite of their denial of a link, do incorporate into their ritual activities seances (i.e., blessing services) that are more commonly associated with Spiritualism. Through these sessions, members of the congregation receive messages from deceased family and friends as well as spirit "guides." These messages are provided as the deceased speak through members of the congregation—mediums or prophets—who are able to bridge the material world and the spirit world. Mediums, healers, and advisors often hold private consultations—usually for which they are compensated—with members of the church and members of the larger community who are interested in advice concerning their health, finances, and relationships. Such sessions, both private and public, are meant to address physical and spiritual causes of disorder or problems generated by physical sources and problems resulting from unseen, evil forces. There are stories of miracles (healings for the most part) stemming from the work of various spiritual leaders. However, there is little in the way of documentation for these events. For example, Mother Catherine, the founder of a Spiritual church in the southern United States, is said by some to have healed a small child for whom medical treatment had not produced an ability to walk.[3]

There are undoubtedly differences in Spiritual church practice and teaching from congregation to congregation, and in some instances even the term *spiritual* has been replaced in the name of churches with more socially accepted terms such as *holiness*. Those making this change tend to do so as a way of distinguishing their commitment to living a life that separates them from the evils of the world. In this sense, they understand themselves as committed to a life marked by holiness—by an attitude and set of behaviors that distinguish them from the sinful nature of society. They understand themselves as being set apart from worldly interests. The term *spiritual* has connotations that often attach it to Spiritualism, although it is often meant to imply a righteous life, one marked by a deep concern with one's soul. To avoid confusion and to reduce the possibility of being associated with Spiritualism and its work with the dead, some churches have found it easier to avoid the term *spiritual* altogether.

Development of Spiritual Churches

Most scholars conducting research on black Spiritual churches suggest that they begin to develop through the efforts of a few charismatic figures. Much of the conversation concerning these churches centers on Chicago and New Orleans, where there are reports of Spiritual churches very early in the twentieth century. According to one report, in Chicago alone there were seventeen churches in 1928. Within ten years the number had increased to fifty-one, with approximately one out of every ten black churches in the Bronzeville section of Chicago being a Spiritual or Spiritualist church.[4] In order to maximize resources and build regional strength, Spiritual churches formed associations such as the

Metropolitan Spiritual Churches of Christ, Spiritual Israel Church and Its Army, and the Mt. Zion Spiritual Temple. From the first of these three associations Clarence Cobbs stands out.

Beginning with four members in a small church in Chicago, Cobbs's ministry grew to include a large congregation with numerous outreach programs. He was a charismatic figure who combined prophecy and grand rituals to attract a primarily working-class audience. Cobbs's appeal was massive in that he was said to have brought together some ten thousand people in a Chicago auditorium for a service. In part his appeal was based on his ability to connect financial reward to proper conduct, exemplified by his prosperity. According to one account, at the end of a service people were given "an opportunity to be the beneficiaries of his spiritual powers: after each believer came forward to confide to Cobbs his innermost desires, he or she received a candle from the prophet; as compensation for this favor, each one was expected to place a monetary offering on the altar."[5]

Another leader whose charisma resulted in a large following was King Louis H. Narcisse, who founded the Mt. Zion Spiritual Temple, Inc., in the early 1940s. The association of churches headed by King Narcisse contained only ten congregations spread across the country, but his style demanded notice. For example, his typical attire included capes, rings, and a bright crown. Attention-grabbing attire, composed of elements representing various traditions, such as clerical robes from the Roman Catholic tradition, was not unique to Narcisse in that many if not most Spiritual church leaders wear elaborate outfits. His attire, however, was combined with theatrics that most leaders could not duplicate. According to Hans Baer: "King Narcisse was chauffeured to the temple in a shiny black Cadillac limousine with his title and name inscribed upon the door. As he proceeded down the center aisle of the sanctuary, the congregation stood to welcome its majestic leader. During the remainder of the service, except when he was preaching and conducting various rituals, King Narcisse sat on a throne in the front, occasionally sipping a beverage from a golden goblet." Furthermore, Narcisse alluded to a deep connection between himself and God: "God is great and greatly to be praised in the sovereign state of Michigan in the Kingdom of 'His Grace King' Louis H. Narcisse."[6]

Although Narcisse is noteworthy, perhaps the best known and most thoroughly researched church leader to make claims to divine authority is Father George Willie Hurley, who founded the Universal Hagar's Spiritual Church in 1923. After three years as a minister in the International Spiritual Church, Hurley organized his own church, and one year after

One of Detroit's many Spiritual churches.

its opening he initiated a school for mediums where he taught individuals how to advise on spiritual matters. With time, Hurley's ministry increased from this first church to an association—the Universal Hagar's Spiritual Church—with thirty participating congregations in Michigan, New York, New Jersey, Pennsylvania, West Virginia, Delaware, and Illinois.

Hurley developed an elaborate theology and ritual structure centered on his personae as God. He, however, did not argue that he alone contained the spirit of God. In fact, he taught that all of his followers had in them the spirit of God, but he, Father Hurley, was the "major God," with a mission others had not been granted.[7] That is to say, Hurley was God with a capital "G" and his followers were gods with a lowercase "g." In this sense, one might say that while his followers were godly, he was God. The idea that God was manifest in black flesh held religious ramifications in that it dovetailed with an understanding of African Americans as actually having an exalted status that the social arrangements and teachings offered by some of European descent sought to deny. African Americans had been misled by whites, had em-

A Spiritual church located in Detroit, Michigan.

braced false religions, and were in need of Hurley's guidance to secure their proper status as the descendants of the original people—the Ethiopians. This status involved full inclusion in the best the United States had to offer. To achieve this end Father Hurley did not limit his work to spiritual rituals and esoteric knowledge. Rather, he combined spiritual development with attention to political issues.

Hurley's job, as the most recent incarnation of God, he argued, was to provide better doctrine. In this capacity, his teachings took precedence over all other religious teachings and systems.[8] Hurley, often referred to as the "black God of this Age," argued that existing religious systems outside his church involved manipulation and distortion of the teachings initially provided to prophets such as the Buddha and Jesus. His rejection of what he considered misinformed and distorted doctrines is expressed in his sermons and also in the celebrations recognized by members of the Universal Hagar's Spiritual Church. For example, rather than celebrating Christmas, which Hurley argued was a holiday instituted for and by whites, his followers celebrated "Hurley's feast" annually with activities starting on February 11 and ending with a major event commemorating the birth of Father Hurley on February 17. As part of the week of festivities, members of the church exchange gifts, hold special meals, and participate in religious services.

In addition to ritual activities, there is an elaborate system of positions and auxiliaries within the association. One such auxiliary incorporating basic church functions with esoteric knowledge is the "Knights of the All Seeing Eye." Even the description offered for this organization plays into its secrecy and esoteric nature: "The K. Of the A.S.E. is a Mystical Benevolent Order that has been ushered in on the sands of time tracing the footprints of the Ancient Initiates and Brothers down through the ages. Each loyal member of the U.H.S.C. [Universal Hagar's Spiritual Church] will become a member of this mystical society in order to promote the elevation of the race to a higher calling."[9] Other elements of the church's structure, including deacons and ushers, resemble those of other Spiritual churches and many of the other African American denominations. Although Father Hurley died in 1943, the work of the association continued, but did so in the context of other Spiritual churches and flamboyant leaders.

Hurley's combining of theatrics, charismatic personality, grand ritual, and guarded knowledge was also present in Detroit's Prophet Jones, who had a substantial following through much of the twentieth century. Initially licensed to preach at six years of age within the Holiness Movement, Jones, who developed a reputation as a prophet, eventually ministered within the Triumph the Church and Kingdom of God in Christ, in Birmingham, Alabama. According to his obituary, he moved to Detroit in 1938 in order to "run a short meeting, but his gracious words and dynamic prophecies were such cool water and good bread for thirsty and hungry souls, that Detroit claimed him as her very own." After teaching in Detroit for six years, Prophet Jones organized the Universal Triumph, the Dominion of God, Incorporated with locations in fifteen states. The headquarters remains in Detroit and is named the "Church of Universal Truth, the Dominion of God, Incorporated." The development of this organization, never referred to as a church by Prophet Jones, did not go without notice. In fact, *LIFE* magazine (November 27, 1944) ran a story with photographs concerning Jones's Detroit ministry.

His teachings revolved around "respect for oneself, then love of all mankind, regardless of race, creed, color or ethnic background, an honest day's work for an honest day's pay, love of country and of God."[10] The organization's web site indicates that the Prophet's objectives fit into the general framework established by these ethical principles: "(1) to disseminate the whole truth of God throughout the world; (2) to provide for the widows and orphans, the poor and the needy; (3) to establish churches, schools and seminaries throughout the world; and (4) to ordain and appoint missionaries and evangelists."[11] His teachings were summed up in the organization's motto: "Life, Our Most Precious Possession." Proper response to Jones's teachings entailed action summarized, for example, in 1947 as follows: "First—Obey God in everything and after you live right, contact God and ask Him to give you work to do to help build up the Dominion and after you have your job then go ahead and work without ceasing, constructively, and then see Dr. Jones smile upon you."[12]

Jones's central place within this organization's hierarchy was noted in the title used—"His Holiness, Rt. Rev. Dr. James F. Jones, Dominion Ruler." Men within the organization were referred to as "Sir, Lord, and Prince," and the women were known as "Lady and Princess." The association with divinity that marked Father Hurley's self-perception is also expressed by members of Universal Triumph, the Dominion of God when referring to "His Holiness": "We feel that Christ (the Power of God, and the Wisdom of God) has made his return or second coming in the embodiment of the Rt. Rev. Dr. James F. Jones (Christ's first embodiment was Jesus)."[13] Even the way in which Prophet Jones was addressed when entering a service speaks to this exalted position. Members sang: "Here comes our saviour; he came to set us free."[14] In a manner similar to that of King Narcisse, Jones's title was accompanied by elaborate outfits consisting of fur coats, expensive suits, and jewelry.

Like other Spiritual church leaders, Prophet Jones supplemented established Christian holidays with celebrations reflecting his teachings. For example, Jones added the following celebrations to his organization's calendar: "November 24 (Jones's birthday)—Philiamethyu—meaning open gate to a city. December 1—Hushdomecalama—meaning comes another day." According to Prophet Jones, the first is similar to Yom Kippur and Christmas and the latter is similar to New Year's and Rosh Hashanah. These two dates mark the start and the end of a period involving feasts and other communal activities.

In addition to special celebrations such as the two just mentioned, Prophet Jones required members of his organization to hold a minimum of five services each week: Wednesday night, Thursday night, and three on Sunday (1:00 P.M., 3:00 P.M., and 8:00 P.M.). With respect to the Sunday services, Prophet Jones gave the following framework to participating congregations:

The services are to begin with four songs, then everyone stand, and clap their hands to express thanksgiving to God for your individual blessings. Then everyone lift their head, look up in a realm of thought (silent concentration). This takes the place of prayer. The director of the devotional services will end the thought realm by uttering these words: "May the God of the universe bless us, and grant our desires in the name of His Divine Holy Prophet." One more song, then space will be given for expressions (testimonies). After the expressions the services will be turned over to the local administrator or speaker who will then administer the truth (message of truth) or lecture. After the message, the local administrator or the person in charge of the services shall appoint someone to get the offering.[15]

When Prophet Jones preached in Detroit's Oriole Theater—the home of Universal Triumph, the Dominion of God—it was not unusual for him to hold the audience for five or six hours. Furthermore, the esoteric nature of his message was exemplified through the use of "chanting, rhythmic 'unknown tongue' peppered with phrases like 'cosmic illuminability' and 'the lubritorium of lubrimentality.' Services would eventually culminate in 'shouting, stamping' and other energetic activities."[16]

Members of this organization were taught to obey the "twelve divine immutable Laws of the Universe" in order to secure happiness—the creation of their "own Heaven on earth." These laws involve a type of esoteric knowledge that seeks to explain the place of humans in the universe, the nature of human life, as well as the proper thoughts that help humans change their circumstances. They are: (1) the Law of Intimation—regulates reproduction for humans. Mating only during the proper season (January 1–December 31) avoids the production of children with illness and an improper instinct. For example, "Man would never have had an airplane but his Mother and Father mated in the fowl's mating season—then he was born with an instinct to want to fly. Now man is using the airplane as a weapon of destruction"; (2) the Law of Making and Forming—controls "everything that is or was formed or made" in accordance with the story of creation in Genesis 2:7. That is to say, this law explains the material realities that compose the universe, as we know it; (3) the Law of Bringing Forth—is responsible for those things that do not appear to have been created. This law is meant to control and allow followers of the law to make sense of those things that do not have a clear origin. For example, the biblical account of creation begins with the existence of certain things such as the ocean. This law addresses such situations; (4) the Law of Darkness—is responsible for night and evil. This law explains the existence of evil and the darkness or night countered by God's creativity activities in the Book of Genesis; (5) the Law of Light—manages the movement of the sun, moon, and stars. This law explains the pattern of movement recognizable in

Order of Services for the
Universal Triumph, the
Dominion of God

- Four songs
- Congregants stand and clap their hands
- Congregants lift their heads
- Closing of devotional services "May the God of the universe bless us, and grant our desires in the name of His Divine Holy Prophet"
- Songs
- Expressions
- Lecture by local administrator
- Offering

the planets and stars that make up the universe; (6) the Law of Life—monitors all living things. This law explains the behavior and activities of all creatures; (7) the Law of Death—corresponds to the destructive processes associated with evil and Satan. This law explains the negative dimensions of life and does so in terms of invisible and evil forces that impinge upon human life; (8) the Law of Gravitation explains gravitation as a force of the universe; (9) the Law of Increase—can be dealt with through proper thoughts. This law indicates that those things we seek in life (health, etc.) are first secured by believing we have them, recognizing we have them through positive thinking, and then acting accordingly; (10) the Law of Time—addresses the reality of eternity. This law helps those who are members of this organization understand the full scope of life—the limitations of human existence and the never ending reality that marks God's existence; (11) the Law of Eternity—explains the nature of God as a being without beginning or end. That is to say, it describes God as a being who was not created by another being; (12) the Law of Creation—similar to the law of making, this law that is controlled by God addresses the creation of all living things. This law explains the nature of God as the creator of the universe.[17]

Readers may find some of these laws difficult to "unpack," while others are scientific realities, such as gravity. It is important to note, however, that according to organizations such as Jones's Universal Triumph, the Dominion of God, a proper understanding of esoteric teachings comes only with time and training. In part, the Prophet Jones's importance within the organization revolves around his ability to explain and exemplify the practice of these teachings, to lead the faithful toward a new day free from ignorance and its ramifications of poverty, sickness, and other misfortunes.

There is a millennialist tone to some of Prophet Jones's teachings that is similar to the "end of the world" remarks made by his contemporaries like the Honorable Elijah Muhammad of the Nation of Islam. According to Jones:

Jesus' birth ushered in this present world which is known as the Gentile world. Jesus is the leader or Savior. This present world at the end of this year 1945 will have stood 1945 years. Add this to the other four thousand years that have passed and you will have 5945 years or five days and 945 years in another day. Fifty-five more years and the six days will be ended (6000 years). Jesus tells of the signs of the end of this world in Matthew 24:3–14. The seventh day will soon be ushered in. In that day, the seventh day which will be one thousand years, humanity will rest from sickness, sorrow, pain, and death. For then death's reign will end. The devil, old satan who has caused sickness, sorrow, pain, and death will be bound.[18]

The new way of life undertaken by the faithful, under the direction of the Dominion Ruler, leads to "Divine Health," making unnecessary rituals for temporary healing practiced by many other organizations. In this way, the mind is alerted to "its creative functioning principles or activities,"[19] and members of the Dominion are able to move beyond the false teachings and attitudes associated with traditional churches.

The membership of this organization is difficult to determine, particularly in light of the grand claims made by Jones who, on December 19, 1952, claimed six million members in the United States, Caribbean, and West Africa. Talk of an international membership is somewhat questionable when one considers that in 1947 the "Third International General Assembly" for the Universal Triumph, the Dominion of God did not list any non–U.S. resident administrators. Membership and Jones's influence began to decline somewhat after 1956. Nonetheless, within the United States, particularly the Detroit area, Prophet Jones is still mentioned in spiritual circles, and spiritual leaders trained by him continue to be somewhat prominent within the Spiritual Movement.

Notwithstanding the significance of cities such as Chicago and Detroit for the growth of Spiritual churches, most scholarly treatments of black Spiritual churches give a great deal of attention to New Orleans and the work of Mother Leafy Anderson. She developed Chicago's "Eternal Life Christian Spiritualist Church" in 1913 and also organized New Orleans's the "Eternal Life Spiritualist Church in the Crescent City" before the end of the decade, probably around 1920. Some in New Orleans—or the "Crescent City"—argue that Anderson actually initiated Spiritual practices in their city. Yet scholars Claude Jacobs and Andrew Kaslow note that prior to her arrival in Louisiana there were already elements of the Spiritual Movement in place. It seems that the best explanation for Spiritual churches in New Orleans involves a combination of factors: (1) the city's diverse religious environment; and (2) the teachings of Mother Leafy Anderson within that complex religious context. Mind-

The Divine Twelve
Immutable Laws

1. Law of Intimation
2. Law of Making and Forming
3. Law of Bringing Forth
4. Law of Darkness
5. Law of Light
6. Law of Life
7. Law of Death
8. Law of Gravitation
9. Law of Increase
10. Law of Time
11. Law of Eternity
12. Law of Creation

ful of this, one can safely say that teachers, prophets, and healers who appealed to esoteric knowledge and terrific rituals in doing their work existed in Louisiana prior to Mother Anderson. But it is not until her arrival that an institutional basis for such practices and beliefs developed in earnest.[20]

There is basic agreement on certain aspects of ritual and doctrine as they revolved around the need for deep spiritual connection to the divine in order to secure physical happiness. Nonetheless, there is disagreement concerning the incorporation of certain practices. For example, while Anderson rejected Voodoo, many others embraced (not always by name) aspects of Voodoo, such as recognition of certain spiritual forces or deities associated with it. Anderson did advance, however, the notion of spirit guides and agents of assistance for the spiritually minded. One of her major guides was Black Hawk, who many argue was first introduced to Spiritual circles through Anderson. Black Hawk was an early nineteenth-century leader from the upper Mississippi Valley who fought against the Americans in the War of 1812. Those familiar with Mother Anderson also note her interest in "Father Jones," a powerful spirit guide who is said to have "appeared to Mother Anderson in full dress clothes one dark and dreary night and instructed her how to master all evil, promising to stick by her at all times."[21] In addition, it was not unusual, and this remains the case, to see statues of various Catholic saints, with the understanding that they also assist members with spiritual and material growth. In some cases, Catholic saints such as the Virgin Mary have greater visibility than Native American guides such as Black Hawk. Furthermore, while Jesus Christ has significance within Spiritual churches, his place is not always the same as his role in Methodist, Baptist, and Pentecostal churches. For traditional African American churches, Jesus Christ is the God/Man. That is to say, there is a creative tension between his physical form and the spirit of God contained in that form. Some argue that Mother Leafy Anderson's teachings, however, included an understanding of the physical presence of Jesus as unimportant. What was essential about Jesus was the manner in which his physical form housed "Spirit," the divine.[22]

Like churches in other denominations, Spiritual church activity centers around services conducted throughout the week. For example, while limited information is available concerning the details of Anderson's worship practices, scholars have noted that there were typically five services each week: two on Sunday, a class on Tuesday to train church leaders, and one each on Thursdays and Fridays. In keeping with what was noted earlier concerning the content of Spiritual church services, Anderson's services contained prayers, scripture readings, songs, a sermon, and encounters with the spirit world.[23] The process of worship did not differ drastically from the typical order of service within most churches. Typically, participants gained the correct frame of mind for worship through the singing of devotional songs, which are musical selections meant to bring about the proper atmosphere for the religious service. In addition, worship leaders provided readings from the Bible, with commentary concerning the significance of the passage given. This type of information concerning the underlying meaning and purpose of scripture for securing a good and prosperous life continued in the form of the sermon given by the minister-in-charge. After the sermon, those present received an invitation to come to the altar at the front of the church. There they were able to pray for assistance with particular life issues. In addition, ministers present prayed with those at the altar and provided scripture passages to be read for strength and wisdom. During this time at the altar, as members of the congregation prayed, it was not unusual for spirits to make their presence felt. During these times of possession, an individual was "taken over" by a particular spirit (typically one of the spirit guides or the Holy Spirit), and that spirit gave messages to members of the church using the body and voice of the possessed person.

Mother Leafy Anderson was a gifted leader who combined spiritual power with a keen sense of the mechanisms for institutional growth through the training of many women who established congregations based on the model Anderson provided. These new congregations eventually formed an association that was under Anderson's leadership until her death in 1927. This organization covered a territory stretching throughout the South and portions of the North (e.g., Chicago, Little Rock, Memphis, Houston, and New Orleans). It is interesting to note that unlike the Methodist, Baptist, and Pentecostal churches, many black Spiritual churches recognized early the ministerial and leadership talents of women. And, as one might assume based on the centrality of Mother Leafy Anderson, women held significant positions of leadership including the pastorate of their own churches.

According to some accounts, the 1930s marked a watershed of growth in Spiritual church activities and personalities resulting in roughly one out of six African American churches in New Orleans claiming to be spiritual.[24] Statistics suggest that by 1995 there were approximately one hundred spiritual churches, of varying size, in New Orleans alone.[25]

Basic Spiritual Church Beliefs

What is clearly evident about Spiritual churches is their borrowing of rituals and doctrine from various religious systems (i.e., Pentecostalism, Roman Catholicism, Voodoo, and Spiritualism) without reflecting strong links to any one source of religious knowledge. Spiritual churches borrow from Roman Catholicism, but they are not Roman Catholic churches; they borrow liberally from Pentecostalism without becoming Pentecostal churches, and so on.

Some Spiritual churches over the years incorporated what might be considered subtle African American cultural nationalist notions, or more precisely Ethiopianism. (Readers will note similarities between the understanding of African Americans espoused by some Spiritual churches and that advocated by groups such as the early Nation of Islam.) For example, the Spiritual Israel Church and Its Army in Detroit and several other cities argued that its members were connected to Ethiopia culturally and to Israel spiritually. In fact, they considered themselves the spiritual offspring of the ancient Israelites. Both their Ethiopian and Israelite connections point to the religious and historical significance of blacks because: "the first human beings were Black people, starting with Adam, who was created from the 'black soil of Africa.' All of the great Israelite patriarchs and prophets, including Noah, Abraham, Isaac, Solomon, David, and Jesus, were Black men."[26] This connection between African Americans and the ancient biblical world is important for religious reasons in that some Spiritual churches argue that their religious tradition has roots in the ancient Near East.

While examples of ritual practices and beliefs are easily provided, this does not point to the existence of a unified structure within the Black Spiritual Movement. To the contrary, like Baptist churches, Spiritual churches may belong to associations, but they maintain a great deal of autonomy and are often more heavily influenced by the local pastor than by the hierarchy of the association. One might expect there to be a premium on autonomy if for no other reason than that "tradition" is not of much importance within Spiritual circles because what one believes and practices is in large part premised on what one learns through contact with spiritual forces. That is to say, spiritually directed behavior takes precedence over structure and order.[27]

Independence, as is the case in Baptist circles, can result in schisms over doctrinal, ritual, or politico-organizational disagreements. Autonomy is the general rule, but in some instances associations have worked to establish doctrinal statements and guidelines. For instance, the Southwest Association of Spiritual Churches developed a series of sixteen statements (in 1937) meant to outline the general structure of belief as a way of clarifying what Spiritual churches believe and to also distinguish them from Spiritualism and Voodoo. The principles can be summarized as follows: (1) God is a Spirit manifested in the form of the Trinity; (2) the Son of God is the Word of God manifest in flesh; (3) the resurrection of Jesus the Christ as outlined in Scripture is historically accurate; (4) the Holy Spirit is the third member of the Trinity; (5) the Scriptures (Old and New Testaments) provide all information necessary to secure salvation; (6) humans are sinful by nature and can be redeemed only through Jesus Christ; (7) speaking in tongues, prophecy, and healing are signs that one has received the Holy Spirit; (8) the true Church is a Spiritual Church—one that worships God in spirit and in truth; (9) through prayer the deceased can intercede for the living; (10) images of Christ and the saints are useful reminders of religious and spiritual obligations and help the spiritually minded properly orient themselves; (11) church ritual should be conducted using robes; (12) things used to glorify God are good; (13) baptism is an important church ritual; (14) baptism and communion are the sacraments given by Christ to the Church; (15) ministers are free to marry; (16) "secular" rules and regulations that do not contradict the teachings of God should be obeyed.[28]

The fundamental meaning of these statements is recognized in the workings of many Spiritual churches inside and outside the Southwest. One should not assume that these principles are articulated by all Spiritual churches, however. It is important to remember that the autonomy of individual congregations includes the ability to determine ritual structures, doctrines, and relationships to other congregations.

Besides the issue of autonomy, individual spiritual churches are similar to Protestant churches in terms of church organizational structure. Their internal structure and organization are similar in that ministry within a local church is composed of the pastor and other ministers and church officials responsible for various aspects of the church's daily activities. They differ, however, in that most Protestant churches make use of fewer titles when referring to officers or members of the church.

For example, in the African Methodist Episcopal Church, there are Reverends, Church Mothers, and so on. Similar titles are present within Baptist circles. However, in Spiritual churches, it is not uncommon to have key, influential members referred to as Prince or Princess; female ministers, rather than simply being called Reverend might be called Reverend Lady; and the leader of the congregation or association might be called King or Queen in some cases.[29]

There is overlap between Sunday services in denominations discussed in this volume and Spiritual churches. A case of this involves feast days for particular saints observed by many Spiritual churches and by Roman Catholic churches, or the foot washing services—used as a sign of humility and as a reenactment of Jesus washing the feet of his disciples—found in both some Pentecostal churches and some Spiritual churches. In both cases, services include the singing of hymns, communal prayer, scripture readings, a sermon, moments during which testimonies concerning an individual's spiritual growth are given, and offerings collected for the work of the church. Like more Pentecostal or charismatic churches, Spiritual churches give considerable attention to healing the sick and prophecy through which the community of the faithful is equipped to live in the world outside the church walls.

There are also services within some Spiritual churches that are not duplicated within the other traditions discussed in this book. An example is the "Uncle Bucket Service." It is not clear that this figure was an actual historical person. Some suggest he is Saint George; others argue he was a confederate soldier. During this service, the musician plays "When the Saints Go Marching In" and the minister directs "the worshippers to form a line and proceed to the rear of the church where there [is] a small table with the pail on it. At this altar each person [makes] a silver offering and [is] then instructed to place three fingers into the pail of sand, while 'making a wish'" after which the person goes back to his or her original place.[30] This ritual holds great importance in that it provides a way for believers to secure spiritual and material health. By following the steps of this ritual and making a wish, the person involved is able to secure a more promising future. Through a small offering, those participating in the "Uncle Bucket Service" believe they can change their circumstances and improve their lives. Furthermore, although there is a shared interest in being "filled" or possessed by spiritual forces, Spiritual churches differ from their Pentecostal counterparts in that they have a more liberal moral outlook. For example, while Pentecostal churches such as the Church of God in Christ discussed in Chapter 2 oppose premarital sex and secular modes of entertainment such as "worldly" music, some—but not all—Spiritual church leaders do not condemn sexual relationships outside of marriage, and secular modes of entertainment were not discouraged for the most part.

Concluding Thoughts

It is fairly clear that the Spiritual Movement has lost strength over the decades, and it is not certain what will happen to particular associations and individual churches. Over the course of their history, these churches have attracted a multilayered audience—middle class as well as working class, the young and senior citizens, and former members of various mainstream African American denominations as well as those who were previously "unchurched." As is the case with other religious communities, the demographics continue to change over time, and the number of members within any given association is difficult to document. It is possible that some of these churches will continue to maintain minimal membership and also provide services (e.g., healing and advice) to nonmembers. Others once considered spiritual may move into more mainstream status by altering some of their practices and beliefs and by claiming status as either Pentecostal or Holiness churches.

While the general fate of Spiritual churches is unclear at this point, it does seem somewhat certain that practices from this tradition will continue to find a place in the religious lives of African Americans. This is because Spiritual church theology and practices have provided some African Americans with a way to address the hardships of life and a way to celebrate the achievements within their lives. The teachings are often mysterious and esoteric, and the practices are often a blending of elements from various religious traditions. In this way, these churches have opened their members to an understanding of the world as thick with forces, both visible and invisible forces, that give some shape to human life experiences. By learning the inner meaning of scripture and learning how to recognize and tap into the spiritual forces that surround humans, it is possible to increase one's enjoyment of life through spiritual and material growth. Through such teachings, Spiritual churches in particular and spiritual practices in general have played a role in the religious self-understanding of some African Americans.

Notes

1. Hans A. Baer and Merrill Singer, *African-American Religion in the Twentieth Century: Varieties of Protest and Accommodation* (Knoxville: University of Tennessee Press, 1992), 38–52.

2. Hans A. Baer, *The Black Spiritual Movement: A Religious Response to Racism* (Knoxville: University of Tennessee Press, 1984), 9.

3. Jason Berry, *The Spirit of Black Hawk* (Jackson: University Press of Mississippi, 1995), 73–74.

4. Drake and Cayton (1945): 642. Quoted in Hans A. Baer, *The Black Spiritual Movement: A Religious Response to Racism* (Knoxville: University of Tennessee Press, 1984), 23.

5. Baer, *Black Spiritual Movement*, 26.

6. Ibid., 28.

7. Ibid., 93.

8. Ibid., 92.

9. Ibid., 88.

10. Obituary for Prophet Jones, August 12, 1971.

11. http://www.utdog.org/.

12. *Dominion Messenger*, December 1947.

13. The Rt. Rev. Dr. James Jones, *Ritual—Universal Triumph, the Dominion of God* (n.p., 1946), 17.

14. Ibid., 10.

15. Ibid., 5–6.

16. Zena Simmons, "Detroit's Flamboyant Prophet Jones," *The Detroit News* found at: http://info.detnews.com/history/story/index.cfm?id=182& category=people.

17. The Rt. Rev. Dr. James F. Jones, *The Mind Awakener* (n.p., 1945), 2–4.

18. Ibid., 8.

19. Ibid., 12.

20. Claude F. Jacobs and Andrew J. Kaslow, *The Spiritual Churches of New Orleans: Origins, Beliefs, and Rituals of an African-American Religion* (Knoxville: University of Tennessee Press, 1991), 19, 30–32.

21. Berry, *Spirit of Black Hawk*, 70.

22. Jacobs and Kaslow, *Spiritual Churches of New Orleans*, 52.

23. Ibid., 34–35.

24. Ibid., 43.

25. Berry, *Spirit of Black Hawk*, 11.

26. Baer, *Black Spiritual Movement*, 28.

27. Berry, *Spirit of Black Hawk*, 152.

28. Jacobs and Kaslow, *Spiritual Churches of New Orleans*, 53–58.

29. Ibid., 47.

30. Ibid., 115–16.

Chapter 4

Buddhism

For a good number of years now, action films laced with the martial arts have drawn substantial crowds and have inspired attention to religious traditions coming out of the East. Hollywood depictions are not the only motivations for this infusion of Eastern sensibilities into life in the United States, however. As some scholars have noted, as early as the 1940s and gaining increased energy in the 1960s, many living in the United States appealed to loose configurations of Eastern philosophy and practices as a way to make sense of life in a country perceived as spiritually empty and consumed with material acquisition. While many of these practices revolved around superficial adaptations, others involved a strong commitment to Buddhism, first as an institutional reality in the form of the Buddhist Churches of America.

While the Buddhist Churches of America represents possibly the oldest institutional form of Buddhism in the United States, it is unwise to assume that this organization sets the tone and determines the texture of Buddhism within this context. Buddhism, the name given by Westerners to the tradition associated with Siddhartha Gautama's teachings, has grown to take numerous forms and presentations. Furthermore, it has grown to include Americans of various socioeconomic, racial, and ethnic backgrounds. As Buddhist scholar Richard Seager notes, "there are white collar Buddhists; Buddhist cab drivers, mechanics, and chefs; and Buddhist artists and musicians. Some Americans are highly self-conscious about being Buddhist, while others take the fact that they are Buddhist for granted."[1]

This diverse and complex Buddhist community is composed of immigrants who establish the tradition in their new home as well as American converts. According to some accounts, there may be as many as four million Buddhists in the United States, more than in any other Western country. Of that number, almost one million are American converts. What may surprise some readers is that, as of the late 1990s, of these converts a noteworthy number, perhaps somewhere around 30,000, are African American. The vast majority of these African American Buddhists are members of Soka Gakkai International-USA, the most racially diverse form of Buddhism in the United States.[2] A proper understanding of Soka Gakkai International-USA and its African American membership requires context, a general understanding of Buddhism's development.

Buddhism

The story of Buddhism begins with Siddhartha Gautama, the historical Buddha, born during the sixth century BCE in what is now known as Nepal. Siddhartha Gautama was born into an important warrior class responsible for protecting the people, and as a result of its responsibilities this class held great social importance. Based on the stature and social ranking of his clan, he would have experienced a comfortable life, free from most discomforts.

At the age of twenty-nine, Siddhartha Gautama rejected this sheltered life and began a quest to understand and end human suffering. As part of this quest, he worked to control his body through extreme ascetic practices learned from various teachers encountered during his travels. These practices did not, however, serve to end suffering. It was not until seven years after he began this process that Siddhartha Gautama found the enlightenment he sought while meditating under a pipal tree. Engaged in deep meditation, or *dhyana*, he worked through his various past lives, and from this rehearsing of his past he realized the manner in which *karma* (fate, or the force determining the nature of one's next life) influences the nature and contours of life. This awakening, the realization of suffering's causes and the way to eliminate it, resulted in his becoming enlightened—the Buddha.

Siddhartha Gautama did not only recognize the nature of suffering and its causes, he also discovered the proper way to obtain liberation from suffering, *nirvana*, through the surrender of desires that produce suffering. This proper way is referred to as the "middle way." It moves between surrender to the senses and the attempt to control ourselves through harsh, ascetic practices. In order to help others, the Buddha began teaching this new path, the *dharma* or doctrine, as well as *vinaya* or discipline. He first announced this new way during a sermon given outside Varanasi.

With time the Buddhist tradition grew throughout India, with written texts developing to form a canon of teachings and philosophy. Various schools emerged, with the three dominant being Theravada (the most traditional and strict form), Mahayana (the "Great Vehicle," so called because it considered Theravada too narrow for most), and Vajirayana, which involves an embrace of esoteric scriptures (*tantras*). These traditions differ in numerous ways, including: (1) disagreement on the nature of connection between nirvana (liberation) and *samaara* (this world); (2) the idea of the Bodhisattva (one who vows to assist others to become liberated from suffering);[3] and (3) the appeal to particular texts as vital on the path to liberation. Besides disagreements related to teachings, the complexity of this growing Buddhist tradition was also found in the formation of its ritual activities and the visual images associated with it. These differences would generate internal disagreements and spark various movements, but they did not stifle the religion's growth. Although Islam would supplant Buddhism in India, the tradition continued to grow over the centuries, reaching the United States prior to the twentieth century.

Buddhism in the United States

According to accounts by his followers, Nichiren, a Buddhist in Japan from the Mahayana tradition, lamented what he considered the decline of dharma, and attempted to correct this through emphasis on devotional practices geared toward laity who were not from the more socially elite groups. He emphasized chanting and the Lotus Sutra (a sacred text in Mahayana Buddhism) because he considered it the most complete Buddhist teachings. The supreme importance of the Lotus Sutra is expressed in the name change through which Zenshobo Rencho becomes Nichiren (Sun-Lotus).[4] Missing from this approach was attention to the four noble truths and the eightfold path defined later in this chapter. Those involved in Nichiren Buddhism also participated in *kosenrufu*, or the push toward world peace. Nichiren was not content to address the needs of Japan alone as they relate to practice and the study of Buddhism. In fact, he desired to take his understanding of Buddhism, which he considered the only true form of Buddhism, across the globe. While one can debate Nichiren's personal success as a missionary, it is quite evident that his movement eventually developed into various Nichiren Buddhism schools, including Soka Gakkai International, in various areas of the world.

Some trace the presence of Buddhism in the United States back to the mid-1800s through the rather superficial understanding promoted by transcendentalists such as Henry David Thoreau, who published in 1844 a translation of the Lotus Sutra.[5] As scholar Charles Prebish notes, by 1882 "America was the site of more than simply an edifying discussion about Buddhism as a religious tradition." With the arrival of immigrants, including some missionaries, Buddhism's presence only increased.[6]

In addition to the early efforts of missionaries Shuei Sonoda and Kakuryo Nishimjimo, who came to the United States in 1899, D.T. Suzuki (a student of Buddhism from Japan) and Alan Watts (an Episcopal priest) aided the expansion of Buddhism's influence. The writings of Suzuki reached a diverse audience across several decades, as the experience of Angel Kyodo Williams, an African American Buddhist, suggests. Williams writes that her first acquaintance with Buddhism stems from an intense appreciation for the aesthetic of Japanese notions of home that led her in search of materials on Japanese culture. "What I found," she writes, "was a classic Zen book called, what else, *Zen and Japanese Culture*, by a scholar named D.T. Suzuki who happened to also study Zen. . . . His writing did a lot to bring Zen to the West and to America, but I didn't know that then. All I knew was that it wasn't Japanese culture that I was having a love affair with . . . it was the culture and sensibility that came from Zen."[7]

One of the Buddhist organizations that began to flourish during the 1960s was Nichiren Shoshu of America. This organization, composed of priests and laity, was associated with the Nichiren Buddhist movement of Japan mentioned earlier. Nichiren Shoshu of America experienced tremendous growth, with estimates as high as 7,500 new members each month in 1969. And by 1976, Nichiren Shoshu Temple claimed some 200,000 members, with branches in cities such as Los Angeles, San Francisco, Philadelphia, Phoenix, Washington, DC, and Seattle.[8] Internal conflict within this organization, however, eventually fueled a schism in 1991, resulting in the Nichiren Shoshu Temple led by priests and Soka Gakkai International-USA led by the laity.

Soka Gakkai was founded by Tsunesaburo Makaguchi, who became a teacher in Sapporo and eventually in Tokyo. In developing his ideas on Soka (or value creation), he drew on three fields of study: sociology, pragmatism, and geography. He was impressed by the manner in which these disciplines shed light on the nature of relationship and the reciprocal interaction between groups. Drawing on these disciplines and the teachings of Nichiren Buddhism, he set out to form an educational system bringing together individual improvement and social commitment—an effort to transform society through the practice of Buddhist teachings. By 1937, he had worked out the basic principles of value creation education and Buddhism, giving it institutional form as the Soka Kyoiku Gakkai (Value Creation Education Society). The society lasted only six years because of pressure from the Japanese government, with Makaguchi and other members of the society's leadership being imprisoned on charges of treason because they rejected state-supported Shintoism. Makaguchi died in prison, but the movement he initiated continued under the leadership of Josei Toda, and with a new name: Soka Gakkai (Value Creation Society).

In 1951 Toda worked to have Soka Gakkai recognized as a religious organization, under the authority of the Nichiren priesthood. Prior to his death in 1958, he used an aggressive approach to proselytizing to increase the organization's size, and he gave Soka Gakkai a doctrinal base which it lacked in its earlier years by appealing to the Lotus Sutra and the writings of Nichiren. Toda's goal for Soka Gakkai was to increase individual happiness within the context of a world marked by harmony.

Saisaku Ikeda became the next president of Soka Gakkai. Although aggressive proselytizing benefited Soka Gakkai, Ikeda diminished this aspect of spreading the organization's teachings while transforming the movement from a regional, Japan-based religion (with political involvements through its *Komeito* or "Clean Government Party" founded in 1964) into an international movement. This process of internationalization in regard to the United States began in 1960 with Ikeda's first trip. This trip resulted in the formation of Soka Gakkai of America (Nichiren Shoshu of America). Initially, its membership was primarily Japanese immigrants, with meetings conducted in Japanese. The first meeting in English took place three years later.

Rather loosely organized, Soka Gakkai of America's leadership structure grew through the appointment of George Williams as the American General Chapter Chief in 1968. Invitations were extended to strangers to attend meetings during which they were introduced to the practice of chanting. They also heard testimonies from group members concerning the spiritual and material benefits of chanting. On a larger scale, the organization hosted "culture festivals" during which neighborhoods were introduced to the activities and teachings of Soka Gakkai. In terms of organization, "the basic organizational unit of Soka Gakkai International-USA is known as a district. The districts are composed of smaller segments known as units and groups. Moving upward organizationally and geographically, one can identify larger units known as chapters, headquarters, territories, and joint territories, which encompass the regional and national design of Soka Gakkia International-USA. Administrative authority is generally based on length of practice and capability to teach others within the unit. Within the local units, activities are structured according to age and gender, and thus one finds a men's division, women's division, young men's division, and young women's division."[9]

By 1976, aggressive efforts to introduce Soka Gakkai to an American public were suspended because of the negative ramifications of the mass suicide and murder in Jonestown by followers of Jim Jones. In spite of this setback, the organization has paid attention to the racial and ethnic diversity of the United States and developed various initiatives (e.g., the Boston Research Center for the Twenty-first century in Cambridge, Massachusetts and the Soka University of America in southern California) to increase the diversity of its membership as well as to promote religious dialogue and understanding.

African Americans and Buddhism

For some, the recognition that African American Buddhists exist is linked to the movie about Tina Turner's life in which she is shown chanting. Others might be aware of Herbie Hancock's link to Buddhism (see Appendix 2). However, these are only two of the many African Americans who claim Buddhism as their religion.

Soka Gakkai International-USA, a component of the larger Soka Gakkai International organization with members in over 100 countries, typically claims a membership of roughly 100,000 and maintains a headquarters in Santa Monica, California. Although actual membership is hard to calculate for this movement, what is significant is the fact that Soka Gakkai has a larger African American membership than any other Buddhist group in the United States. In fact, African Americans constitute 20,000 of Soka Gakkai's total membership.[10] Although most Buddhist communities are rhetorically committed to diversity, only Soka Gakkai has lived this out in ways that are reflected in the makeup of the membership.[11] For example, regarding district leadership (one of the basic units within Soka Gakkai), African Americans by 1990 "represented 26.74 percent of the district leaders: Atlanta—43 out of 67; Boston—24 out of 180; Chicago—75 out of 160; Los Angeles—101 out of 458; Miami—5 out of 64, New York—141 out of 465; Philadelphia—60 out of 1120; San Francisco—103 out of 599; Washington, DC—103 out of 336. Whites make up 38.67 percent, Japanese 18.66 percent and Hispanics, for example 5.69 percent."[12] While the executive committee for Soka Gakkai traditionally had been Japanese and male, this began to change when African Americans gained prominent

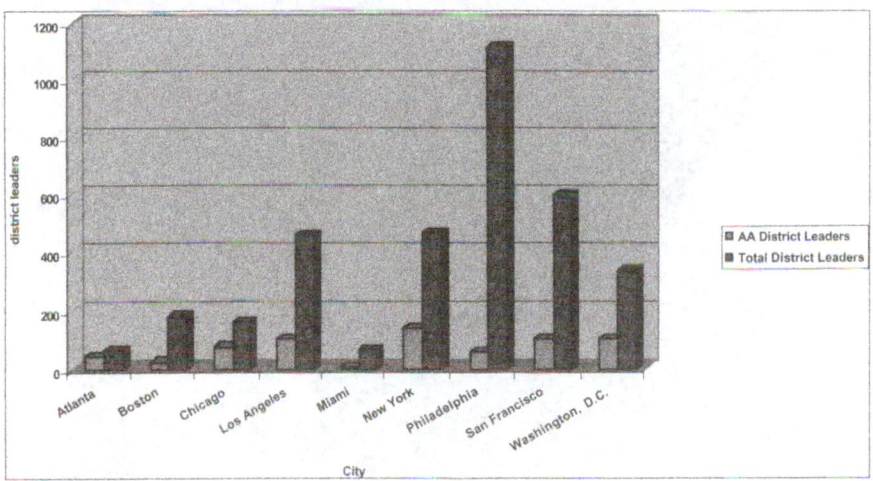

Figure 4.1
African American District Leadership, 1990
Created by Stephen Finley.

positions: Sheilah Edwards became a vice-general director in 1997 and Ronnie Smith in 1998 (see Fig. 4.1).[13]

With such a long history of Christian church involvement, why have so many African Americans turned to Buddhism? (See Fig. 4.2.) This question is extremely pertinent when one considers that irrespective of conversation to the contrary, many American Buddhists have a difficult time actually applying notions of equality and "raceless" movement through the world that marks much of the Buddhist tradition. In an article titled "American Buddhism (What Does It Mean for People of Color?)," frustration over this very issue is expressed in graphic terms: "Separatism and mutuality are equally free to emerge in the splendor of freedom in America. For some Buddhists, this causes confusion. Some American Buddhists who believe in the mutuality of all beings conversely find themselves practicing racial, cultural, and economic segregation in their Dharma activities. Mere mention of this contradiction makes them very upset and can cause them to condemn, cold shoulder, and even reject someone from their Dharma center."[14] For Euro-American Buddhists, the article continues, this dilemma is at times dealt with in far from productive ways, through what the author refers to as a "loosely formed majority consensus" by which selection for inclusion involves: "(1) people of color are allowed in as long as they do not bring up the heritage issue; (2) people of color who have no connection to the heritage issue, such as Tibetans, are welcome because their preoccupation is with Chinese heritage rather than American heritage;

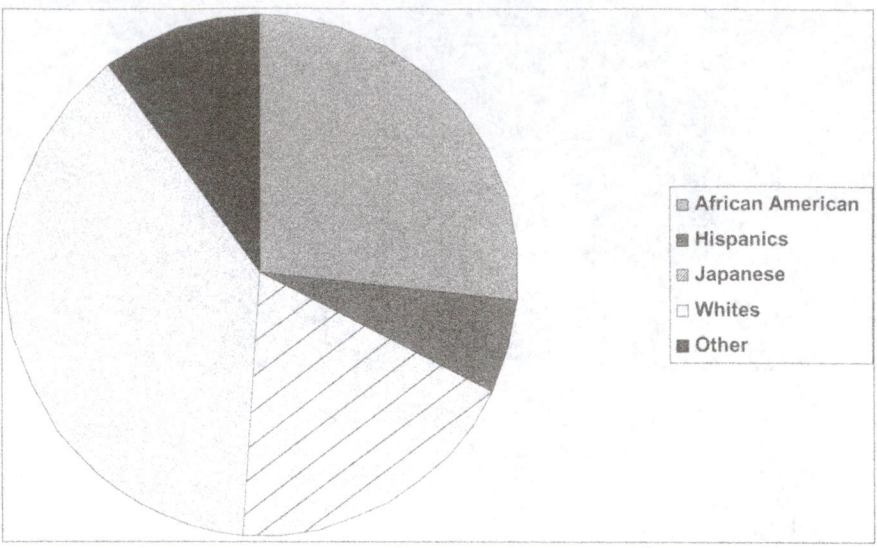

Figure 4.2
District Leadership
Created by Stephen Finley.

(3) anyone, regardless of race or culture who speaks of these issues must subject him/herself to a verbal caution from a dominant culture senior student." Those who fail to adhere to the no-race-talk requirement after an initial reprimand are subject to dismissal for "non-Buddhist activity."[15] In another portion of the "American Buddhism (What Does It Mean for People of Color?)" article, a rather troubling encounter based on American stereotypes was played out. The author notes, "I had one newly arrived Asian Teacher tell me he was afraid of me when we first met. He said he had heard that black people were violent, and challenged me to a battle of his Asian magic against my black magic."[16] The extent of such problems and the precise manner in which issues of race and ethnicity are handled are not exactly clear.

In spite of such problems, African Americans have found in Soka Gakkai a somewhat tolerant approach to multicultural religiosity, one that allows them to embrace both their African American heritage and the Buddhist teachings, fostering a synergy of sorts. According to Ronnie Smith, who has been a Buddhist for almost thirty years: "In Buddhism there's a sense of equality because all people can attain enlightenment. . . . People like the idea that this is something everyone can do. . . . Within about five months I had changed so much that my mother started practicing it too. She was raised as a Baptist, but she's been a Buddhist ever since then."[17]

In keeping with the more recent strategy of individual contact, word of mouth has been a primary way by which African Americans have come to embrace Buddhism through Soka Gakkai, seeing and responding to members of their family and friends who claimed major life changes through the tradition. Some scholars claim that Soka Gakkai is attractive to African Americans because its social sensibilities are in line with the dominant mind-set of progress that emerged out of the Civil Rights Movement. That is to say, "Soka Gakkai maintains an ethos of individual power, the freedom to change one's life no matter what one's circumstances, and the support of the mission for world peace."[18] Put yet another way, "after the civil rights movement many African Americans were seeking ways out of poverty and new spiritual alternatives to the racism that they had found in Christianity."[19] As Joe Parks notes, "as an African American young man, this organization of people is the only group aside from my family where I have felt fully accepted, and acknowledged."[20]

African American members also at times speak of the "fit" between Buddhism and African American life in terms of Ikeda's appreciation for the plight of African Africans and those in the African Diaspora. Hence, joining Soka Gakkai did not result in cultural disconnect, a surrender of black pride, or an eclipsing of a desire for social transformation. For example:

> African-American members in Chicago remember how Ikeda was angered during his first visit to America in 1960 by seeing the hurt in a little black boy's eyes when he was kept out of a baseball game in Lincoln Park by a white adult. . . . African Americans also often quote the remark by Ikeda that Africa is the continent for the twenty-first century. . . . It is well known across Soka Gakkai International-USA that Ikeda specially honored Rosa Parks, the southern black woman who refused to give up her seat on the bus and was arrested on December 1, 1955. . . . It is also well known across Soka Gakkai International-USA that when Rosa Parks was asked to choose a single picture to represent her life, she chose a picture not of her arrest or civil rights demonstrations, but a picture of her shaking hands with Ikeda in 1993.[21]

Soka Gakkai understands race as a social construct lacking deep or fundamental merit. There is a recognition of the impact this social construct has had on life in the United States, while struggling to live in ways that move beyond race and ethnicity. This seems a general Buddhist principle presented in numerous places, including Internet conversation such as those on Rainbowdharma.com. On this web site it is stated that "through faith, labels designating our country of birth, race, culture, and social status, etc., finally can be reduced to road signs from a past journey. Faith ultimately casts aside attachment to concepts like 'people of color.'"[22]

Basic Buddhist Beliefs

With time, the teachings of the Buddha were combined with various forms of devotion. For example, according to Richard Segal, "Buddhists gathered together under pipal trees to recall the night of the Buddha's enlightenment. These trees became known as bodhi trees, trees of awakening, and continue to be a major element in Buddhist iconography. Stupa mounds (a circle or square monument containing relics of the Buddha) became major cult sites in Asian Buddhism. . . . The Buddha is also symbolized by an empty throne or footprints, images signifying that although the dharma remains on earth, Shakyamuni himself attained ultimate liberation. The lotus, a beautiful flower with roots planted firmly in mud, is a reminder that while nirvana is a transcendent goal, it is attained from within the realm of human suffering. By the first century BCE, the human image of the Buddha . . . came into widespread use."[23] While those who have achieved enlightenment provided texts or sutras that explain the Buddha's teachings, the elemental nature of Buddhism that guides most Buddhists is often described in terms of the "Four Noble Truths": (1) life is marked by suffering or dukkha, and this reality should not be lamented but rather acknowledged simply as a reality to be addressed and overcome; (2) dukkha is caused by desire or *tanha* through which people misunderstandingly seek happiness through temporal realities and this attempt to secure happiness through those things that cannot in actuality produce lasting happiness causes suffering; (3) dukkha or suffering ends when desires are surrendered; (4) dukkha ends through the eightfold path, the "middle way" described by the Buddha.

In addition to the four noble truths, there is the path that leads to the ending of suffering and nirvana through eight realizations: (1) right view—understanding that our actions have felt consequences that shape our lives through the production of bad or good *karma* or action; (2) right resolve—commitment to avoid all perceptions and actions that block movement toward complete liberation; (3) right speech—recognition that what we say has felt consequences in that it produces bad karma that harms us and others; (4) right action—avoiding activities that harm ourselves and others; (5) right livelihood—undertaking economic activities that are in keeping with the production of good karma;

(6) right effort—consistent practice of right thinking; (7) right mindfulness—recognition of the importance of the connection between the mind and the body highlighted in the process of meditation; (8) right concentration—proper focusing of the mind so as to achieve liberation.

Followers of the Buddha's teachings formed a community (*sangha*), based on various levels of engagement with the Buddha's principles of proper living. Monks (*bhikkhus*) and nuns (*bhikkunis*), who are most deeply devoted to the middle way—the path to liberation outlined by the Buddha—surrender all worldly attachments. While all followers of the middle way are expected to adhere to a particular life marked by a refusal to kill, steal, and so on, monks and nuns live an even more rigorous life involving many strict regulations concerning dress and so on. Those who maintained connections to family and the larger world express their devotion in part through efforts to care for monks and nuns. Monks, nuns, and laity play a role in the spread of the Buddha's teachings, sharing the middle way, with converts. This movement into Buddhism involves "taking refuge": "I take refuge in the Buddha. I take refuge in the dharma. I take refuge in the sangha."

Soka Gakkai embraces Nichiren's teaching that there are three secret laws of Buddhism: (1) *gohonzon*—a small scroll (resembling the one written by Nichiren) containing the *diamoku* and embodying the dharma that is the primary object of devotion for Buddhists who follow the teachings of Nichiren; (2) *kaidan*—the sanctuary of Buddhism often associated with the temple, Taisekiji, founded by Nikko Shonin; (3) the true chant of the daimoku, at times said to be "hail to the wonderful dharma Lotus Sutra" or "Homage to the Lotus Sutra." It is chanted quickly and for roughly thirty minutes. According to those in Soka Gakkai, the meaning of the chant—Myohorenge-kyo—is as follows: "Myoho is the mystic law of the universe, the underlying principle of duality which is the basis of human life. Renge is the lotus flower, which can be understood as a metaphor for the simultaneity of cause and effect (karma) and the pure flower which blooms in a swamp. Kyo is the sound or vibration one creates in chanting which attunes the individual to the law of the universe."[24] Various individual and communal concerns play into the general guidelines of Soka Gakkai International: "1—To work for the prosperity of society by being good citizens who respect the culture, customs, and laws of each country; 2—to promote humanistic culture and education based on the fundamental, humane principles of Buddhism; 3—to join our efforts for world peace, for instance, with those of the United Nations by supporting the spirit of its charter, thereby helping achieve our ultimate goal of the abolition of nuclear arms and universal renunciation of war."[25]

Concluding Thoughts

Buddhists in America define themselves in various ways and, as this chapter suggests, participate in various traditions all linked in some way to the initial teachings of Siddhartha Gautama, the Buddha. Related to this, American Buddhists are involved in a diverse and complex community, one that at times is composed of an uneasy tension between various cultural backgrounds, socioeconomic positions, and political commitments.

The participation of African Americans in Buddhism adds to the rich religious landscape that marks their religious history. Buddhism has become one of the religious orientations allowing African Americans to make sense of the world and forge a firm and healthy sense of self within the context of a larger community of living beings. In short, it promotes a deep sense of happiness, and points toward a path by which the various modalities of suffering or the cycle of suffering—and Buddhism allows African Americans to acknowledge the various ways in which injustice has meant suffering—can be understood and ultimately overcome.

Notes

1. Richard Seager, *Buddhism in America* (New York: Columbia University Press, 2002), 9.
2. Ibid., 11.
3. Angel Kyodo Williams in *Being Black: Zen and the Art of Living with Fearlessness and Grace* [(New York: Penguin Compass, 2000), 83, 84] seems to think through the existence of Bodhisattvas in a way that connects the concept to the best of various struggles for liberation. She writes: "To inspire our way we have in our history a fine legacy of people who voiced a commitment to live more responsible lives. They were awakening warriors in their own time and many of them sacrificed what we consider elements of their personal freedom in the course of remaining true to their commitments of waking up the world. Sojourner Truth was one of the first voices of both women's rights and human rights. . . . The list of people that have made a conscious choice to be more responsible in life goes on and on. Their warrior-spirits transcended all boundaries of race, class, gender, sexual orientation, culture, and religious affiliation."
4. Jane Hurst, "Nichiren Shoshu and Soka Gakkai in America: The Pioneer Spirit," in Charles S. Prebish and Kenneth K. Tanaka, eds., *The Faces of Buddhism in America* (Berkeley: University of California Press, 1998), 82.
5. Charles S. Prebish, *Luminous Passage: The Practice and Study of Buddhism in America* (Berkeley: University of California Press, 1999), 3.
6. Ibid., 3, 4.

7. Williams, *Being Black*, 4.

8. Prebish, *Luminous Passage*, 23–25.

9. Ibid., 121.

10. Shelvia Dancy, "Buddhist Influence Grows Among African Americans," *The News & Observer*, Raleigh, North Carolina, August 25, 2000.

11. David W. Chappell, "Racial Diversity in the Soka Gakkai," in Christopher S. Queen, ed., *Engaged Buddhism in the West* (Boston: Wisdom Publications, 2000), 184.

12. Chappell, "Racial Diversity in the Soka Gakkai," 190.

13. Ibid., 203.

14. "American Buddhism (What Does It Mean for People of Color?), Part One," http:www.Rainbowdharma.com/commentaries.html#Part1.

15. Ibid.

16. "American Buddhism (What Does It Mean for People of Color?), Part One," http:www.Rainbowdharma.com/commentaries.html#Part2.

17. Ibid., 2.

18. Hurst, "Nichiren Shoshu and Soka Gakkai," 90.

19. Chappell, "Racial Diversity in the Soka Gakkai," 188.

20. Ibid., 195.

21. Ibid., 194.

22. http://www.Rainbowdharma.com/teaching.html.

23. Ibid., 19.

24. Hurst, "Nichiren Shoshu and Soka Gakkai," 84.

25. Prebish, *Luminous Passage*, 120.

Chapter 5

Humanism

A film starring Hollywood legend Al Pacino called *The Devil's Advocate* portrayed humanism in a manner many in the United States hold to be true.[1] The film deals with the Devil's attempt to produce the anti-Christ and bring about the end of the world using a successful law firm as his cover. He has spent eternity impregnating women hoping that one would be the perfect "specimen." In the late twentieth century, one of his sons—a lawyer—is the perfect one, the chosen one. Near the end of the film as the Devil outlines the plan that his son is reluctant to follow, the Devil argues that he has always been on the side of humanity. As he continues his speech, the Devil argues that he, the Devil, is in fact the last of the humanists. Many in the late twentieth century make similar assertions concerning humanists: they are a hopeless lot who have rejected God and are bound for hell. To the contrary, humanism has provided meaning for many throughout the history of the United States. Even during the early years of the New Republic, figures such as Thomas Jefferson pushed to move beyond superstition and embrace reason as the guiding force of life. A great religious zeal would overtake much of the United States during the nineteenth century, but even so, some argued for reason over religious superstition and a reliance on human creativity and ingenuity over dependence on divine forces.

While few would automatically think of a strong humanism growing within the soil of the African American religious landscape, humanism has existed in African American communities for centuries. Early evidence of African American humanism is found in the blues, a musical formed developed early in African American culture which often made light of Christian claims and commitments. In the worried words of Daniel Alexander Payne one also finds evidence of humanist leanings in African American communities (see Appendix 7). Payne writes concerning his work in the South:

the slaves are sensible of the oppression exercised by their masters and they see these masters on the Lord's day worshipping in his holy Sanctuary. They hear their masters professing Christianity; they see these masters preaching the gospel; they hear these masters praying in their families, and they know that oppression and slavery are inconsistent with the christian religion; therefore they scoff at religion itself—mock their masters, and distrust both the goodness and justice of God. Yes, I have known them even to question his existence. I speak not of what others have told me, but of what I have both seen and heard from the slaves themselves. . . . A few nights ago between 10 and 11 o'clock a runaway slave came to the house where I live for safety and succor. I asked him if he was a christian; "no sir," said he, "white men treat us so bad in Mississippi that we can't be christians." . . . In a word, slavery tramples the laws of the living God under its unhallowed feet—weakens and destroys the influence which those laws are calculated to exert over the mind of man; and constrains the oppressed to blaspheme the name of the Almighty.[2]

While individual humanists have existed in African American communities throughout the history of the African presence in North America, the participation of African Americans in humanist-oriented organizations is a more recent development.

Humanist Beginnings

Among the earliest African American humanists to express themselves within a public forum were members of the artistic movement of the early twentieth century referred to as the Harlem Renaissance. Concerned as it was with the presentation of African American life in its full complexity, the Harlem Renaissance produced some literature that raised questions concerning the importance of theistic forms of religious expression. This is most pointedly the case with respect to African American churches. As Arthur Faust notes: "the church, once a sine qua non of institutional life among American Negroes, does not escape the critical inquiry of the newer generations."[3] In autobiographical writings, some artists of this "newer generation" made explicit their freethinking stance in the form of humanism. James Weldon Johnson, a Harlem Renaissance writer known for *God's Trombones: Seven Negro Sermons in Verse* and the words for "Lift Every Voice"—the black national anthem—is a case in point. Those who argue that African American writers making use of African American religious idioms in their work are themselves committed to the religiosity expressed in their work are mistaken. While the sermonic style of African American churches is celebrated in *God's Trombones*, it is clear that Johnson's interest is in the tropes, idioms, and aesthetics of African American churches. This presentation of African American culture in the garb of Christian expression does not speak to his personal

What Is African American Humanism?

Definition: Humanism is a system of thought and conduct based on a commitment to humans as the shapers of human destiny.

commitments because, as he tells readers, "my glance forward reaches no farther than this world. I admit that I throughout my life have lacked religiosity. I do not know if there is a personal God; I do not see how I can know; and I do not see how my knowing can matter."[4]

In what might be considered a second wave of the Harlem Renaissance, or a movement in black realism, James Baldwin spoke to a similar reliance on human capabilities and creativity as opposed to reliance on claims of the transcendent and the supernatural. In *Go Tell It On the Mountain*, Baldwin explained his early, Pentecostal church commitments resulting in his call to the preached ministry. Reflecting on that early career as a preacher some years later, he presented a much more pragmatic or functional reason for his participation in the church. It was not so much a deep reliance on the supernatural. Rather it had to do with a space in which to deal with socially generated fears. That is, in his words, "all the fears with which I had grown up, and which were now a part of me and controlled my vision of the world, rose up like a wall between the world and me, and drove me into the church."[5] He was clear in that growing up in the world of Harlem required belonging, belonging to something, to some expectation of the life that surrounded him. He, like everyone in that world, had to surrender to something. Hence, growing up, he knew that "one doesn't, in Harlem, long remain standing on any auction block. It was my good luck—perhaps—that I found myself in the church racket instead of some other."[6]

Baldwin preached for three years, but he ultimately discerned that the workings of the church did not promote wholeness and health, but rather bred denial of humanity's full worth through its failure to engage the world. In his writing, Baldwin finds the ability to humanize life, and in this way he engages humanism by replacing claims of the transcendent and its workings in human affairs with a firm embrace of human responsibility to create a livable world. He puts this perspective in sharp relief: when asked by the Honorable Elijah Muhammad about his religious commitments, Baldwin said, "I'm a writer. I like doing things alone."[7]

Not all African American humanists do things alone. Of the African American humanists who expressed their commitments in the context of organizational structures, those in the Communist Party as of the 1920s were probably among the first. The atheistic stance of the Communist Party and its rhetorical appeal to African Americans (thin as it was) provided a forum and institutional home for African American humanists who found churches hopelessly out of touch with the times. Although the Communist Party was reluctant to attack African American churches because of the strength of these churches, some African Americans who joined the party were more than willing to provide this critique, even when they held membership in the church.[8]

African American communists, like Hosea Hudson, were active in the church, but some ministers attempted to prevent the use of churches for what they considered trouble-making speeches and activities. At one point, in light of such sentiments, Hudson stopped attending church, but he recalls starting to attend again between 1937 and 1938. His comments to church members, most likely meant to spark discontent with the church's otherworldly stance, were as follows:

> I challenge one or two deacons one Sunday afternoon. We all sitting around talking. I told them, I said, "It ain't no such thing as no God. You all go around here singing and praying," I said, "and they regular lynching Negroes, and you ain't doing nothing about it."[9]

Again, Hudson's remarks—based on his church involvement—were most likely meant to initiate thought. However, Hudson recounts that this type of belief was actually held by some members of the Communist Party who never attended church. Hudson says:

> I had heard other Party people talking. Some of them had never been members of no church, talking about there wont no such thing as God: "Where is he at? You say it's a God, where is he at? You can't prove where he's at." Negro Party people said that to me, Murphy and Horton and Raymond Knox. We'd have big discussions. One Sunday I said I was going to church. "What you going for? What you going for?" I said, "I'm going to serve God." They said, "Where is God at? You can't prove it's no God nowhere." They said, "Where is God?" I said, "In heaven." "Well, where is heaven?"[10]

In rejecting God, the African American humanists Hudson knew gave humanity responsibility for social transformation.

By the time African Americans participated in noticeable numbers, the Communist Party had withdrawn from a strong interest in the "negro question" and was concerned primarily with the "Moscow line."[11] Some African Americans undoubtedly remained within the party hoping for a change, while others moved in the direction of black nationalism as a means by which to embrace a materialist critique of U.S. society and the question of race. In the late twentieth century the Black Power Movement, particularly the second wave of the Student Nonviolent Coordinating Committee (SNCC) and the Black Panther Party, served as an example of this turn toward black cultural nationalism. The shift away from the Christian-based Civil Rights Movement marked by the second wave of SNCC and its thundering call for "Black Power!" pointed to deep differences. The theistic motivations for marching and for explanations of abuse suffered espoused by Dr. Martin Luther King Jr. did not adequately address the concerns and ideas of some of the more radical elements of the movement. The break, therefore, marks a transition from the theism of the Civil Rights Movement toward materialist analysis and human-centered solutions. Gone were SNCC's integrationist goals that made it compatible with the Civil Rights Movement. Gone was its reliance on Christian doctrine and paradigms for action. Key leaders of SNCC exemplified this new line of reasoning.

James Forman, a SNCC leader, in his autobiography *The Making of Black Revolutionaries* describes his conversion to humanism as a move that did not hamper but rather informed praxis (action based on thoughtful reflection). He notes that during his time at Wilson Junior College in Chicago his doubts concerning the existence of God grew, and this process was intensified by contact with questionable black preachers whose self-centered and selfish ways resulted in his distaste for ministry and the church. Such interactions are summed up by this comment from Forman: "God was not quite dead in me, but he was dying fast."[12] After returning from military service some years later, Forman came to a final conclusion concerning the existence of God. He writes:

> The next six years of my life were a time of ideas. A time when things were germinating and changing in me. A time of deciding what I would do with my life. It was also a time in which I rid myself, once and for all, of the greatest disorder that cluttered my mind—the belief in God or any type of supreme being.[13]

This was not a matter of personal frustration for Forman. He did not reach this conclusion simply because God had not responded to self-centered requests. Rather, this conclusion was based on the historical condition and needs of a large community. Furthermore, this rejection of God was not surrender to absurdity. To the contrary, it was a call to arms. For him, humanism required a strong commitment on the part of people to change their condition.[14]

Critiques of African American churches based on materialist approaches to social transformation were also present in the ideological platform of the Black Panther Party. In fact, the attraction of some SNCC workers to the Black Panther Party led by Huey Newton, Bobby Seale, and Eldridge Cleaver revolved around a common concern with transformative activity that held as its measuring stick the welfare of African Americans and other oppressed groups. The Black Panther Party had a clearly materialist platform and was certain of its armed and revolutionary stance. This commitment to human struggle as the key to social transformation housed theological underpinnings that were humanistic in nature. Reflecting on the ultimate demise of many Black Panthers, Bobby Seale sums up the goals of the Black Panther Party in ways that speak to humanist desires:

> We need activists who cross all ethnic and religious backgrounds and color lines who will establish civil and human rights for all, including the right to an ecologically balanced, pollution-free environment. We must create a world of decent human relationships where revolutionary humanism is grounded in democratic human rights for every person on earth. Those were the political revolutionary objectives of my old Black Panther Party. They must now belong to the youth of today.[15]

The Black Panther Party softened its position when it recognized the central role African American churches played in the African American community's life. Like the Communist Party, the Panthers recognized recruitment would be difficult if open hostility existed between the Black Panther Party and churches. Therefore, the Panthers fostered a relationship of convenience and sociopolitical necessity, but without a firm commitment to African American church doctrine. Newton rationalized this involvement by arguing a different conception of God, God as the "unknown" whom, interestingly enough, science will ultimately resolve. In this sense, God does not exist in the affirmative because God is the absence of knowledge. Whether successful or marked by misguided movement, the Black Panther Party's humanism is notable. Attention is taken off divine assistance as talk of God is ignored.

African Americans for Humanism

In more recent years, the nationalistic impulse that marked the humanism of SNCC and the Marxist sensibilities of African American humanists in the Communist Party have given way to a more politically mainstream orientation. An example of this is the organization African Americans for Humanism (AAH), directed by Norm Allen and housed at the offices of the Council for Secular Humanism in Buffalo, New York.

Norm Allen started a conversation with the Council for Secular Humanism that resulted in his relocating to Buffalo, New York, in 1989 to develop AAH. AAH dealt with outreach as a means of spreading information to potentially interested parties through travel, lectures, articles, a book (*African American Humanism: An Anthology*), and the AAH newsletter. AAH, composed primarily of urban middle-class males, has developed branches in Kansas City, Seattle, and other U.S. locations as well as Ghana, Zaire, Uganda, and Kenya.

In establishing the grounds for an African American shift to humanism, Norm Allen Jr. remarked on the duplicity of Christianity. From his perspective, while African American churches have played a significant role in the struggle against social injustice, these problems develop as a result of slavery and racism that were supported by Christians.[16] Allen does acknowledge the seeming benefit of Christianity with respect to the survival of African Americans. Even this, however, points to human tenacity, not the correctness of Christian praxis. Allen writes: "Throughout history poor people have tended to be deeply religious; their beliefs have often made them apathetic to their plight and easy for the rich to dominate. This was the case with blacks during slavery."[17] Furthermore, "blacks are very proud of their deep religious convictions, but convictions are usually obstacles to new and productive ideas. The ultimate value of a religion is not how long it has helped a people to survive, but how far it has helped them to advance."[18]

Instead of relying on such "convictions," Allen suggests furthering human thought and inquiry based on the potential of human ingenuity to transform life. This, he acknowledges, is not a matter of guaranteed progress; such optimism is unwarranted. Nonetheless, Allen asserts that humanism suggests a viable alternate moving humanity toward its own fulfillment.

The African-American Humanist Declaration presented in 1990 provides useful insight into the nature, content, and function of humanism as a praxis-oriented religious system. The writers of this declaration proclaim: "Today the world needs a critical, rational, and humane approach to living. This is what humanism is all about."[19] Humanism provides a systematic response to major problems plaguing U.S. society, such as alcohol and substance abuse and economic development issues. It does so by increasing recognition of human accountability and potential for fostering useful change. AAH is committed to a mature and complex community in which individuals are respected and exposed to vital and viable life options. It seeks improvement of life options for African Americans through a series of informed actions:

- Fight against racism in every form.
- Incorporate an Afrocentric outlook into a broader world perspective.
- Add depth and breadth to the study of history by acknowledging the great contributions made by people of African descent to the world, with the purpose of building self-esteem among African Americans and helping to demonstrate the importance of all peoples to the development of world civilization.
- Develop eupraxophy, or "wisdom and good conduct through living" in African American community by using the scientific and rational methods of inquiry.
- Solve many of the problems that confront African Americans through education and self-reliance, thereby affirming that autonomy and freedom of choice are basic human rights.
- Develop self-help groups and engage in any humane and rational activity designed to develop the African American community.
- Emphasize the central importance of education at all levels, including humanistic moral education, developing a humanistic outlook, and providing the tools for the development of critical reason, self-improvement, and career training.[20]

The Unitarian Universalist Association

African Americans have embraced humanism in a variety ways over the years, but the most visible, substantial, and institutional form of this commitment is probably their involvement in the Unitarian Universalist Association.

The Unitarian Universalist Association is a nationally recognized body, developed through a merging of Unitarian and Universalist churches in the late twentieth century. The former, Unitarianism, founded in 1825, was a movement with European roots insisting upon the oneness of God and the humanity of Jesus Christ. Unitarianism in the United States was carried forth by influential figures such as Theodore Parker and Ralph Waldo Emerson. Unitarianism as such was not explicitly humanistic, but its theological liberalism contained openness to inquiry that easily incorporated the activism that marked humanism and social reform efforts of this period. In addition, this openness allowed those who believed in God as well as those who de-nied God a place in the church as well as in social transformation.[21] Unitarians, however, were not alone in their radical appeal to the value of humanity. Universalist churches emerged in the eighteenth century and provided another forum for humanist endeavors. Having rejected notions of eternal punishment based upon failure to accept the "cor-rect" faith, Universalists—as the name implies—believed God would embrace all of humanity and bring about democratic existence of all. A common need for a stronger organizational base combined with theo-logical connections between these two organizations resulted in a 1961 merger: the Unitarian Universalist Association (UUA).[22] The timing of this merger is important in that the 1960s mark a period of strong in-tellectual openness and disillusionment with African American churches that might account for the interest of some African Americans in the UUA. The theological openness of this organization allowed the rejec-tion of the basic principles of theism suggested by figures such as James Forman to take more concrete and institutional form. While the num-ber of African Americans involved remains small, they have been vocal and have sparked changes within the organization.

The use of black humanism as a label or tag is fairly recent, and it is associated with the presence of African Americans in the UUA. Be-cause this organization was already open to the label of humanism, it makes sense that one of the first, if not the first, references to black hu-manism took place within its struggles over the advancement of black power within the UUA. *Empowerment: One Denomination's Quest for Racial Justice, 1967–1982* provides the following information con-cerning the use of this term, black humanism, linking its use with the Black Unitarian Universalist Caucus (BUUC) created to respond to racial issues within the UUA. In February 1970, the BUUC's newsletter (*BUUCVine*) announced this label and defined it this way: "Black Hu-manism calls for a seizure of decision making and implementation for oneself. Gaining power is an essential element of humanism."[23]

Such a statement allowed for the fundamental elements of religios-ity—ultimate concern in the form of human development and ultimate orientation humanizing empowerment. That is to say, humanism as a religion replaces a devotion to God with a commitment to human progress, and bases this hope for human development on signs of human potential for doing good. This religiosity brings into play the unique demands and existential context of African Americans; the value of their "blackness" was brought into human-centered thought and ac-tion. Such a posture was possible because the UUA's appeal to social justice is similar to that used historically within African American Christian churches minus one ingredient: justice is demanded and premised upon an appeal to human accountability and progress, and not on the dictates of scripture lived through a commitment to God. The UUA is embraced by some African Americans, and this relationship can be traced to at least the early twentieth century through Egbert Ethelred Brown and Lewis McGee.

Frustrated with Unitarians in Jamaica, Brown traveled to Harlem in 1920, hoping to bring liberal religion to African Americans in New York City. Brown found Harlem engulfed in progressive possibilities related to the NAACP, Marcus Garvey's UNIA, and the Communist Party. He held numerous jobs in an effort to support his family while attempting to establish a Unitarian church, with little support from the American Unitarian Association. Brown devoted a significant amount of time to his ministry and fostered a sense of religiosity that was connected to a longing for justice and political-social equality while drawing on the few socialists, communists, and Garveyites who crossed his path.

Gatherings usually consisted of thoughtful talks, rebuttals, and discussion. Missing was the emotional outburst and otherworldly orientation that marked many churches in this same section of New York City. The format and focus of the church created a problem for those wanting traditional African American Church worship. Brown's answer was variation. That is to say, "he reported that services were modified from year to year, always with the hope of attracting new people. Over the years they varied between a traditional religious service, with hymns, prayers, scripture readings, doxology, sermons, and benediction, and a forum situation, with a strongly secular orientation that included a brief service before the sermons and a discussion afterward." In addition, "it was largely upon the forum element that the reputation of the Harlem Unitarian Church was built. It drew people through the quality of its speakers and the open dialogue, yet its character as a forum also left it vulnerable to the kind of disruption described earlier. Moreover, it left some members desiring a service that was more religious in content and format."[24]

Some who desired a more religious, meaning theistic, service complained to Unitarian officials about the atheistic tone of the church. Nonetheless, the atheist ethos was a natural outgrowth not only of Brown's leadership but the perspective of many participants—the communists and socialists among them. In keeping with this perspective, Brown believed African Americans needed to be freed from "the emotionalism and superstition and otherworldliness of the old time religion." Furthermore, he understood the Harlem Unitarian church as "a church-forum where the honey-in-heaven and harassment-in-Hades type of religion is not tolerated. There are no 'amen corners' in this church, and no 'sob sister bench.' " Rather, this church called for human action and accountability for the condition of the world.[25] Its self-understanding is present in its charter statement:

> This Church is an institution of religion dedicated to the service of humanity.
>
> Seeking the truth in freedom, it strives to apply it in love for the cultivation of character, the fostering of fellowship in work and worship, and the establishment of a righteous social order which shall bring abundance of life to man.
>
> Knowing not sect, class, nation or race it welcomes each to the service of all.[26]

In the 1940s Brown lost the few members he had to larger, more prominent churches such as Community Church. Until his death in 1956, Brown continued to struggle with this church.

Lewis A. McGee began the Free Religious Fellowship (initially named the Free Religious Association) in Chicago in 1947 after having been a part of the Chicago Ethical Society. He developed this fellowship in response to a lack of liberal religion on Chicago's South Side. It began as a discussion group composed of African Americans, and from that it grew. Most of the members of this fellowship, unlike Brown's church in Harlem, were African Americans from the United States (not the Caribbean) with some white and Japanese members.[27] McGee's fellowship consisted of people who came to humanism from more traditional Christian communities. Many argued that they left traditional Christian churches because those churches failed to explain adequately why oppression existed in the world, and the theology of those churches often conflicted with science. For those in McGee's group, science was a more solid basis for thought and action than were unsubstantiated theological claims. Furthermore, the exclusive nature of African American church community and the general segregated nature of Christian community (and the larger society) posed a problem for them. In short, "these were people whose lives were no longer confined to the black community. Their broadening outlook required a religion that supported their quest but did not confine them as orthodoxy had."[28] First held in the home of Harry Jones, whom McGee met at the Chicago Ethical Society, the services consisted of twenty-minute talks by McGee on issues such as "What Is Unitarianism" and "Why Make a New Approach to Religion."[29]

Some members of McGee's fellowship were involved with the Communist and Socialist parties, reenforcing a humanist perspective within the fellowship. This, however, during the years of U.S. communist hunting, caused problems resulting in surveillance of fellowship activities. Yet, in spite of increased stress created by external forces, McGee's fellowship was more successful than Brown's church for several reasons, the most obvious being a changed attitude within the Unitarian Association concerning integrated churches and concerning African American Unitarians in general. McGee built on this growing acceptance.

McGee's fellowship was committed to social action. Members of this organization, under McGee's leadership, acknowledged that religious involvements necessitate social activism. And so McGee and other members of the fellowship involved themselves in the NAACP, Civil Rights Movement, and other transformative efforts. In the words of McGee:

> We believe in the human capacity to solve individual and social problems and thus to make progress. We believe in a continuing search for truth and hence that life is an adventurous quest. We believe in the scientific method as valid in ascertaining factual knowledge. We believe in democratic process in our human relations. We believe in ethical conduct. We believe in a dynamic universe, the evolution of life, the oneness of the human family and the unity of life with the material universe. . . . We believe in the creative imagination as a power in promoting the good life.[30]

The fellowship maintained as its goal the application of humanist principles within African American communities. After McGee's retirement the fellowship continued to function on Chicago's South Side.

Unlike the makeup of these two early churches led by Brown and McGee, African Americans in the UUA currently are spread throughout predominantly white congregations. The involvement of African Americans in the Unitarian Universalist Association does not rival the number of African Americans who make African American churches their home. At best roughly one percent of the total membership of the UUA (approximately 150,000) is African American. Nonetheless, even this limited involvement represents a strand of religious experience within African American communities. Progress was made, however, in 2001, when William Sinkford was elected the first African American president of the Unitarian Universalist Association.

What Humanists Believe

African American humanism is not a blind rejection of God and traditional religious community; it is not aimless, nor is it without moral and ethical sensibilities. Clearly, humanism is not composed of the same ritual, doctrinal, and theological sensibilities as one finds in African American churches. Nonetheless, humanism in African American communities provides orientation for life, frames a sense of meaning and purpose, and provides answers to the deep and ultimate questions of existence.

Individual humanists will articulate basic commitments in differing ways. The other religious modes of experience discussed in this volume are subject to the same differences in personal perspective, yet it is possible to suggest broad principles that appeal to most African American humanists. This tradition is difficult to define. It can be characterized, however, as a system of thought and conduct based on a commitment to humans as the only shapers of human destiny. It is a religious system that develops its understanding of life and proper ethical and moral conduct based on the following principles: (1) a critique of claims of the transcendent and the supernatural; (2) reliance on human creativity and ingenuity for the development of proper moral and ethical codes of conduct; (3) recognition of human responsibility and accountability for the betterment of the world; (4) optimism generated by a measured sense of realism with regard to the progression of history in productive ways; (5) suspicion toward or rejection of the idea of God or gods.

> **Basic Humanist Principles**
>
> 1. Critique of claims of the transcendent and the supernatural
> 2. Reliance on human creativity and ingenuity
> 3. Recognition of human responsibility
> 4. Measured realism
> 5. Suspicion concerning the existence of God

Concluding Thoughts

Humanism exists in various forms. Some of those forms revolve around the perspective and commitments expressed by individuals, and some involve organizational arrangements. In either case, this mode of religious experience provides meaning and life structure for a segment of the African American population. African Americans who embrace humanism and live in accordance with this sense of accountability and responsibility do not live in isolation. They are able to draw on the wisdom of African American humanists who have come before them, who embraced this perspective centuries ago and before it was labeled African American (or black) humanism.

Openly embracing humanism has always held its dangers. Some

who do so are rejected by friends and families, and in some cases jobs are lost because of an open commitment to this system of belief. Nonetheless, some African Americans, we cannot be certain of exactly how many, find humanism enriching. For them it provides a way of moving through the world with a full sense of accountability for their own destiny, and with a sense of responsibility for living in ways that enhance life for the larger community. Whether practiced individually or within the context of a community such as the Unitarian Universalist Association, humanism provides a way of life that has appealed to African Americans, and because of this it is an important dimension of the religious landscape of African American communities.

Notes

1. This chapter is drawn from and expands upon the discussion of African American humanism in "What If God Were One of Us?: Humanism and African Americans for Humanism," used with permission from *Varieties of African American Religious Experience* by Anthony B. Pinn (Minneapolis: Fortress Press, 1998), chap. 4. Copyright © 1998 Augsburg Fortress.

2. Daniel Alexander Payne, "Daniel Payne's Protestation of Slavery," in *Lutheran Herald and Journal of the Franckean Synod* (August 1, 1839), 114–15.

3. Arthur Fauset, *Black Gods of the Metropolis: Negro Religious Cults of the Urban North* (Philadelphia: University of Pennsylvania Press, 2002), 7.

4. In Roy D. Morrison II, "The Emergence of Black Theology in America," *The A.M.E. Zion Quarterly Review* vol. 94, no. 3 (October 1982): 6.

5. James Baldwin, *The Fire Next Time* (New York: Dell Books, 1962), 42.

6. Ibid., 44.

7. Ibid., 97.

8. Robin D. G. Kelley, "Comrades, Praise Gawd for Lenin and Them! Ideology and Culture among Black Communists in Alabama, 1930–1935," *Science and Society* vol. 52, no. 1 (Spring 1988): 65–66.

9. Kelley, "Comrades," 133.

10. Nell Irvin Painter, *The Narrative of Hosea Hudson: His Life as a Negro Communist in the South* (Cambridge, MA: Harvard University Press, 1979), 133–34.

11. See Harold Cruse, "Jews and Negroes in the Communist Party," in *The Crisis of the Negro Intellectual: A Historical Analysis of the Failure of Black Leadership* (New York: William Morrow and Company/Quill, 1967, 1984), 147.

12. James Forman, "Corrupt Black Preachers," in *The Making of Black Revolutionaries* (Washington, DC: Open Hand Publishing, 1985), 58.

13. James Forman, "God Is Dead: A Question of Power," in *The Making of Black Revolutionaries* (Washington, DC: Open Hand Publishing, 1985), 80–81.

14. Ibid., 83.

15. Bobby Seale, *Seize the Time* (New York: Random House, 1991), intro., 3. Although on the individual level the objectives often gave way to

problematic and abusive behavior, the humanist tone of the Black Panther Party's platform is still noteworthy:

1. We want freedom. We want power to determine the destiny of our Black Community.
2. We want full employment for our people.
3. We want an end to the robbery by the white man of our Black Community.
4. We want decent housing, fit for shelter of human beings.
5. We want education for our people that exposes the true nature of this decadent American society. We want education that teaches us our true history and our role in the present-day society.
6. We want all black men to be exempt from military service.
7. We want an immediate end to POLICE BRUTALITY and MURDER of black people.
8. We want freedom for all black men held in federal, state, county and city prisons and jails.
9. We want all black people when brought to trial to be tried in court by a jury of their peer group or people from their black communities, as defined by the Constitution of the United States.
10. We want land, bread, housing, education, clothing, justice, and peace. And as our major political objective, a United Nations–supervised plebiscite to be held throughout the black colony in which only black colonial subjects will be allowed to participate, for the purpose of determining the will of black people as to their national destiny.

16. Norm Allen Jr., "Humanism in the Black Community," in *The Sunrays* vol. 1, no. 1 (October–December 1991), 12.
17. Ibid.
18. Ibid.
19. "An African-American Humanist Declaration," in *Free Inquiry* vol. 10, no. 2 (Spring 1990), 13.
20. Ibid., 14–15.
21. Corliss Lamont, *The Philosophy of Humanism* (New York: Frederick Ungar, 1965), 53.
22. Humanist organizations such as the American Humanist Association founded in 1934 also merit consideration. This organization has been extremely important, although it has not consistently given attention to overtly religious issues.
23. Unitarian Universalist Commission on Appraisal to the General Assembly, *Empowerment: One Denomination's Quest for Racial Justice, 1967–1982* (Boston: Unitarian Universalist Association, 1983), 24.
24. Mark D. Morrison-Reed, *Black Pioneers in a White Denomination*, 3rd ed. (Boston: Skinner House Books, 1994), 92.
25. Quoted in Morrison-Reed, *Black Pioneers*, 94.
26. Ibid., 95.
27. Ibid., 130.
28. Ibid., 132–33.
29. Ibid., 120.
30. Ibid., 135.

Chapter 6

Judaism

African American history is peppered with conversation concerning the connection between African Americans and Jews. In large part this connection is described in terms of a common understanding of suffering based on the atrocities of the slave trade, the holocaust, and continued racially and ethnically based discrimination. This general understanding of commonality-based oppression is given more specific expression by African American Christians throughout history who speak in terms of a religious connection: both groups have a profound connection to God based on what both perceive as a special relationship to God, a type of chosen status. That is to say, "the Jewish components of American Christianity were appealing to slaves and to post-abolition blacks. They identified with the stories of the embondaged children of Israel and had hopes of God's leading them out of their state of slavery in a similar manner."[1] For the descendants of slaves in the United States, the story of bondage and freedom outlined in the Old Testament provided hope for a better time to come, and so African Americans gravitated toward these stories and saw in their experience commonalities with the protagonists of the Old Testament stories—the Jews.

Most African Americans have expressed this sense of kinship within the context of the Christian faith by giving great attention to the biblical story of the Exodus, the Psalms and Proverbs, and by appealing to the biblical prophets for ways to understand the demands of a proper relationship with God. Others have expressed this connection through involvement in predominantly white Jewish synagogues. As early as the Civil War some blacks participated in white Jewish synagogues in southern states.[2] Still others such as Arnold Ford, who was associated with Marcus Garvey's UNIA, have gone further to argue not only a general religious connection to Jews but also a claim on Judaism. In other words, "after 1900 a plethora of groups who characterized themselves as black Jews, black Hebrews, and black Israelites expanded the metaphorical kinship between black religion and Judaism."[3] Many of these early, separate communities developed in New York City, in Harlem, and in large part this was the case because Harlem, early in the twentieth century, was a heavily Jewish area. This made for ideal contact between African Americans, who worked in Harlem's neighborhoods, and Jews who lived and worshipped in those areas.

Questions can be raised concerning how strongly these African American groups adhered to Judaism, in that for instance most of these groups walked a line between the Old Testament's laws and customs and the New Testament's celebration of Jesus Christ. Few of these congregations extended their appreciation for Judaism beyond the Bible to the oral law and commentaries (Talmudic tradition) that inform traditional Jewry.[4] One of the groups hinted at in the preceding quotation is the Church of the Living God, Pillar of Truth for All Nations.

The Church of the Living God, Pillar of Truth for All Nations

The dating of these various communities is difficult, but it is often suggested that Prophet F. S. Cherry was one of the first to institutionalize this appeal to Judaism when, in 1866, he organized the Church of the Living God, Pillar of Truth for All Nations. Originating in Chattanooga, Tennessee, Cherry moved his organization to Philadelphia some time in the 1940s. Concerning the development of the Church of the Living God, Prophet Cherry told his followers that "years ago, when he was far from his native land, the Lord approached him in a vision and touched him, thereby appointing him His prophet. Thereafter he was led back to America and to Philadelphia, where he was directed to establish the Church of God."[5] With this story of origin, it becomes clear that Prophet Cherry is the final authority in all matters within the church, but, like other charismatic leaders mentioned in this book, he has developed a hierarchy of assistants, including deacons, elders, secretaries, and preachers, who help him manage the church.

Cherry proclaimed that divine visions instructed him to undertake the work of bringing African Americans to a proper understanding of themselves as the true Jews. Cherry's message was aggressive and nationalistic in that he argued that God and biblical figures such as Adam, Eve, and Jesus were physically black. Furthermore, he argued that whites, including white Jews, altered this information concerning the blackness of biblical figures to fit their purposes. African Americans are representative of the true people of God. Prophet Cherry's teachings are premised on his reading of the Hebrew Bible, which is the ultimate source of knowledge for his church.

Much of this doctrine is explored and explained within the context of worship. Prophet Cherry's services took place on Saturday, the Sabbath. Members of the church also gathered on Fridays and Wednesdays, but the most important was the Sabbath, Saturday, service. Those who gathered started the service with songs, and after a few selections had been sung, Prophet Cherry took the pulpit and called the service to order. After the congregation sang another song and prayed, Prophet Cherry read from the Bible and provided commentary on the meaning of the biblical passage.

Members of the congregation did not simply listen and absorb the Prophet's teachings. To the contrary, members of the congregation were invited to raise questions concerning the Prophet's teachings or to provide their insights concerning the biblical passages under study. After this portion of the service was completed, another song was sung, and this was followed by a sermon from the Prophet during which he expounded on the organization's teachings, including the status of his followers as the true people of God. He criticized Christian churches for embracing the incorrect teachings of white Christians and Jews, first by accepting the idea that Jesus is white. Also exposed to critique were white Jews, who, according to Prophet Cherry, are guilty of not understanding the true significance of Jesus Christ. Clearly, Prophet Cherry combined elements of Judaism such as the Passover with Christian commitments such as the centrality of Jesus Christ.

After the sermon, another song was sung and the congregation was dismissed. These weekly teachings were supplemented on a daily basis by moral and ethical guidelines heavily dependent on the Ten Commandments. Requirements were strict, including no dancing, no heavy drinking of alcohol, avoidance of pork, and a prohibition of photographs of church members or having pictures on the walls of their homes.[6]

Prophet Cherry's work as leader of this organization continued until his death in 1965. After his death, Prophet Cherry's son, Benjamin Cherry, led the organization. Information concerning the church after Prophet Cherry's death is unavailable, but what is more certain is the manner in which Prophet Cherry's ministry served to buttress the work of those who came after him.

The Church of God and Saints of Christ

Shortly after Prophet Cherry began his work in Philadelphia, William Saunders Crowdy's life changed. He began a path of religious awakening similar to Cherry's.

Born in 1847, in Charlotte Hall, Maryland, Crowdy spent the first fifteen years of his life as a slave. Once an opportunity presented itself in 1863 to leave his position of servitude, he journeyed to the North and became a cook for the Union Army. With the conclusion of the war, he held various jobs in Guthrie, Oklahoma, and Kansas City, Missouri. Accounts of his life indicate that it was while living in Guthrie for the second time that his religious life took a turn from a rather uneventful connection to the Baptist Church to contact with the divine that changed his behavior.

In 1893 he began having visions. The first occurred while he was farming: "He heard a loud sound that was similar to that produced by a large flock of birds. Amidst this noise he thought he heard a voice saying 'run for your life.' On hearing this he dropped his axe and cleared a trail into the forest. . . . There he fell into a deep slumber during which the vision came to him as a dream." This dream, the account continues, involved him being "in a large room and that tables were descending from above. The tables were covered with filthy vomit. . . . Each table was labeled with the name of a church. . . . At one point in the vision a small, clean white table came down with the name Church of God and Saints of Christ on it."[7] Crowdy understood the vision to mean a divine mission to start a tabernacle, as he called his congregations, rejecting the problems of the other denominations. His tabernacle would be true to the teachings of God, as provided in scripture and through subsequent visions experienced by Crowdy.

In a manner meant to resemble the ministry of biblical prophets, Crowdy took to the streets and began sharing his vision for a new tabernacle with anyone who would listen. This ministry was based on the demands placed on him during that first vision. The organization's web site describes the command to preach felt by Crowdy:

> When afterwards I heard a voice speaking unto me; saying, as he had so said unto Ezekiel, "Son of Man, I send thee to the children of Israel, and to all nations of the earth that hath rebelled against me. They and their Fathers have transgressed against me, even unto this very day; for they are imprudent children and stiff-hearted. I do send thee unto them and thou shalt say unto them, thus saith the Lord God; not Elder Crowdy, or any other man or minister, but thus saith the Lord

God who is Supreme above all, and in all; whether they will hear or whether they forbear, yet shall they know there has been a Prophet among them. The Lord let me know that I should look for trouble and tribulation, but be not afraid of them; neither be afraid of their words; though briars and thorns be with thee. And thou dost dwell among scorpions, be not afraid of their words or be dismayed at their looks and thou shalt speak my words unto them, whether they will hear or whether they will forbear.[8]

From 1893 through 1895, he spread the teachings he received in the visions to his family and receptive members of the community. Feeling a need to spread these teachings beyond Guthrie, Crowdy made his way to Chicago and stayed there a short time teaching both African Americans and whites.

Wanting to give his converts and the doctrine they embraced an institutional framework, he moved to Lawrence, Kansas, in 1896 and established his first organization. By 1898, he had more than twenty fellowships throughout Kansas. These somewhat loosely arranged fellowships took the form of a church in 1899 during the second general assembly organized by Crowdy. From this point until his death in 1908, the organization maintained a presence in various cities and established its headquarters in Belleville, Virginia, in 1917. The tabernacles varied in size, but it has been suggested that some, including one in New York City established in 1899, had roughly 1,000 members. Beyond efforts to reach potential converts in the United States, the church also established missionary outposts in the Caribbean and in South Africa.

To foster the smooth functioning of these various congregations, Crowdy arranged them into regional districts, each headed by one of his ministers. The elders, or ministers, who supervised these districts formed a group referred to as the Presbytery. These elders played an important role, but the organization clearly revolved around Crowdy who, in addition to being called the "Black Elijah" because of the prophecy and healing he offered his followers, was understood as the primary teacher. In order to manage the affairs of the organization, Crowdy was assisted by C. S. Skinner and W. H. Plummer, who served as counselor for and business manager of the organization, respectively.[9]

Crowdy, who was understood to be one of God's prophets, taught his followers that African Americans were members of the lost tribes of Israel. Based on this, he pushed for strong adherence to various elements of Judaism. For example, Crowdy's churches followed the Jewish Sabbath by centering activities around Friday evening and Saturday. On Friday evening, the service began with the Rabbi (teacher), assisted by the Cantor, leading the congregation in silent meditation and prayer. Afterward, the Rabbi led the congregation in various readings, some of them from scripture. Songs were sung throughout the service, and the service concluded with a sermon by the Rabbi.

On Saturday, members of the various tabernacles gathered early, and after a time of fellowship during which songs were sung, people divided into Sabbath school classes. These classes provided information concerning the church's distinctive doctrine taught and significant scriptural stories. After Sabbath school, the main service began. As with the Friday service, singing was an important dimension of worship. However, the focus of the Saturday service was the presentation of the Torah and the rabbi, and this was followed by the sermon that outlined the origin and teachings of the organization. After the sermon, those present were given an opportunity to either join the tabernacle (if they were visitors) or renew their relationship with God if they were current members. Additional singing and a benediction brought the service to an end, but those gathered did not go to their homes until after a communal meal was eaten.[10]

Crowdy's organization recognized various rituals as central to church life, including Rosh Hashanah (Jewish New Year), Yom Kippur (the day of Atonement), and Passover. Within this church, the Passover celebrations were distinguished by color. There was a purple Passover during which members of the church wore that particular color. There was also a black Passover, so called for the same reason. Members of the various local congregations were encouraged to travel to the headquarters for the denomination, and there they would celebrate the Lord's safekeeping of the children of Israel when the angel of death killed the firstborn of the Egyptians (Exodus 11:4–6). Furthermore, the Passover allows for a recounting of the Exodus story in which the Jews were freed from bondage in Egypt. During the week of celebration, members of the organization attended services consisting of singing and sermons. Meals consumed during this period centered around unleavened bread, and the week of activities culminated in a communal meal of bread and lamb.

While Crowdy's followers understood themselves to stand within the tradition of Judaism, their practices were not pure in that Crowdy sought to blend Judaism with Christianity. He gave a great deal of attention to Jesus Christ as the model of conduct. Crowdy does not refer to Jesus as the messiah, but the perception of Jesus seems to extend beyond traditional Jewish understandings of him:

The scripture says when you are converted old things passed away. Now if you are converted, leave lying, whoremongering, idolatry, witchcraft, hoodooing, and all manner of isms, you want to leave that behind and take up the new things of Jesus Christ which by no means will suffer to do any of those things. I want members to stop evil speaking of one another, and don't care to undermine one another and let me know it, if you can't speak a good word for your neighbor, even if he is a sinner, hold your peace [sic].[11]

In addition to the life of Jesus Christ and an appreciation for other dimensions of the prophetic tradition as expressed in Judaism, Crowdy developed rituals unique to the church, including Re-establishment Day, which honors Crowdy and recounts the church's history.

These activities were practiced within the context of established doctrine, drawn loosely from the Bible, by which tabernacle members lived. Central among these innovations were the "Seven Keys":

1. The Church of God and the Saints of Christ.
2. Wine forbidden to be drunk in the Church of God forever.
3. Unleavened bread and water for Christ's body and blood.
4. Foot washing is a commandment.
5. The Disciple's Prayer.
6. You must be breathed upon with a Holy Kiss.
7. The Ten Commandments.

The Seven Keys speak to the significance of Crowdy's work by highlighting the truthfulness of the Church of God and the Saints of Christ. This church, unlike traditional churches and based on the revelations received by Crowdy, is in line with the will of God and is teaching the truth about God and God's relationship to African Americans. The Christian undertones of this religious organization are apparent in the centrality given to Jesus Christ. The Third Key speaks to this by describing the appropriate items to be used in celebration of what Christians refer to as communion, the ritual enactment of Jesus Christ's blood and body sacrificed on the cross. Most Christian churches celebrate communion using some type of bread to represent the body and wine (or grape juice) to represent the blood of Jesus Christ. However, as the Second Key stipulates, wine is not consumed by members of this community, not even as part of the communion ritual. Other important components of the organization's code include the ritual of foot washing through which members show their humility and community by washing the feet of other members of the group. It is meant to represent the biblical tradition of cleaning the feet of guests as they entered the home. Jesus Christ does this for his disciples as a sign of humility in that the proclaimed Son of God lowers himself and provides this service. Also of symbolic importance is the Holy Kiss given to members as a sign of community and proper relationship. The final two elements of this code are the Disciple's prayer that plays a role in the worship experience of members of the church, and the Ten Commandments drawn from the Old Testament. Even after Crowdy's death, the principles that he outlined hold sway over the Church of God and Saints of Christ.

Currently the organization's chief executive officer is Bishop Robert D. Grant. While the total membership is uncertain, the Church of God web site indicates that Bishop Grant oversees a network of thirty-two tabernacles in cities in the United States such as Buffalo, New York; Detroit, Michigan; and Newark, New Jersey; as well as in the Caribbean, South Africa, and England. In an effort to continue to advance its work, the Church of God argues that its "vision is presently focused on community development. The Church of God and Saints of Christ ha[s] embarked upon a multi-million dollar project, a multi-faceted building on 110 acres of land owned by the church in Galestown, Maryland. This project will include worship edifice, recreational and educational facilities."[12]

The Commandment Keepers Congregation of Harlem

While attention to Talmudic tradition within Crowdy's movement is suspect at best, Arnold Ford, who was affiliated with Marcus Garvey's movement, studied Hebrew and made an effort to enrich African American acquaintance with Judaism through attention to the Talmud. Unable to convince Garvey that Judaism should be the religious underpinning of the Universal Negro Improvement Association (UNIA), Ford did his best to encourage the practice of Judaism in Harlem, and he is credited with playing a significant role in the development of several congregations. Ford disappeared, some arguing that he moved to Ethiopia and others suggesting that he moved to Detroit. Little is known about him after he left Harlem.

His work continued through the efforts of numerous figures including Wentworth A. Matthew, who in 1919 organized and led the Harlem community known as the Commandment Keepers Congregation of the Living God. This organization was incorporated in 1930, and eventually relocated to Brooklyn, New York.

As is the case with numerous traditions discussed in this volume, the Commandment Keepers Congregation's teachings begin with a rejection of African American identity grounded in a history of slavery, and offer a counter identity centered on Africa. They were not "negroes," or "blacks" and "coloreds," as African Americans were commonly called. An identity connected to these labels was degrading. Rather, members of this group argued that African Americans are Ethiopian Hebrews, a part of the original Israelites spoken of in the Bible: "During slavery they took away our name, language, religion, and science, as these were the only possessions the slaves had, and they were pumped full of Christianity to make them more docile. . . . All so-called Negroes are the lost sheep of the House of Israel which can be proved from scripture and they all have birthmarks that identify their tribe. Jacob was a black man because he had smooth skin."[13] According to their reading of the Bible, "smooth skin" is synonymous with blackness, and their blackness results from their heritage as the offspring of King Solomon and the Queen of Sheba, who was black, an African.

Because of this lineage, according to this group's belief, the proper religion of African Americans is Judaism, not Christianity. Judaism is the religion of African Americans, and Christianity the religion of whites. Those adhering to the latter will face destruction because of their evil deeds and their perverting of the true religion through the breaking of the Ten Commandments. But those who embrace Judaism, the true people of God, will be restored to greatness. Not only do members of this religious group claim an identity based on connection to Ethiopia. Rabbi Matthew, as he was called, claimed that he spoke with the authority granted him by "the Chief Rabbi of the Falasha and the National Coptic Church of St. Michael." He claimed to be the only teacher with this credential.[14]

This relationship to Ethiopia put Rabbi Matthew in the best position to lead the "black Jews" in the United States. Those who were willing to embrace the teachings of Judaism as presented by the Rabbi began by recognizing the centrality of the Hebrew language. Members of this community understood Hebrew to be the language of God, the proper language of God's people. Hence, instruction in Hebrew was offered to the members of the Commandment Keepers. In addition to use of the proper language, to the extent they were able to do so, they were required to maintain a strict diet. This was not a traditional kosher diet, in that it excluded foods such as duck that are not forbidden to orthodox Jews. However, Rabbi Matthew asserted that duck was forbidden to his followers because this animal is within the same family as the pig.[15] The avoidance of the foods the Rabbi labeled forbidden—pork, crab, catfish, lobster, duck, hotdogs, and bear—promoted good health and the proper mindset for learning.

Much of what members of the Commandment Keepers believed was summarized by Rabbi Matthew in what he called the "twelve principles of the doctrine of Israel." These principles can be summarized as follows. Members of this community believed in creation as outlined in the Bible. In addition, they understood that the life well lived involved obedience to the laws given by God through Moses, and the dietary restrictions outlined in scripture. The people of God were also required to tithe. The goal of God's people, in light of attention to scripture, was holiness. Proper attention to the laws of God resulted in healing and everlasting life. The working of God for God's people, particularly with respect to their freedom from bondage, must be remembered and celebrated by those within the community. The most important ceremony of remembrance was understood to be the Passover, and this was to be observed along with the ritual of the washing of feet. God promises that when God's people are faithful, Israel will be restored, and the dead (the black Jews) can be raised at the proper time. God's will includes the coming of the Messiah for God's people and the inauguration of the age of rule by God.[16] Rabbi Matthew provided scriptural references for these principles, and he taught them on a regular basis. The aim was to produce, based on a highly disciplined and strict code of conduct, a community that lives in an ethically and morally responsible way to God and to each other.

Rabbi Matthew provided instruction not only during the course of Sabbath services, but also through what was called the Ethiopian Hebrew Rabbinical College of the Royal Order of Ethiopian Hebrews and the Commandment Keepers Congregation of the Living God, Inc. The Rabbi taught based on the training he claimed to have received while in Virginia. What he provided was a type of esoteric knowledge, based on the "hidden" truths of Judaism—the "Cabbalistic Sciences." Classes included languages (Hebrew, Greek, Latin, and French), biblical studies related to learning about the meaning of various books of the Old Testament, Jewish history, and the Talmud. Members of the congregation took classes related to these topics over the course of several years. At the end of their training, students received degrees such as "Master of Hebrew Doctrine." This training in the hidden wisdom of Judaism, according to Rabbi Matthew, allowed the well trained, through the assistance of angelic forces, to cure various illnesses, bring about prosperity through control over those with evil intentions, and bring children back from the dead.[17] Rabbi Matthew claimed to have healed and performed miracles based on the Cabbalistic Sciences. While undocumented, these claims were made during classes offered through the college and through sermons.

Like Crowdy and Cherry, Rabbi Matthew insisted on observation of the proper Sabbath—Friday evening and Saturday—in addition to Jewish holidays such as Passover, which they considered the most important of the holidays because both the Jews and enslaved Africans experienced an exodus. Weekly services began with the singing of a hymn, followed by prayer in unison. Selections from their prayer book written by the Rabbi were then read in both English and Hebrew, followed by readings from the Torah in Hebrew. The service concluded with hymns and the reciting of prayers in Hebrew. This Saturday morning service was followed by an afternoon service that was similar in format with the exception of testimonials offered by members of the congregation and a sermon given by Rabbi Matthew.[18]

Rabbi Matthew led the organization until his death in 1973. After Rabbi Matthew's death, his members gained a new leader in his grandson, David M. Dore. It is unclear exactly how many members there are in the Commandment Keepers Congregation of the Living God. However, it is known that Rabbis trained by Matthew organized congregations that maintained an allegiance to Matthew's teachings. Examples include the work done in Chicago by Rabbi Abihu Ben Reuben and Rabbi Lazarus. Furthermore, Rabbi Capers C. Funnye Jr., who assisted Rabbi Reuben, participated in the merger of several congregations that resulted in the formation of Beth Shalom B'nai Zaken Ethiopian Hebrew Congregation, which was led by Rabbi Funnye.

The Hebrew Israelites

Of the communities discussed in this chapter, none has received more national and international attention than the Hebrew Israelites. Ben Carter (aka Ben Ammi), the leader of this community, was a member of the Abeta Hebrew Israel Culture Center in Chicago, Illinois. This organization held a deep belief in the movement of African Americans back to Africa. According to the Hebrew Israelites, Ben Carter had a vision in 1966 through which it became clear that it was time to establish the kingdom of God by leaving the United States. In 1968, Carter and others from the organization were sent to Liberia to investigate the possibility of relocation. The organization was able to secure land through a third party, and the sharing of this information upon their return sparked the organization's growth as pro-emigration African Americans made their way to the Abeta Hebrew Israel Culture Center. It did not take long for members to abandon their connections to the United States and make their way to Liberia. This movement began in 1969, shortly after the return of Ben Carter and the others.

The work was hard, and the clearing of land for the planting of crops was foreign to the emigrants who came from the urban context of the United States. Breaking all ties with the United States was difficult at best, and life in their new home was tough. Sickness, poor supplies, and growing disillusionment with their Liberian context fueled tensions between members of the community. Troubles mounted as members of the community found it hard to complete what they understood as required religious rituals such as Passover. Snares like this might have caused even deeper divisions without the counsel of Ben Ammi, but Ammi was able to persuade the community to downplay the significance of traditional requirements for rituals, such as the lamb sacrifice for Passover, by arguing that God demanded only the loyalty of God's people—not the external trappings of religious worship. His insights not only served to keep the community intact, they also pushed him to the forefront of organizational leadership.

While committed to the correctness of their departure from the United States, Ben Ammi was no longer certain that Liberia was anything more than a temporary location for the preparation of the community for its final home—Israel. With this in mind, Ammi took a few members of the group with him and went to Israel seeking permission to relocate. Although the Israeli government initially resisted this request, in 1969 members of the organization were able to move in small groups and receive housing, jobs, and other benefits. Ultimately, however, they were told that permission to stay in settlements such as Dimona required proper conversion to Judaism. Some members of the small group who had been granted temporary visas agreed to convert, but Ammi argued that they should not because they were not Jews, but Hebrews. For Ammi the distinction was doctrinally significant in that his group, as the true people of God, gave allegiance only to the Torah, not the commentaries and other materials developed after the revelation of the Torah. Why should they convert, Ammi reasoned, when they were the true people of God and more entitled to the land than were its current inhabitants?

Troubles mounted as new emigrants arrived, some with questionable allegiance to the rules and regulations governing the community. To stem the tide of trouble and solidify the conduct of group members around a unified will, Ammi instituted new codes of conduct and stiffened the punishment for breaking the rules: those who did not abide by the regulations were expelled. Although it would take time, the Hebrew Israelite community was able to secure privileges: employment, social services, and permanent housing. This community in Israel is matched by branches of the movement in Chicago and several other major cities in the United States. Clear numbers are unavailable for the United States, but recent estimates for the Israel community range between one thousand and twenty-five hundred members.

Ben Ammi's status within the organization continued to grow. Ultimately he became the group's messiah, bringing them out of the troubled land of the United States to the promised land of Israel. This change in status was reflected in the name he was given after 1972: Rabbey and Adoni Rabbey, meaning "My Lord and Master."[19] As head of the community, he is responsible for outlining the beliefs and practices of Hebrew Israelites. While his perspective on the Hebrew Israelites as true Jews over against others who claim Judaism has softened somewhat, the aesthetics and doctrine of the group remain a rough combination of African American cultural sensibilities and Judaism. No longer arguing biological links to the tribes of Israel, Ben Ammi began to argue that one's connection to true Israelite identity is marked only by proper behavior and comportment.

This connection based on actions as opposed to genealogy is played out both in the way Hebrew Israelites present themselves and how they conduct themselves. For example, the clothing worn by men and women within the community represents a combination of African styles of dress and Jewish aesthetics: "Men wear long African print shirts with the biblically prescribed fringes known in Hebrew as tsitsit, as well as head covering called kippot. Women wear long, modest dresses."[20] This style of dress, an external marker of religious commitment, is combined with a vegetarian diet in order to keep the body pure and healthy, and in this way match a presentation of the body as religious through clothing with a commitment to proper nutrition as religious obligation. Regularly observed rituals such as Passover, Yom Kippur, and the Sabbath (Friday and Saturday) round out the obligations of Hebrew Israelites. These traditionally Jewish ritual activities, however, are altered by the community and combined with African American Christian activities such as the use of Gospel music.

Religious activities are combined with the typical elements of communal existence, including a school, health clinic, and community center. All of these activities and services are meant to separate Hebrew Israelites from all others through a more disciplined and balanced life.

Basic Beliefs

It is difficult to state the basic beliefs of these Jewish communities in general terms. However, there is enough overlap to suggest that these organizations recognized themselves as serving to bring African Americans into an understanding of their proper religion. In all cases it was suggested that Judaism is a tradition associated with Africa, and that African Americans are connected to the original Children of Israel discussed in the Old Testament. They are not blacks, not African Americans. They are the descendants of the Children of Israel, whether they live in the United States or Israel. To make this connection, great attention was given to a fairly literal reading of the Old Testament, and this sacred text tended to take precedence over Talmudic tradition for most of these communities. This is to say, what might be considered traditional texts within the Judaic tradition are utilized in a rather selective fashion. These communities argue for a historical and spiritual connection to God that sets them apart and affords them access to guarded knowledge. Such a position, however, requires rigorous discipline and attention to laws that included the Ten Commandments, but that also extended beyond these commandments.

Each of the communities discussed made an effort to separate its membership from nonmembership through attire and ritual. For example, members dressed in modest clothing that was often based on a combining of Jewish aesthetics and African American culture. In addition, each community prided itself on adherence to ritual celebrations such as Passover and Yom Kippur and to the dietary restrictions associated with biblical Judaism (at times with more stipulations on proper foods than one finds in the biblical dietary laws). In some cases traditional celebrations such as Passover were supplemented by rituals revolving around the leaders of particular communities. This combination of traditional and new rituals marked the manner in which these communities sought to make Judaism meaningful within the context of the particular details of African American life. These groups made Judaism "their own," even when this involved breaks with traditional perceptions of the faith.

Concluding Thoughts

Some came from African American Christian churches, others from organizations premised on black nationalism. Whatever their initial religious orientation, African Americans who eventually embrace some form of Judaism do so because it offers, for them, the best way to organize life.

The rituals of Judaism, as expressed in the tradition's literature, combined with new practices based on their historical and cultural context nurture their religious inclinations. They find in the aesthetics and rituals of the faith a language and pattern of behavior that helps makes sense of the world. Although expressed in various ways, and with differing life spans, forms of Judaism have found a place on the African American religious landscape.

By the time some African Americans prepare for Sunday service in their Christian churches, some have long completed Friday prayers, and still others have completed the religious obligations associated with the Sabbath observed on Friday evening and Saturday. How many embrace some version of Judaism is uncertain. But regardless of the number involved, Judaism (whether traditional or not) is the religion of choice for some African Americans.

Notes

1. Elly M. Wynia, *The Church of God and Saints of Christ: The Rise of Black Jews* (New York: Garland Publishing, 1994), 13.

2. Merrill Singer, "Symbolic Identity Formation in an African American Religious Sect: The Black Hebrew Israelites," in Yvonne Chireau and Nathaniel Deutsch, eds., *Black Zion: African American Religious Encounters with Judaism* (New York: Oxford University Press, 2000), 57.

3. Yvonne Chireau, "Black Culture and Black Zion: African American Religious Encounters with Judaism, 1790–1930, an Overview," in Yvonne Chireau and Nathaniel Deutsch, eds., *Black Zion: African American Religious Encounters with Judaism* (New York: Oxford University Press, 2000), 21.

4. Howard M. Brotz, *The Black Jews of Harlem: Negro Nationalism and the Dilemmas of Negro Leadership* (New York: Schocken Books, 1970), 10.

5. Arthur Huff Fauset, *Black Gods of the Metropolis: Negro Religious Cults of the Urban North* (Philadelphia: University of Pennsylvania Press, 2002), 32.

6. Ibid., 37–39.

7. Wynia, *Church of God and Saints of Christ*, 21.

8. http://www.churchofgod1896.org/founder.html.

9. Wynia, *Church of God and Saints of Christ*, 32–33.

10. Ibid., 60–64.

11. Ibid., 52.

12. http://www.churchofgod1896.org/MISSION%20&%20VISION.htm.

13. Brotz, *Black Jews of Harlem*, 16.

14. Ibid., 22.

15. Ibid., 28.

16. Ibid., 40–41.

17. Ibid., 31–32.

18. Ibid., 35–38.

19. Singer, "Symbolic Identity Formation," 67–69.

20. Ethan Michaeli, "Another Exodus: The Hebrew Israelites from Chicago to Dimona," in Yvonne Chireau and Nathaniel Deutsch, eds., *Black Zion: African American Religious Encounters with Judaism* (New York: Oxford University Press, 2000), 75.

Chapter 7

Nation of Islam

The twentieth century was full of dramatic cultural achievements, two of which relate to the religious community under consideration in this chapter: Spike Lee's adaptation of Malcolm X's autobiography and the Million Man March orchestrated by Minister Louis Farrakhan. With respect to Spike Lee's film, Americans, some of whom knew virtually nothing of the former national spokesperson for the Nation of Islam, paid a good sum of money to explore segments of Malcolm X's (born Malcolm Little) complex journey from criminal to convert. The Million Man March, drawing from the teachings of the Nation of Islam, brought African American men together for atonement, to acknowledge ways in which they have fallen short of their responsibilities to themselves, their families, and the larger community. As part of this gathering, they pledged themselves to greater effort regarding the successful shouldering of their commitments. Both the film and the march focused national attention on the Nation of Islam and sparked interest in the modes of nationalism that informed the Nation of Islam's development. While the Nation of Islam has received a great deal of media attention because of its nationalistic rhetoric, it is important to remember that its sense of nationalism is based on a long-standing tradition.

Religiously Infused Nationalism: Three Pre–Nation of Islam Examples

Perspectives on Nineteenth-Century Emigrationism

While churches grew and African Americans made some progress during the period of Reconstruction, this growth was not long lasting.

In fact, as soon as federal troops were no longer in place to enforce the rights of African Americans, white supremacy resurfaced. "Jim Crow" regulations replaced slavery as a mechanism for maintaining inequality and the privileges of whiteness. Within this social context, Henry Mc-Neal Turner, a leader within the AME Church, developed a brand of nationalism that pushed for recognition of the importance of physical blackness through a theologically informed denunciation of racism. Turner, beginning his ministry with a milder appeal to the full human-ity of African Americans, over the years witnessed the demonic nature of racism and radicalized his appeal. Ultimately, he argued that African Americans would secure opportunities for advancement and reach their full potential only by emigrating back to Africa. In fact, this movement back to Africa was, according to Turner, providential—the unfolding of God's will.

This perspective raised a question: If African Americans should be in Africa, why did God allow their forced removal in the first place? Turner provided a theological response to this question by suggesting that God allowed slavery as a *temporary* institution to introduce Africans to civil forms of government and the Christian faith. In Turner's words:

> There is no more doubt in my mind that we have ultimately to return to Africa than there is of the existence of God. . . . The four millions of us in this country are at school, learning the doctrines of Chris-tianity and the elements of civil government. And as soon as we are educated sufficiently to assume control of our vast ancestral domain, we will hear the voice of a mysterious Providence, saying "Return to the land of your fathers."[1]

While there are undoubtedly problems with this perspective in that it is religiously chauvinistic and Eurocentric, during the nineteenth cen-tury it was a position suggesting that slavery (which whites sinfully tried to make a permanent arrangement, a sin they will be punished for by God) prepared African Americans with the faith and sociopolitical skills necessary to transform Africa, to restore it to its former glory in keep-ing with scripture: "and Ethiopia shall stretch forth her hands unto God" (Psalm 68:13).

Turner was clear: only in Africa could there be healthy community in which those of African descent prosper. He was convinced that the resources existed in Africa for this providential development based on his travels, during which he witnessed Africans managing businesses, offices, churches, schools, and so on. There was, from his perspective, a ready framework for self-reliance and independence in Africa. Hence, separation from white Americans and the development of a new community in Africa were the keys to the progress of African Americans. While Africa held great allure for many emigration-minded African Americans, some also noted the possibility of nurturing the formation of a strong nation within the context of the New World, perhaps in the Caribbean or South America, which are heavily populated with people of African descent.

Although this theologically informed version of nationalism was rhetorically powerful and convincing to some, few actually went to Africa. Those who did go sent back mixed messages. There were numerous complaints demonstrating that African Americans were not prepared for the cultural differences that separated them from Africans, nor were they prepared for the natural environment. Many became ill, and others found it difficult to make a living off the land. Some stayed and made the best of their situation, praying that God would fulfill God's will through their presence. Others returned to the United States. The inability of some to succeed in Africa did not, from Turner's perspective, cause the importance of emigration to be fundamentally questioned.

Turner was convinced that movement to Africa was the best conceivable plan, a providential plan, but he also argued that those who did not want to go—as ridiculous as he thought this was—had earned all the rights and privileges that whites enjoyed as citizens. As Turner's most recent biographer notes, Turner's understanding of God's ultimate plan for African Americans allowed for success on two continents, Africa and North America. In either case, whether in the United States or Africa, African Americans were entitled to a fruitful existence marked by prosperity and freedom from the terror of discrimination.[2]

Henry Turner's rhetoric made him a major spokesperson for emigration within religious circles. He was certainly not the only African American of prominence to hold this perspective, however. He was not the first when one considers figures of the 1800s such as merchant Paul Cuffee, Methodist minister Daniel Coker, and Baptist missionary Lott Carey, who worked to bring the Gospel of Christ to Africa and in that way redeem the continent. Furthermore, a discussion of nationalism within the religious context must also include mention of Edward Wilmot Blyden.

Although he was born in 1832 to free parents on the Caribbean island of St. Thomas, Blyden was aware of the destruction to the human body and spirit caused by slavery. Blyden, like Turner, recognized that the condition of African Americans did not speak to their nature and capabilities. That is to say, those of African descent were not oppressed because they were inferior to whites. Both Blyden and Turner recognized in African Americans the seeds of a destined greatness, and the glory or genius of this people would be manifest as they worked to uplift Africa. Regarding Liberia in West Africa, a primary location for emigrants and holding particular significance for him, Blyden makes the following appeal: "Liberia, with outstretched arms earnestly invites all to come. We call them forth out of all nations; we bid them to take up their all and leave the country of their exile. . . . We summon them from the States, from the Canadas [*sic*], from the West Indies, from everywhere, to come and take part with us in our great work."[3]

Unlike Turner, whose acquaintance with Africa was based on occasional trips and reports returned through church-based media outlets, Blyden made an appeal to African Americans to emigrate based on his time lived in Africa. Blyden differed from some other proponents of migration in that he not only desired the building of a new society in Africa but also strove to develop a unified Africa extending beyond West Africa. In this sense, Turner was an emigrationist while Blyden became a Pan-Africanist. An emigrationist in this context is interested in a movement of people to Africa, and a Pan-Africanist is interested in the uniting of the various countries and peoples (in Africa and the African diaspora) who have a connection to the land.

Some whites, through various colonization schemes and organizations, used the relocation of African Americans to Africa as a way of removing a problem. That is to say, rather than addressing discrimination and reshaping the sociopolitical fabric of the United States in ways that responded to the needs of all its citizens, they sought to simply discard African Americans. Nationalists, through various emigration projects, whether geared toward Africa or somewhere in the Caribbean or South America, did not view the quick removal without resources of African Americans as the solution to the race problem. In some instances, they were willing to temporarily work with whites, resisting their racism but utilizing their resources (and skills at times) to restore the greatness and past glory of those of African descent. Impassioned debate, energetic apologetics, philosophical inconsistencies, and uneven results mark the work of these nationalists. But on the heels of their efforts, an arguably more popular attempt to unify African Americans around a new home developed.

Those opposed to emigration saw God at work in the circumstances of African Americans. As was noted earlier in this book, some whites argued that African Americans were of less value than whites, and that they were fitted for servitude. Those making this argument suggested that this perspective was not simply a matter of convenience, a rationale for inequality. No, to the contrary, they made a case for understanding African Americans as inferior using scripture to push for a divine sanction on the status of African Americans as second-class citizens. Emigrationists responded to such arguments by rejecting the United States, understanding this nation to be beyond redemption. Other African Americans, however, attempted to counter versions of this argument put forth by some whites as a justification for inequality by flipping it on its head. They advocated an understanding of African Americans as a special or chosen people, whom God was using to improve the United States. God's movement in human history was understood as entailing a special development, one that rendered African Americans a chosen people.

Marcus Garvey's Universal Negro Improvement Association

While many high profile figures, such as Turner and Blyden, promoted a sense of nationalism premised on emigration, it must be noted that the largest nationalistic campaign ever mounted in the context of the United States came after the death of Turner and Blyden. It was developed by Marcus Garvey, a Jamaican intrigued by the self-help philosophy of Booker T. Washington. Garvey called the organizational underpinning for this mass movement the Universal Negro Improvement Association (UNIA), and this organization held sway over nationalists between 1917 and 1972.

After traveling through Central and South America as well as London, Garvey embarked on a trip to the United States to meet with Booker T. Washington. He was too late, however. Washington passed away in 1915 and Garvey arrived in 1916. Recognizing the deplorable socioeconomic, political, and psychological conditions under which African Americans lived, Garvey began sharing his plans for African American renewal and self-reliance, framed by his Universal Negro Improvement Association. This strategy quickly sparked a mass movement tied to several central premises, including the following assertions: (1) African Americans are a chosen people, selected by God for greatness; (2) Africa is destined for glory based on Psalm 68:13; and (3) the fulfillment of God's plan for African Americans and Africa necessitates the emigration of the former to the latter.

The UNIA was similar to other modalities of African American nationalism in that it fostered a revised and subversive sense of history by presenting African Americans as great contributors to world civilization beyond slavery, but the UNIA provided an aesthetic dimension to its nationalism that was sorely missing in the versions noted earlier. The organization was marked by an elaborate system of offices and rituals that entailed the display of finely arranged and arrayed members. In part, this attention to the presentation of African American bodies as beautiful through comportment and attire—elaborate uniforms and so on—spoke in subtle but powerful ways to the philosophy behind the organization's efforts to develop "Negro independent nationalism [a nation] on the continent of Africa."[4] "Africa for the Africans" was the UNIA catch phrase.

While the presentation of African Americans with dignity and beauty argued their worth in nonverbal ways, the stated goals and aims of the UNIA articulated this perspective more forcefully: "It must be the mission of all Negroes to have pride in their race. To think of the race in the highest terms of human living. To think that God made the race perfect, that there is no one better than you; that you have all the elements of human perfection. . . . Love yourself better than anybody else. All beauty is in you and not outside of you."[5] In this way, like Turner before him, Garvey placed those of African descent within the context of what is best about the universe. Both Garvey and Turner—and one could include Blyden here—understood that history has a positive purpose and those of African descent play a significant role in its unfolding.

Attention to aesthetics, theological underpinning for the movement, and commitment to a non–United States–centered identity for African Americans persisted in various forms after the decline of Garvey's movement. In fact, one could feasibly argue that Garvey's philosophy and the work of another organization called the Moorish Science Temple played a significant part in the development of the Nation of Islam's theological and social agenda. The links between the UNIA and the Moorish Science Temple of America were not lost on the founder of the latter: "In these modern days there came a forerunner, who was divinely prepared by the great God-Allah and his name is Marcus Garvey, who did teach and warn the nations of the earth to prepare to meet the coming Prophet, who was to bring the true and divine Creed of Islam, and his name is Noble Drew Ali."[6]

Noble Drew Ali's Moorish Science Temple

In 1913, Noble Drew Ali (born Timothy Drew) established the Canaanite Temple in Newark, New Jersey, later called the Moorish Science Temple in America. Concerning his ministry and the Temple's work, Noble Drew Ali told his followers that the King of Morocco, the original home of African Americans, gave him instructions to educate African Americans in the religion of Islam. This was his mission in life, his calling as the last in a line of great prophets. Noble Drew Ali sought to reenvision African American identity and consciousness through a rejection of white supremacy on theological or religious grounds. Rather than argue against discrimination using the Christian tradition, however, Noble Drew Ali pushed for an interpretation of Eastern philosophy framed by the experience of African Americans. This reimagining of African American identity involved a name change in that they were to be regarded as "Moors," or "Moorish Americans." The reasoning behind the adoption of a new name was forcefully presented: a name or identity precedes a nation.

Like Garvey, change in terms of identification and self-consciousness was mirrored externally through a shift in decorative aesthetics: new clothes for a new person. So those affiliated with the Moorish Science Temple carried their identification cards marking them as members. They walked through their neighborhoods with men wearing red fezzes and women wearing turbans and long dresses. Through their attire and conversation they professed the teachings of their leader:

> Drew did not allow himself to be troubled by the inconveniences of history. He simply decreed that, thenceforth, American blacks were to be known as "Asiatics." . . . To document this ethnic transformation, he issued "Nationality and Identification Cards" to his followers. Each card bore the Islamic symbol (the star and the crescent), an image of clasped hands, and a numeral "7" in a circle. . . . Each card was validated by the subscription, "NOBLE DREW ALI, THE PROPHET." . . . The members of the [group] felt an exaggerated sense of security and importance in their new "Asiatic" status, symbolized by the red fezzes that the male members were required to wear at all times.[7]

The Moorish Science Temple gained ground, expanding well beyond its initial beginnings in Newark. But it also underwent a rather messy split only a few years after its founding. Some left and organized the Holy Moabite Temple of the World, and others maintained the original name and their allegiance to Noble Drew Ali.[8]

The sense of group unity, that is, nationalism, developed by the Moorish Science Temple was not unique. It was a fundamental element by definition of all African American nationalist groups. Nonetheless, it was an expanded sense of nationalism in that Noble Drew Ali wanted to bring together the Asiatic peoples living in the Americas, Asia, and Africa as a cultural whole, under one religion. Yet as a contradiction to this effort to unite under one religion, members of the movement often spoke of themselves as Muslim members of the Moorish Science Temple who embrace all the great prophets—Jesus, Muhammad, Buddha, Confucius, and of course Noble Drew Ali. There are numerous elements of their religious orientation that prevent the label of Islam from fitting comfortably. One of the most glaring distinctions is the manner in which Noble Drew Ali is considered the reincarnation of the Prophet Muhammad. The doctrine of the Moorish Science Temple speaks to a blending of various traditions including, according to historian Richard Brent Turner, Garvey's philosophy, Islam, Freemansonry, Theosophy, and the basic principles of African American nationalism.[9] The theological details of this religious system are provided in the *Holy Koran of the Moorish Science Temple* (not the Qur'an).

At the organization's height of influence, there may have been as many as 30,000 African Americans committed to the teachings of Noble Drew Ali.[10] The membership of the Moorish Science Temple declined over time, due to internal schisms and external pressures from the government. Some within the organization saw membership as an opportunity for financial gain, and they took advantage of members of the organization who expressed an interest in buying items that connected them to their "Asiatic" heritage. However, Noble Drew Ali saw the selling of charms and other items as a perversion of the organization's aims. His resistance to such money-making schemes resulted in his murder in 1929.

Although the original Moorish Science Temple would never match the status it held in African American communities during his leadership, the teachings of Noble Drew Ali remain very much alive in cities such as Baltimore and Detroit. That is to say, "while the group declined sharply in membership and appeal during the 1930s, the religious foundation it had laid . . . lasted long enough to be exploited by others."[11] Noble Drew Ali is reincarnated, it is believed, in each "Sheik" who leads a temple associated with the movement. For example, although the Nation of Islam denies it, some argue that Master Fard Muhammad represented one of many reincarnations of Noble Drew Ali. Of less questionable status are the suggested links between the Honorable Elijah Muhammad and the teachings of Noble Drew Ali. Whether through Master Fard Muhammad or the Honorable Elijah Muhammad, the Nation of Islam's teachings include portions of Moorish Science Temple doctrine, as well as the nationalist sensibilities of figures such as Turner, Blyden, and Garvey.

Master Fard Muhammad and the Nation of Islam

A mysterious man appeared in Detroit in 1930, selling silk and other items door to door. Some of those he approached invited him into their homes, and W. D. Fard (Master Fard Muhammad), during the course of conversation, explained that he had come to them from the land where the silks were produced and worn. This intrigued his customers, who faced the difficult times of the Great Depression and the dilemmas of life in the segregated North. To their queries concerning the place from which he had come, Fard responded with a history lesson grounded in a dietary pronouncement: "Now don't eat this food. It is poison for you. The people in your own country do not eat it. Since they eat the right kind of food they have the best health all the time. If you would live just like the people in your home country, you would never be sick any more."[12]

The answers Fard Muhammad provided were mysterious yet feasible enough to grab the attention of listeners. With time, and through word of mouth, his audience grew beyond what could be accommodated in any living room. To continue the teachings concerning the true history and destiny of African Americans begun during those informal gatherings, a public space was rented. As he grew closer to members of Detroit's African American community, he intensified his lessons regarding proper moral and ethical sensibilities, admonishing them to avoid unhealthy practices such as adultery and drug use. Master Fard, as he was called by some of his followers, grew to know a great deal about the community in which he worked, but his identity remained rather mysterious. He would tell those who asked that he was from Mecca, but more information about him could not be given at the time. Yet, if they were patient and faithful, his greatness and their destined glory would manifest.

With time, his identity was revealed to the faithful. They came to know him as one from the tribe of the Prophet Muhammad, the child of a black father and a white mother as foretold in the Christian scriptures, the Book of Revelation: "After this I saw another angel coming down from heaven, having great authority; and the earth was made bright with his splendor" (18:1).

Using the Bible and teachings revealed to him (containing information from Freemasonry and Seventh Day Adventist teachings), Fard explained that African Americans were a special people. By extension, he argued, their treatment in the United States was based on lies concerning their nature. But they, according to this esoteric knowledge, were destined for greatness as the legitimate rulers of the universe.

To achieve this destiny required African Americans to recognize the lies perpetuated by whites and to embrace their true religion and its regulations. In short, African Americans prepared for their future through knowledge of self and knowledge of the true nature of the white person as a deceiver who, through "trickology," attempted to prevent them from uncovering their ultimate value.

African Americans were "lost" within the "wilderness" of the United States, but Master Fard had been sent to "find" them and restore them to their former glory. He would accomplish this through his teachings and written materials known as the Supreme Lessons, a blending of basic educational skills and metaphysics. The basic principle was simple: African Americans are the Lost-Found Nation. They are not true citizens of the United States. Rather, they are "Asiatics," and Mecca is their true home.

Those who accepted Master Fard's teachings surrendered their slave surnames—Peterson, Johnson, Pinn—and began a new life marked by a strict code of ethics and morality. These rules associated with this code of conduct first addressed physical appearance. Members of Master Fard's Nation of Islam were to dress modestly and be well groomed. They were to present themselves through attire and demeanor in ways that spoke to their strong discipline and the seriousness with which they approached life. Their clothing, "natural hair" (i.e., hair styles that required straightening the hair through chemicals were forbidden), and the overall manner in which they presented themselves publicly spoke to a desire to avoid the stereotypes that marked public perceptions of African Americans as lazy, irresponsible, poorly groomed, and so on. This seriousness was further demonstrated through a rejection of sports and other forms of popular entertainment such as gambling and movies. Their code of ethics and morality prevented the use of alcohol and tobacco because these substances enslaved the body and prevented the proper functioning of the mind. Furthermore, members of the Nation of Islam were to avoid certain foods such as pork because they did damage to the body and destroyed the mind. According to the main dietary restriction, the prohibition on consumption of pork, which was believed to be a hybrid of cat, rat, and dog, Master Fard's teachings were explained eventually this way: "Eating bad food: it forms your features, and your characteristics." More to the point, "pork was created by God to attract the diseases and germs which the white man traditionally carries and wants to transmit to Blacks with the aim of poisoning them, in order to weaken their race."[13]

With time, members would be taught to control their diet and their weight by not only limiting the types of food eaten, but also limiting food consumption to one meal each day. Recognizing that these dietary restrictions and other codes of conduct were difficult to follow within the context of the dominant society, the Nation of Islam opened restaurants, markets, and organized activities for young people that involved proper forms of entertainment centered on the teachings of the Nation of Islam and often involving community-based evenings of study.

In terms of proper relationships, members were encouraged to marry, and divorce was discouraged. Related to marriage, followers of Master Fard were not to marry outside their race because interracial marriage was considered dangerous in that it meant entanglement in white society, a condition considered problematic for reasons that will become clear to readers. In short, however, the Nation of Islam envisioned proper families in which new members of the Nation of Islam were produced as a primary concern. Such families reinforced the obligations of the individual to the larger Nation of Islam community, and also strengthened the resolve of the community through the production of individuals who placed the will of the group above their own. The Nation of Islam was concerned, in simple terms, with the production of a new nation committed to the teachings of Master Fard Muhammad.

Members were instructed in their new code of conduct during meetings in the temple and through the University of Islam. The University of Islam opened in 1930 as a way of spreading the teachings of the Nation of Islam's founder, Master Fard. Instruction was provided to adult members of the Nation of Islam as well as the organization's children. In either case, instruction revolved around basic academic subjects as well as the organization's theology and practices. In spite of early efforts by Detroit officials to disrupt its operations because of its unorthodox teachings, the University advanced its educational agenda. Its curriculum included basic instruction on African and African American history and culture, math, science, and the Nation of Islam's religious teachings. In addition to instruction in these areas, Muslim girls received training in home economics—how to raise children, proper care of the home, and personal hygiene.[14] Much of what girls were taught outside the academic curriculum was captured in the "Laws of Islam":

1. Do not use lipstick or makeup.
2. Do not wear hair up unless wearing long dress.
3. Do not smoke or drink alcohol.
4. Do not commit adultery.
5. Do not use pork in any form.
6. Do not cook in aluminum utensils.
7. Do not wear heels over 1½ inches.
8. Do not dance with anyone except one's husband.[15]

These regulations speak to the sense of morality espoused by the Nation of Islam in that the laws were meant to present Muslim women as industrious, disciplined, and devout members of their families and the larger Nation of Islam community. The young men were also given instruction beyond their academic coursework. The basic principles of these extracurricular materials revolved around their mandate:

1. To protect organizational officials and property
2. To reinforce the doctrine and objectives of the organization
3. To prepare for the race war known as Armageddon.[16]

These regulations also speak to the ethical and moral outlook of the Nation of Islam in that they reinforce the organization's commitment to protect the family, the religious community, and the larger African American community as a part of proper living.

The discipline and sense of African American pride that the teachings of Master Fard provided appealed to many African Americans during the socially and economically trying times of the early 1930s. Some estimates suggest that Master Fard's temple grew to roughly eight thousand members. Harassment by local police authorities who disliked the separatist activities of the Nation of Islam simply reinforced the importance of Master Fard's teachings. For recruits, the attempt of the dominant society to destroy Master Fard's work pointed to the truth of his teachings in that Fard must have posed a threat to the unjust workings of society. If this were not the case, local authorities would have left the Nation of Islam alone. One of Master Fard's most important supporters during this time was Elijah Poole.

Like so many others, Poole left the South, Georgia, following the trail of the Great Migration—the massive movement of African Americans into southern and northern cities from the late nineteenth century through the mid-twentieth century—to urban possibilities. Yet, with little formal education and a family to support, Poole found Detroit a difficult place. In part he worked through his frustrations by maintaining an interest in being a preacher, a Christian preacher sensitive to the teachings of Marcus Garvey. These two elements, the teachings of Garvey and a desire to preach, came together through an encounter with Master Fard Muhammad's temple.

The critique of white supremacy couched in Master Fard's notion of "trickology" and his reconstruction of self-worth and self-esteem trampled by the harshness of discriminatory practices in the United States appealed to Poole. This philosophy of life articulated the pain he felt but had not expressed publicly in strong and transforming ways. Upon first hearing Master Fard, it was clear to Poole that the teacher's words were true, representing a greatness that Poole wanted to better understand. "You are that one we read in the Bible that he would come in the last day under the name Jesus," Poole said with confidence. Fard's response only added to the draw of this mysterious figure: "Yes, I am the One, but who knows that but yourself, and be quiet."[17] There was a quick and clear connection between the two, a bond of sorts that would culminate in Poole's name being changed to Elijah Muhammad, and his being called to minister on behalf of Fard. "Tell him," Fard said to Elijah Muhammad's wife, Clare Muhammad, during a temple meeting, "that he can go ahead . . . and start teaching, and I will back [him] up."[18] Master Fard's authorization of Muhammad's preaching made him a significant figure within the Nation of Islam in that Muhammad became Master Fard's second in command. This, however, did not sit well with some within the movement who had ambitions of their own.

In 1934 Master Fard disappeared mysteriously. With Master Fard gone, a power struggle developed, and it became clear that Elijah Muhammad's rivals would kill him if he remained in Detroit. The movement splintered into various camps, each with a different understanding of Master Fard's teachings. The most significant group was the organization the Honorable Elijah Muhammad developed in Chicago. He told his followers that this Chicago temple, "Muhammad's Temple of Islam," was the new headquarters of Master Fard's movement.

Traveling to cities such as Chicago, Elijah Muhammad preached that Fard was God (Allah) incarnate and that he, Elijah Muhammad, was the messenger of God commissioned to teach African Americans about their true nature as the original people of the earth, god-like and destined to rule the universe. Mr. Muhammad ritualized this new statement concerning Fard as Allah through the institution of "Savior's Day." On this day, February 26 of each year, members of the Nation of Islam come together to celebrate the birthday of their savior, Fard Muhammad. Each Savior's Day is highlighted by speeches outlining the aims and achievements of the Nation of Islam. This celebration also forms another opportunity to reinforce the Nation of Islam's teachings.

Perhaps the most graphically troubling dimension of the Nation of Islam's theology for most Americans was the reference to whites as devils, created by a wise, yet mad, scientist named Mr. Yakub. During the early years, members of the Nation of Islam were taught that Allah and the "wise scientists" who construct human history in twenty-five-thousand-year cycles, with one scientist serving as judge and monitor, allowed the creation of this actual and historical devil race to rule people of African descent for a set number of years. Domination of African Americans was allowed to happen, according to the Nation of Islam's theology, because they, the original people created by Allah,

What the Muslims Believe

1. WE BELIEVE in the One God whose proper Name is Allah.
2. WE BELIEVE in the Holy Qur'an and in the Scriptures of all the Prophets of God.
3. WE BELIEVE in the truth of the Bible, but we believe that it has been tampered with and must be reinterpreted so that mankind will not be snared by the falsehoods that have been added to it.
4. WE BELIEVE in Allah's Prophets and the Scriptures they brought to the people.
5. WE BELIEVE in the resurrection of the dead—not in physical resurrection—but in mental resurrection. We believe that the so-called Negroes are most in need of mental resurrection; therefore they will be resurrected first.
6. WE BELIEVE in the judgment; we believe this first judgment will take place as God revealed, in America.
7. WE BELIEVE this is the time in history for the separation of the so-called Negroes and the so-called white Americans. We believe the black man should be freed in name as well as in fact.
8. WE BELIEVE in justice for all, whether in God or not; we believe as others, that we are due equal justice as human beings. We believe in equality—as a nation—of equals.
9. WE BELIEVE that the offer of integration is hypocritical and is made by those who are trying to deceive the black peoples into believing that their 400-year-old open enemies of freedom, justice and equality are, all of a sudden, their "friends."
10. WE BELIEVE that we who declare ourselves to be righteous Muslims, should not participate in wars which take the lives of humans.
11. WE BELIEVE our women should be respected and protected as the women of other nationalities are respected and protected.
12. WE BELIEVE that Allah (God) appeared in the Person of Master W. Fard Muhammad, July, 1930; the long-awaited "Messiah" of the Christians and the "Mahdi" of the Muslims.

We believe further and lastly that Allah is God and besides HIM there is no god and He will bring about a universal government of peace wherein we all can live in peace together.

strayed from their true religion, Islam, and had to be punished and prepared for their return to greatness. Again, whites would be allowed to reign through their trickology for a set number of years, until African Americans through the work of the Nation of Islam were educated as to their true nature and religion, and then judgment would occur. Whites would be punished, but Nation of Islam doctrine fluctuates between the complete destruction of whites and a measure of hope for the redemption of whites. Changing opinion on this issue is perhaps attached to a fundamental question: Can a community that was created for the sole purpose of harming people of African descent be punished with total destruction for fulfilling its divinely ordained purpose?

The nationalist vision offered by the Nation of Islam culminates in an apocalypse of fire. After the earth is purged, the faithful of God (i.e., the Nation of Islam's membership) will build a new nation, with a government "based upon truth, freedom, justice, and equality." Within this new nation, "the lost-found black people would appear sixteen years of age and would be able to live a thousand years or longer. . . . After the Judgment, the reason for Allah's creation of the devil [white race] would be clear, and his righteous people would know that he gave the white man power to rule the earth for six thousand years to show that he could 'destroy the devil in one day without falling a victim.' The new paradise, more than anything else, would be a testament to God's omnipotence and his new Islam."[19] The Honorable Elijah Muhammad taught that work toward this new paradise had to start immediately, and attacks by the dominant society could not destroy the destiny of Master Fard's people.

Self-sufficiency was a hallmark of the Nation of Islam, expressed through the farm, restaurants, and other business ventures established during the time of the Honorable Elijah Muhammad. But one would expect attention to the nurturing of economic independence from an organization that argues for separation from whites through the development of a nation within a nation—an independent nation geographically comprised of some choice land within the United States. The Honorable Elijah Muhammad taught that this separate nation, his version of nationalism, was necessary in that it provided freedom from whites necessary in order for African Americans to revive themselves and prepare for their reign over the universe. In terms of financing this new nation, the Honorable Elijah Muhammad called for the United States government to provide funds enough to sustain it for 20–25 years, until it was self-sufficient. From the Nation's perspective this was not a loan or a handout; rather, it was overdue wages for centuries of uncompensated slave labor.

In spite of setbacks and difficulties with local authorities, by the 1950s the Honorable Elijah Muhammad's work as the "Spiritual Head of the Muslims in the West" began to bear fruit as the Nation of Islam grew to include temples in numerous large cities. While Elijah Muhammad was alive, those who accepted the teachings wrote a letter to the headquarters in Chicago: "I have been attending the teachings of Islam by one of your Ministers, two or three times. I believe in it, and I bear witness that there is no God but Thee, and that Muhammad is Thy Servant and Apostle. I desire to reclaim my Own. Please give me my Original name. My slave name is as follows . . ."[20] Until a new name was provided, members made use of the "X," the unknown. The "X" involved a rejection of the former self, and the embrace of a new identity associated with a new relationship with Allah and his messenger, Elijah Muhammad.

The infrastructure of the Nation of Islam expanded to accommodate new members, particularly professional and formally educated members who joined during the late 1950s. For example, each local temple contained a minister who spread the Honorable Elijah Muhammad's teachings. To facilitate this increased work, the local minister was assisted by the captains of the Fruit of Islam (the collective of men who hand down discipline and provide security for the Nation of Islam) and the Muslim Girl's Training and General Civilization Class (MGT-GCC). Taught within the context of the University of Islam mentioned earlier, the latter involved instruction for girls on topics such as cooking and caring for children. In both cases, the Fruit of Islam and the MGT-GCC, the goal was protection. The former protects the Nation of Islam from external threats posed by members of the larger society who challenge the legitimacy of the Nation of Islam as well as members of the organization whose activities run contrary to the Nation of Islam's teachings. The latter, according to the Nation of Islam's teachings, protects the Nation of Islam by training women to assume their proper roles and as a consequence produce families that are committed to the Nation of Islam's agenda.

The conversion of new members did not involve an emotional event. Rather, it involved a reasoned and thoughtful embrace of the teachings of the Honorable Elijah Muhammad. The Nation of Islam's growth occurred in large part as a result of "fishing," the practice of reaching out to members of the community through public events and a well-known prison ministry. In fact, through personal contact with prisoners, the Nation of Islam gained one of its most well-known leaders: Malcolm X.

Malcolm X was the perfect convert in that his move into the Nation of Islam entailed a movement between extremes. Having lived a

What the Muslims Want

1. We want freedom. We want a full and complete freedom.
2. We want justice. We want justice applied equally to all, regardless of creed or class or color.
3. We want equality of opportunity. We want equal membership in society with the best in civilized society.
4. We want our people in America whose parents or grandparents were descendants from slaves, to be allowed to establish a separate state or territory of their own—either on this continent or elsewhere.
5. We want freedom for all Believers of Islam now held in federal prisons.
6. We want an immediate end to the police brutality and mob attacks against the so-called Negro throughout the United States.
7. As long as we are not allowed to establish a state or territory of our own, we demand not only equal justice under the laws of the United States, but equal employment opportunities—NOW!
8. We want the government of the United States to exempt our people from ALL taxation as long as we are deprived of equal justice under the laws of the land.
9. We want equal education—but separate schools up to 16 for boys and 18 for girls on the condition that the girls be sent to women's colleges and universities. We want all black children educated, taught and trained by their own teachers.
10. We believe that intermarriage or race mixing should be prohibited. We want the religion of Islam taught without hindrance or suppression.

life of crime, which resulted in a prison sentence, Malcolm Little discovered the teachings of the Honorable Elijah Muhammad. Turning his back on his criminal past, he embraced the strict discipline of the Nation of Islam. Upon his release from prison in 1952, he went to Detroit: "My going to Detroit instead of back to Harlem or Boston was influenced by my family's feeling expressed in their letters. Especially my sister Hilda had stressed to me that although I felt I understood Elijah Muhammad's teachings, I had much to learn, and I ought to come to Detroit and become a member of a temple of practicing Muslims."[21] His commitment to the Nation of Islam was so strong that he became one of its ministers:

It simply had never occurred to me that I might be a minister. I had never felt remotely qualified to directly represent Mr. Muhammad. If

> someone had asked me about becoming a minister, I would have been astonished, and told them I was happy and willing to serve Mr. Muhammad in the lowliest capacity. I don't know if Mr. Muhammad suggested it or if our Temple One Minister Lemuel Hassan on his own decision encouraged me to address our assembled brothers and sisters.[22]

He was named assistant minister of Detroit Temple Number One in 1953.

He was no longer Malcolm Little. He was now Malcolm X, the man who would give all his time and energy to spreading the Honorable Elijah Muhammad's teachings. Malcolm's charismatic personality and media exposure benefited the Nation of Islam as new temples were added to the organization, and international attention was garnered. Because of his hard work and role in the growth in membership, Malcolm X moved through the ranks and eventually held the position of the Honorable Elijah Muhammad's national spokesperson—Mr. Muhammad's second in command.

However, the Honorable Elijah Muhammad's failure to abide by the moral and ethical guidelines he established and the Nation of Islam's failure to actively participate in the Civil Rights Movement ultimately resulted in Malcolm's break with the Nation of Islam and his conversion to Sunni Islam in 1964. Malcolm X spoke about his disillusionment with the Nation of Islam in these terms:

> Around 1963, if anyone had noticed, I spoke less and less of religion. I taught social doctrine to Muslims, and current events, and politics. I stayed wholly off the subject of morality. And the reason for this was that my faith had been shaken in a way that I can never fully describe. For I had discovered Muslims had been betrayed by Elijah Muhammad himself.[23]

Mr. Muhammad had committed adultery and fathered children outside his marriage. Malcolm X had a difficult time with this, but he tried to find ways to move beyond it. However, his reaction to it and the existing jealousy of his position by other ministers in the movement influenced Mr. Muhammad to place restraints on Malcolm's work. With the assassination of President John F. Kennedy on November 22, 1963, and Malcolm's remark that this event involved the violence perpetuated by the United States coming back to haunt the United States, Mr. Muhammad made a move that would result in Malcolm's break with the organization. Mr. Muhammad silenced Malcolm, forbidding him to speak publicly. It became clear to Malcolm that the censure would never be lifted. This silencing, combined with attempts on his life, made it clear that the Nation of Islam was no longer his home. He would have to develop a new way of addressing the plight of African Americans in the United States: "I reasoned that the decision already had been made for me. The ghetto masses already had entrusted me with an image of leadership among them. I knew the ghetto instinctively extends that trust only to one who had demonstrated that he would never sell them out to the white man. . . . I felt a challenge to plan, and build, an organization that could help to cure the black man in North America of the sickness which has kept him under the white man's heel."[24] This new organization, however, would not be based on the teachings of Mr. Muhammad. Rather, through travel, particularly his participation in the hajj—the Muslim's pilgrimage to Mecca—Malcolm gained a deeper sense of Islam, and this influenced his perception of issues of injustice in the United States and elsewhere. In a letter to be distributed to the press, Malcolm said, "you may be shocked by these words coming from me. But on this pilgrimage, what I have seen, and experienced, has forced me to re-arrange much of my thought-patterns previously held, and to toss aside some of my previous conclusions. . . . Each hour here in the Holy Land enables me to have greater spiritual insights into what is happening in America between black and white."[25]

Malcolm X was assassinated in 1965 as his Organization of African American Unity and Muslim Mosque Incorporated were beginning to forge an identity and place within the ongoing work of social transformation. Malcolm X, during his years with the Nation of Islam, played a major role in its growth. Although the numbers are questionable, testaments to this growth were given throughout the remaining years of the Honorable Elijah Muhammad's life. For instance, in 1974, during the last Savior's Day celebration held under the leadership of the Honorable Elijah Muhammad, those gathered in honor of the birth of Master Fard Muhammad and the working of his messenger, the Honorable Elijah Muhammad, were told about the Nation of Islam's tremendous growth. Beginning with a few interested parties in 1930, the Nation of Islam increased, they were told, to five hundred thousand members. The organization's net worth was estimated to be $75 million, including various businesses and pieces of property.[26]

After the Honorable Elijah Muhammad's death in 1975, his son Wallace Deen Muhammad (Imam Warith Deen Muhammad) was named head of the Nation of Islam. Attempting to bring the Nation of Islam in line with the larger, worldwide Islamic community, Wallace Deen Muhammad rethought the aesthetics of the temples, calling them mosque and removing the inappropriate elements. As one former member of the Nation of Islam remarks in her autobiography of life in this organization, during this period of reconstruction "the brothers got rid of our flag and blackboard with all our symbols, then they tore down the stage so our minister could stand on even ground with the rest of us when we prayed. . . . All the chairs had been taken out, replaced by carpet for us to sit on."[27] In addition, Wallace Deen Muhammad modified practices, removing syncretistic elements and increasing attention to the fundamental five pillars of Islamic faith and the ensuing practices. (These are discussed in Chapter 11.) One year after taking over, the name Nation of Islam was changed to World Community of Islam in the West, and changed again in 1982 to the American Muslim Mission.

The aesthetic changes, alterations in practice, and the inclusion of Muslims from outside the African American community were troubling, and resulted in some leaving the organization. Even more troubling for some was Wallace Muhammad's restructuring of the Nation of Islam's cosmology: Master Fard was not Allah, simply a Muslim teacher in California. The Honorable Elijah Muhammad was not a divine messenger, the last prophet. The Prophet Muhammad was the last prophet, and Elijah Muhammad was a man who sought to help African Americans, even if much of his theology was fundamentally flawed.

One who found these changes to the Nation of Islam's structure and theology unacceptable was Minister Louis Farrakhan (born Louis Walcott). Malcolm X trained Farrakhan, and after Malcolm's departure from the Nation of Islam, Farrakhan became a central figure in its ministry. Under the leadership of Minister Farrakhan, the theology of the reconstituted Nation of Islam formed in 1978 would change. An effort was made by Farrakhan to be true to the Honorable Elijah Muhammad's vision, but with theological changes and a new perspective on social activism in keeping with the needs of African Americans in the late twentieth century. For instance, more charged claims such as the demonic nature of whites were reconceived as a metaphorical attack on white supremacy. That is to say, members of the Nation of Islam do not hate white people. Rather, they hate the *deeds* of supremacy and repression committed by white people. In addition, members of the Nation of Islam are currently encouraged to play a role in politics, and Farrakhan modeled this through his controversial involvement in Reverend Jesse Jackson's first bid for the presidency in 1988. Prior to this, Farrakhan supported Harold Washington's candidacy for mayor of Chicago, and he "encouraged Chicago Muslims to campaign, register to vote, and to cast their ballots for Washington."[28] This is clearly a break with the Honorable Elijah Muhammad's rejection of political involvement in a society that is marked for destruction.[29]

The Minneapolis (Minnesota) Study Group.

Furthermore, the shift away from the original teachings involved a softening of Elijah Muhammad's theory of separation—the development of an independent nation—through an appeal for involvement in the life of this country as a way of stemming off final judgment. There has been increased effort on the part of the Nation of Islam to rework its image and present itself as a religious community with a constructive contribution to make to life in the United States. The charged rhetoric of nationalism has been toned down in some cases, and observation of traditional Islamic practices has increased. For example, after 1986 members of the Nation of Islam began observing the month of Ramadan and its required fasting from sunup to sundown.

Perhaps in part because of tremendous growth in the Sunni Muslim presence in African American communities (see Chapter 11) and the importance of participation in the larger community of Islam across the globe, the Nation of Islam is working to revamp its image and its theological connections with orthodox practices. Nonetheless, charges of anti-semitism were heightened by the publication of *The Secret Relationship between Blacks and Jews*[30] by members of the Nation of Islam in Boston. *The Secret Relationship between Blacks and Jews* argues that the Jews were heavily involved in the slave trade and continue to harm African Americans. The Nation of Islam added this text to its arsenal, although it was condemned by noted scholars such as historian Robin Kelly of Columbia University and Darlene Clarke-Hines of Michigan State University. Beyond this, inflammatory remarks by a former leader within the Nation of Islam, Khallid Muhammad, during a speech at Kean College, only served to heighten public outrage against the organization.

The Nation of Islam and the World Community

Failing to make significant changes in the Nation of Islam's relationship to the Jewish community, Minister Farrakhan worked to improve relations with the larger Islamic world. Through his knowledge of Arabic, his participation in the hajj in 1985, his growing relationships with Sunni Muslims in the United States and elsewhere, and the opening of membership in the Nation of Islam to all interested parties, Farrakhan pushed for a broader audience and a deeper recognition as a Muslim. As a symbolic gesture related to the reorientation of the Nation of Islam, at the 1986 Savior's Day celebration Minister Farrakhan and Imam Warith Deen Muhammad renewed relations and pledged mutual support. This healing of earlier animosity continued when the two figures embraced at the 1992 Savior's Day celebration.[31]

Some of the Nation of Islam's international activities and relationships have been controversial. For example, its relationship with Libya's Colonel Qadhafi and the Libyan leader's efforts to provide the Nation of Islam with financial assistance have met with resistance from the U.S. government. Shortly after the 1995 Million Man March, Farrakhan was invited by Qadhafi to organize a meeting of the World Islamic Peoples Leadership Conference, which consisted of workshops on issues such as health. The success of this event, meant mainly for Arab and Persian Muslims living in the United States, strengthened Minister Farrakhan's connections to the Middle East and the larger Muslim community in the United States. It failed, however, to strengthen his position with African American Sunni Muslims, who did not attend in notable numbers. Will Minister Farrakhan's growing relationship with Islam in the Middle East bring an even sharper turn from the original teachings of the Nation of Islam? Only time will tell.

Periods of tension and questionable allegiances have been mixed with more productive moments. One such period of positive media attention for Minister Farrakhan personally and the Nation of Islam in more general terms involved renewed relations between the late Betty Shabazz (Malcolm X's widow), her family, and Farrakhan. For decades it was assumed by many that Farrakhan's stance against Malcolm X's departure from the Nation of Islam at the very least created the atmosphere necessary for Malcolm's assassination. Malcolm X's daughter, Qubilah Shabazz, was arrested in 1995 on charges of plotting to have Minister Farrakhan murdered. The Nation of Islam, however, argued that the plot was a fabrication of the government meant to further deepen bad feelings between segments of the African American community. Farrakhan's embrace of Malcolm X's family and the Nation of Islam's work to raise money for Qubilah Shabazz's legal expenses restored friendly relations.

Minister Farrakhan and the Nation of Islam remain somewhat marginal within the religious landscape of African American communities, and are despised by segments of the larger United States. Regardless of internal and external struggles, however, the Nation of Islam continues to maintain its viability through events such as the Million Man March of 1995 which, according to some estimates, brought over one million African American men from all backgrounds and walks of life to Washington, DC. Thousands of others watched the event from their homes. No African American leader prior to Farrakhan, controversial or popular, had been able to mobilize such a large gathering. The Nation of Islam has been unable to fully capitalize on the success of this march, with more recent ventures (e.g., World Day of Atonement in New York City, 1996) unable to secure the number of participants one might expect. Struggle to maintain high numbers at sponsored events has resulted in a rethinking of its structure. For example, while the Nation of Islam once used the strategy of personal and frequent contact as a recruitment tool, more attention is currently given to the Nation of Islam's ability to spread Farrakhan's teachings not through local temples and study groups, but via satellite speeches and distribution of his lectures and books through regular post.[32] There is an effort on the part of the Nation of Islam's hierarchy to instill its principles without the formal, localized structures that are expensive to maintain and always vulnerable to the excesses of local leaders.

What the Nation of Islam Believes

Nation of Islam's teachings and activities expound upon four basic areas: (1) religious sensibilities concerned with both spiritual health and social advancement within a troubled historical context; (2) a theological platform that associates the will of God with African Americans as God's chosen people; (3) full expression of this religious/theological framework tied to providential establishment of a new and unified

African American community, within a new "space"; and (4) punishment for those who work against the establishment of this new African American "nation." Some attention should be given to the content of these four points, which are captured to some extent in a statement by historian C. Eric Lincoln, the first person to study the Nation of Islam: "They have developed black consciousness into a confession of faith. They teach that blacks have a manifest destiny and characterize whites as the personification of the evil that separates them from their freedom, their moral development, and their God."[33] While insightful, such a statement requires unpacking, and what Lincoln proposes can be concisely stated as follows: The Nation of Islam exemplifies a commitment to both the social and spiritual development of African Americans.

Whereas, by the late nineteenth century and early twentieth century, many African American Christian churches gave priority to either social transformation or spiritual development, the Nation of Islam's doctrine and activities united these concerns. The Nation of Islam premised this commitment to the progress of the person within the world and in relationship to spiritual dimensions of life on an understanding of this commitment as the will of God. That is to say, the Nation of Islam argued that God required improvement of life conditions and the development of a closer relationship with God as the primary focus of God's will. According to the Nation of Islam, this agenda is played out in relationship to African Americans because God favors them. They are the group of humans that most concerns God. Those who seek to harm this chosen people, according to the Nation of Islam, will face God's wrath. During the early years of the Nation of Islam, these enemies of God's chosen people were called "devils." God's plan for God's chosen people involves not only their progress, but their progress within the geographical context of a land—a nation—they can call their own. Under the leadership of Warith Deen Muhammad and now Minister Louis Farrakhan, the teachings have been modified. No longer does the Nation of Islam condemn white Americans as devils. Now the Nation of Islam focuses on social injustice as a demonic attitude that seeks to harm people of color. Furthermore, Farrakhan altered the Nation of Islam's cosmology in 1978. Farrakhan argued that Fard was Allah; the Honorable Elijah Muhammad, the Messiah; and he, Farrakhan, the prophet carrying on the work until the return of the Messiah and judgment.

Much of what the Nation of Islam achieves with respect to its reception and growth within the United States and its links to Sunni Muslims around the globe will depend on the ways in which its theology is modified over time. At points, Minister Farrakhan seems committed to the Nation of Islam embracing the traditional Islamic pillars of faith and theological commitments, but at other times the more controversial teachings of the Honorable Elijah Muhammad are preached. One can only assume that time will ultimately sharpen what is now a theologically, rhetorically, and in terms of its praxis unfocused Nation of Islam. The direction taken will have great significance because greater participation in the world community of Islam will require a firm and consistent denouncement of the Nation of Islam's teachings concerning Master Fard and the Honorable Elijah Muhammad as Allah and the last prophet, respectively. Farrakhan has shifted theologically to some extent, as evidenced during the 2000 Savior's Day celebration when he moved away from the cosmology presented by the Honorable Elijah Muhammad. Will this last? These doctrines, controversial as they are, have served to distinguish the Nation of Islam within the context of the United States. The resulting controversy has been a source of attention and in some cases membership. Which road will the Nation of Islam select: world community of Islam or headline-sparking separatism?

Concluding Thoughts

Drawing on earlier organizations and individuals committed to religiously influenced nationalism, the Nation of Islam highlights the plight of African Americans and offers what many consider questionable solutions. From figures such as Marcus Garvey, the Nation of Islam gained recognition for community building based on a celebration of race. From Noble Drew Ali, the Nation of Islam developed a sense of Africa's importance as a geographic and intellectual home for African Americans, as well as a deep interest in non-Christian traditions as the basis for African American religious belief. Clearly, the Nation of Islam borrowed from various movements, but it took materials and made them dimensions of its controversial agenda.

Whether one agrees with the Nation of Islam's teachings or not, it is difficult to think about religion in African American communities and the larger United States without at least mentioning the activities of the Nation of Islam. As one scholar notes:

> Those who unequivocally condemn Minister Farrakhan and the Nation of Islam should pause to reflect on what they actually are attacking. Farrakhan is not so much a problem as he is a symptom of the problems presently tearing apart American society. Should Farrakhan disappear, he would be replaced by another voice produced by

the same conditions that produced Farrakhan. The Nation is a consequence of the black experience, it is a social product stamped with a
"Made in the U.S.A."[34]

Television stations broadcast Mr. Louis Farrakhan's sermons. On the
streets of major cities in the United States and other countries such as
Canada, France, Ghana, and England, representatives of the teachings
of the Honorable Elijah Muhammad recruit aggressively, distributing
newspapers and other materials that speak to the interests of the Nation of Islam. It is clearly a part of the religious fabric of African American communities in particular and the United States in general.

Notes

1. Henry McNeal Turner, *The Negro in All Ages* (Savannah, 1873), quoted
in Stephen Ward Angell, *Bishop Henry McNeal Turner and African-American
Religion in the South* (Knoxville: University of Tennessee Press, 1992), 264–65.
2. Angell, *Bishop Henry McNeal Turner*, 265.
3. Edward Blyden, "The Call of Providence to the Descendants of Africa
in America," in *Liberia's Offering*, 76; quoted in Hollis R. Lynch, *Edward
Wilmot Blyden: Pan-Negro Patriot, 1832–1912* (London: Oxford University
Press, 1967), 30.
4. Marcus Garvey, "Lesson 3: Aims and Objects of the U.N.I.A," in
Message to the People: The Course of African Philosophy, ed. Tony Martin
(Dover, MA: Majority Press, 1986), 33.
5. Ibid., 28.
6. Noble Drew Ali, *The Holy Koran of the Moorish Science Temple of
America* (Chicago, 1927), 59; quoted in Richard Brent Turner, *Islam in the
African-American Experience* (Bloomington: Indiana University Press, 1997),
90.
7. C. Eric Lincoln, *The Black Muslims in America*, 3rd ed. (Grand
Rapids, MI: Wm. B. Eerdmans, 1994), 48–49.
8. The collective of temples was referred to as the Moorish Divine and
National Movement of North America, Incorporated.
9. Turner, *Islam in the African-American Experience*, 90.
10. Claude Andrew Clegg III, *An Original Man: The Life and Times of
Elijah Muhammad* (New York: St. Martin's Press, 1997), 19.
11. Ibid., 20.
12. Quoted in Turner, *Islam in the African-American Experience*, 149.
13. Gilles Kepel, *Allah in the West: Islamic Movements in America and
Europe*, trans. Susan Milner (Stanford, CA: Stanford University Press, 1997),
30.
14. Clifton E. Marsh, *From Black Muslims to Muslims: The Resurrection,
Transformation, and Change of the Lost-Found Nation of Islam in America,
1930–1995* (Lanham, MD: Scarecrow Press, 1996), 44.
15. Ibid.

16. Ibid.

17. Clegg, *Original Man*, 22.

18. Ibid., 23.

19. Ibid., 66, 67.

20. Louis E. Lomax, *A Report on Elijah Muhammad, Malcolm X, and the Black Muslim World: When the Word Is Given* . . . (Westport, CT: Greenwood Press, 1963), 26.

21. Malcolm X, *The Autobiography of Malcolm X* (New York: Ballantine Books, 1973), 220.

22. Ibid., 230.

23. Ibid.

24. Ibid., 360.

25. Ibid., 392.

26. Vibert L. White Jr., *Inside the Nation of Islam: A Historical and Personal Testimony by a Black Muslim* (Gainesville: University Press of Florida, 2001), 97.

27. Sonsyrea Tate, *Little X: Growing Up in the Nation of Islam* (San Francisco: HarperCollins, 1997), 132.

28. White, *Inside the Nation of Islam*, 100.

29. Louis Farrakhan, *Torchlight for America* (Chicago: FCN Publishing Company, 1993).

30. Historical Research Department (Chicago: The Nation of Islam, 1991).

31. White, *Inside the Nation of Islam*, 151.

32. For details on this see White, *Inside the Nation of Islam*, chap. 11.

33. C. Eric Lincoln, *The Black Muslims in America*, 3rd ed. (Grand Rapids, MI: Wm. B. Eerdmans, 1994), 63.

34. Mattias Gardell, *In the Name of Elijah Muhammad: Louis Farrakhan and the Nation of Islam* (Durham, NC: Duke University Press, 1996), 349.

Chapter 8

Protestant Churches

On a bright and inviting Sunday morning, I hopped on the famous "A" train and I made my way to Washington Temple Church of God in Christ, in Brooklyn, New York.[1]

Starting with a tent revival in 1951, Reverend Frederick Douglas Washington began a ministry in Brooklyn. News of this revival spread through New York City and as new converts increased, new housing for this religious revival was necessary. Reverend Washington secured temporary sites and finally purchased, with the assistance of the Church of God in Christ, the Loews Bedford Theater. On May 4, 1952, he marched his congregation into its new home.

Initially incorporated as the Bethel Temple Church of God in Christ, the name was changed in 1954 to honor its founder: Washington Temple Church of God in Christ, Inc. This church understands itself as:

[reaching] out to the world through missions and by weekly broadcast over television and radio, spreading the Gospel of Jesus Christ. At one time Washington Temple broadcasted live from its sanctuary weekly over Channel 9 Television Station as well as a live broadcast from the Sanctuary from 9:00PM to 10:00PM every Sunday Night. The message emanating from Washington Temple over radio has been heard as far away as Monrovia Liberia, Africa, Bermuda, Mexico, and into other far reaching areas via satellite.[2]

Consecrated a bishop in 1955 by the founder of the Church of God in Christ denomination, Bishop Washington served as pastor of Washington Temple until his death in 1988. After a short period, Elder Robert L. Madison, the assistant pastor, was named pastor of the congregation. Elder Madison preached the day I visited the church. The building is a massive structure, taking up nearly a city block. What is more impressive, however, is the sounds that greet visitors the moment they enter the general area of the church: "Good Morning!" "God bless you!" "It's good to see you!" "Welcome to our church!"

The service and mission of Washington Temple Church of God in Christ, although part of a relatively new denomination, are within a tradition of African American Christianity that is almost three hundred years old, and this larger tradition covers the emergence and growth of numerous denominations.

Predominantly Black Denominations

African American Baptist Churches

By the early 1770s, the Baptist church in Boston began to reflect in its records African membership. This would suggest that some enslaved Africans were given religious attention, but for the most part these were slaves within cities and towns. What is interesting is the fact that somehow the Baptist faith reached enslaved Africans beyond those in urban areas who in turn embraced it, began to preach it, and built churches devoted to it in various areas of the southern seaboard and western states. Some of these churches were forced to disband as a result of a perceived threat to the slave system, while others continued to grow, and in some cases their memberships reached well over 1,000.

The first black Baptist church is most commonly identified as the Silver Bluff Church (of Silver Bluff, South Carolina), founded by George Leile and managed by one of his converts, David George. The history of this congregation is far from certain in that it is usually dated between 1773 and 1775, although the cornerstone claims a date of 1750.[3] What is more certain is that this Silver Bluff Church was forced to disband due to the Revolutionary War. David George and other members of the Silver Bluff Church left for Savannah, Georgia, hoping that the British would grant them freedom. George Leile, who was eventually freed by his owner, moved to Savannah where he reunited with members of the old Silver Bluff Church. Leile did not remain in Savannah, and upon his departure he left behind a group of converts who, led by Andrew Bryan and former Silver Bluff member Jesse Peters, also founded the First African Church of Savannah (1788) on a piece of land granted by Jonathan Bryan.

Bryan's work was recognized by white Baptist ministers in the area, and the church was given official standing within Baptist circles by Reverend Thomas Burton and Reverend Abraham Marshall. Two years after its founding, First African Church of Savannah was admitted to the Georgia Association of Baptist Churches and remained a part of this association until participating in the formation of the Savannah Association in 1803. These associations are church collectives based on a particular geographical area, perhaps a city or state. They are organized in order to maximize resources and to allow for more far-reaching activities than any one church can undertake alone. When the membership of First African Church reached roughly 800, it was decided that the congregation should be divided and Second African Baptist Church organized (1802).

Black Baptist churches also developed during the early 1800s in Kentucky, Tennessee, Alabama, Mississippi, and Louisiana. Outside the South, historians note the emergence of black Baptist churches in Virginia as early as 1774, Massachusetts as of 1805, Pennsylvania in 1809, New Jersey in 1812, Manhattan in 1808, and Brooklyn in 1847. These are just a few examples of the push toward independent black Baptist community within the years before the Civil War.

The appeal of independent black churches—some making use of white ministers—is clear in that participation in such a church was a step toward complete personhood and freedom in an oppressive land. Many of these churches, under the leadership of forward-thinking ministers, thought about religious life as connected to sociopolitical realities such as the slave system (Appendix 1). These churches and others like them functioned as best they could under the restrictions placed on blacks. Fear that such gatherings would result in open and violent rebellion, combined with growing pressure on slaveholders from northern abolitionists, made the development of independent black Baptist associations impossible. Furthermore, the existing ethos of white supremacy made involvement in white churches and associations of limited benefit. Circumstances grew even worse when white Baptists underwent a North versus South split over the issue of slavery.

The Civil War and Reconstruction benefited black Baptist churches. Growth was quick, although hard fought in that much of this period is marked by feuds between white and African American churches over church property in the South (who gets the property abandoned by confederate loyalists?) and between blacks of different denominations. With respect to the latter, African American churches fought over the recently freed, trying to convince them that a particular denomination best served their needs. For instance, it was not uncommon for Baptist ministers to lampoon the rigid, educational preoccupation for ministry espoused by the African Methodist Episcopal (AME) Church. In turn, Methodists would often make light of the lack of formal organization and the energetic style of worship found in Baptist churches. In the worst cases, ministers from competing denominations would attempt to "steal" members and appropriate property, often seeking assistance from the Freedmen's Bureau that regulated the "New South" during Reconstruction. In spite of animosity and hard competition, churches grew.

Although Baptist congregations frowned on the highly structured denominational style of the Methodists, they recognized the need for some type of organizational structure beyond the makeup of local churches. Over the course of the nineteenth century, various regional Baptist conventions formed in an effort to combine and better utilize resources. In 1895, the National Baptist Convention, USA formed through a merger of three religious bodies: the Baptist Foreign Mission Convention of the United States of America, the American National Baptist Convention, and the National Baptist Educational Convention of the USA. It took as its mission not only the promotion of spiritual health of African Americans, but also the development of the skills and attitudes necessary to claim their full humanity and act accordingly. Complete with both foreign and domestic mission boards and a publishing house as of 1897, the convention under the leadership of Elias C. Morris sought to continue the Baptist goal of uplifting African Americans through strategies and programs developed and operated independent of white involvement and control.

One would think the growing hostility toward African Americans expressed by formal laws and extralegal mob activities such as lynchings would result in the strengthening of Baptist solidarity as a way of safeguarding the interests of African Americans. In spite of this reason for unity, however, the convention experienced its first schism in 1897, resulting in the Lott Carey Foreign Missionary Convention. This new convention was named after one of the most important black Baptist missionaries of the nineteenth century. While the two conventions were autonomous, limited cooperation between this new convention and the National Baptist Convention on issues related to foreign missions remained a possibility for some time.

Because affiliation with either of these two conventions, National Baptist or Lott Carey, was voluntary and in no way a compromise of local church autonomy, efforts to unite continuously failed, resulting in a variety of new organizations. For example, efforts to unite the Lott Carey Foreign Missionary Convention and the National Baptist Convention failed in 1905, and this action was followed by two schisms within the National Baptist Convention. The first of these two schisms took place in 1915 and the second in 1961.

The first of the two resulted in the emergence of the National Baptist Convention of America. As readers might imagine, the ability to address societal and religious issues in print, free from white control, was a vital tool for emerging African American Baptist organizations. But such operations were not without tension. Conflict over the direction and ownership of the convention's publishing board in fact fueled the 1897 schism as well as the 1915 split. The National Baptist Convention, USA describes the 1915 split in these terms:

> Of all of the agencies of the convention, the Publishing Board was the most successful, under the leadership of R. H. Boyd. Leaders and pastors of the convention became suspicious of the actions of the Publishing Board when they did not receive the reports they thought the convention ought to receive. A debate ensued concerning the ownership of the Publishing Board.[4]

Before this split, the National Baptist Convention contained roughly three million members housed within some twenty thousand churches. The original convention, the National Baptist Convention USA, Inc., after the split was the larger of the two and currently claims a membership of over 5 million. The National Baptist Convention of America claimed, as of 2000, roughly 3.5 million members.

Regarding the second schism, opposition to church involvement in the Civil Rights Movement played a role in the eventual formation of the Progressive Baptist Convention in 1961, although the seeds were sown much earlier. In 1952, the National Baptist Convention, USA, Inc. adopted a policy limiting a president's term of office to a maximum of four years. In 1957, several ministers took the president, Joseph H. Jackson, to court in an effort to prevent him from overturning the 1952 regulation. The Federal court found in favor of Jackson, and in payment for their efforts, Jackson had his opponents expelled from the convention. This episode pointed to a glaring problem within the convention: the president exercised too much power and had held this power for far too long.

In an effort to break Jackson's hold on the convention, several prominent members including Martin Luther King Jr. and Sr., Ralph D. Abernathy, and Benjamin Mays put Gardner Taylor's name forward as a candidate for the presidency during the convention meeting in 1961.[5] In a move that troubled the "Taylor team," Jackson was nominated by the nomination committee and quickly elected without consideration given to Taylor's candidacy. When those who held power in the Jackson camp made it clear that the election would not be reevaluated, those opposed to this move by Jackson's supporters remained after the convention "officially" ended and held another election with Taylor as the victor. The convention, of course, refused to acknowledge this second election, and the court case filed by the Taylor group failed to force Jackson out of office. With few alternatives and little hope for reconciliation, Martin Luther King Jr. and the others who supported Taylor met in Cincinnati in 1961 as the "Volunteer Committee for the Formation of a New National Baptist Convention." This group put in place the Progressive National Baptist Convention, with T. M. Chambers as its first president.

Free from Jackson, the Progressive National Baptist Convention quickly became involved in the Civil Rights Movement and the antiwar efforts of the 1960s. Although smaller than the two conventions already discussed, six years after its founding the Progressive Baptist Convention claimed over 500,000 members in some 655 churches. In recent years it has been active in foreign missions in Africa and the Caribbean. By 1995, it claimed a membership of over 2 million members.

Dexter Avenue Baptist Church, Montgomery, Alabama.

African American Methodist Churches

Many enslaved Africans and free Africans found the teachings of Methodism interesting because of the energetic worship and great access to the pulpit. Methodism, as expressed during the revivals and camp meetings, could be used by both free and enslaved Africans to make sense of the world and forge a more humane way of life. In this way, some Methodist ministers made an effort in their sermons to speak to the sufferings endured by blacks.[6] Nonetheless, issues of segregation mounted in the Methodist societies after the late 1700s. Whereas 1816 marked the end of sustained efforts by Methodists, now rather mainstream, to fight slavery on all fronts, it also marks the development of the AME Church as an independent denomination, emerging in part as a result of the Methodist Episcopal Church's inability to adequately address the issue of racial injustice.[7]

The story of the AME Church, the oldest African American denomination in the United States, actually begins not in 1816 but in 1787 with the founding by Richard Allen, Absalom Jones, and others of the forty-two-member Free African Society within the city of Philadelphia. Through this society a black Methodist presence at least seventeen years old was consolidated around the notion of religious freedom. Determined to improve the spiritual and mundane existence of blacks in the city, the Society drew on the energy and vision Richard Allen exemplified from his first encounter with the black Christians of Philadelphia.

Allen, upon the invitation of Methodist Church leader Francis Asbury, made his way to Philadelphia to preach in one of the city's established churches. In keeping with the Methodist effort to evangelize, Allen's attention quickly turned to blacks in the larger Philadelphia area, addressing their needs through the creation of a prayer meeting service. Recognizing that regular church gatherings and social opportunities eluded many blacks, Allen proposed the establishment of a separate place of worship for the city's black Methodists. Despite opposition from white Methodists, in 1787 Allen and several others formed a mutual aid and religious society. This was not a move toward separation from St. George's Methodist Episcopal Church, the place of worship for most of the city's black Methodists. Continued neglect and racial hostility, however, would eventually force a break with white Methodists. One offense in particular had to be addressed: while praying in St. George's, Allen and several others were pulled from their knees and told to wait until all white members had been to the altar. In protest of their treatment they withdrew from the church and committed themselves to the formation of their own house of worship.

Allen's group continued to grow and received word from other areas of the country (e.g., New Jersey and Maryland) where black Methodists experienced similar hardships and sought a way of freeing themselves from religious and social constraints. These various congregations, representing roughly 1,000 black Methodists, united under the banner of the African Methodist Episcopal (AME) Church in Philadelphia, April 9, 1816.

Uniting these various societies entailed more than taking on the AME Church name; rules and regulations were also necessary. Because leaving the Methodist Episcopal Church was not based on a doctrinal disagreement, they chose to keep the Methodist Episcopal Church's *Book of Discipline*, with the addition of a stronger antislavery stance.

The AME Church concerned itself with uplifting the perception of blacks with respect to morality, ethics, and social sensibilities. By so doing, the church believed blacks could prove themselves worthy of full citizenship, and American society would be forced to grant them all rights and complete equality. To accomplish this, ministers and their churches sponsored programs to address the behavior of young people and adults through attention to temperance, public conduct, and other issues. It was clear that this new denomination connected religious growth to socialization and saw this merger as the basis for citizenship. Racial prejudice in the North made this work difficult, and prior to emancipation it was virtually impossible in the South.

The Civil War and Reconstruction opened possibilities but did not completely remove barriers to evangelization in the South. Nonetheless, by the end of the Civil War and Reconstruction (1877), the AME Church was firmly established in the South and Midwest. The church was not content, however, to preach the Gospel only on familiar soil, because it recognized the need for global evangelization. This desire to extend the denomination's reach and influence marked its activities and thought throughout the nineteenth century and into the twentieth century.

Growth was slow at times, and the denomination faced many challenges as it moved into the twentieth century. The Great Migration, the movement of blacks from rural areas to cities in the southern states and the northern states during the late nineteenth century through the mid-twentieth century, placed a strain on church finances and raised questions concerning the denomination's ability to address the socioeconomic and spiritual needs of newly arrived blacks. Regardless of such problems, the denomination increased its membership over the twentieth century, planting new churches in the United States, Caribbean, Europe, and Africa. Through both domestic and international missionary efforts,

Persimmon Grove AME Church, Montgomery, Alabama.

the AME Church grew to include several million members worldwide by the end of the twentieth century. By 1999, the denomination claimed 2.5 million members.

Drawing on a tradition of spiritual and material progress, from the 1960s to the present, local AME churches have committed themselves to alleviating some of the problems facing the neighborhoods in which these churches are located. For example, many churches have developed day care facilities, low-cost housing, health clinics, employment services, voters' information services, and schools.

The African Methodist Episcopal Zion Church

Those in New York who eventually constituted the African Methodist Episcopal Zion (AMEZ) Church initially worshipped at John Street Church. As the size of John Street Church's congregation increased, proper accommodations for white members made the presence of blacks uncomfortable and problematic. Both St. George's Church and John Street Church decided on the same solution: segregated seating and restricted access to important rites and rituals for blacks—prayer in the case of St. George's Church and communion for John Street Church.

In response to this discrimination, Peter Williams and others representing the black membership petitioned Bishop Francis Asbury for

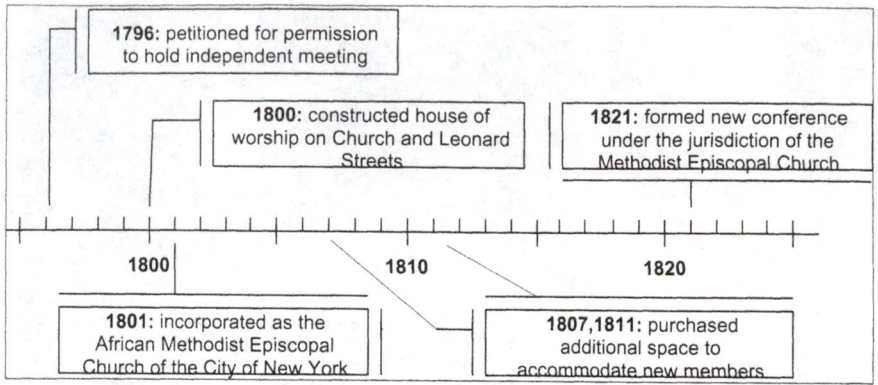

Figure 8.1
The Beginning of the African Methodist Episcopal Zion Church
Created by Stephen Finley.

permission to hold regular meetings of their own beginning in 1796. In 1800, a new house of worship was constructed on Church and Leonard Streets, and it was incorporated in 1801 as the African Methodist Episcopal Church of the City of New York. The church purchased additional space in 1807 and 1811 to accommodate the new members of Zion Church, as it was popularly called (see Fig. 8.1). When another church developed, with former Zion member William Miller preaching, the circuit was expanded to include both Zion and the new congregation called Asbury Church. The development of this growing connection of churches was not without its share of difficulties, as white Methodists sought to control these congregations through the placement of preachers and by determining the financial resources available to these new churches.

News of Zion and Asbury churches' plight brought word of similar concerns elsewhere. Interested churches from New York, Connecticut, and Pennsylvania—representing over 1,410 black Methodists—met in 1821 in New York and formed a new conference under the continued jurisdiction of the Methodist Episcopal Church. This meeting was followed by a second held one year later at which there were nineteen delegates representing churches in New York and Philadelphia, with a combined membership of 1,426. The General Conference of the Methodist Episcopal Church considered the activities of this new conference—seeking ordination of its own ministers and establishing its own *Book of Discipline*—a break with the denomination. The denomination considered these activities an ultimatum to the denomination: end segregation, or black members will simply disregard church bylaws.

In response, the new conference was told to either drop its ambitious program or develop a separate denomination without the support of the Methodist Episcopal Church. The black Methodists who formed the conference decided that restrictions on their activities were unacceptable. The African Methodist Episcopal Zion Church ("Zion" to separate it from the denomination begun in Philadelphia) was born.

The new denomination experienced tremendous growth during the Civil War and Reconstruction years by building churches and instituting programs. By 1900, the church claimed roughly 500,000 members in over 3,600 churches, served by roughly 2,500 ministers. This growth marked progress, but it did not result in a relaxed attitude toward the denomination's mission. Like their AME cohorts, these ministers were sensitive to the same pressing issues. Both northern and southern blacks had to be incorporated into a changing nation. The Civil War and Reconstruction had given, from their perspective, the United States an opportunity to move beyond racism and provide full citizenship to African Americans. But African Americans would have to prove themselves worthy. Often torn between W.E.B. DuBois's demand for participation in U.S. life on all levels—political, cultural, social, and economic—and Booker T. Washington's push for economic inclusion through self-help,

Butler AMEZ Church, Tuskegee, Alabama. Birthplace of Tuskegee Institute.

the AMEZ Church, like the AME Church, pushed African Americans to apply the morals and ethics found in scripture to every aspect of life. They saw the church as the best hope for African Americans in that it provided a safe space in which to discuss and work on both their spiritual and material standing. From issues of full citizenship, to temperance, to the structure of the family, to socialism, both the AME and AMEZ churches strove to guide the development of African Americans' self-consciousness and social acceptability.

Through the work of numerous missionaries and preachers, the AMEZ Church grew in numbers through southern and western mission activity. During the nineteenth century, work in the South and West faltered at times due to factors such as the lack of missionaries resulting in conferences (many of them containing several states or territories) going uncultivated. But overall the church grew by building churches and instituting racial uplift programs, and by 2002 the denomination claimed slightly more than 1.43 million members.

Although missions in the United States were the priority for Zion, like the AME Church, it worked in foreign fields. So, for example, although this work had its high and low points, the Zion denomination, by 1932, counted roughly 18,000 members in West Africa. With time, foreign missions would grow to encompass work in the Caribbean as well as areas of Europe such as England.

The Christian Methodist Episcopal Church

With the end of slavery, the Methodist Episcopal Church, South, realized African American churches coming from the North would ultimately take many of its members. This fear was well warranted in that better than half of the African Americans involved in the Methodist Episcopal Church, South, left the denomination after the Civil War. It was clear that a separate body for African Americans was necessary and desirable if the Methodist Church, South, wanted to maintain a presence in African American communities.

At a meeting held in 1870, in Tennessee, southern Methodists worked out plans for a new African American church, the Colored Methodist Episcopal (CME) Church, with the named changed to the Christian Methodist Episcopal Church in 1956. A leadership plan was put in place during that meeting, beginning with the election of two bishops: William H. Miles and Richard H. Vanderhorst. This denomination is similar to the two denominations already discussed in that it too embraced the *Book of Discipline* used by the larger body of Methodists, with only minor changes.

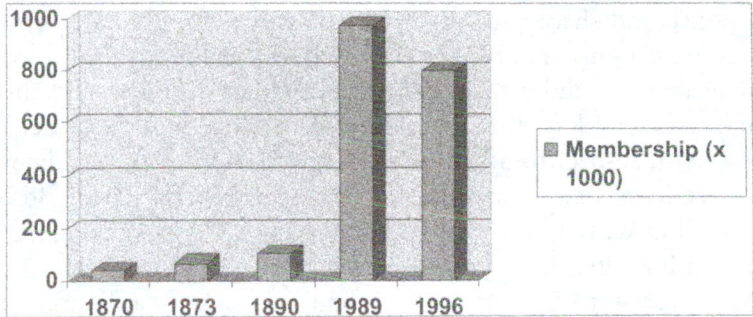

Figure 8.2
The Growth of the CME Church
This chart includes statistics from http://www.blackandchristian.com/
blackchurch/cme.shtml. Created by Stephen Finley.

The CME Church's connection to the Methodist Episcopal Church, South, had some benefits, but this connection was often used against the church during its mission efforts in the South. Both AME and AMEZ missionaries remarked that the CME Church was the church of those who had favored slavery, and joining it therefore would not be an exercise of freedom and liberation. When this tactic did not work, AME and AMEZ ministers at times attempted to take over CME Church property. Even with these annoyances, the CME Church began operating without some hardships faced by both the AME and AMEZ churches because, at its moment of inception, it already held 40,000 members and the financial support of the Methodist Episcopal Church, South. As of 1873, three years after its founding, the denomination claimed a membership of over 67,000, and in 2002 it claimed 850,000 members worldwide (see Fig. 8.2). However, it was not until the 1960s that the CME denomination undertook substantial missionary work in Africa. As of 1990, there were ten districts, composed of thirty-six annual conferences, within the denomination with ten active bishops, and by 1996 the number had grown to 3,000 churches in thirty-four U.S. conferences.

Why Three Methodist Denominations?

Although developed for different reasons, the CME Church shared the same interests and concerns as the AME and AMEZ denominations. All three recognized the need to bring African Americans into full participation in the life of the nation, and the church was seen as a significant tool by which to prepare them for this level of involvement.

In polity and theological doctrine the three churches are virtually identical, with ministers able to move between them with full recognition of ordination and rank. With respect to an origin in response to religious racism and a desire for independence, they are the same. That is to say, with respect to all three, the organization of the local church and connectional church stem from the Methodist Episcopal *Book of Discipline*, but with an increased sensitivity to the issues facing African Americans. Initially, this entailed sensitivity to the issue of slavery, but with time it grew to include a more complex push for full citizenship. Theologically, all three have embraced an understanding of the Gospel that fosters African American consciousness and pride. For example, it is not uncommon to see in local churches depictions of a black Jesus. Furthermore, African American Methodism across lines has embraced a version of black theology of liberation that addresses the full range of human needs in light of the teachings of Christ. Black theology of liberation developed during the late 1960s as a way of radicalizing the Gospel of Jesus Christ. Leading theologians such as James H. Cone attempted to do this by bringing the thought of Martin Luther King Jr. together with the social critique of Malcolm X. In so doing, Cone and others like him argued that God (through Jesus Christ) was concerned with the liberation of the oppressed. This line of theology is an extension of the effort of ministers during the late nineteenth century and the early twentieth century to bring the Gospel of Christ to bear on the daily experiences of the poor. This thought was referred to as the "Social Gospel" in that the teachings of Christ were used to address pressing social concerns. Many other examples are possible, but the bottom line remains the theological and doctrinal similarities of these three churches. With this in mind, one might wonder why they have not merged in order to strengthen African Methodism by pooling resources.

Recognition of the merits of merger is long standing, and efforts to accomplish the merger date back to 1864 when AMEZ and AME representatives met at Bethel Church in Philadelphia to consider the possibility of unification. Furthermore, talks in the early twentieth century between the AMEZ Church and the CME Church seemed promising but made no progress. Leading figures in both denominations spoke about the benefits of merger, but midcentury movement in that direction never materialized. Serious conversation did not resume until the period of the Civil Rights Movement, but not even the unification sparked by a common quest for racial justice was strong enough to pull these denominations together.

It is likely that the idea of merging met with initial excitement because it meant the sharing of financial resources and the ability to better organize the Methodist community without the drawbacks of competition among various African American Methodist groups. The realities of the merger probably prevented true efforts to enact it, however, because merger would mean the need to reduce staffs, including bishops, and none of the denominations were willing to make this type of sacrifice. The last decade of the twentieth century found these three denominations in conversation with the United Methodist Church concerning the possibility of merger, a move that would have needed to address centuries of racial friction.[8]

The topic of merger continuously surfaces in the major publications of each denomination. For example, a recent issue of the AME Church's *Christian Recorder* contained a front-page story on the planned merger of the AMEZ and CME churches in which the merits of unification were explored.[9] In the words of Thomas L. Hoyt, Jr., a New Testament scholar and bishop within the CME Church: "Without losing sight of our hope for the larger union which will include all persons without penalty of race, Black Methodists are challenged to continue their efforts toward union among themselves. Such unions, if realized, will be a significant step toward union involving the whole church."[10] This vision for a united Christian Church, however, has not materialized.

Black Pentecostal Churches

Concern with the spiritual condition of the United States dominated the thought of many Methodists during the late nineteenth century. Some of the more aggressive holders of this mindset took it upon themselves to spark a "holiness" campaign to enliven a national devotion to God, thereby recapturing the revival fervor felt earlier that century. This push toward holiness—a life that rejects worldly distractions and one that is in full keeping with the will of God—ultimately moved in two directions. Some maintained the original perspective and concentrated on perfection in this life. Others took this process of righteous living a step further and argued for a holy or sanctified life based on the presence of the Holy Spirit in one's life, evidenced through speaking in tongues. Those holding to the second perspective argued that Christians were saved, set apart from the world for the glory of God (i.e., perfected), and only then filled with the Holy Spirit. Those filled with the Holy Spirit were granted spiritual power and authority evidenced through speaking in tongues as noted in the New Testament story of Pentecost recorded in the Acts of the Apostles. To paraphrase, Jesus is resurrected and meets with the disciples, giving them instructions to await the arrival of the "comforter," the Holy Spirit. The disciples gathered as commanded, and with time the Holy Spirit descended on those gathered, and they spoke in languages they did not know but that were recognized by others. Wanting to be as close to God as possible, many sought the gift of the Holy Spirit as described in scripture. One such person was William Seymour.

Seymour based his theology in part on the teachings of Charles Fox Parham, a minister in Kansas who is typically credited for introducing this baptism with the Holy Spirit as a necessary component of Christian life. Seymour began preaching in a small Holiness church named Church of the Nazarene in California. His theology, however, was not to the liking of the pastor, and Seymour was barred from further involvement with the congregation. Determined to continue his ministry, Seymour began holding meetings in the home of Richard and Ruth Asberry, on Bonnie Brae Street in Los Angeles. An event occurred at this new location that forever changed Seymour's impact on the Pentecostal Movement, so named because of its attempt to re-create the indwelling of the Holy Spirit described as Pentecost in the New Testament.

During one of the meetings, Seymour began speaking in tongues, to the delight of the congregation. Word spread concerning this event. Soon the gatherings were too large for the Bonnie Brae Street location, and Seymour moved his group in 1906 to an old building (once owned by the AME Church) at 312 Azusa Street. Starting with a group primarily composed of women, Seymour's congregation grew, and the famous Azusa Street Revival was underway. Despite ridiculing of the revival by several papers and unsympathetic religionists, interested Christians came from diverse U.S. locations as well as from other parts of the world. All were welcome, treated equally, and allowed to participate. Without musical instruments and devoid of any concern with time, revival services on Azusa Street were guided by Seymour but were in essence without a rigid order of service. Visitors were certain to hear testimonies and a sermon. They sang and prayed for themselves and those in need. Of course, the major point of concern was the coming of the Holy Spirit with speaking in tongues.

The revival at Azusa Street caused a fire of religious commitment and Pentecostal fervor that spread through congregations across the country. Even after the demise of the Azusa Street experience (eventually institutionalized as the Azusa Street Mission) in 1931, nine years after Seymour's death, the impact of its work continued as Pentecostal churches continued to grow. The most widely recognized of these churches is the Church of God in Christ, founded by Charles Harrison Mason.

Mason was initially a member of a Baptist church in Arkansas. Mason's Holiness experience in 1893 resulted in his dismissal due to unacceptable teachings. Continuing to preach on sanctification in Mississippi as a revival evangelist resulted in Mason and fellow evangelist Charles P. Jones being denied fellowship in the Baptist association of the state. Unable to find a welcoming pulpit in Mississippi, Mason returned to Arkansas only to find a similar situation. Like Seymour in Los Angeles, Mason began holding services in various homes until space proved inadequate. Assisted by Charles Jones and W. S. Pleasant, Mason moved his services to an old cotton-gin. Steady growth made possible the organization of a Holiness church referred to as the Church of God. It was the first in what would quickly become a collective of like-minded congregations under the leadership of Mason and Jones. This church, founded in 1897, was renamed the Church of God in Christ (COGIC) in 1906.

One year after God revealed the proper name for this church—Church of God in Christ—Mason convinced two others to accompany him to the Azusa Street Revival. Once there Mason received the Holy Spirit and, upon leaving Los Angles, his preaching took on Pentecostal overtones and his revival services were marked by the manifestations of the Holy Spirit (e.g., speaking in tongues, healing, and deliverance from demons) he had been taught to expect while in Los Angeles.[11] This experience resulted in a shift in his theology from Holiness to Pentecostalism, the latter marked by insistence on believers being filled with the Holy Spirit accompanied by proper evidence as a necessary third step in the process of Christian growth.

During a meeting of the General Assembly held in Memphis, Mason requested that COGIC embrace this Pentecostal doctrine. Most of its members rejected the shift as did Jones, the man who had played a major role in the development of the church. A schism occurred with Jones and the majority of the member churches forming the Church of Christ (Holiness) USA, and Mason continuing as head of the COGIC. At a meeting of the COGIC's General Assembly held in November 1907, Mason was made the "General Overseer and Chief Apostle" of the denomination (composed of twelve congregations). Later named senior bishop, Mason maintained control over every aspect of the denominational life. He was convinced that the technique of sending out preachers used during the great revivals of the early 1700s and early 1800s would prove useful in the twentieth century. So his ministers went out, made converts, and formed churches. The Great Migration provided an ample supply of displaced Christians in need of an institutional home, a religious family that COGIC was eager to provide.

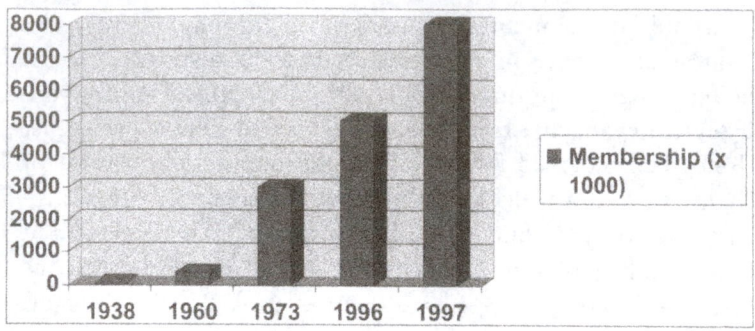

Figure 8.3
The Growth of the COGIC
This chart includes statistics from http://www.cogic.org/history.htm.
Created by Stephen Finley.

Enthusiastic COGIC ministers transformed Mason's regional movement into something much more expansive. Congregations developed
in major northern cities such as New York and Chicago were added to
the strong base of support in states such as Tennessee, Mississippi,
Arkansas, Oklahoma, Texas, and California. What resulted from this
growth entailed a shift from a primarily rural to an overwhelmingly
urban denomination. In 1938, COGIC had slightly more than 30,000
members in 733 churches. Figures available show tremendous growth,
with the denomination claiming almost 400,000 members in 1960 and
more than 5 million members as of 1996 (see Fig. 8.3).

What Baptists, Methodists, and Pentecostals Believe

The heated exchanges and reshaping associated with the history of the
various Baptist conventions might lead readers to believe these conventions are highly influential on all levels of Baptist life. This, however, is
far from the case. The cherished autonomy of the local congregation
with respect to theological issues, doctrinal sensibilities, and polity prevents conventions from exercising strong control over local congregations and their ministers. In fact, the laity in general has few dealings
with the various conventions because most lay members never serve as
delegates to convention meetings. In this respect, the minister is more
likely to pay attention to happenings on the national level than anyone
else in the congregation, but this national involvement is balanced with
a strong concern for the minister's congregation because, unlike the
Methodist system, Baptist ministers are not assigned by the national
body but are hired by the local congregation. Because ministers serve at

the pleasure of the local congregation, they must remain sensitive to the concerns and perspective of their immediate membership.

The central authority of the local church is also witnessed with respect to the development of ministers. Although a sense of divine calling is a prerequisite for entering the ministry, local Baptist churches, unlike their local Methodist counterparts who are ordained by a bishop, have primary responsibility for the licensing and ordination of ministers. This is not to say that the local association of Baptist churches has no say over the requirements for ministry. Those seeking ordination, in addition to proving themselves before the local congregation through a "trial" (or first) sermon, also have their knowledge of church polity and the Bible examined through a written test. Training for this test is provided in seminary settings through regularly offered courses on Baptist polity, or through classes offered by ordained ministers on the regional level. While Methodist ministers must also preach a trial sermon before the local congregation, they must also prove themselves before regional church officials and a collective of local ministers who comprise a church-based educational initiative referred to as the Ministerial Institute. This institute was initially developed to provide training in church history, polity, and so on when seminary access was difficult at best. Currently, ministers are still required to attend this annual program, but those who are interested in the itinerant ministry—ministers who can pastor anywhere within the connectional church—are also encouraged to attend seminary.

The autonomy of the local Baptist church with respect to theology, doctrine, and polity does not mean that those entering ministry across local church lines share nothing other than a desire to preach. Baptist churches do share basic doctrinal sensibilities and polity. With respect to the latter, there is a common organizational structure that gives primary responsibility for the functioning of the church to the trustees and deacons who, among other functions, maintain the physical plant and the financial operations of the church. Local Methodist churches also have trustees, deacons, and other officials, but they operate in accordance with a centralized and national hierarchy of authority. The work of these church officers is important, but it does not give them authority over the wishes of the congregation. Baptist tradition ensures all major decisions concerning the life of a church are made through meetings of the entire adult church membership. In addition to this structural similarity, there is a shared doctrinal base that stems from the religious sensibilities that formed the foundation of the early Baptist congregations.

Doctrine shared by black Baptists across the country includes the following: (1) like Methodists, they believe proper conduct is guided by the Bible; (2) like Methodists, they believe salvation is based on a personal commitment to Christ; (3) immersion of adults who have made a confession of faith is the only biblically based mode of baptism; (4) like their Methodist counterparts, a commitment to the priesthood of all believers enables all believing adults who are members of the church to vote on church affairs with equal authority; (5) as Methodists, they believe the church is the collective body of the redeemed established by Christ; (6) Baptists, unlike Methodists, believe the autonomy of each church must be preserved above all else; (7) similar to Methodists, Baptists believe religious rights and liberties must be protected.

Although Baptists and Methodists share a common acknowledgment of scripture's adequacy for religious life and the importance of baptism as a sign of redemption from sin, Methodists do not restrict the form of baptism to immersion. Converts can be sprinkled or fully immersed, depending on the resources available to a given local congregation. Furthermore, whereas both acknowledge the priesthood of all believers, Baptists extend this to a sense of autonomy that is foreign in the highly connectional and authoritarian Methodist organizational structure. Structures differ for both, but a common history of struggle against racial prejudice and its negative effects on religious liberty forge a common commitment to the preservation of religious rights and liberties as a pillar of African American Christian life.

Noting that many Pentecostal churches had their origins within African American Methodist and Baptist churches, it is not unreasonable that there would be similarities. One might think, based on the denominational structure and the strength of the presiding bishop, that COGIC resembles African American Methodism's strong hierarchy and connectional authority. However, it is closer to the truth that the relationship between local churches and the denomination fits more comfortably somewhere between Methodism's central authority and Baptist autonomy. On one hand, local churches must make financial contributions to the denomination similar to the assessment that African American Methodist congregations pay. On the other hand, Pentecostal churches and their ministers have a degree of independence in that they might have the founder of the church as pastor for decades and this pastor can appoint a successor. This differs from the Methodist itinerant system that, according to the *Book of Discipline*, requires bishops to periodically move ministers to new churches. The rationale behind this movement, according to Methodists, involves a desire to make certain that churches do not become overly attached to particular leaders but instead maintain an allegiance to the larger church.

With respect to ministry, similarities and differences abound. One might start with the title of choice, which in the COGIC is not the "reverend" typically used in Baptist and Methodist circles. Rather, ordained ministers are more typically called "elder" or "pastor." However, what one will find when church members and ministers converse casually is a host of other titles. In such circumstances, it would not be uncommon for ministers to be referred to as "doc" or "doctor," for example. The use of such titles is a sign of respect through recognition of the minister's spiritual expertise and authority.

Concerning the process of ordination, unlike Baptist churches, COGIC pastors license people to preach, but only the Ordination Committee of the jurisdiction can ordain ministers. Like the Methodists, COGIC has various levels of ministry—licensed or local preachers, ordained elders, pastors, and bishops. Although these categories are not identical to Methodist categories, there is a much stronger sense of ministerial progression than one finds in the Baptist churches. Yet Pentecostal pastors have a degree of freedom and length of service to a particular congregation that more closely resembles the nature of ministry in Baptist churches. For example, the strength of the founding pastor's connection to a church is often overtly present in the name of the church—for example, *Washington* Temple Church of God in Christ. A slow drive through African American communities throughout the country provides numerous examples of this practice—churches named after contemporary founders—in both the COGIC and the various Baptist conventions. One would, however, be hard pressed to find this practice within Methodist circles, outside examples of churches named after founding figures of African American Methodism—(Richard) Allen AME Church, for instance.

There are, of course, distinctions between what COGIC teaches and what Methodists and Baptists are taught. First, all three preach the need for salvation from sin through the acceptance of Jesus Christ as one's personal savior, followed by the attempt to live a sin-free life. But only COGIC argues that baptism in the Holy Spirit is necessary in order to have a complete and effective spiritual life. Baptists and Methodists are more likely to acknowledge various steps toward closeness to God. As current COGIC materials state: "the doctrine of sanctification or holiness is emphasized, as being essential to the salvation of mankind."[12] The Pentecostal perspective promoted by COGIC is based on a particular reading of scripture, and scripture is understood by this church as the infallible word of God. This depiction of scripture is not as consistently held within Methodist and Baptist circles. Furthermore, Methodist ministers, in keeping with the *Book of Discipline*, will baptize children or adults. However, Baptists and Pentecostals reserve baptism for adults who have made a profession of faith. Whereas some Christians across denominational lines believe in the final judgment and the second coming of Jesus Christ, the uniformity of this belief is generally much stronger in COGIC than it is in Methodist and Baptist churches. The same is true regarding other elements of doctrine such as divine healing and exorcism (or the general belief in evil spirits) that are more consistently recognized by COGIC than by Methodists and Baptists. Some elements of Pentecostal belief, however, seem to flow between the various denominations.

Although, in general, there remain strong doctrinal differences, there is a growing similarity in that many churches remain true to their denominational affiliations while advocating a strong interest in baptism in the Holy Spirit. Some refer to this as a charismatic move initiated to enliven the spiritual energy and authority of their local churches: In the last days before the return of Jesus Christ to judge the world, God will pour out blessings and spiritual gifts on the faithful. This includes the power and spiritual authority that comes with the indwelling of the Holy Spirit. Within Baptist and Methodist churches that abide by this philosophy, it is not uncommon to see ministers anointing parishioners with oil, or hear prayers in tongues, or have a member of the church prophesy.

There is much left to learn about this phenomenon—the charismatic movement—but what is of immediate interest is the manner in which increased interest in spiritual gifts and talents comes in the late 1970s, on the heels of the Civil Rights Movement. As the nation "processed"— often with a sense of despair—the events, the battles, triumphs, and setbacks that marked the mid-twentieth century, Christians across the country in churches such as Agape AME Church, Prince of Peace Church of God in Christ, and Friendship Baptist Church recognized the transforming power of the Holy Spirit. They used this spiritual power to address daily concerns. Occasionally this turn to spiritual renewal and religious authority was an attempt to avoid pressing social dilemmas awaiting church members outside their sanctuaries. For others it meant recognition that the Christian faith at its best calls for and provides tools to transform the world. The charismatic movement was an attempt to bring religious power to bear on a world in trouble.

Predominantly White Denominations

When Christianity in African American communities is mentioned, the typical image is of people gathered in one of the predominantly African

American denominations—living out the religious heritage of Richard Allen, Sojourner Truth, Martin Luther King Jr., and Fannie Lou Hamer, among others. To think this way, however, entails a myopic view of African American religious life, a perspective that ignores a good percentage of African Americans and their Christian commitments.

African American Christians dominate the religious landscape of African American communities in the United States. But one should not assume that all African American Christians are affiliated with historically African American denominations. Nothing could be further from the truth. They are spread across numerous denominations, and while the presence of African Americans in all these various communions is important and deserving of attention, the remainder of this chapter is limited to a discussion of African Americans within the Lutheran Church, Presbyterian Church, and Episcopal Church.

African Americans and the Lutheran Church

From its initial beginning in Europe, the basic patterns of Lutheranism spread, eventually moving into the North American context as Europeans sailed to the colonies beginning in the 1600s. Lutheranism, like other forms of Protestantism—so named because those associated with the general movement protested against what they considered problems in the Catholic Church—spread across a great territory.[13] In 1649 a group of Lutheran colonists established themselves in an area stretching from what is currently Manhattan to Albany. In spite of this movement, congregations had a difficult time recruiting clergy willing to undertake the dangerous and frustrating work of leading new congregations in the New World. The few ministers available had to spread their services over large geographic areas, attempting to meet the basic needs of several congregations at one time—each receiving a few sermons during a year. Based on this shortage of clergy for the growing Lutheran presence, it was not until 1669 that those in New York celebrated communion.

It would take roughly a century for these small congregations to solidify into a formal network. The first synod (the Ministerium of Pennsylvania), a regional grouping of congregations, was developed in 1748 when Henry Muhlenberg gathered together a group of Lutherans for the purpose of better organizing their activities and developing communication between various churches. This push toward firm organizational structure was matched in 1786 by liturgical conformity through the production of a book of service and a hymnal.

At this point in the eighteenth century, Lutherans numbered roughly seven thousand spread across seventy churches.[14] The number of Lutherans would grow with time, as would the mechanisms (e.g, schools, magazines, mission organizations) used to conduct their work. This growth, however, was not without controversy and splits. For example, debate over the extent to which the uniqueness of the North American context should impact the presentation and application of traditional Lutheran doctrine—should there be a liberal application of Lutheran doctrine, or should there be a more orthodox application—resulted in the formation of various synods. In 1847, as a result of this debate, the Lutheran Church Missouri Synod formed with an interest in preserving a traditional or conservative application of doctrine. Other synods formed were the General Synod and the United Synod.[15]

Such difficulties and divisions only intensified during the early twentieth century as a new wave of Lutheran immigrants reached the United States with their assumptions concerning church life in tow.

The twentieth century was marked by continued disagreement and splits over theological issues, but also efforts to merge like-minded Lutherans. In either case, the significance of Lutheranism and its appeal remained. The numbers tell the story in that two of the largest denominations in the United States are Lutheran: the Evangelical Lutheran Church in America with over 5 million members as of 2002, and the Lutheran Church Missouri Synod with roughly 2.5 million members. This membership is diverse, representing various racial and ethnic groups. Within this communion of Lutherans who work to safeguard and enhance their church are African Americans. Theirs is a history of involvement that moves through numerous difficulties, always striving for a richer participation in Lutheranism. It is a story of religious commitment beginning during the period of slavery.

In 1669 an African was baptized into fellowship within the Lutheran Church in New York.[16] Starting out with a few scattered conversions and baptisms, Africans slowly gained excess to Lutheran churches with a noticeable increase as a result of the revivalism and pietism that marked the 1730s and the early 1800s, in the northern colonies and southern colonies, respectively.

Not all Africans became members of predominantly white congregations. For example, Jehu Jones formed an African Lutheran church in New York in 1832. But much of this work took place within the context of tension over slavery, with many Lutherans seeking to aid Africans without disrupting the system of slavery. Daniel Payne, a Lutheran of African descent who eventually joined the AME Church, spoke to this contradiction and called for Lutherans to fight against slavery because of the manner in which it damages the God-human relationship:

To treat a man like a brute is to brutalize him. We have seen that slavery treats man like a brute, therefore slavery brutalizes man! But does slavery stop there? Is it content with merely treating the external man like a brute? No, sir, it goes further . . . it lays hold of the immortal mind, seizes the will, and binds that which Jehovah did not bind—fetters that which the Eternal made as free to more and act as the breath of Heaven! It destroys moral agency! . . . So it subverts the moral government of God. In view of the moral agency of man, God has most wisely and graciously given him a code of laws, and certain positive precepts, to control and regulate moral actions. This code of laws, and these positive precepts, with the divine influence which they are naturally calculated to exert on the mind of man, constitutes his moral government. Now, to nullify these laws—to weaken or destroy their legitimate influence on the human mind, or to hinder man from yielding universal and entire obedience to them is to subvert the moral government of God. Now, slavery nullifies these laws and precepts—weakens and destroys their influence over the human mind, and hinders men from yielding universal and entire obedience to them; therefore slavery subverts the moral government of God. This is the climax of the sin of slavery![17]

The strategies used to approach Africans certainly involved a compromise with slavery. Yet in some areas such as the Southeast there was a noteworthy increase in African membership, with estimates approaching ten thousand before 1860.

Consensus did not exist in Lutheran circles concerning the proper response to slavery, although most Lutherans in the nineteenth century were not concerned with what might be considered the political ramifications of religion. Some objected to it, while others endorsed segregation and did nothing to change the social status of Africans. There was little interest in using Lutheranism as a way of transforming the socioeconomic and political nature of American life. The segregation model fueled developments such as support for the formation of separate regional conventions. Creation of the Alpha Evangelical Synod of Freedmen resulted from such an effort, but its independence was rather limited as black leadership was replaced by white leadership.

The relationship of African Americans to Lutheranism was troubled at times, but efforts were made sporadically to ease this tension. One such attempt involved the Lutheran Church in America's, prior to its merger with two other Lutheran churches, consultation on Minority Group Interests. African Americans and other representatives of the minority presence in the church suggested goals for improving the relationship between people of color and Lutheranism. Some of the goals were rather ambitious, such as a call for aggressive evangelization of minorities until the makeup of the church represented the population makeup of the United States.[18] In such efforts the American Lutheran Church devoted resources to educational opportunities for African Americans, and in the early 1980s the Board of American Lutheran Church Women put in place a policy requiring the presence of women of color on the board as a way of insuring the development of policies and plans that were sensitive to the needs and wants of women of color. Lutherans would approve the ordination of women, and the first woman would become a bishop in 1995.

The efforts of the American Lutheran Church, the Lutheran Church of America, and the Association of Evangelical Lutheran Churches were combined to some degree through the development of the African American Lutheran Association, an organization of the Evangelical Lutheran Church in America (a 1988 merger of the American Lutheran Church, the Lutheran Church of America, and the Association of Evangelical Lutheran Churches). The perspective of the Association is clear:

> We, the African American Lutheran Association, are the people of God, rooted in the gospel and redeemed by Jesus Christ. We are committed to living out faith by expressing our love for one another and affirming ourselves and our cultural heritage as gifts to the church (Evangelical Lutheran Church in America). God, our Creator, has richly endowed each individual with gifts. Humanity, however, has fallen into bondage to sin and stands separated from God. This sin expresses itself in many ways, including exclusivism and separation among people manifested in racism. We believe Jesus Christ is our true Liberator, having come into the world proclaiming a Gospel which gives sight to the blind and releases the captives. We believe that we have been called to a ministry of reconciliation (II Cor. 5), serving as ambassadors for Christ. The church is to be a fully inclusive fellowship which celebrates the contributions of all members.[19]

Conferences related to the experiences of African Americans in the Lutheran Church, financial support of mission activities, and other means are used to push Lutheranism to confront issues of race. This work includes fostering an ongoing conversation concerning the legacy of slavery and the reparations debate.

Progress has been slow with respect to an increase in black membership. As of 1999, the Evangelical Lutheran Church in America—the largest Lutheran church in the United States with some five million members—reported African American membership of less than 54,000, roughly one percent of the total membership of the denomination.[20]

What Lutherans Believe

While it is not completely accurate to argue that Lutherans, in spite of the name of the denomination, are committed to the teachings of Martin Luther, it is reasonable to suggest that the Book of Concord containing some of Luther's religious thought guides the theological sensibilities of most Lutherans in the United States.[21]

Luther began to ask questions concerning the nature of the Roman Catholic faith and the activities of the church. In keeping with the traditional academic practice of his time and location, Luther posted ninety-five theses for debate in Wittenberg, in 1517. Church officials considered this a challenge, and he was eventually asked to recant his views. Luther refused because to do so would be to reject scripture and the ministry of Jesus the Christ as he understood them. Luther did not reject the Catholic Church per se; rather, he rejected what he considered its troubled teachings and attitudes.

Luther developed a reformation of the Catholic Church's position on the nature of salvation. The church's theology and actions suggested that salvation could be secured through good works, but Luther's reading of scripture posed an alternative: Salvation is simply a gift from God, given to humans through divine Grace and accepted by faith. Humans do not merit salvation, nor can they behave consistently in a way that would earn it. Furthermore, Luther believed preoccupation with the monastic system and priesthood as exceptional modalities of service to God did not recognize the manner in which people could serve God in productive ways through their daily lives, within the context of their secular employment.

Luther believed that each individual was capable of developing a relationship with God and was capable of understanding scripture with the aid of the Holy Spirit, when sermons and liturgy were made available in the language of the common people.[22] That is to say, there is something to be said for the notion of a calling from God to service, but Luther understood this call as a general process by which people should attempt to live righteously within all professions and all dimensions of life. Hence, all believers should be active in the worship experience because all believers are equal in the sight of God, regardless of their socioeconomic circumstances. In essence, Luther argued for what is commonly called the priesthood of all believers. In addition, Luther argued only baptism and communion should be recognized as sacraments.

The Augsburg Confession (1530) outlined the underpinning of this new theological and liturgical position, and it provided the framework for the doctrinal commitments of Lutherans. Shaped by the Augsburg Confession, the most recent statement of faith found on the Evangelical Lutheran Church in America (the largest Lutheran communion in the United States) web site summarizes basic dimensions of its theological heritage. It does so by highlighting the saving work of God through Jesus Christ, who "is the Word of God incarnate, through whom everything was made and through whose life, death, and resurrection God fashions a new creation." Furthermore, "the proclamation of God's message to us as both Law and Gospel is the Word of God, revealing judgment and mercy through word and deed, beginning with the Word in creation, continuing in the history of Israel, and centering in all its fullness in the person and work of Jesus Christ." The nature and purpose of Jesus Christ is presented, according to Lutherans, through the canonical scriptures, which tell the story, inspired by God, of God's work through Jesus Christ. These scriptures provide all information necessary for salvation.[23]

African Americans and the Presbyterian Church

Some in England sought to purify the Church of England through attention to John Calvin's theology. Calvin was a reformer of the Catholic Church who, from Geneva, sought to bring the church in line with the will of God. Ultimately, those who embraced Calvin's teachings articulated their vision in what is called the Westminster Confession: a statement of their beliefs that in modified form continues to have influence. Their efforts, which took institutional form through the development of a presbytery in 1572, gained them the name Puritans.

Presbyterianism, with its Calvinist sensibilities, spread to the North American colonies through English Puritans who sought escape from religious intolerance. They planned to develop a community in the New World premised on their religious sensibilities, and given institutional form in keeping with the principle of "representational leadership."[24] The first presbytery in the North American colonies was founded shortly after the start of the eighteenth century, in 1706, and the first General Assembly—the gathering of the full church's representatives—took place eighty-three years later in 1789. This body, the General Assembly, remains the most significant governing body in the Presbyterian Church.

Over the course of the Presbyterian Church's presence in North America, it, like Lutherans, Methodists, Baptists, and other denominations, faced numerous splits and schisms related to both doctrinal issues and social realities such as slavery. For example, most Presbyterians did not question the institution of slavery. However, a small percentage did think of the "peculiar institution," as slavery was often called, as damaging. To address this disagreement, a rather tame compromise was attempted by which the Presbyterian General Assembly condemned slavery in principle, but left it up to local divisions of the church to implement (or not) this policy as they saw fit.[25] In essence, the church did little to nothing to address slavery in substantive ways, and so slavery divided the church as it divided the larger society. Because of this tension the Presbyterian Church established two general assemblies in 1838 over the issue of slavery—one proslavery and the other opposed to slavery. This development also stemmed from theological doctrine and organizational structure such as a proposed unification with the Congregational Church (a denomination in part based on strong concern for the control of church functions on the local parish level).

Differences between Presbyterian churches in the South were worked out to some extent, and those between churches in the North were also smoothed over. There was unity between the churches in each section of the country, but still disagreement between northern churches and southern churches largely revolving around the issue of slavery. But how does a church divided on issues such as the significance of blacks undertake the type of evangelization consistent with its rhetoric?

Presbyterians wrestled with the ramifications of this question—the position of African Americans in the church—for many years. Both local churches and the larger denomination felt the consequences of such pressing concerns. Issues related to the racial makeup of the denomination and other social concerns over the course of the nineteenth and twentieth centuries influenced patterns of decline and growth with respect to membership. As was the case with many denominations during the late twentieth century, for example, the number of Presbyterians declined. However, as of 2002, the denomination still claimed over 3.4 million members. Some of those within this number are African Americans, many of whom have family connections to the church that extend back to the period of slavery.

Initial efforts to more systematically address the evangelization of Africans date back to the mid-1700s and the work of minister Samuel Davies. Presbyterian ministers labored among enslaved Africans, helping them to establish Presbyterian fellowships in northern cities such as Philadelphia. First African Presbyterian Church, founded in Philadelphia in 1807, was one of the first in the denomination. It was followed by two others also in Philadelphia. In addition to work in the North, Presbyterians attempted to evangelize on southern plantations, particularly in Virginia where numerous Presbyterians settled. According to available records, John Chavis was the first missionary sent south by the General Assembly. He began his work in 1801. The best known white Presbyterian preacher to enslaved Africans, however, was Charles C. Jones, who left his pastorate in 1833 in order to work with Africans. Although the work of various missionaries was energetic at times, in terms of actual numbers it was rather limited with no more than 2,800 Africans in the Presbyterian Church as of the mid-nineteenth century. Nonetheless, certain areas of the South experienced noteworthy growth only a few years after the reported membership of 2,800.[26] This growth was related to a surge in religious energy.

The energy was unmistakable as reports to General Assembly suggested, highlighting as they did the "spontaneous revivals, accompanied by emotional public conversions, speaking in tongues, and testimonies of physical healings [that] swept across the young nation."[27] Ministers working in this environment were influenced by this religious fervor and made it their mission to bring both whites and blacks into the Christian Church. The acceptance of the socially contrived racial hierarchy influenced even church practice, however, resulting in Africans holding second-class status exemplified by segregated seating and limited opportunities for ordained ministry. What to do with Africans was a topic of conversation, but most white Presbyterians held little interest in making the issue a central concern of the church.

Presbyterian policies retarded efforts and put them behind Methodists and Baptists, who accommodated requirements for membership and ministry to the social environment. For example, educational opportunities were limited at best for Africans, but membership required attention to creeds and rituals that assumed some level of reading proficiency that Africans were denied by law. Even for free Africans in the North, the formal requirements for Presbyterian Church membership were achieved only with great effort. There was also another difficulty, an underlying assumption on the part of many northern white Presbyterians that separate churches for Africans under white control were best. Such an attitude could stimulate only limited achievement with regard to converting Africans, and it certainly did not generate many opportunities for Africans to advance within the church. In the South, separate churches and full participation in white churches were both unthinkable for most white Presbyterians. Yet, Presbyterians of African descent in both the North and the South made impressive, individual marks on Presbyterian history. One need only think of figures such as Lucy Craft Laney, who founded a school for African Americans; Daniel Jackson Sanders, who became the first African American president of Biddle University (now Johnson C. Smith University); or Albert Byron McCoy, who directed Sunday school missions in the important Presbyterian area of North Carolina.[28]

With the emancipation of slaves in 1863 and the end of the Civil War shortly after that, Presbyterian churches as well as other denominations had to rethink their behavior or run the risk of losing African American membership to more liberal communions. Dynamic ministers of African descent such as Francis Grimke, Samuel Cornish, Theodore S. Wright, Henry Highland Garnet, and J.W.C. Pennington were doing impressive work on the local level to improve the religious and sociopolitical position of African Americans, but also making efforts to connect Presbyterians of African descent in more expansive ways through the formation of the Afro-Presbyterian Council (the Council of the North and West). In 1897, members from the Southern Presbyterian Church created the Afro-American Presbyterian Synod with a membership of slightly over 1,300. The name was changed to Snedecor Memorial Synod, but the prevailing attitude toward African American members hampered the ability of this new synod to thrive. It was disbanded in 1951, with participating congregations placed in other synods. One year prior to this, the African American congregations that made up the Catawba Synod (Virginia and North Carolina) suggested all synods be integrated.[29] Little was made of this suggestion.

Efforts in the North such as the creation of the Negro Cumberland Church did not fare any better.[30] Matters were only complicated when northern Presbyterians began working in southern regions. This created a sense of competition that southern Presbyterians met with resentment. While the efforts of northern missionaries resulted in substantial growth in the number of African American Presbyterians, this growth pales in comparison to the large African American population within the areas worked by missionaries. In short, most African Americans either were not reached by the message of these missionaries or found the Presbyterian Church unattractive. Those who did join probably found the educational opportunities afforded as attractive as the doctrine and religious practices, if not more so.

There was much at stake as African Americans migrated to northern and southern cities looking for economic opportunity, with many also looking for places to worship. Presbyterian churches made an effort, developing churches and centers geared toward meeting social needs. Segregated synods and presbyteries (a grouping of ministers and elders from various congregations within a district of the church) were addressed with time. An effort was made to better include African Americans in the life of the church by, for example, electing Edler Hawkins moderator of the General Assembly. In addition, some white churches actively sought out African American pastors. Some twenty years ago, long-time Presbyterian and noted historian Gayraud Wilmore lamented this complex problem facing the church. Although strides have been made to address issues of race within the church since Wilmore's comments in the 1980s, the Presbyterian Church continues to wrestle with his question: "There are not only racial and class prejudices—on both sides—but more subtle problems arising from patterns of institutionalized racism of long standing—paternalism and servile self-abnegation, apathy and repressed anger, ignorance and cynical nonparticipation, under representation and the consequent under utilization of gifts. . . . How should Blacks and whites be together in the same church . . . given the history of racial oppression in the American churches and in the nation?"[31]

Until a solid answer to this pressing question is given, the situation looks daunting. The inclusion of African Americans in the full life of the church remains a problem. According to William H. Hopper Jr., as of 2000, "anyone with eyes to see soon perceives that African American Presbyterians have little voice in the Presbyterian Church (USA) governing bodies today, despite the fact that a few African Americans hold important staff positions at various governing body levels in the church."[32]

Furthermore, according to Rosalie Potter, associate director for evangelism and church development in the National Ministries Division, "147 of the denomination's 390 black churches do not have ministers. At the same time . . . many black Presbyterian women have been ordained but can't find a pastoral call."[33] In response to such problems, Pat Brown, moderator of the General Assembly in 1997, suggests that the National Black Presbyterian Caucus (NBPC) work to fill up existing churches and to educate the church's young people on Presbyterianism.[34]

While Presbyterians have worked to provide answers to pressing religious and social problems, changing attitudes toward religion and shifting religious allegiances of Americans have had an impact on the membership of the Presbyterian Church (USA), the largest Presbyterian church in the United States and the ninth-largest denomination in the United States. Since 1997, there has been a decline in membership of roughly 500,000. Recent reports suggest that African Americans make up roughly two percent of the denomination's membership of roughly 2.6 million.[35]

What Presbyterians Believe

Presbyterianism, like the Lutheran tradition, is a product of the sixteenth-century effort to reform religious belief and practice of the

Roman Catholic Church. In part this was based on an effort to bring church structure in line with the scripture as the ultimate authority. It was understood that this could be accomplished in part through attention to the proper function of the pastor in line with the biblical position of the elder, or presbyter. The pastor's role was that of teacher, one who monitored the celebration of the sacraments. But this person was not to control or rule the church. The priesthood of all believers meant a more active role in church life for the laity than the idea of a priesthood of elite rulers allowed.[36] More involvement in church ritual for the laity meant development of an institutional structure that was guided by pastors and elders rather than bishops, popes, and other such figures. In short, religious leaders conducted the worship and sacraments of the church, but God was the ultimate authority and the scriptures served as God's blueprint.

John Calvin in Geneva, and later John Knox in Scotland, used Reformed (i.e., a rethinking of Roman Catholic theology) theological work to ground a new governance for the church, one that moved quickly from Geneva to other parts of Europe. Living and working in Geneva, Calvin explored the teachings of the church and came up with several conclusions that ran contrary to dominant Roman Catholic doctrine. There are four major theological points made by Calvin that impact deeply the development of Presbyterianism and that continue to shape the faith stance of contemporary Presbyterians: (1) the sovereignty of God; (2) the authority of scripture; (3) justification by grace and accepted by faith; and (4) the priesthood of all believers. The Presbyterian Church (USA) says this concerning these early and foundational theological precepts:

> What they mean is that God is the supreme authority throughout the universe. Our knowledge of God and God's purpose for humanity comes from the Bible, particularly what is revealed in the New Testament through the life of Jesus Christ. Our salvation (justification) through Jesus is God's generous gift to us and not the result of our own accomplishments. It is everyone's job—ministers and lay people alike—to share this Good News with the whole world. That is also why the Presbyterian church is governed at all levels by a combination of clergy and laity, men and women alike.[37]

Presbyterians believe that God's saving work was accomplished through Jesus Christ, and that God's continuing presence is felt through the Holy Spirit. The Bible provides God's revelation, or God's presence in human history, and in this way it offers all necessary information for proper living. Furthermore, all humans are guilty of sin against God in that all humans are estranged from God. However, through acceptance of Christ, humans are able to renew their relationship with God.

These theological ideas, initially presented by John Calvin, provide the framework for Presbyterian Church doctrine. The confession of this faith is found in the Book of Confessions, and these statements, according to the Presbyterian Church, "reflect our understanding of God and what God expects of us at different times in history, but all are faithful to the fundamental beliefs described above. Even though we share these common beliefs, Presbyterians understand that God alone is lord of the conscience, and it is up to each individual to understand what these principles mean in his or her life."[38]

African Americans and the Episcopal Church

The reconfiguration of the church in England took place over the course of several royal administrations, with citizens who were considered too zealous for radical change being persecuted periodically. Some escaped persecution by moving elsewhere in Europe, and others saw the New World as their proper place.[39]

One of the early examples of this reconstitution of the church expressed in the colonies was the Protestant Episcopal Church. The name *Protestant Episcopal* distinguished it from the Roman Catholic Church in that, even though like Catholicism its structure included bishops, it was Protestant. It was unlike some of the other Protestant churches, however, in that it believed in the system of bishops as the scriptural given church structure. With time, "Protestant" was dropped from the name of the church; hence the Episcopal Church of the United States of America is the name currently used.[40] The Episcopal Church is a part of the Anglican Communion, meaning it is connected to the churches that have their roots in the Church of England.

Even before the founding of this church, Anglican services were conducted in Virginia, which was the first Anglican settlement in the American colonies. From this beginning in Virginia, the Episcopal tradition took root and expanded. Virginia played a major role in the development of Episcopal churches, but not to the exclusion of other southern colonies such as South Carolina or North Carolina and Georgia, where growth was slow but Episcopal churches were present.

Anglican churches were also planted in middle colonies such as Pennsylvania, Maryland, New York, New Jersey, and Delaware. Some of this work was encouraged and supported by the Society for the Propagation of the Gospel developed in England in 1701 as a vehicle for assisting the spread of the Anglican tradition in the New World through the work of hundreds of ministers who established missions through-out the colonies. However, even a year before the society formed, there were roughly one hundred Anglican churches in the colonies, from New England to the southern colonies.[41] By the time of the Revolutionary War, the Anglican Church was the second largest denomination in North America, claiming over four hundred churches.[42]

An evangelical impulse in Episcopal circles was exemplified through figures such as George Whitefield, who, while disliked by many from his own Anglican communion, pushed with great enthusiasm the need for personal salvation, repentance from sin, combined with the accept-ance of Jesus Christ as savior that marked the "true" Christian. Some objected to such an emphasis on strong emotion, but the energetic and evangelical perspective ultimately gained adherents. It was not unheard of for some influenced by Whitefield to leave the Anglican Church for other denominations, but many maintained both evangelical sensibili-ties and Episcopal membership.[43]

As students graduated from institutions such as the College of William and Mary, the number of American-born ministers slowly in-creased. The church began to take on an American tone as ministers preached and led congregations based on the social and cultural con-ditions of life in the colonies, as opposed to religious life reflecting the European training and cultural sensibilities of imported ministers. Be-fore the end of the eighteenth century, it was clear that stronger orga-nizational bonds were necessary, but without the presence of bishops selected within and consecrated for North America such unity was vir-tually impossible.

In exchange for the consecration of American bishops, congrega-tions in North America agreed to restrict revisions to the Prayer Book that might cause tension with England as they might be regarded as a departure from the Anglican tradition. In 1787, a couple of years after the first General Convention was held in Philadelphia, two American bishops, Samuel Provoost and William White, were consecrated. The General Convention in 1789 developed a common constitution, *Book of Common Prayer*, regulating laws, and an organizational structure for religious leadership. In this way it was possible to doctrinally and ritually unite churches across regional and state lines.

The energy that went into solidifying organizational structure was matched by an interest in both domestic and foreign missions and re-newed religiously informed education opportunities. After the first decade of the nineteenth century, the church experienced growth as de-termined ministers and missionaries canvassed various sections of the United States holding meetings and seeking converts. These efforts had limited consequences in the Deep South and the western territory, but other areas experienced growth.[44]

Unified activity based on the 1789 Convention ran into the slavery question. The slavery question divided the church, sapping its energy and blurring its ecclesiastical vision. Members of the church tried to deny the problem being caused by the slavery question, but ultimately the schism between northern churches and southern churches could not be ignored. The division did not last as long as it did in some of the other denominations. Before the end of 1865 it was over. Debate and disagreement over issues of doctrine, wars, urban flight, and shifts in approaches to scripture persisted, however.

The influx of immigrants beginning in the mid-nineteenth century only complicated church politics inspired by questions of race and ethnicity within a changing America. In some instances, and at times using a sense of the Christian faith as having social implications, church leaders such as Phillips Brooks worked to incorporate the challenges of new thought and a changing sociopolitical environment. He and others like him sought to maintain the numerical strength of a church that had persisted in North America for centuries. By 1960, the Episcopal Church claimed 3.4 million members, but the church, like many others during the late twentieth century, experienced membership decline, so that in 2001 the church reported membership of roughly 2.33 million members.[45] Among those who have remained loyal to the Episcopal Church are African Americans. As was the case with the Lutheran Church and the Presbyterian Church, some of these African Americans have family links that run back to the early years of the church's presence in North America.

It was not long after the Anglican Church established itself in Virginia that enslaved Africans were brought into its fellowship, the first entering the church in 1623.[46] This, however, would not mark a sustained effort. Episcopalian slaveholders were not different from their counterparts in other denominations in that they also refused missionaries and pastors regular access to their plantations. But at the turn of the nineteenth century, the Anglican Church used the Society for the Propagation of the Gospel to attract and convert enslaved Africans. Its success was mixed in that this evangelism was accompanied by an unwillingness to question the system that held Africans as chattel. During the antebellum period, the years prior to the Civil War, the number of African Episcopalians reached 35,000.[47]

The great revivals noted several times in this chapter helped Episcopalians reach citizens of the new country—the United States—as well as slaves. But the number of converts paled in comparison to those attracted to Baptist and Methodist churches in part because the Episcopal Church's regulations made it difficult for Africans with no educational opportunities to enter ministry or hold other important offices. While the church did not consider social equality, some of African descent did receive ordination and were permitted to start separate congregations. One of the early and best known of these ministers was Absalom Jones, who prior to becoming the Episcopal pastor of St. Thomas Church had walked out of St. George's Methodist Episcopal Church with Richard Allen.

One would think that the Episcopal Church experienced discord and schism as a result of the slave question. This is not the case, although southern congregations did form a united body during the time of the Confederacy. Episcopalians had no desire to understand this temporary break in relations as a formal schism. While church business was not as messy as in some other denominations, the issue of slavery and what to do with Africans in America was debated and did impact church membership. It also inspired African missions. In 1850, this effort took institutional form through the election of John Payne as the first bishop in Africa.

As was the case with the Presbyterian and Lutheran churches, Episcopal congregations experienced a crisis with the end of the system of slavery in that many former slaves left and entered independent African American denominations. Why would they stay in churches that had addressed the question of African membership without disrupting the social restrictions that shaped the existential situation of enslaved Africans? The Episcopal Church had to come up with an answer to this. In response the Protestant Episcopal Freedman's Commission developed in 1865. Among its initiatives was the creation of educational institutions.

Some dioceses in the South attempted to address the departure of African Americans by creating separate convocations for them. African American Episcopalians such as Alexander Crummell and George Freeman Bragg Jr. worked to nurture the presence and participation of African Americans in the life of the church. They also called on the church to embrace its responsibility for the improvement of life for African Americans in a holistic sense. In the wake of this, in 1918 Edward T. Demby was elected the denomination's first African American bishop, and in 1945 Bravid Harris was named its second. John Burgess became the first African American to control a white group of churches when he was made bishop of Massachusetts in 1962. In 1989, the church broke another barrier by electing a woman, an African American woman, Barbara Harris, a bishop of the church.

In terms of numbers, as of the 1920s, the Episcopal Church could claim only 31,000 African American members. By 1933 less than two percent of all African American churches in urban areas were Episcopal churches, and in rural areas the figure was less than one percent.[48] Rhetoric concerning the problem of segregation within the church and other matters continued, but it was not until 1954 that important, concrete steps to address them were taken. The first such step was the admission of African American parishes into the South Carolina Convention. Also during the 1950s, the church reached consensus concerning the granting of African Americans full voting rights, but it would be another decade before women would be granted the same rights.[49]

As the Civil Rights Movement gained momentum, many Episcopalians lived out their religious commitments through participation in the struggle for a transformed society. African American clergy, such as Quinland Gordon, who represented only a small percentage of active clergy in the church, extended this commitment to social transformation and used it to rethink the church's basic theological stance through the growing Black Theology Movement. This was a theological development within African American communities that sought to bring the Gospel message into the fight for civil rights. In keeping with the principles of black theology, Gordon argued that there was no contradiction between the aggressive struggle for civil rights and the teachings of Jesus Christ. In fact, a commitment to the Christian faith, to be Christlike, necessitated full commitment to the end of racism. In addition to the more general work of a black theology that cut across denominational lines, Gordon and others brought the basic premises of this theology into the Episcopal Church through "A Declaration by Priests Who Are Negroes," presented to the church and the media in 1967. It called for an end to the poor treatment of African Americans in the church. One of the outgrowths of this aggressive critique of the church was the General Convention Special Program meant to "transfer power from the powerful to the powerless."[50]

African Americans hoped this would mark the beginning of a permanent presence for them in the church's affairs. As was the case with the other churches addressed in this chapter, the push from African Americans and supportive whites has resulted in changes within the Episcopal Church. As a result, African Americans have made some gains in the pastorate, other forms of leadership, and as lay persons involved in the functioning of the denomination (Appendix 4).

What Episcopalians Believe

The Episcopal Church claims over 2.3 million members, making it, like the Presbyterian Church (USA) and the Evangelical Lutheran Church in

America, one of the twenty-five largest denominations in the United States. It shares more than size with the Presbyterian Church and the Lutheran Church, however. All three emerged in response to what are considered doctrinal and practice-related shortcomings that prevent proper relationships and that hamper human fulfillment.

There developed a strong dislike for the attempt of the Roman Catholic Church to control all matters of life, whether they were explicitly religious or having to do with secular government. This perceived intrusion combined with high taxes imposed by the Roman Catholic Church and the questionable conduct of some church officials eventually resulted in open conflict.

King Henry VIII had a disagreement with Roman Catholic officials over his ability to annul his marriage and marry another. For the king this was somewhat personal, but for the citizens of England it spoke to a general need to keep the church from damaging the political system. These issues were ultimately resolved through the formation of a new church, the Church of England. Through an act of the English Parliament, the Church in England was freed from the Pope's authority. It became the independent Church of England, or the Anglican Church, yet in most ritual matters it remained similar to the Roman Catholic Church. According to the contemporary Episcopal Church: "The Episcopal Church, having its roots in the Church of England, is also an Anglican Church. Like all Anglican churches, the Episcopal Church is distinguished by the following characteristics: Protestant, yet Catholic. Anglicanism stands squarely in the Reformed tradition, yet considers itself just as directly descended from the Early Church as the Roman Catholic or Eastern Orthodox churches. Episcopalians celebrate the 'Mass' in ways similar to the Roman Catholic tradition, yet do not recognize a single authority, such as the Pope of Rome."[51] In this regard Episcopalians claim to belong to "a fellowship of Churches at one and the same time Catholic in seeking to do justice to the wholeness of Christian truth, in emphasizing continuity through the Episcopate and in retaining the historic Creeds and Sacraments of undivided Christendom; and Evangelical in its commission to proclaim the Gospel and in its emphasis on personal faith in Jesus Christ as Saviour."[52]

Another dimension of the Episcopal Church's faith involves the use of the Book of Common Prayer containing the liturgy in English as well as the fundamental elements of church doctrine and belief. The Episcopal Church's web site says this concerning the Book of Common Prayer: "Unique to Anglicanism, though, is the Book of Common Prayer, the collection of worship services that all worshipers in an Anglican church follow. It's called 'common prayer' because we all pray it together, around the world. . . . The prayer book explains Christianity, describes the main beliefs of the Church, outlines the requirements for the sacraments, and in general serves as the main guidelines of the Episcopal life."[53] As is the case for Lutherans and Presbyterians mentioned earlier, Episcopalians also place great emphasis on the Bible, arguing that our study of scripture using the ability to reason God provides us offers the knowledge necessary for salvation and for a good life. Sin involves the human's rejection of God and God's will. Salvation, however, was made available by God through Jesus Christ.

Concluding Thoughts: Predominantly Black Churches or Predominantly White Churches: Does It Make a Difference?

Some might argue that African American congregations within predominantly white denominations are not part of the "Black Church." This argument tends to revolve around the overwhelmingly white makeup of the leadership of these churches and the manner in which so many African Americans in these denominations are part of churches that are predominantly white, shaped by the social sensibilities of white Americans. This argument is superficial in that there is no typical way of being African American and Christian within predominantly African American denominations. There are no particular styles of worship—types of songs, types of prayer, types of sermon styles, or patterns of celebration such as speaking in tongues—that are universally accepted within African American denominations.

Furthermore, it must be stated that what renders unique African American participation in white denominations is not style of worship. What serves to distinguish African American participants and African American congregations from their white counterparts within the same denominations is the struggle of African Americans for full inclusion in the life of the denominations and the manner in which this struggle for inclusion shapes their participation within these predominantly white denominations. Therefore, what was highlighted in the preceding discussion was not doctrinal or stylistic differences, but rather the history of the struggle for inclusion in the Christian faith.

African Americans in predominantly white denominations share this desire for full inclusion in the life of the church with their counterparts in historically African American denominations. The difference is that the latter struggle resulted in the development of independent denominations. It is safe to say that huge doctrinal differences do not exist between African Americans and whites in predominantly white denominations. However, such a statement can also be made with respect to African American Methodists, African American Baptists, and African American Pentecostals, and their white counterparts. The basic framework of faith is consistent.

Regardless of which particular denominations are embraced, African Americans have found within the Christian faith a way of developing spiritually, challenging social injustice, and forging healthy community.

Notes

1. This chapter draws from and builds on historical presentations found in Anthony B. Pinn and Anne H. Pinn, *Fortress Introduction to Black Church History* (Minneapolis: Fortress Press, 2001), copyright © 2002. Chaps. 1–3; and Anthony B. Pinn, *The Black Church in the Post–Civil Rights Era* (Maryknoll, NY: Orbis Books, 2002), chaps. 1–2.

2. Washington Temple Church of God in Christ Church, *Anniversary Booklet* (1998), 1.

3. C. Eric Lincoln and Lawrence Mamiya, *The Black Church in the African American Experience* (Durham, NC: Duke University Press, 1990), 23–24.

4. National Baptist Convention, USA web site: http://www.national baptist.org.

5. In 1984 the convention restricted the president's maximum term of office to ten years.

6. Cythnia Lynn Lyerly, *Methodism and the Southern Mind, 1770–1810* (New York: Oxford University Press, 1998), 52.

7. As Gayraud Wimore and James Campbell noted, Bethel Church founded by Richard Allen is not the first black Methodist church. That honor belongs to the African Union Church of Wilmington, Delaware (1807). Furthermore, the AME Church, CME Church, and the AMEZ Church are the topic of this discussion not because they are the only African American Methodist churches. Rather, space limitation and available information make it impossible to provide a discussion of all African American Methodist churches. With this in mind, I decided that attention should be limited to the three largest African American Methodist denominations.

8. "Methodist Groups Talk of Merger," *Christianity Century*, November 15, 1995, 1071–72; Mary R. Sawyer, "Efforts at Black Church Merger," *Journal of the Interdenominational Theology Center* vol. 13 (Spring 1986). Also available at: http://www.bu.edu/sth/BTI/edudocs/ja.htm.

9. "AME Zion and CME Church Leaders Announce Plans to Merge by the Year 2004," in *The Christian Recorder* vol. 149, no. 18 (May 2000): 1, 7. Also: *The Christian Recorder* vol. 149, no. 19 (June 2000): 1, 4.

10. Thomas L. Hoyt Jr., "Theological Themes and Pan-Methodism," in the *AME Church Review* (Spring 2000), 25.

11. Other gifts of the spirit include prophecy, interpretation of tongues, teaching, preaching, and healing.

12. Church of God in Christ official web site: http://www.cogic.org/hist.htm.

13. Mark A. Noll, *The Old Religion in a New World: The History of North American Christianity* (Grand Rapids, MI: Wm. B. Eerdmans Publishing Company, 2001), 12.

14. L. DeAne Lagerquist, *The Lutherans* (Westport, CT: Greenwood Press, 1999), 55.

15. Noll, *Old Religion in a New World*, 21.

16. Lagerquist, *The Lutherans*, 26.

17. Daniel Payne, "Daniel Payne's Protestation of Slavery," *Lutheran Herald and Journal of the Franckean Synod* (Fort Plain, NY: Committee of Publication of the Franckean Synod, 1839): 113–15.

18. Lagerquist, *The Lutherans*, 142.

19. http://www.aala-online.org/nuaala81.htm.

20. http://stlconline.org/elcanews/200308/2003080806.html.

21. Lagerquist, *The Lutherans*, 5–6.

22. Randall Balmer and Lauren Winner, *Protestantism in America* (New York: Columbia University Press, 2002), 37.

23. http://www.elca.org/co/faith.html.

24. http://www.pcusa.org/101/.

25. Andrew E. Murray, *Presbyterians and the Negro: A History* (Philadelphia: Presbyterian Historical Society, 1966), 18.

26. Ibid., 55, 59–60.

27. R. Douglas Brackenridge, *The Presbyterian Church (USA) Foundation: A Bicentennial History, 1799–1999* (Louisville, KY: Geneva Press, 1999), 17.

28. Gayraud S. Wilmore, *Black and Presbyterian: The Heritage and the Hope* (Philadelphia: Geneva Press, 1983), 55.

29. William H. Hopper Jr., *Authentic Congregations* (Louisville, KY: Geneva Press, 2000), 129.

30. Murray, *Presbyterians and the Negro*, 151–52.

31. Wilmore, *Black and Presbyterian*, 15.

32. Hopper, *Authentic Congregations*, 124–25.

33. Worldwide Faith News Archives, "Black Presbyterians Urged to Reclaim Their Heritage," from PCUSA>NEWS@psusa.org (April 4, 1998), found at: http://www.wfn.org/1998/04/msg00106.html.

34. Ibid.

35. Ibid.

36. Wilmore, *Black and Presbyterian*, 56.

37. http://www.pcusa.org/101/.

38. http://www.pcusa.org/101/101-theology.htm.

39. David L. Holmes, *A Brief History of the Episcopal Church* (Valley Forge, PA: Trinity Press International, 1993), 20.

40. Ibid., 50–51.

41. Ibid., 28.

42. Ibid., 37.

43. Besides internal battles over the usefulness of the evangelical perspective in church work, the Revolutionary War brought into question for many Episcopal churches their connection to England's Anglican Church. During this period it was more common for it to be referred to as the Church of England

than the Episcopal Church. The term *Anglican* was not really popular until the nineteenth century as a more subtle way of expressing connection to the churches associated with the Church of England.

44. Holmes, *Brief History*, 69.

45. Ibid., 175.

46. Ibid., 78.

47. Ibid., 79.

48. Gardiner H. Shattuck Jr., *Episcopalians and Race: Civil War to Civil Rights* (Lexington: University Press of Kentucky), 31, 32.

49. Ibid., 55.

50. Ibid., 180.

51. http://www.episcopalchurch.org/17041_17013_ENG_HTM.htm?menu-menu16975.

52. Powel Mills Dawley, *The Episcopal Church and Its Work* (New York: Seabury Press, 1961), 5–6.

53. http://www.episcopalchurch.org/17041_17013_ENG_HTM.htm?menu-menu16975.

Chapter 9

The Roman Catholic Church

Some time ago, I attended a Roman Catholic Church in St. Louis, Missouri. I had heard wonderful things about the pastor and the congregation, about its social activism and the manner in which the larger community embraced this church—St. Alphonsus Church, or the "Rock" as it is commonly called.

The service was marked by energetic singing, enthusiastic preaching, African art and textiles, and a general ethos of vibrant celebration. What was even more intriguing than the tone of worship, however, was the makeup of the congregation. It was predominantly African American. I talked with some of the members after the service and discovered that their families had attended this church for decades.

While not all African American Catholics worship in predominantly African American settings, they do claim the same faith and understand themselves as an important part of the Roman Catholic presence in the United States. The style of expression may differ in some cases, as St. Alphonsus demonstrates, but there are no significant differences in liturgy between white and African American Roman Catholics. Differences are more a matter of perspective—viewing the faith from the vantage point of African American culture—than the theological or ritual content of the church's practices. In short, the story of African American involvement in Roman Catholicism is more a story of the struggle for inclusion in the full life of the church, rather than a story of diverse practices. In other words, it is the story of the struggle to "make it possible to be Black, Catholic, and American without being cursed and spit upon, devalued and marginalized."[1]

African Americans and the Roman Catholic Church

As of the 1500s the Roman Catholic Church was present in the New World, with a diocese, or geographic area overseen by a bishop, established in the U.S. territory of Puerto Rico as of 1511. French and Spanish missionaries also worked to gain converts in Texas, Louisiana, and California, among other locations. With time, some Catholics from England made their way to locations such as Maryland and established congregations. Although faced with anti-Catholic feelings from other colonists, Roman Catholics maintained a presence in the colonies. With time, Catholics in North America made an impact on the church's hierarchy.

The first American bishop, John Carroll, was elected in 1789, and he eventually organized what became Georgetown University and St. Mary's Seminary with the hope, unfulfilled for some time, of "training" religious leaders in the United States. In time new dioceses developed and men and women committed themselves to serving the church as priests and nuns (i.e., women religious). While these developments were important, it was clear up to the twentieth century that the church's strength—financially and otherwise—lay outside the United States. The Roman Catholic Church in the United States was young and uncertain of its direction: should it push for a uniquely American version of the church, or should it embrace a European model and its accompanying religious sensibilities? The church's movement in North America ebbed and flowed. With time conversions and the immigration of Catholics from other areas of the world (such as Italy, Ireland, and Poland) changed the Roman Catholic Church's strength in the United States. Ethnic and territorial parishes developed in diverse communities of the country. With time, Roman Catholics in the United States would come to represent better than 20 percent of the total population, and these Catholics play a major role in financially supporting the Vatican and the overall life of the church.

As of 2000, it was reported that the Roman Catholic Church had over one billion members. This is not to say that Roman Catholics all have the same relationship to the church. To the contrary, scholars argue that there are various types of Roman Catholics, ranging from those who abide by all the established regulations to those who claim membership in the church but are only remotely aware of its doctrine and ritual structures. The latter are nominal Catholics, who attend mass only on occasion and live life in ways that are devoid of strong church influence.[2]

In all fairness this is not a situation unique to the Roman Catholic

Church, but it may say something about the recent shift in this church. I am referring to the Second Vatican Council, or Vatican II (1962–1965), the ecumenical council called by Pope John XXIII. The Pope called for this gathering in order to address concerns related to the church's relationship to the modern world. As part of sweeping changes, Catholic practices became more inclusive of the church membership by, for example, no longer requiring that mass be conducted in Latin. This change in terms of the language of mass is significant in that, for instance, in Los Angeles alone mass is now celebrated in forty-seven languages, clearly marking the diversity of the church. On the level of symbolism, this move spoke to the church's openness to the social realities of its diverse membership.[3]

This openness was also marked by the repositioning of the priest during mass; no longer did he conduct the service with his back to the congregation. Now he faced those gathered. There was also opportunity for increased participation by nonclergy as well as more open or public discussion between conservative and liberal segments of the church on church policy regarding sensitive issues such as interreligious dialogue, reproduction ethics, sexuality, and suicide. The manner in which Catholics were now encouraged to read scripture as part of their devotions also opened new conversation concerning the church's embrace of God's will in modern life. However, as is the case in historically African American denominations, debate concerning the place of women in ordained ministry continues to be a heated issue.

It is possible, if not highly likely, that those active in the church prior to Vatican II and those involved afterward have somewhat different takes on what it means to be Roman Catholic. Accordingly, a recent survey indicated "72 percent of pre–Vatican II Catholics claim to go to mass weekly, but only 44 percent of post–Vatican II Catholics say they go weekly and the real numbers are probably closer to 33 percent attending."[4]

The Roman Catholic Church has changed over the years with respect to how members approach doctrine, ritual, and life based on them. The Roman Catholic Church in the United States has also struggled with issues of identity and its relationship to the authority of Rome versus the spirit of freedom that marked the emergence of the United States and guided its growth: how can one be American and Catholic? This question has been particularly heated with respect to African Americans, who have a long and complex history with the Roman Catholic Church. People of African descent have made a significant impact on the Roman Catholic Church, its teachings, and its ritual life. From some of the African church fathers to more recent priests, nuns, and laypersons, people of African descent have given their time and energy to the life of the church.

In the context of the United States, the first Catholic of African descent was Estebam, a slave who in 1536 was brought to the territory comprising present day Florida, Texas, and Arkansas.[5] It was not uncommon for Spanish and French colonists to baptize their slaves into the Catholic faith. In addition, in the eighteenth century, conflicts between the Spanish and the English in the southeast resulted in some slaves converting to Catholicism as they were encouraged by Spaniards to flee their English slaveholders and live free in Florida, if they converted. The strength of Catholicism in Florida fluctuated for some of the eighteenth century depending on who controlled the territory at any given moment. Even so, by 1791 there were roughly one hundred African Catholics in Pensacola alone.[6]

There was a rhetoric of conversion regarding enslaved Africans, but as was the case with Protestants, this did not mean that most slaves owned by Catholics received sustained religious instruction. A suspicion concerning the consequences of instruction combined with a limited number of priests to serve the needs of slaves and whites made outreach difficult. William Henry Elder speaks to this dilemma:

> Catholic masters of course are taught that it is their duty to furnish their slaves with opportunities for being well instructed, and for practicing their religion. And here is my anxiety, that I cannot enable those masters to do their duty because there are not Priests enough. The negroes must be attended in a great measure on the plantation . . . because in our case there are so few churches; and even where there is a church, the negroes of four or five plantations would fill it up, and leave no room for the white, nor for the other negroes of the neighborhood.[7]

Attention to Africans was spotty at best, and ability to practice their faith was often hindered: "From the viewpoint of evangelization, slavery was a hindrance to the preaching of the gospel. From the viewpoint of the apostolate, Catholic slaves often were deterred from the practice of their religion by the ill will of the slaveowners."[8] In spite of this dilemma, blacks joined the Roman Catholic Church.

Estimates suggest that there may have been one thousand African Catholics in Louisiana prior to the start of the Civil War. Growth of the church's African membership, however, was not limited to Florida and Louisiana, although they represent an early African Catholic presence. To get an accurate picture of the movement of Catholicism within early African communities in North America, one must also note the growth that took place in what would become Missouri, Kentucky, Pennsylvania, and Maryland. For example, before the end of the eighteenth century, there were roughly 3,000 African Catholics in Maryland. The number of Africans who communed in the Roman Catholic Church grew in the Mid-Atlantic area and the South. Scholars generally agree, however, that the first African Catholic parish, Chapel of the Nativity, developed in Pittsburgh in 1844.

Such growth is impressive, and it provides a sense of the makeup of Roman Catholic community, but numbers do not suggest very much with respect to the religious life of enslaved Africans. Nonetheless, enslaved Africans and free Africans who were part of the Catholic Church, according to historian Albert Raboteau, "were attracted to the centuries-old rituals of Catholicism. They found deep meaning in the Mass, the sacraments, and in personal devotion to the Virgin and the Saints."[9] Regarding this, it is likely that most African Catholics had a worship experience in keeping with the dominant social sensibilities that meant segregated worship in white churches.

Prevailing social attitudes made it difficult for Africans to undertake the sacrament of ordained church ministry, and African women were not encouraged to become women religious. In fact, it is not until roughly 1829 that African women, who had developed a school for young girls, made their profession and successfully entered religious life through the formation of the Oblate Sisters of Providence. The four women—Marie Madeleine Balas, Rosire Boegue, Almeide Ducheniea Maxis, and Elizabeth Lage—and their work were recognized and approved by Pope Gregory XVI in 1831. Some years after being approved by the Pope, the Oblate Sisters of Providence expanded by opening a short-lived school for African children in Philadelphia in 1863. In addition to providing this educational opportunity, they also worked with orphans in New Orleans.

Thirteen years after the formation of the Oblate Sisters of Providence, the Sisters of the Holy Family formed in New Orleans to take care of destitute Africans. Three of the women associated with the Sisters of the Holy Family took their canonical vows in 1852. Life for these women was intense, as free as possible of worldly distractions: "The sisters arose at 4:30am and they retired at 8:45pm. At 5:00am there was morning prayers, after half an hour of meditation, followed by Mass. . . . The meals were in silence with reading. Individual spiritual reading in French or English preceded supper."[10] Other communities of African sisters developed over the course of time, each with a commitment to focusing life on service to God through attention to others.

The work of these women is important in itself, but it is also significant in that it points to the striving of the African Catholic population, marking its efforts to experience the full life of the church and to bring the best of the Catholic heritage to those of African descent. This striving for participation in the life of the church did not simply involve women religious. It also entailed the efforts of African men to enter the priesthood.

The practice of ordaining Africans was adopted in the eighteenth century in keeping with the vision of the Congregation for the Propagation of the Faith. Pope Gregory XV developed this organization for the purpose of organizing ministry within the various mission areas. For the most part, however, the work of this organization involved Africans outside the United States. In North America, the idea of ordaining blacks met with opposition through the early twentieth century. Early efforts to bring black men into ministry date back to the late 1800s when the Congregation of the Holy Ghost received three men interested in preparing for the brotherhood.[11] Marking the concern of a minority of the church, such efforts met with very limited success.

The first Africans ordained as priests in the United States happened to be brothers, born the slaves of Michael Morris Healy. With the encouragement of the bishop of Boston, John Fitzpatrick, James Augustine, Patrick Francis, and Alexander Sherwood were educated at Holy Cross College. James Healy not only became a priest in 1854, but also became the first African American bishop, in Portland, Maine. Alexander was ordained in 1858, and after receiving a doctorate in canon law he joined the faculty of a seminary in New York State. Patrick, after further study but before receiving his doctorate in philosophy, was ordained in 1864. After holding several posts, Patrick eventually became the president (1874) of Georgetown College (now Georgetown University).

Mention must also be made of Augustus Tolton, who was born a slave but without the socially derived benefit of skin that could pass as white. He, because of his dark complexion, unlike the Healys had the fact of his African ancestry presented during his efforts to obtain training and ordination. After demonstrating an interest in ordination and after struggling for enrollment in college, Tolton was ordained in Rome in 1886 (see Fig. 9.1). The initial idea was for Tolton to train for missionary work in Africa, but this did not happen. Instead he was sent to the difficult pastorate of a small African American church in Quincy, Illinois. After a short time in Illinois, Tolton was transferred to a new African American parish in Chicago, one with limited resources. His reputation for commitment to African American Catholics spread be-

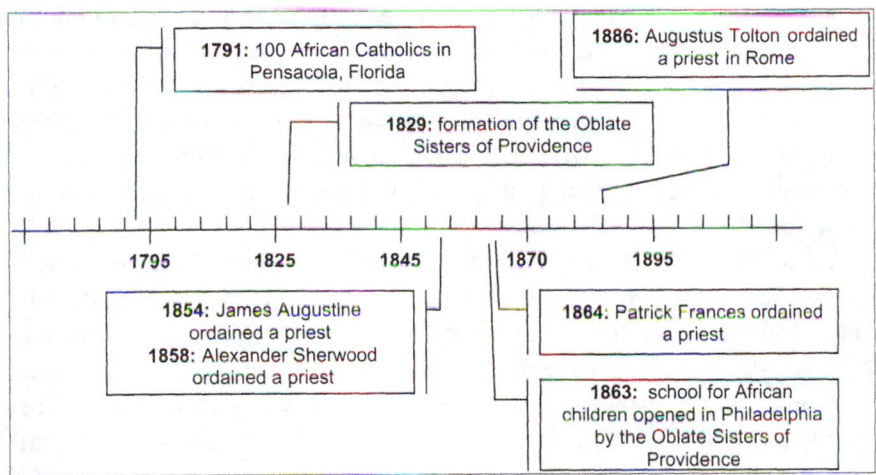

Figure 9.1
Highlights of the Early Involvement of Africans in the Roman Catholic Church
Created by Stephen Finley.

yond Chicago and, according to historian Cyprian Davis, "more than he realized, he was the inspiration for the remarkable movement of faith and evangelization among the African American Catholic laity in the last decade of the 19th century."[12] Tolton's ordination was followed by that of others such as Randolph Uncles. This slow increase in the number of African American priests inspired the creation of a seminary in Mississippi for the training of African Americans. African Americans were interested in the priesthood and were making efforts to secure ordination, but a nagging question persisted: What should be done with African American priests and African American Catholic laity?

The number of black Catholic parishes increased during the late nineteenth century, but the problem of racial discrimination persisted. The Roman Catholic Church of the nineteenth century was not certain about what to do with its African membership. So, it was often the case that treatment varied from one diocese to another as each bishop determined what constituted the proper place for those of African descent in the church. There was no interest on the part of most in losing African American members to Protestant churches, but there was no agreement on a strategy for making fellowship in the Catholic church attractive and rewarding for African Americans. How and by whom should African Americans be evangelized? Should there be separate churches for them? Should they be included in ordained ministry?

African American Catholics did not rely on the good graces of white Catholics to promote their full inclusion in the life of the church. Figures such as Daniel Rudd, who founded the *American Catholic Tribune*, worked to organize a national conversation concerning the state of the church and the work of African Americans within the Catholic community. It was argued that a national conversation, beginning in 1889, spearheaded by African Americans would increase their visibility and would foster substantive changes within the church in the United States. There was also an implicit assumption that the increased visibility of African American Catholics might have significance with respect to the general perception of African Americans, and might contribute to the push for the larger social transformation. That is to say, the presentation of African American Catholics' spiritual and moral commitments might contribute to a national shift with respect to civil engagement between the races in that it would point to the merits and capabilities of African Americans.

Through a series of congresses the objectives for the better treatment of African Americans outlined by Rudd and others were expressed. These objectives were very similar to those expressed by African Americans in Protestant churches. In both cases the emphasis involved the church as a religiously oriented clearinghouse of sorts for a synergy of spiritual, educational, economic, political, and moral growth and opportunity. In short, religious commitments well lived should foster transformation on all levels of individual and communal existence. Good Catholics should be good citizens who strive for racial equality. One can easily argue that African American Catholics sparked a self-evaluation of Roman Catholicism in the United States based on a strong commitment to religiosity sensitive to the unique U.S. cultural context and historical moment. This process involved both an affirmation of the Catholic Church's potential and a critique of its shortcomings with respect to issues of racism both inside and outside the church.

In response to the work of the congresses initiated by Rudd, the church formed the Catholic Board of Negro Mission. However, the issues it was charged with addressing, such as mixed churches versus segregated congregations, were so intense that the board accomplished little. Some church leaders, including Pope Benedict XV, made an effort to address the concerns and needs of African American Catholics. But the church relied so heavily on the good will of individual bishops and congregations that little systemic progress was made. Irrespective of shortcomings, there were signs of promise including the development of educational opportunities for African Americans interested in service to the church.

The middle of the twentieth century marked a change in the status of African Americans in the Roman Catholic Church. This shift was part of a larger trend toward diversity as the descendants of immigrants gained authority and positions of privilege within the church. Neighborhoods changed. The descendants of immigrants moved out of the inner city and African Americans moved in. Former immigrants who once simply identified themselves as Catholics from a particular place in Europe now understood themselves as white in keeping with the racial structure and hierarchy of the United States. This phenomenon was a sociological fact with religious ramifications in that churches experienced changes in membership and were forced to address issues of race. According to John T. McGreevy, "change from a Euro-American Catholic to an African-American neighborhood moved to a different rhythm. . . . These developments—neighborhood changes, a growing distinction between 'black' and 'white' and a blurring of lines between Euro-American Catholic groups" occurred across the urban landscape.[13] Racial issues within the church notwithstanding, African Americans continued to find the ritual and teachings of the church spiritually appealing and a key source of what they considered the most appropriate manner for connecting to God.

As the African American membership increased, it became difficult to continue thinking of African American Catholics as an "add on," an aberration in the fabric of Catholic community. This did not mean that discrimination against African Americans ended, nor did it mean the kind of active participation in the struggle for equal rights the church could have mustered. (For example, Catholic schools were only integrated slowly and this was typically done over strong objections.) Rather, it entailed greater space within the church structure for African Americans to express their concerns and exercise their gifts and talents.

As the Civil Rights Movement heated up and in light of Vatican II, some, but certainly not most, African American priests and laity—figures such as Chicago's Father George Clements—fought (often against both the church and the larger society) for a more liberationist agenda with regard to civil rights and to develop a religious identity that was true to the growing concern with black consciousness that marked the late twentieth century. These more progressive Catholics developed various organizations such as the Black Clergy Caucus founded by George Clements to provide a structure for the immediate action they felt was necessary if the Church wanted to be relevant to the lives of African Americans (see Appendix 5). Some African American priests gave this effort an aesthetic dimension by using artistic representations of an African Christ and Virgin Mary, as well as by appealing to the importance of African saints.[14] Such structural and aesthetic action was not without opposition.

The church addressed issues of racism through pastoral letters coming from American bishops and also from the African American bishops (who numbered more than ten by the late twentieth century). Subtle moves were made to improve the visibility and power of African Americans in the Catholic Church, including the establishment in 1988 of Eugene Marino as the first African American archbishop in the United States, in Atlanta, Georgia. Some of the roughly two million African American Catholics wanted more than the addition of African Americans to a troubled system, one that still contained only a small number of African American priests—roughly one for every five thousand African American Catholics.[15] Churches were being closed, African American churches included, and there was little from the perspective of many to suggest a deep concern on the part of church hierarchy. Some African Americans called for fundamental theological and ritual changes that recognized and celebrated the history and talents of African Americans. It is this call for the inclusion of African American culture into religious life that accounts for the style of worship at churches such as St. Alphonsus. Some, however, pushed for more, and one of the more noteworthy advocates for radical change is George Stallings.

Stallings, educated in Rome and ordained in 1974, gained attention in the late 1980s because of his fiery rhetoric directed at the Roman Catholic Church for its failure to creatively address moral issues such as the celibacy of priests and its failure to develop rituals in keeping with the cultural heritage of African Americans. Stallings's services in Washington, DC, drew thousands of African American Catholics (as well as African Americans from other religious communities) interested in the Afrocentric style of worship that greatly resembled the energy-full services associated with African American Pentecostalism. Afrocentrism is a philosophy of life premised on the idea that people of African descent should view life from the perspective of Africa. That is to say, Africa and the welfare of those of African descent should be at the center of their thought and actions. According to Stallings, "I realized the church is a white racist institution controlled by a preponderantly Euro-American white male hierarchy that for a century had decided the fate of black people in the Catholic Church. . . . My blackness could no longer tolerate it!"[16]

He developed a new congregation without the approval of the bishop. The first mass at this new church, Imani Temple (The African American Catholic Congregation), took place on July 2, 1989. Following this, it declared its independence from Rome on January 31, 1990.

St. Alphonsus Church, St. Louis, Missouri.

The mission of this new organization was stated on the church program as follows: "It is the mission of the African American Catholic Congregation to be a preeminent holistic provider of spiritual and educational development. The African-American Catholic Congregation, an autonomous and independent Catholic institution, understands that a people who do not take control of their destiny, moved by the genius of their culture, can never achieve full spiritual, economic, social, cultural, and psychological maturity. Therefore, the African-American Catholic Congregation and its parishioners and [sic] committed to the movement and struggles of our days, in hope of preserving our tomorrows."

More troubling for church hierarchy than the worship style referred to as the "Gospel Mass" was Stallings's theological position on the issue

Imani Temple, Washington, DC.

of ordination that marked a clear rejection of church authority and tradition. Rejecting restrictions on who could be ordained, Stallings ordained a former nun in 1991, and boldly stated that his church was pro-choice, supportive of the gay and lesbian lifestyle, in favor of marriage for priests interested in it, and committed to the right of couples to divorce. In taking this position Stallings knowingly disregarded canon law. He rejected the general authority of the Pope and the local authority of the bishop.

It should come as no surprise that Stallings's teachings and actions which resulted in the development of a religious movement led to his excommunication from the Roman Catholic Church. But his removal from Roman Catholicism did not stop him from fulfilling his religious agenda in that he developed an independent church housed in six locations, serving as its archbishop (consecrated by Richard Bridges of another independent church). It is estimated that his organization has a total membership of over three thousand.

Stallings's activities have taken an odd twist. In recent years, and over the objections of some of his followers, Stallings has developed a relationship with Rev. Sun Myung Moon, going so far as to marry a member of Moon's Unification Church. In response to questions concerning the marriage, Stallings said: "Jesus was an Asiatic Jew with black blood flowing through his veins. Look at me, a man of African descent about to marry a woman of Asian descent. We are about to have some new Jesuses."[17] This connection to the Unification Church marks a theological shift within Stallings's organization. He seems to be moving even further way from anything recognizable as Roman Catholicism. Where he and his followers will ultimately settle in terms of theology and ritual structures remains to be seen.

What Roman Catholics Believe

Stallings's work involves a break with many of the traditional beliefs and practices of Roman Catholicism. A major distinction between Roman Catholicism and Stallings's position as well as that of other Christian denominations revolves around the infallibility of the Pope with respect to issues related to the faith and its practice. Declared during the First Vatican Council in 1870, this perspective on the Pope is significant in that it promotes a strong hierarchical structure within the Church and centralizes formal authority within one figure, whose authority stems from the Apostle Peter as the first leader of the church. This understanding of Peter and his ministerial descendants is drawn from Jesus Christ's comments regarding Peter:

> When Jesus came into the region of Caesarea Philippi, He asked His disciples, saying, "Who do men say that I, the Son of Man, am?" And they said, "Some say John the Baptist, some Elijah, and others Jeremiah or one of the prophets." He said to them, "But who do you say that I am?" And Simon Peter answered and said, "You are the Christ, the Son of the living God." And Jesus answered and said to him, "Blessed are you, Simon Bar-Jonah, for flesh and blood has not revealed this to you, but My Father who is in heaven. And I also say to you that you are Peter, and on this rock I will build My church, and

the gates of Hades shall not prevail against it. And I will give you the keys of the kingdom of heaven, and whatever you bind on earth will be bound in heaven, and whatever you loose on earth will be loosed in heaven."[18]

This authority held by the Pope is deeply important in that it results in the Pope having the right at times to teach what Catholics are to believe regarding the faith in ways that are not open to question because they contain no errors.

The Pope is not the only figure in the church permitted to teach Catholics what to believe and how to conduct themselves. Bishops can teach the principles of Catholic life, but this involves teachings that are subject to revision and change. That is to say, what bishops teach is subject to alteration; if this were not the case their authority would in fact challenge that of the Pope. In both cases—teachings open to change and teachings not subject to alteration—the fundamental source of information is the revelation from God housed in sacred scripture and more contemporarily in the working of God's spirit in the modern world.

Much of what is taught within the church results from councils called by the Pope to discuss with the bishops important and pressing issues. The teachings generated by these councils can be declared infallible. Members of the church, to varying degrees, are familiar with the basics of the councils' work, but less well known is Canonical Law, revised in 1983, that provides a code for the general processes guiding the Roman Catholic Church. This law is not as directly theologically framed and formulated as are the workings of the various councils. Furthermore, Canonical Law is the product of the Pope in consultation with a small group of canon lawyers as opposed to the gathering of the Pope and bishops that defines the work of a council.

In a sense the importance and authority of the bishops and the Pope speak to the Roman Catholic Church's deep appreciation for those who have committed themselves to the service of God and God's church on the highest levels. This type of appreciation might also play into the significance of saints—individuals who displayed unusually strong devotion to God expressed through extraordinary events associated with their lives—within Roman Catholicism. For Roman Catholics, the saints are important on some level because they are able to intercede for the living and thereby help them in their effort to live a proper life. Of particular importance with respect to the saints is the Virgin Mary, the mother of Jesus.

There are similarities between Roman Catholicism and many of the other traditions outlined in this volume in that doctrine and ritual are of fundamental importance for the insurance of good spiritual health.

Participation in the life of the church requires markers, ceremonies, or rites, that denote the movement of the individual into the community of the faithful. There are seven ceremonies or sacraments in Roman Catholicism: baptism, confession, confirmation, matrimony, communion, and holy orders (priesthood), extreme unction (last rites). I highlight the three most frequently discussed by scholars: baptism, communion, and confirmation. The first involves a symbolic "death" of the sinful person through the sprinkling of water on the child or adult. This ceremony opens the person to relationship with God within the context of the community of believers. One of the activities made available to the person through baptism is communion. This ritual involves recognition of the crucifixion of Jesus Christ for the sins of the world. Jesus Christ died for the sins of the world on the cross, and the ritual of communion is a remembrance of this event. Communion is a part of the ritual of the churches in Chapter 8 as well, but unlike most Christian churches presented in this book, Roman Catholics argue that the wine and bread consumed during this ceremony become the actual body and blood of Jesus Christ. This belief is referred to as transubstantiation. Confirmation involves a public pronouncement of the person's embrace of Catholic teachings, and it takes place after the person has studied the doctrine of the church. It is what one might consider the final phase of initiation into the Roman Catholic Church.

In addition to the above sacraments, there are ritualized activities that are quite important to Roman Catholics. Confession is one such ritual through which the believer is given the opportunity to confess shortcomings and receive instructions for overcoming sin. Since Vatican II, the nature and frequency of confession have changed. Fewer people undertake it on a regular basis, and limited church resources (including a declining number of priests) make it difficult for priests to provide this service regularly. Furthermore, the shift follows a theological change regarding perceptions of sin through which "sin is less juridical, so that the faithful focus upon their fundamental life's direction toward God rather than evaluating every act independently."[19] Much of the connection to God's will that some might have felt through the process of confession is undertaken by many through the process of prayer in both formal and informal spaces set apart for this activity.

Concluding Thoughts

Roman Catholicism is complex, with elaborate rituals and doctrine. While most people, when asked to describe the makeup of this division of Christianity, will not think in terms of African Americans, the Roman Catholic Church membership represents a part of the diversity of the United States population. Many African Americans express themselves religiously within the context of this church, finding in its rituals and theology a good way of defining themselves spiritually. The number of African Americans who are members of the Roman Catholic Church is small, when one considers the overall size of the church. Yet, they represent a noteworthy segment of the population of African American Christians.

The practices of Roman Catholicism offer a sense of awe, an awareness of the majesty of the divine, through which to approach God. The elaborate prayers, the songs, the attire of religious leaders, the smell of incense, communion, and the other elements of Roman Catholicism offer its adherents a depth of religious experience that they believe best exposes them to a relationship with God.

For African Americans who embrace Roman Catholicism, their connection to this tradition does not take them away from a sense of what it means to be African Americans in the United States. Rather, it allows them to place themselves within a larger community, with more complex identifications. The connection to God and the community of believers found within the church gives them a greater sense of themselves within the context of a worldwide community of believers, a complex community composed of many colors and cultural backgrounds.

Notes

1. Jamie T. Phelps, "African American Catholics: The Struggle, Contributions, and Gifts of a Marginalized Community," in Jamie T. Phelps, ed., *Black and Catholic: The Challenge and Gift of Black Folk* (Milwaukee: Marquette University Press, 1997), 18–19.
2. Chester Gillis, *Roman Catholicism in America* (New York: Columbia University Press, 1999), 16–19.
3. Ibid., 21.
4. Ibid., 22.
5. Cyprian Davis, *The History of Black Catholics in the United States* (New York: Crossroads, 1991), 28.
6. Ibid., 31.
7. Ibid., 44.
8. Ibid., 43.
9. Albert J. Raboteau, *A Fire in the Bones: Reflections on African-American Religious History* (Boston: Beacon Press, 1996), 119.
10. Davis, *History of Black Catholics*, 108.
11. Ibid., 145–46.

12. Ibid., 162.

13. John T. McGreevy, *Parish Boundaries: The Catholic Encounter with Race in the Twentieth-Century Urban North* (Chicago: University of Chicago, 1996), 35, 36.

14. Ibid., 224–25.

15. Raboteau, *Fire in the Bones*, 117; McGreevy, *Parish Boundaries*, 381.

16. http://www.bccandidates.com/StallingsBio.htm.

17. Center for Studies on New Religions, "Could It Be Love?" found at http://www.cesnur.org/2001/moon_may23.htm.

18. Matthew 16:13–19 (King James Version).

19. Gillis, *Roman Catholicism in America*, 171.

Chapter 10

Santería

Many individuals listen to the soothing yet energetic voice of the late Celia Cruz, or the passionate rhythms of the late Tito Puente's drums. But how many are aware of the rumors concerning their religious practices? On numerous occasions, while enjoying these and other artists, I have been told the same story: Puente and Cruz are practitioners of the African "way," of Santería, the New World religion derived from the Yorùbá tradition. I cannot speak with certainty to the truth of statements concerning the involvement of Cruz and Puente in this religion. Whether true or not, the conversation points to the fascination with Yorùbá-derived religion in the Americas. It undoubtedly points to the fact that interest in this religion extends beyond the academy and a select few and reaches into popular culture. Television programs, both documentaries and sensationalized accounts, spark public interest in this tradition and at times provide a glimpse into the world of the *orishas* (the saints or deities).[1] In addition, songs and music videos make use of imagery associated with the orishas. Several years ago, within the context of this public exposure, this religion, the "way of the saints," received media attention as a result of legal action concerning the Church of the Lukumi Babalu Aye in Hialeah, Florida, and its alleged involvement in animal sacrifice. As a result of their legal victory, Santería houses in Florida and elsewhere increased in popularity and visibility.

Santería in Cuba

As was the case with Voodoo, Santería, the way of the saints, developed through a blending of various African religious practices and sensibilities. The primary source for this religious tradition, however, is drawn from the Yorùbá of modern-day Nigeria. In the New World, Santería is associated with the Yorùbá transported to Cuba. The Yorùbá in Cuba—referred to as *Lucumi* because of their greeting, *oluku mi* ("my friend")—developed significant communities (nations), or *cabildos*, in which they kept alive their cultural identity, including elements of their religious heritage.[2] Cabildos were clubs organized by slaves as a way of maintaining their associations with particular cultural groups connected to beliefs and practices from their homes in Africa. These clubs were later referred to as *reglas*, and with time they became less associated with particular ethnic groups and came to include members from various ethnic backgrounds.

The Spanish who controlled Cuba were required by their regulations and codes to baptize slaves and introduce them to the teachings of the Roman Catholic Church. While church officials should have worried about the activities in the social clubs or cabildos, they assumed that Roman Catholicism was superior to any cultural practice Africans might maintain within these organizations. The religious instruction that the Africans received in these clubs was filtered through their persisting African religious memory. As a result, these organizations aided in the development of Santería by facilitating the combination of Roman Catholicism and African religious sensibilities. Enslaved Africans continued to embrace the orishas, which are manifestations of cosmic energy known as *ashé* (*ache*), associated often with elements of the natural environment such as tornados, the oceans, and rivers. The orishas interact with humans, providing health and other benefits in exchange for attention and sacrifice.[3] The Yorùbá gave their orishas the identity of Catholic saints in order to avoid trouble with church officials. This process involved recognition that orishas and Catholic saints were similar in that they both represent cosmic energy and relate to various patterns of interaction with humans. For example, St. Barbara and the Yorùbá deity Shango are linked in that both are depicted wearing red, and both are associated with soldiers.

The cosmological structure of Santería begins with Olodumare, who is the high God, the supreme deity. Because Olodumare is responsible for the universe, he has no time to respond to human wants and needs. Hence, Olodumare receives no cult attention and has no shrines or priests. The orishas, who represent aspects of Olodumare, have direct contact with humans. Furthermore, each deity is associated with a certain aspect of life, a certain component of existence. Each has certain celebrations in keeping with events, feast days, and other rituals or ceremonies. All these events, feast days, and other rituals or ceremonies related to the orishas are concerned with balance. They involve the meeting of obligations, the correction of wrongdoing, and the celebration of good events. There are many orishas, but the following are the major gods within the cosmology.

Obatala is an elder deity associated with great wisdom and honor. Because of his great age, he is also considered senior to the other orishas. Obatala is also credited with defining the shape of human beings during the process of creation. Eleggua is the trickster figure, the messenger between the orishas and humans. He allows communication and exchange to take place. In addition, there is Ogun, the god associated with war and the working of iron; he is often connected to Oshosi, who is known for his hunting abilities. This connection in part stems from the manner in which both Oshosi and Ogun are known for their abilities with weapons. Associated with the art of warfare is Shango, the god of thunder and wrath. Shango, a former king of Ile-Ife, is also connected to romantic love and fertility. Shango's favorite spouse is Oya, the goddess of the wind who is thus related to storms. Oya also controls cemeteries. There is also a relationship between Shango and Oshun, who is the goddess of rivers, love, and beauty. While Oshun controls the rivers, Yemaya is associated with the upper levels of the ocean, and Olokun is associated with the deep and darker levels of the ocean—where the bodies of the slaves thrown overboard slave ships came to rest. Orunmila is a major orisha because he controls divination and is capable of revealing information concerning one's destiny. In this way, he plays a significant role in the process of maintaining the balance that defines a life well lived. Through Orunmila one learns what needs to be done to restore order, and the restoration of order often involves using herbs to address issues of disease (associated with Babaluaye) or other concerns. These herbs are controlled by Osanyin.

Selected Santería Divinities: Names, Functions, and Colors

Yorùbá Name	Santería Name/ Saint	Function/Color
Olodumare	Olodumare/Olofi —Christ	Aspect of Supreme God who controls the World
Orisa-nla/Obatala	Obatala/Virgin of Mercy	Elder orisha connected with wisdom/morality (White)
Eshu-Elegba	Eleggua/Child of Atoche	Messenger of Olodumare/keeper of the gates (Black and red)
Ogún	Ogun/St. Peter	Associated with iron tools and war (Green and black)
Oschoosi	Oshosi/Norbert	Associated with the forest and hunting (Blue and orange)
Orunmila/Ifá	Orunmila/Francis of Assisi	Controller divination (Green and yellow)

Yorùbá Name	Santería Name/ Saint	Function/Color
Obaluaiye	Babaluaye/Lazarus	Associated with disease (smallpox) (Black or light blues)
Osanyin	Osanyin/Joseph	Controller of herbs and herbal medicine (Green)
Sángó	Shango/St. Barbara	God of thunder/battle (Red and white)
Oyá	Oya/Virgin of La Candelaria	Associated with whirlwinds/ cemeteries (Maroon, red, brown)
Yemojá	Yemaya/Virgin of Regla	Associated with ocean/motherhood (Blue and white)
Olókun	Olokun/Virgin of Relga	Associated with lower levels of the ocean (Blue and white)
Oshún	Oshun/Virgin of Cardiad del Cobre	Associated with water/sensuality (Yellow)

Furthermore, those who follow the way of the orishas must be cognizant of the presence of the ancestors (*egun*), who are reborn in their descendants as well as other spiritual forces that influence human life in numerous ways.[4]

How one works with these various manifestations of ashé involves divination through which the will of a particular orisha is discerned and proper action outlined. An imbalance in one's life through improper action can be corrected through sacrifice of some kind—including various animals such as chickens. Such imbalances are understood as temporary and correctable. The idea of permanent punishment or reward similar to the Christian notion of heaven and hell does not play a role in Santería. In addition, divination can be used to find one's proper place within the religion. For example, an orisha may require an individual to undergo various initiations, at times leading to the priesthood. Initiation into the priesthood would typically end with some variation of the following:

> The culmination of the ceremony, which is also called *asiento* or *hacer santo* ("making saint"), is a three-day fast during which the neophyte is presented to the community as a new brother or sister. In Cuba, it was usually at this time that the orisha that had been "seated" first possessed the neophyte. Actual orisha possession, obligatory in Cuban Santeria, is becoming rarer in America, possibly because consecrated batá drums, which have to be played for the orishas to possess the neophyte, are also very rare. After initiation, both males and females

Person dressed as Elegba and dancing (Cuba).

are known by the feminine name iyabó (in Yoruba, iyawó), which literally means "bride" but is understood in Santeria to mean "novice." During the one-year novitiate that follows, [they] must wear white and observe numerous taboos, some of which they must continue to respect for the rest of their lives. [This information is attained through divination, referred to as the itá.] . . . During their first year . . . santeros also learn the technical and practical aspects of their new status as fully initiated priests or priestesses.[5]

Orishas select individuals for initiation without consideration of gender. For example, a man can become a priest of Oshun, and a woman can become a priestess of Shango. Issues of gender become somewhat blurred in that the gods represent energy, cosmic force, and are not necessarily bound to gender. Hence, Shango is represented by St. Barbara because what connects them is their common relationship to humans. That is to say, how the gods function is more significant than societal thinking on issues of gender. There is one exception, however, in that only men become babalowas (babalaos), who are the priests of Orunmila.

Santería in the United States

At times, the practice of this religion (*le regla de ocha*, or the rule of the orishas) was opposed by political forces governing Cuba. Yet, whether underground or not, the tradition maintained its vitality and appeal. With the movement of Cubans into the United States at the start of the Cuban Revolution in 1959, the religion gained ground in North America. But even before then, many accounts suggest that Francisco (Pancho) Mora, a priest of Ifa, was active in New York as of 1946. Mora is credited with initiating the first santera (priestess) in Puerto Rico in 1954 and organizing the first American drum dance in 1964.[6]

From the late 1950s to the present, better than one million Cubans have made the United States home, particularly Miami. Some brought with them the religious sensibilities associated with Santería. Others embraced the religion once they arrived in the United States. "It is not surprising," George Brandon remarks, "that some Cuban Americans should go to *santeros* [religious leaders] for help." This is because "in the santero they find a healer who speaks their language, shares their basic culture and world view, is able to describe and explain the problems they have, and can set in motion a course of action to deal with them."[7] It is important to note that while this religion was first associated with Cubans, it has grown to include people of various racial and ethnic backgrounds. Researcher Mary Curry sheds light on this when saying "membership in the Religion is extremely diverse and continues to diversify; at the time of my first writing, there were Cuban Houses, Puerto Rican Houses, Black Houses and Multi-ethnic houses. Now, depending upon the part of the country one considers, there are Polish Houses, Mexican Houses and Houses of other ethnic groups."[8] For example, the first African American priestess initiated fully into the tradition was Margie Baynes Quiniones in 1961. She eventually led her own house and initiated some twenty-one priests. Those she initiated have initiated others, resulting in the development of a third generation of African American priests and priestesses completely initiated in the United States.[9] The development of new houses and the movement of the tradition into new communities have not meant complete openness. There remains a need to maintain a level of secrecy because of continuing perceptions of the tradition as dangerous by those who misrepresent it as a tradition used to harm people.

There are few structures that alert the general public that Santería rituals take place in any given location. It is more likely that rituals and other ceremonies take place in the home of the priest or priestess, or in spaces that are also used for other purposes.

Physical space in which religious activities take place, combined

Altar containing St. Barbara (Shango), in Cuba.

with the general secrecy adhered to by most involved in the religion, make active recruitment of members unthinkable. Some African Americans enter the tradition because they have sought out a priest or priestess in order to address needs that have not been adequately addressed through other religious traditions.[10]

Over the course of time, some African Americans altered Santería based on the political and cultural concerns of black nationalist movements of the 1960s and 1970s. For traditionalists, this is a problem, a sign of disrespect and an ill-formed knowledge base. Respect for and deference toward those with more knowledge and deeper commitment to the tradition are a major expectation. But for those making the changes, they are willing to ignore such expectations because the changes serve as a way to better understand and embrace their African roots. Much of this early effort to celebrate the tradition's African base was sparked by Walter King, later known as Oba Oseijeman Adefunmi.

Oba Oseijeman Adefunmi, the king of Oyotunji African Village (Sheldon, South Carolina), was the first African American initiated into the religion in Cuba (1959). He described the initiation this way:

When we go there [Mantanzas, Cuba] they took us into a room, as I recall, and they then began to divine. They wanted to do their own. . . .

> They read me as Obatala. . . . It took a week then to buy all kinds of stuff that we needed, to purchase the animals and other live stock and to get us psychologically prepared. . . . I understood absolutely nothing because I was waiting for them to ordain me some kind of way but with words. But they got everything together. . . . So they did then my entire initiation without interruptions. . . . Then we [he and Christopher Oliana who was also initiated] stayed in the room for six days. We had to perform and everything like that. . . . I wanted everything to be African. They had some type of spanish clothes, they wanted us to wear. I didn't want to wear those, not on a daily basis. So I use to wrap my sheet around me the way the Akan people do. . . . The only part that I didn't really find African there was, one final day when we had to visit a church. We had to get some holy water. [11]

With time, Oba Adefunmi became uneasy with the Christian "covering" shrouded over this African-based religion. In response, he decided to remove Roman Catholic attributes related to the orishas. From his perspective, doing so was the only way to avoid "cultural amnesia" and be true to the religion's African roots. In order to achieve this, Oba Adefunmi began developing ritual structures he believed were more in keeping with the practice of Yorùbá religion in Nigeria. In his words: "numerous other Afro-Americans were entering the traditional Cuban Santo system and only timidly and surreptitiously substituting Yorùbá images in place of Christian images. These for the most part avoided Yorùbá attire which was angrily prohibited by their Afro-Cuban Godparents [those who guide and train those who are new in the religion]."[12] In addition to questioning the Catholic elements of "the way of the saints," Oba Adefunmi also angered some members of the Santería community by removing the secrecy that surrounded the tradition since its early days in Cuba. Furthermore, he gave Yorùbá names to those who had not been initiated into the tradition, and this created tension because "knowledge of an initiate's Yorùbá or Lucumi name was the mark of being an insider and the names were used only among priests." Dismissing this traditional use of Yorùbá names, "he encouraged blacks to use these names publicly and to substitute them for their English or 'slave' names." He also broke the tradition of secrecy by holding open performances and *bembes* (parties), and by actively recruiting participants.[13]

The community representing those in agreement with Oba Adefunmi's practices went through several transformations, beginning with the Shango Temple (in Harlem, New York City) and culminating in Oyotunji African Village (Sheldon, South Carolina).

Others never left the way of the saints as presented to them by

Statue of Olokun at Oyotunjia Village.

Cuban priests and priestesses (*santeros/santeras*). In recent years, how-ever, even those who have maintained allegiance to the religion as taught to them by traditionalists still raise questions concerning Euro-pean holdovers like the appearance of Catholic saints on altars. Subtle distinctions began to develop. For example, "one of the earliest indi-cators that such differences exist was the different vocabulary employed by Latin and Black American practitioners. Books and dissertations use a Latin vocabulary while Black Americans prefer English or Yorùbá nomenclature. . . . Another terminological difference is that it is Latins who call the Religion Santería and Black Americans who call it the Yorùbá Religion."[14] One trait of the religion that allows for differences in doctrine and ritual is the lack of a standard model of practice. Like Voodoo and black Spiritual churches, there is variety in that various houses will establish sets of procedures corresponding to the teachings of particular priests or priestesses.

Those who remain in the tradition as transmitted via Cuba involve themselves in a house or ilé, headed by a priest or priestess, and con-taining others of varying degrees of commitment to the orishas. Priests and priestesses are not obligated to establish houses and initiate others, but those who take responsibility for training others within a new house are commonly referred to as *babalocha* in the case of men, or *iyalocha* in the case of women.[15] Styles of leadership will vary from one priest or priestess to another, some exercising more forceful control than others. The rather loose configuration of the religion and the independence of houses from each other influence the shape of the religion in the United States. One priest describes his situation this way:

> Generally a person comes to you and they're troubled about something. You give them a reading and tell them that the reading says that, "You should do A, B or C and, if you do, your problem will be resolved or dissipated or won't be a problem at all." And then people want to join, and you can include them in your house if you feel that they want to progress with you. It's a very loosely organized religion. It's not an organized religion per se. As godfather, I try to be an influence, or a guide. But in terms of saying, "You must do this, or you can't do this," that's not my way. I'm only going to show him a better way, how his spiritual thing can unfold or spark so he can reach self-awareness.[16]

Contemporary houses are marked by diversity, as researcher Joseph Murphy discovered: "I . . . begin to edge my way around the crowded house. I find old and young people, Afro-Americans, Puerto Ricans, and Cubans. Little children run by at play; teenagers sit together, some boisterous, some withdrawn. Very old women are leaning on cane and on each other. There seem to be about four women for every man."[17] Difficulties based on social and cultural differences between various racial and ethnic groups have surfaced over the years. This problem has been fundamental because of the significance of the spoken word. Steven Gregory gives an example of this dilemma within the context of a house in New York City: "Language, however, remains a significant barrier to the full integration of African American and other English-speaking members of the house. For example, English speakers tend to mix among themselves during ceremonial events and Spanish speakers even if bilingual, tend to speak only in Spanish."[18] As more African Americans develop houses, this issue of language may shift in that for some it will become a matter of importance to use as much Yorùbá, as opposed to English or Spanish, as possible because the tradition has roots in Yorùbá.

Houses are named for the priest or priestess in charge. Those who belong to a house under the leadership of a particular priest or priestess are the "god-children" of that religious leader, and all those related to a particular leader in this sense are god-brothers and god-sisters. While related in a sense as brothers and sisters in the faith, there are particular ways in which they must interact. What determines the nature of their interaction as well as their general bond as members of a house centers on the process of initiation—a movement symbolizing growing acquaintance with the workings of the tradition. There are restrictions on which ceremonies and rituals one can attend and participate in. Those who are *aleyo*—strangers—attend more "public" events and get assistance from the orishas through work with a priest or priestess, but they have weak ties to the house. On the other hand, *omoricha* have been initiated as priests or priestesses within the tradition and have long-lasting commitments to the community and the deities.

Initiations are essential to the religion because Santería "must be understood as an initiatory religion; initiations punctuate the changes and elevation of a person in the tradition."[19] But there are various types. One of the first ceremonies, often secured for protection or at the request of an orisha discerned through divination, is the giving of the *eleke*. The person receives the colored beads associated with various orishas as well as "sacred objects used to create and maintain a shrine for these protective deities."[20] Those undergoing the process of receiving eleke—the first step one takes in becoming a santero's or santera's godchild—encounter events similar to those described regarding the practice in Cuba:

> To prepare the *collares*, each necklace is ritually washed in an herbal infusion consisting of water and the sacred herbs of each of the orishas represented. The string used in the collares must be cotton or some other absorbent material . . . , for sacrificial blood must be absorbed through the thread, to charge the necklace with ashé. The color patterns of each necklace indicate which orisha is being represented. . . . The actual ceremony in which a person receives the collares . . . is very involved; the collares recipient is ritually bathed and must shed his or her old clothes for new white ones. [There are prayers and incantations that accompany this.] . . . The first necklace to be conferred is usually, but not always, that of Eleggua, who as the Lord of the Gate opens each Santeria ceremony. . . . A few ilés give Obatalá's . . . first, since Obatalá is the greatest of all orishas. The number of collares given at the ceremony varies slightly, and santeros may keep on adding necklaces as needed. Most of the time, however, the first five necklaces conferred are Eleggua, Obatalá, Yemayá, Shangó, and Oshún. Other orishas commonly represented are Ogún and Babalú Ayé.[21]

Beyond the receiving of eleke, the ceremony involving a lifelong commitment to the orisha entails initiation into the priesthood. Beyond signs such as the white clothing worn for a year after initiation and restrictions on food, alcohol, and other items taboo to the particular orisha, movement into the priesthood is a process of religious growth not completely understood or known by those who have not undergone it. However, it is safe to say that the process involves the use of divination to determine which orisha controls the head of the person to be initiated. This information is used to determine which orisha's priesthood the person will be initiated into. After completing this process of discernment, the orisha who "owns" the person's head is ceremonially implanted in the head. This connection between the orisha and the initiate is symbolically significant in that it marks a deep relationship between the two, one that involves mutual obligation and responsibility. All members of a house understand the importance of this process, and they respect the demands imposed on those who undergo initiation.

One way to distinguish levels of authority in a particular house involves initiations undergone: Has the person received the warriors? Has the person been initiated into the priesthood of a particular deity? Those who have been initiated into the priesthood have seniority based on how long they have been in the priesthood. This is so because length of service as a priest corresponds to the degree of knowledge of the tradition possessed. Those within a house must give serious attention to issues of seniority in order to make certain that they greet or salute properly their elders. It is within the context of this community of persons with varying levels of knowledge and commitment to the religion that rituals and ceremonies take place.

Celebrations, or *bembes*, for orishas can be elaborate events drawing large numbers of people who come to pay their respects to the orishas and religious leaders. These gatherings take place periodically throughout the year and relate to feast days for the orishas in relationship to the corresponding Catholic saints—for example, December 4 for Shango (St. Barbara). They involve elaborate decorations in the colors of a particular orisha and large quantities of food related to the likes of particular deities, and they culminate in possession by orishas.

Drums are played corresponding to rhythms associated with particular orishas. Songs are sung, and some members of the house dance in keeping with the rhythm. In one case, "one woman in particular is carried by this energy, and other begin to channel theirs toward her. The dancing circle clears for her alone, and the drums focus directly on her. Her eyes are closed, and she is whirling and whirling." This process began the moment of possession, when the orisha arrived. After falling to the ground and being helped up, the woman's "eyes are open now and gigantic, their focus open to the whole world. Her face is illuminated with an enormous smile, and she moves her shoulders and hips with sensuous confidence. Oshun has arrived."[22] The person possessed by Oshun was dressed in garb in keeping with the colors of the orisha. And she, Oshun, through this woman, interacted with those present. The celebration ended with the orisha leaving its human host, but conversation among those gathered continued for some time afterward.

Items needed for rituals or ceremonies are not always available in local supermarkets. For these events, practitioners make use of *bontánicas*—the hundreds of stores from the East coast of the United States to the West that sell supplies associated with rituals and ceremonies of the religion: "to the uninitiated, their merchandise must look mysterious indeed: candles and beads, herbs and oils, cauldrons and crockery, and plaster statues of Catholic saints. . . . Shelves and glass cases are crammed full of religious articles. One large case is devoted entirely to necklaces of brightly colored beads, each coded to a particular orisha. . . . Piled high in unlikely corners are large crockery tureens in a variety of colors. These are *soperas,* great lidded bowls that will contain the most fundamental symbol of the orishas' presence—their holy stones." These stones, because they embody the orisha, are "fed" during ceremonies by having the blood of the sacrificial animals poured over them.[23] In addition to stones, each orisha has items—*fundamentos*—that speak to their characteristics and functions. For example, Ogun, who is associated with ironwork and war, has as one of his fundamental elements the machete. Oshosi, the hunter, has as one of his fundamental elements the bow and arrow. These important items and others line the shelves and back room of the store, but those who pass by without an attachment to the religion simply see just another corner store. For those faithful to the religion, these stores and the items sold are the building blocks for celebrations and sacrifices.

Sacrifice is extremely important in that it allows members of the religion to shift cosmic energy and circumstances in beneficial ways. The orisha receives ashé and in return those presenting sacrifices of various kinds receive spiritual and physical benefits. Divination is also important as a ritual step prior to sacrifice in that it allows humans to get information concerning the root cause of difficulties and needs and provides information concerning the necessary corrective (i.e., a sacrifice of some kind). Divination unpacks information concerning one's destiny (*ori*), selected in heaven but forgotten with birth. This is a central and complex element of the religion, one connected to ideas of predestination, reincarnation, and the path one chooses to walk through life. Destiny says something about what one will do in terms of employment, love, and also how long one will live. But none of this information is fixed, unchangeable. It involves potential that one can meet, or not meet.[24]

> ### Three Forms of Divination in Santería
>
> 1. *Ifa*—conducted by a priest of Ifa
> 2. *Merindilogun*—involves tossing sixteen cowrie shells on a mat
> 3. *Obi*—involves tossing quarters of a coconut in response to questions requiring "yes" or "no" answers

There are three forms of divination practiced in Santería, and two are prominent in the United States. The first, Ifa, can only be conducted by a priest of Ifa (a *Babalawo*). While it can be conducted in the United States, it is not the most commonly used. The second form, *merindilogun*, is more commonly used. This form of divination involves sixteen cowrie shells that are tossed on a mat. The number face up versus face down is counted and provides a sign or pattern that corresponds to a particular *odu*, or story. The story provides information concerning the person's condition and the necessary corrective. The third form of divination, *Obi*, involves use of a coconut cut into four pieces. The pieces are tossed in response to a particular question from the person. The pattern (white up versus brown up) provides information concerning questions requiring a "yes" or "no" answer. Although written materials including the stories (odus) associated with divination are now available in written form, the tradition remains a primarily oral tradition.

Basic Beliefs in Santería

Those committed to this tradition think in terms of life involving balance—an attempt on the part of humans to keep ashé flowing properly through good actions. When an imbalance occurs, it is not a sign of an "original sin," a permanent stain on humankind. Rather it involves a failure on the part of humans (e.g., to honor the ancestors or to keep commitments to the orishas) that can be corrected through a sacrifice of some kind, such as food items given to an orisha or the sacrifice of an animal. In Cuba and also in the United States, the blood is "fed" to the orisha as it is poured on items representing that particular deity.

Although many object to the practice of animal sacrifice, arguing that it is inhumane and barbaric, this is an unjust and problematic assumption. Those serving the orishas and Christians, for example, both recognize that some problems can only be addressed through the shedding of blood. For Christians this is the significance of the death and resurrection of Jesus Christ. For those devoted to the orishas, animal sacrifice plays the same role. Not all required sacrifices involve the shedding of blood. Sacrifices can also involve giving an orisha other food items. The orisha takes from animal sacrifices or other gifts the ashé, the energy present in the item. Also important within the religion is possession by the orisha. Its importance stems from the healing and important information that are given during the presence of an orisha. Possession often takes place during a celebration or *bembe* held in honor of a particular orisha.

Various rituals are important in the religion because they allow people to change their circumstances, to address their needs and wants, through the transference of ashé. That is to say, "at the level of the individual, aché allows people to act with force, intelligence, and impunity," and sacrifice properly done "at the right time in the proper way beneficially changes the objective circumstances of the person who offers it."[25]

Concluding Thoughts

Across the country African Americans gather to practice the "way of the saints." Altars mark their homes as places of devotion to the orishas, and the *eleke* they wear around their necks mark their bodies as connected to the cosmic energy that the orishas represent. They buy items associated with the religion from stores that dot the urban landscape, and they gather with others to celebrate the gods. Through practices such as divination, those involved in this tradition are able to address their needs and respond to the uncertainties of life.

Most of those practicing this religion are concentrated in New York and Miami, although there are smaller communities in Los Angeles, Minneapolis, Atlanta, Houston, Philadelphia, and other major cities throughout the United States. Estimates fluctuate greatly with respect to national participation in the religion because houses do not maintain membership roles as churches might. Yet the influence of this tradition on the life of African Americans cannot be measured simply in terms of the number of participants. While it differs in many respects from other traditions discussed in this volume, this religion is similar in that it provides teachings and activities that a segment of the African American population finds helpful. Regardless of how African Americans practice the tradition, or by what name they call it, there are ways in which they share an appreciation for how the tradition helps to make sense of life, and how it helps African Americans forge a working cultural identity.

Notes

1. See, for example, "The King Does Not Lie."

2. Joseph M. Murphy, *Santería: An African Religion in America* (Boston: Beacon Press, 1989), 27.

3. Ibid., 11.

4. Joseph Murphy indicates Mercedes. Adapted from: Joseph Murphy's *Santería: African Spirits in America* (Boston: Beacon Press, 1988, 1993) and George Brandon's *Santeria from Africa to the New World: The Dead Sell Memories* (Bloomington: Indiana University Press, 1993). This, like the other charts presented in this book, is incomplete. With such a large number of divinities in Santería and Voodoo, a complete outline of the divinities is impractical. However, this chart, like the others, provides a useful framework.

5. Brandon, *Santeria from Africa to the New World*, 33–34. Also see: Joseph Murphy, *Working the Spirit: Ceremonies of the African Diaspora* (Boston: Beacon Press, 1994), chap. 4.

6. Brandon, *Santeria from Africa to the New World*, 104.

7. Ibid., 106.

8. Mary Anthrell Curry, *Making the Gods in New York: The Yoruba Religion in the African American Community* (Dissertation, City University of New York, 1991), ix.

9. Brandon, *Santeria from Africa to the New World*, 106; Curry, *Making the Gods in New York*, 7, 8.

10. Curry, *Making the Gods in New York*, 5.

11. Interview with Oba Adefunmi I, April 1996, Palace of Oyotunji African Village.

12. David H. Brown, *Santeria Enthroned: Art, Ritual, and Innovation in an Afro-Cuban Religion* (Chicago: University of Chicago Press, 1998), 276.

13. Brandon, *Santeria from Africa to the New World*, 118.

14. Curry, *Making the Gods in New York*, 120.

15. Steven Gregory, *Santería in New York City: A Study in Cultural Resistance* (New York: Garland Publishing, 1999), 39.

16. Ibid., 68.

17. Murphy, *Santería: African Spirits*, 52.

18. Gregory, *Santería in New York City*, 48.

19. Michael Atwood Mason, *Living Santería: Rituals and Experiences in an Afro-Cuban Religion* (Washington, DC: Smithsonian Books, 2002), 34.

20. Ibid., 6.

21. Raul Canizares, *Cuban Santeria* (New York: Destiny Books, 1999), 32.

22. Murphy, *Santería: African Spirits*, 96–97.

23. Ibid., 39, 40, 41.

24. Curry, *Making the Gods in New York*, 46, 47.

25. Mason, *Living Santería*, 87, 98.

Chapter 11

Sunni Islam

Abook written before the assassination of Malcolm X reports the opinion of "a high Islamic official in Cairo" concerning the nature of the Nation of Islam's teachings and work: "Of course your Black Muslims are improperly informed. But they are turning men to Allah, away from Christianity, toward Mecca. This is what we want; this is what we must have. . . . If Muhammad can give that new blood we welcome him. As for his teachings . . . we will see to it that the correct view is given to the black man in America. Now the thing is to get them facing toward Mecca."[1] Malcolm faced Mecca and, when the opportunity presented itself, he went to Mecca on pilgrimage.

Malcolm X became El-Hajj Malik El-Shabazz after his *hajj*, the pilgrimage to Mecca required of all able Muslims. He moved away from the teachings of the Honorable Elijah Muhammad and became a Sunni Muslim, one in line with the *ummah*—the world community of Islam. Malcolm was moved in profound and life-altering ways by the sights of the hajj. He saw for the first time a level of equality without pretense and illusion, a unity premised on a sense of community between people from different social and cultural backgrounds. According to the Honorable Elijah Muhammad such a gathering based on equality was impossible.

This recognition of a more complex and ritually sophisticated Islamic world than acknowledged by the Nation of Islam came with its awkward moments. One of these moments involved the proper positioning for prayer:

> Imagine being a Muslim minister, a leader in Elijah Muhammad's Nation of Islam, and not knowing the prayer ritual. . . . I tried to do what he [the guide] did. I wasn't doing it right. I could feel the other Muslims' eyes on me. Western ankles won't do what Muslim ankles have

> done for a lifetime. . . . When my guide was down in a posture, I tried everything I could to get down as he was, but there I was, sticking up.[2]

The problem, however, was not simply the proper posture for prayer. It was also a matter of the language of prayer. As El-Hajj Malik El-Shabazz recalls, "in Elijah Muhammad's Nation of Islam, we hadn't prayed in Arabic. About a dozen or more years before, when I was in prison, a member of the orthodox Muslim movement in Boston, named Abdul Hamed, had visited me and later sent me prayers in Arabic. At that time, I had learned those prayers phonetically. But I hadn't used them since."[3]

From this awkward beginning, El-Shabazz grew into the faith, recognizing the distinctions between the Nation of Islam and Sunni Islam. El-Shabazz recognized the possibility of unity, goodwill, and productive relationships across racial lines. This philosophical shift allowed for recognition of the manner in which issues facing African Americans fit within a global context. In this way, his perspective moved from a rather provincial depiction of life to a concern with internationalism. Once back in the United States, El-Shabazz expressed this change of heart and head through the eventual formation of the Organization of African American Unity, which sought to recast the African American struggle as one for human rights so as to allow for an international hearing through appeal to the United Nations. In addition, he developed the Muslim Mosque, Inc., based on Sunni Islamic sensibilities and doctrine.

By the end of the twentieth century his experience of orthodox Islam, as some call it, was shared by well over one million African Americans, making Islam one of the fastest growing traditions in African American communities and in the United States in general.

Islam

At the age of forty, firmly entrenched in a career within the commercial camel trade in Mecca, Muhammad heard a voice calling him to "Recite!" The voice charged him with being the Messenger of God, a prophet, the last prophet. As such, he was given revelations of the Qur'an over the course of numerous visitations. The Prophet Muhammad received the first revelation of the Qur'an in roughly 610 CE. This date marks the beginning of Islam or, as the name means, submission to God.

Based on the revelations he received, the Prophet Muhammad began preaching in Mecca, condemning the ignorance and idolatry that marked life in Mecca. Supported and encouraged by his wife, Khadija, Prophet Muhammad preached that there was only one God, and that humans must submit to the one, true God and abandon their idolatrous practices. He also preached that all would be judged based on their deeds, and rewarded or punished accordingly by God at the end of their lives. Initially the Prophet's message was rejected by most who heard him. However, a small group of those devoted to the teachings emerged.

In 622, the Prophet eventually moved his group to Medina. Because the revelations and the Prophet's initial work began in Mecca, it is the holiest city in Islam, but it is followed by Medina, which is recognized as the second holiest city for Muslims. It is argued that the Muslim community (*umma*) begins to take shape as a result of this movement to Medina. In this city, the number of followers increased. The Prophet continued to share the revelations he received, and the formal laws governing the community began to take shape during this period as well. Based on the teachings given, the Prophet's reputation grew and he was able to spread Islam beyond its initial boundaries. Based on the growing strength and zeal of the community, the Prophet was able to convert Mecca to Islam in 630. Before his death in 632, the Prophet Muhammad claimed most of the Arabian Peninsula for Islam.

No longer having the Prophet with it, the community had to make a decision concerning new leadership. The situation was a bit tense and complex. Because the Prophet had no sons, the leadership of the community could not be passed through a direct bloodline, through his children. Hence, it was decided that Abu Bakr would become the *caliph*, or head of the community. He was selected because he was an early convert who had been given important tasks such as leading prayer when the Prophet did not. He was followed in leadership of the community by 'Umar and then 'Uthman.

Divisions occurred over issues of leadership, resulting in the development of various groups devoted to the teachings of the Prophet. A few of the more prominent are the Sunni (that is, people of the *sunna*, or the teachings of the Prophet) and Shi'ite (the party of Ali) communities. The former accepted the established line of leadership through the caliphs, beginning with Abu Bakr. On the other hand, Shi'ites argue that the Prophet Muhammad actually selected 'Ali as the next leader of the Muslim community. In addition to these two groups, Sufism (meaning wool in reference to the garment worn by earlier members of this group, also called the people of the platform in reference to their initial meeting place) developed as a rejection of the world and an embrace of the mystical dimensions of the Islamic faith. Sunni and Shi'ite communities developed around the time of the Prophet's death, but some argue that Sufism is much older in that it originated with a group of modest believers who practiced the faith while the Prophet was alive.

Internal conflict, while harsh at times, did not prevent Islam from spreading. Through armed conflict, Muslims moved through areas such as Palestine and Persia, establishing the faith. Islam eventually became not only a religious power, but also a political power, spreading across the globe. It moved across the continent of Africa, from East to West, and with time and partly through the slave trade, it moved into the Americas.

Islam in Africa and the New World

Islam moved across the globe, claiming millions of followers worldwide. Among those who embraced Islam were Africans. Not long after the Prophet's death, believers moved into Ethiopia and gained some prominence in North Africa, and by the ninth century Islam was known in much of East Africa. Islam also spread into West Africa, including areas such as Ghana from which many were forced into the slave trade and shipped to the New World.

It is estimated that anywhere between 5 and 15 percent of the enslaved Africans brought to the New World were Muslims, and some of them were taken to the North American colonies. As one scholar notes, "given that between 400,000 and 523,000 Africans came to British North America during the slave trade, at least 200,000 came from areas influenced by Islam to varying degrees. Muslims may have come to America by the thousands, if not tens of thousands."[4] Unfortunately, there are few records documenting the fine points of their practices, beliefs, and relationship to the larger African American community. Nonetheless, the shadow of this Islamic presence is found in documents by slaveholders that speak to a preference for Muslim slaves from particular regions. Furthermore, runaway slave advertisements (that include Islamic names), personal observations, and property lists that include Muslim names, interviews, and death records include some evidence of Islamic sensibilities. The historical record speaks to an African Muslim community of sorts. In Spanish-controlled areas of North America there was such a presence dating back to the sixteenth century, whereby as of "the middle of the eighteenth century, the third largest African ethnicity in this metropolitan area [St. Augustine, Florida] was . . . a group that certainly contained Muslims." There is also reason to believe that there was some type of Islamic presence in French Louisiana as well.[5] In addition, Moor or Maroon communities in certain sections of the southern British colonies such as Virginia and Tennessee traditionally claimed connections to the early Muslim presence.[6]

There is substantial evidence related to the lives of a few Muslims within the early African American community, including Bilali Mohomet, from Guinea. He lived in Georgia (Sapelo Island) and was quite noticeable in his distinctive dress—a traditional fez as a head covering and a long coat. Living as a slave on the Island from the early to the mid-1800s, he was a religious leader within his community, one who maintained much of Islam's basic doctrine such as prayer (using a prayer rug), diet restrictions, and fasting. These practices, of course, were maintained to the extent possible within the context of life as a slave. In addition to personal practice of Islam, Bilali undertook the writing of a manual dealing with Islam for his community that represented "the only known antebellum African Muslim community in the United States."[7]

Umar Ibn Said (1770–1864), from Fayetteville, North Carolina, although his religious leanings would alter, said the following in his autobiography: "When I came to the Christian country, my religion was the religion of 'Mohammed, the Apostle of God—may God have mercy upon him and give him peace." Elsewhere we are made aware of another enslaved African named Philip who talked of his former home and the customs of his people. Philip "was not a pagan, but a Mohammedan [Muslim]. He greatly interested us by going through all the prayers and prostrations of his native country." Ryna Johnson is said to have prayed in traditional fashion—kneeling on the floor, touching her head to the floor, and it was reported that there was a man on a plantation in South Carolina "who prayed five times every day, always turning his face to the east, when in the performance of his devotion."[8] Finally, Ben Sullivan remarked concerning a slave named Israel that he, Israel, "prayed from a book he kept hidden, on a mat at sunrise and sunset."[9]

It seems that Bilali and others were able to maintain a sense of practice somewhat free of mixing with other traditions. However, from the same time period as Bilal, there is an account related to "Old Lissy Gray" who had been trained in Islamic doctrine but who, probably in part the result of not having an Imam available, attempted to combine Islam with bits of Christian theology.[10] Her syncretistic approach to religious experience runs contrary to other accounts, but it bears some resemblance to the blending of Islam with African-based religious sensibilities that took place as Islam moved across the African continent. In one respect "many West Africans practiced indigenous religions but were nevertheless familiar with and influenced by Islam, having been exposed to Muslim dress, dietary laws, and overall conduct."[11]

African American Islam

The lack of continued production of religious leaders made it difficult to maintain a systematic experience of Islam after the original group of African Muslims died. Elements of the faith survived, but in many cases they did so as indiscriminate pieces of folk culture. There are threads of continuation regarding an Islamic presence from the antebellum period to the twentieth century; however, scholars are not certain of the strength of these strains of religious experience and memory.

The manner in which threads of Islamic experience are claimed in the Moorish Science Temple and the Nation of Islam are explored in Chapter 7 of this volume. In this chapter, the task is to explore Sunni Islam as a thread of religious experience within the context of African American communities. This movement toward traditional teachings was not necessarily an easy journey when one is mindful of the limited information available on Islam to interested African Americans. Making a distinction between Islamic-tinged nationalism and Sunni Islam would be difficult, particularly when charismatic figures presented both options, arguing passionately for their particular movement as the proper religious orientation.

In light of this situation, some African Americans relied on immigrant Muslims, but these new Americans were dealing with cultural and social pressures of a new land. This situation held consequences for the perception of Islamic practice provided. In fact, "much of the counsel they gave to their American brethren reflected Old World views that were being repudiated by their own children, indeed views they might ignore completely themselves when it came to personal or family business."[12] This scenario easily produced feelings of hypocrisy and doctrinal uncertainty that muddied the meaning of Islamic practice. Nonetheless, African American converts to Islam maneuvered through the various possibilities, often by trial and error, and developed communities of meaning and purpose. Some communities were founded upon the teachings of quasi-Islamic teachers. With time, however, in communities such as the First Mosque of Pittsburgh, attention was given to the Sunni tradition as the correct orientation. While seeking to abide by Islam as practiced within the Sunni context across the globe, members of the Pittsburgh mosque as well as the Islamic Mission of America encountered difficulties due to limited knowledge of Arabic.

In 1924, Moroccan Shaykh Dauod Ahmed Faisal started the Islamic Mission of America, Inc., as a way of spreading Islam within the United States. While the mission worked with various immigrant communities, this organization, also called the State Street Mosque or Islamic Brotherhood, believed the original and true religion of African Americans was Islam.[13] In 1939, the organization secured a space in Brooklyn, at 143 State Street. From this location, Imam (religious leader, or teacher) Faisal critiqued American consumerism and encouraged listeners to convert and follow Islam. For fifteen years, between 1950 and 1965, Faisal's efforts were aided by the Institute of Islam housed at the State Street mission. This institute provided basic information related to the teachings of Islam and instruction in Arabic.[14]

Beginning with a mosque in New York, this organization soon developed a group of satellite communities in the northeast, all committed to the orthodoxy missing from the Nation of Islam. Members were expected to abide by the basic elements of faith and their expression through the five pillars—confession of faith, almsgiving, prayer, fasting during Ramadan, and pilgrimage. Those outside the African American community but committed to the faith were welcome to participate. For example, the mosque in New York was often visited by Muslim sailors and immigrants in search of Islamic community.[15]

Until the development of Imam Warith Deen Muhammad's American Muslim Mission, Darul Islam (Dar ul-Islam) represented the largest Sunni Islamic presence in the collective African American community. By 1975, this group claimed over thirty mosques located throughout the United States, Canada, and the Caribbean, with Imam Yahya Abdul-Kareem of Brooklyn providing general leadership. Beginning in the 1960s in Brooklyn, New York, Darul Islam's growth was in part the result of incorporating existing collectives of Muslims into a national organization.

Initial converts often came to Darul Islam through the Black Power Movement. With time, some would leave the Nation of Islam to participate in the Darul Islam community. Energy was not really spent on converting individuals. Instead, attention was given to providing guidance and structure for those already practicing Muslims. Darul Islam operated on the assumption that mission work—the development of this expansive network of believers and mosques—is a part of the expression of one's faith, an extension of one's religious experience. This missionizing impulse was expressed also through attention to the proper training of prison inmates who converted to Islam. While there are records indicating that Sunni Muslims were in the prison system in the early 1960s, it was seldom the case that Islamic prisoners had any formal structure, and Islam was certainly not recognized by prison officials as an authorized religion.[16] Without this recognition, it was impossible to secure necessary supplies and proper space for Islamic worship and study. Darul Islam representatives worked to help Muslim prisoners secure the basic supplies necessary to practice the faith.

Whereas the Nation of Islam and other nationalistic organizations presented modified Islamic practices, Darul Islam rejected separatist ideologies. With a focused concern for orthodoxy, members of Darul Islam were required to study Arabic, the Qur'an, and the Sunna in order to bring their knowledge of Islam in line with the rest of the Muslim world. Furthermore, members were expected to dress in keeping with traditional Islamic aesthetic sensibilities: for women, face covering and loose clothing, and for men, loose clothing. They also were encouraged to limit their contacts to other Muslims. For some children this involved obtaining formal education through the mosque's school rather than attending public schools.[17]

Membership in this community was not easily achieved, perhaps as a way of weeding through those whose motives were not in keeping with the true nature of Islam. According to one scholar, the Philadelphia mosque provided a good example of this exclusivity in that "prospective members were first queried in a kind of anteroom to the main masjid [mosque] facilities. The focus of the questioning was the motivation for the initiate's desire to join the movement. Later, they might be invited to attend Sunday classes."[18] Serious attention to the basics of the faith was required in that before the confession of faith was made, the person had to memorize a great deal of information provided by the organization's leadership, and had to also undertake thorough study of Islam. The focus of study would change with time. As Yahya Abdul Karim, the leader of the Darul Islam community, moved toward Sufism, internal tensions developed resulting in the dismantling of the Brooklyn mosque into various mosques that were smaller but still Sunni. In 1980, Imam Yahya announced the end of the Darul Islam community. A few years prior to the demise of Darul Islam, however, another and unlikely organization moved toward a Sunni orientation.

From the perspective of many within the Nation of Islam, Wallace Muhammad was an unlikely successor to his father. He had his difficulties with the Nation of Islam, resulting in his departure from the organization at one point. Wallace had been close to Malcolm X. Would he be able to lead an organization that many associated with Malcolm's murder? Granted, he reconnected with the Nation of Islam prior to his father's death in 1975, but there remained questions concerning his allegiance to his father's teachings. Should not a more prominent and clearly devoted figure assume leadership of the organization? Perhaps Louis Farrakhan, the national representative for the movement, the man trained by Malcolm X, who eventually condemned Malcolm and embraced the Honorable Elijah Muhammad with unquestioned loyalty? To the surprise of those who assumed someone outside the biological family would take over, the Honorable Elijah Muhammad selected his son, Wallace. During the Savior's Day celebration the day after Elijah Muhammad's death, Wallace was recognized as the supreme leader of the Nation of Islam.

With great deliberation, Wallace began rethinking the theology and structure of the Nation of Islam. He was determined to bring it in line with the Sunni orientation he studied for so many years and had witnessed during his 1967 hajj. The Nation of Islam, as he envisioned it, would mirror Islam as a way of life that did not separate African American Muslims from the rest of humanity based on a special status expressed through separatist rhetoric, but one that incorporated African American Muslims into the ummah. Pride in one's heritage via a connection to Africa remained in place and was symbolically represented through an embrace of Bilal, who the Prophet Muhammad selected to give the first call to prayer. Bilal was understood as being emblematic for the African American Muslim's self-understanding and sense of place. This connection was expressed through reference to African American Muslims as Bilalian.

Removed was the distinctive and mandatory dress code—dark suits and bow ties. Gone was the Fruit of Islam, the paramilitary wing of the movement responsible for discipline and protection of Nation of Islam members. Gone was the original theology through which Master Fard was understood as God and Elijah Muhammad his prophet, the last prophet sent by Allah (Master Fard) to teach the Lost-Found Nation within the context of the wilderness known as the United States. Fard, Wallace Muhammad taught, was simply a Muslim, a teacher living in California. He was not divine. Wallace's father had provided a service for a time, although he was not in actuality the last prophet. Probably the most controversial dimension of the Nation of Islam's theology was also stricken when members were told that talk of the white "devils" was not an indictment of white people; rather, it had only limited metaphorical significance as, according to scholar Richard Turner, "a psychological smoke screen for his [Elijah Muhammad's] community work among the black lower class."[19]

An effort was made to handle the transition with sensitivity. After all, members of the Nation of Islam had recently lost their revered leader. The shift toward orthodoxy was explained in terms of a dualism, a two-pronged evolutionary process resulting in a mature faith and practice. A member of the Nation of Islam during this period reflects on the wording used:

> Our new leader explained that what we had learned and practiced all those years before his father's death was called a First Resurrection. Black people had to be awakened from a mental state of death, from not knowing ourselves and loving ourselves, and move toward doing positive things for ourselves. Now we were moving into the Second Resurrection, and we were supposed to come alive even more and think for ourselves—individually—and read the Holy Qur'an and Bible for ourselves and discipline ourselves.[20]

The Honorable Elijah Muhammad, as the last prophet, maintained strict control over the workings of the Nation of Islam, but Wallace decentralized authority through the creation of a council of Imams responsible for monitoring the movement's teachings and structure. This reformulation of the organization's infrastructure in 1985 culminated in the complete dismantling of the movement. Members were to incorporate fully into the ummah. They were now Muslims, not African American Muslims. Just Muslims.

There remain ways in which the identity of Muslims in African American communities rest on a delicate arrangement of simultaneous identifications. This balancing act can be troubling in that it can leave them without a sense of proper practice and place. Put differently, the commitment to "universal racial brotherhood"[21] as advocated in the Sunni orientation is important for African Americans who embrace this modality of Islam for several reasons, two of which are easily deciphered. It distinguishes them from the racial ideology that marked the Nation of Islam within popular imagination, and it links them with the larger Islamic world through an embrace of faith as opposed to identification via social and biological factors. Yet, Muslims in African American communities continue to live in a society that is to a large degree preoccupied with racial distinctions. How do they navigate between a religious commitment that rejects such superficial determinations and a society that continues to hold them dear? Warith Deen Muhammad (the name taken by Wallace in roughly 1980), with time, talked about a mission to America in general terms. But how would this play out in terms of developing Islamic identity for African Americans, particularly those who once embraced his father's religious nationalism?

Muslims forced to address such questions must continuously work to maintain a creative tension between pride in one's particular cultural or racial heritage and an understanding of this particularity within the context of a much larger sense of community, one without borders and one premised upon a common faith. The Nation of Islam under the leadership of Elijah Muhammad embraced an understanding of all blacks, across the globe, as Muslims by nature. Yet, what Warith Deen Muhammad suggests is a much "more complex" and more comprehensive perspective in that he encourages African Americans to recognize connections to Muslims of various backgrounds. Islam, then, is a religion proper for any willing member of the human race as opposed to being labeled simply a religion appropriate for people of African descent.

While Warith Deen Muhammad's intent is understandable, it might give the impression that there is in fact a unified "practice" of Islam embraced by all. Such an assumption flies in the face of disagreements existing between immigrant Islamic communities within the United States. Pakistani Muslims may not agree on all issues with Indian Muslims, and Indian Muslims may not agree with Saudi Muslims. They may have differing perspectives on what is permissible and what is not. Is a conservative approach to Islamic practice better than a more liberal approach? Where do African Americans, as relatively new arrivals into the Islamic world, fit into this process? Although Warith Deen Muhammad for some time advocated a complete subsuming of African Americans into the world community, in more recent years he has mentioned the possibility of an American contribution to world Islam that entails a somewhat unique intellectual formation. In short, American Islam need not simply be an extension of the Middle East. Regarding this American contingency, Warith Deen Muhammad said the following during an interview:

> I don't belong to any particular school of thought and I don't advise any of my colleagues to begin to promote any school of thought in America. We will eventually have a school of thought in America, that's my hope, that's my belief. . . . As long as our thought represents the essentials in the Quran and life of the Prophet. Islam has had different schools of thought. What's wrong with different schools of thought? We are encouraged to have our own opinion. Islam is not a static religion.[22]

Under his leadership, those who once followed his father took on traditional Islamic names as a symbol of their movement toward communion with Muslims around the globe. As part of this expanding framework of contact and exchange, members of what Warith Deen named the American Muslim Mission made contact with other non-Islamic religious communities in order to start dialogues and forge links that might be helpful in addressing social issues that effect people of color, regardless of faith.

Warith Deen Muhammad encouraged African Americans to embrace a commitment to outreach. For example, in 1994 he developed an organization known as the Junior Association of Muslim Men (in Sing Sing prison) as a way of teaching young Muslims about the proper expression of their faith. Out of a general concern with the growth of Islam in the United States, Warith Deen has worked with other Muslim leaders in Illinois to generate new Islamic schools and mosques. He sees work with prisoners and other Muslim leaders as part of his fulfillment of *da'wa*, which can be understood as the effort to increase the community of Islam through converts, or through the reenergizing of Muslims who have been lax with respect to the pillars of faith.

The former Nation of Islam minister's credibility in the larger Islamic world is represented by his position within the World Mission Council of Imam Administrators. He is the person through whom all Muslims in the United States gain authority to undertake the hajj. He often participates in international conferences as the invited guest of recognized Sunni leaders and organizations. With respect to mission efforts in the United States (within and outside African American communities), he is considered an important presence. This connection to mission efforts puts Warith Deen Muhammad in the center of Islamic community formation within the United States and allows him to serve as an intellectual bridge between Muslims in America and the rest of the Islamic world.

What Muslims Believe

What slowly emerged from the Prophet Muhammad's revelations was the religion of Islam, meaning submission to God, based on five articles of faith: (1) recognition of God's oneness; there is no other being like God; (2) belief in the existence of angels and the presence of angels in human life; (3) faith in Muhammad as the final Prophet and Messenger of Allah (God); (4) acceptance and adherence to the sacred texts provided by God, with the Qur'an being the final revelation from God to humanity; and (5) recognition of a final day of judgment for humanity as an important component of the revelation given by God to the Prophet Muhammad. Islam revolves around surrender to the will of God and various ritualized actions that demonstrate this relationship. These actions flow into the daily living of Muslims because the religion provides a way of life, guided by a foundational principle of peace.

Attached to the basic elements of faith are practical ways of living out one's commitment. This way of practice or life is referred to as the five "pillars" of Islam. They are: (1) witnessing to or affirming the oneness of God and the status of Muhammad as the final prophet of God; (2) prayer five times per day at fixed intervals, preceded by cleansing the head, ears, neck, and feet with water in preparation for prayer; (3) the giving of financial assistance or the alms tax; (4) fasting during the month of Ramadan; and (5) pilgrimage to Mecca, as one is financially and physically capable.

> ### The Five Pillars of Islam
>
> 1. *Shahada*, the affirming the oneness of God and the status of Muhammad as the final prophet of God
> 2. *Salat*, prayer five times a day
> 3. *Zakat*, the paying of the alms
> 4. *Ramadan*, fasting
> 5. *Hajj*, the pilgrimage to Mecca

While Muslims are expected to pray daily, there is also the communal prayer on each Friday. This gathering together, under the direction of the Imam, brings together the Islamic community in collective devotion to God. Men gather with men, the women with women, separated for this ritual activity. In addition to prayer, the Imam gives words related to the teachings of Islam and their application. Financial obligations are also met during this service, with the understanding that the giving of alms is meant to maintain the health of the community by meeting the needs of those who are economically challenged. Traditionally, each Muslim is expected to provide roughly 2.5 percent of his or her wealth to assist others. A voluntary act today in most cases, it is still considered an important component of a Muslim's expression of faith.

Ramadan, the ninth month of the Islamic calendar, is extremely important for Muslims in that the Prophet Muhammad received his first revelation from God during this period. In remembrance of this month's significance, Muslims who are beyond puberty must fast (while there is daylight) during this month. Those observing the fast are not only to refrain from food during the required hours; they are also to avoid tobacco, sex, questionable language, and so on. The fast is broken each evening with family and friends. This is not a time of limited activity or effort to downplay or avoid the physical and spiritual struggles of bodily control. To do so is to misunderstand the value of the experience. The benefits of the fast, from the perspective of Muslims who observe it, are many. Of most significance, it revives the spirit in that it allows for a deeper connection to one's faith through the removal of distractions and through the controlling of physical urges, needs, and wants. Shifting attention away from the fulfillment of one's personal desires is meant to increase one's willingness to understand and meet the needs of others. The nurturing and repairing of relationships is highlighted through the rigors of the Ramadan fast. Those who are ill or elderly are not required to maintain the fast.

A deep connection to the religion of Islam by believers also includes a requirement to undertake a pilgrimage to Mecca during the last month of the Islamic calendar, if one is physically and financially able. Visiting Mecca as a pilgrim involves a variety of tasks and ritual activities. However, one of the more powerful is the movement around the Ka'ba, as Muslims strive to get as close as possible to this important location. In 622 CE, the Prophet Muhammad moved his community from Mecca to Medina. However, he and those following him returned to Mecca and removed its cultural impurities. The Ka'ba, containing the Black Stone said to have been given to the patriarch Abraham by the angel Gabriel, served as the central place of worship for Muslims. According to Muslims, Mecca, the place of this important site, is the most holy place on earth.

The movement around the Ka'ba, however, is only one part of the ritual structure of the hajj. There are various staged events that make up the pilgrimage, and each has significance. These ritual activities speak to and remember the early formation of Islam and reenact events and struggles that shaped the faith. At one point, pilgrims travel "through Mina to the plain of 'Arafat, where the worshiper recalls the struggle of the patriarch Abraham against idolatry. Back in Mina, pilgrims throw seven stones at a small pillar in the main square said to symbolize the recalcitrant Satan. The last act of the pilgrimage is the sacrificing of an animal with its head facing Mecca. . . . At this point the (male) pilgrim's head is shaved," and preparation for returning home is made.[23]

During the pilgrimage, socioeconomic standing becomes irrelevant. All Muslims are at that point equal within the community and before God. All will dress in the same simple clothing, will eat the same foods, and will partake in the same rituals. As one commentator notes, "there is, however, one emphatic passion that is shared by most African Americans who have made their pilgrimage to Mecca: the rapture felt by communing with the multitude of humanity who circle the holy ka'ba. This often becomes the central experience in their lives and produces a contagious effect at home. In this encounter, African American Muslims experience directly the heterogeneous ways of Islam, and the Islamic world comes to know itself as part of the American experience."[24]

Concluding Thoughts

The challenge facing African American Muslims is the maintenance of a healthy balance between the needs of the localized context—people of color in the United States—and the realities of participation in a world religion. That is to say, African American Muslims must work toward the development of local communities and within the context of an Islamic world with its own set of concerns and needs.

The role played by Islam in the religious diversification of the United States continues to grow: A recent survey suggests that there are over four million Muslims in the United States, with almost two million being African Americans. The signs of this Islamic presence in African American communities are numerous. Most clearly representative, however, are the roughly 1,200 mosques that mark the religious landscape.[25]

Notes

1. Louis E. Lomax, *A Report on Elijah Muhammad, Malcolm X, and the Black Muslim World: When the Word Is Given . . .* (Westport, CT: Greenwood Press, 1963), 63.

2. Quoted in Lewis V. Baldwin and Amiri YaSin Al-Hadid, *Between Cross and Crescent: Christian and Muslim Perspectives on Malcolm and Martin* (Gainesville: University Press of Florida, 2002), 55.

3. Quoted in Baldwin and Al-Hadid, *Between Cross and Crescent*, 55.

4. Michael A. Gomez, "Muslims in Early America," *Journal of Southern History* vol. 60, no. 4 (November 1994): 682.

5. Ibid., 684.

6. Allan D. Austin, *African Muslims in Antebellum America: Transatlantic Stories and Spiritual Struggles* (New York: Routledge, 1997), 5, 14.

7. Ibid., 6, 16.

8. Charles Ball, *Slavery in the United States: A Narrative of the Life and Adventures of Charles Ball, a Black Man* (New York: Negro Universities Press, 1969; John S. Taylor, 1837), 165.

9. Austin, *African Muslims in Antebellum America*, 37, 110.

10. Ibid., 40.

11. Gomez, "Muslims in Early America," 683.

12. Robert Dannin, *Black Pilgrimage to Islam* (New York: Oxford University Press, 2002), 53.

13. Richard Turner, *Islam in the African-American Experience* (Bloomington: Indiana University Press, 1997), 120.

14. Marc Ferris, "To 'Achieve the Pleasure of Allah': Immigrant Muslims

in New York City, 1893–1991," in Yvonne Yazbeck Haddad and Jane Idleman Smith, eds., *Muslim Communities in North America* (Albany: State University of New York Press, 1994), 212–14.

15. Aminah Beverly McCloud, *African American Islam* (New York: Routledge, 1995), 21–22.

16. Dannin, *Black Pilgrimage to Islam*, 170.

17. Smith, *Islam in America*, 97–98.

18. McCloud, *African American Islam*, 70.

19. Turner, *Islam in the African-American Experience*, 225.

20. Sonsyrea Tate, *Little X: Growing Up in the Nation of Islam* (San Francisco: HarperCollins, 1997), 133.

21. Richardo René Laremont, "Race, Islam, and Politics: Differing Visions Among Black American Muslims," *Journal of Islamic Studies* 10:1 (1999), 33.

22. Quoted in Turner, *Islam in the African American Experience*, 227.

23. Jane Smith, *Islam in America* (New York: Columbia University Press, 1999), 20.

24. Dannin, *Black Pilgrimage to Islam*, 83.

25. The figures related to the Muslim population and the number of mosques are from Dannin, *Black Pilgrimage to Islam*, 11.

Chapter 12

Voodoo

Some of the public interest in African-based traditions such as Voodoo stems from Hollywood thrillers.[1] Films like "I Walked with a Zombie" (1941) and "The Serpent and the Rainbow" (1986) attempted to hold in tension actual information about Voodoo (or Vodun in the Haitian context) while meeting the desire of movie audiences for the sensational. Other films like the recent "Voodoo" (1995) are content to limit factual representation of the tradition to popular vocabulary—zombies, sacrifice, and so on.

Something, of course, is missing. Popular culture has, in large part, fueled an interest in Voodoo that lacks legitimacy. Even some early "scholarship" lacks proper perspective on the tradition, limiting comments to talk of the bizarre. At best much of this serves to stimulate the minds of tourists, who feed on a diet of Hollywood depictions of the occult. Yet, tracing its roots back to West Africa prior to the slave trade, the history, ritual structure, and theology of this religious tradition are much richer than these depictions would suggest. It is a complex system of belief and practice with roots reaching from Africa into the Caribbean, South America, and the United States.

Haiti and the Vodun

With the importation of slaves to the island of Hispaniola in the sixteenth century, there was a cultural blending of various West African peoples. What is significant about this blending is the manner in which the religious outlooks of these various peoples came to form the tradition known as Voudoun (Voodoo, or Vodun), first called "vaudoux" in 1797 by Mederick Louis Moreau de St. Mery upon observing a ceremony in the land that eventually became known as Haiti.[2] Some scholars suggest that it was somewhere between 1750 and 1790 that Voudoun, outlawed on various occasions during its long history, took form. Although this system of Voudoun shows the markings of the Congo and other areas of Africa, its pantheon and ritual structure are dominated by Dahomeyan (in Benin) influences. Regarding the New World, it is most deeply associated with Haiti.

The word *vo-du* comes from the Fon language of that people in the region of Benin in West Africa and means god. The practices and beliefs that make up the religious tradition of Vodun, however, are drawn from numerous West African cultural groups such as the Dahomeyans, Mandinges, and Ibos.[3] As Africans were captured and forced into the slave trade, they brought to the New World their religious sensibilities and practices. Although religious traditions were not transplanted in total, significant portions were maintained and combined with practices from other regions, and these practices and beliefs were safeguarded and taught by *houn'gans* and *mam'bos*—the priests and priestesses of Vodun. Women in Vodun tend to have greater representation in the religion's hierarchy than one finds in the churches described in this volume, or in many of the other traditions discussed. That is to say, "the adaptability of Vodou over time, and its responsiveness to other cultures and religions; the fact that it has no canon, creed, or pope; the multiplicity of its spirits; and the intimate detail in which those spirits reflect the lives of the faithful—all these characteristics make women's lives visible within Vodou in ways they are not in other religious traditions."[4]

Vodun, within the context of Haiti's slavocracy, attempted to make sense of a world that had seemingly gone wrong. Within this process, information from various African traditions, the Catholic Church (in such practices as communion and attention to the saints), and the religious thought of the indigenous, "Indian" population provided the framework. The religious system was initiated during the eighteenth century (approximately 1750), but many of the ritual structures, beliefs, and activities were in place long before this date. Voudoun is not a centralized tradition; rather, there is flexibility with respect to how one serves the gods who are represented by designs (*vever*) made with cornmeal or red brick powder on the central ground (the *peristyle*) in the place of worship (*hounfor* or *oum'phor*). Like all of the religious traditions described in this volume, Vodun communities house various "offices" or specialized positions necessary in order to conduct rituals and other components of the communities' life. Besides the *houn'gan* and *mam'bo*, the priests and priestesses within the religion, leaders include:

La Place—prepares animals (such as goats) for sacrifice and makes certain that the appropriate foods for the loa (deities) associated with the particular ceremony are in place

Mam'bo caille—apprentice learning to be a priest of the loa

Houn'torguiers—drummers used in ceremonies

Houn'guenicon—person in charge of the chorus responsible for leading chants and dances during ceremonies that are used to call loa to the event

Reine silence—person responsible for keeping ceremonies orderly

Houn'sih ventailleur—secures animals used in ceremonies

Houn'sih cuisiniere—responsible for cooking animals that have been sacrificed during ceremonies

Many of the rituals and deities were taken from the Dahomeyan society, one guided by a highly agrarian system and royal hierarchy. Within that context, the gods provided a sense of protection and balance, helping to maintain order. These "rada" rituals and loa (or *mystere*) are gentle. The context of slavery, however, involved an absurdity and fostered anger over the conditions of slavery that could not be handled through the gentle and balancing attributes of rada rituals and loa alone. The aggression and anger fostered by slavery and the resulting demand for freedom and justice required aggressive loa and rituals, capable of channeling the anger of the slaves and providing for liberating action. Using the example of the slave rebel Boukman, George Eaton Simpson provides a vivid example of how Vodun rites might have served this purpose: "Born in Jamaica, Boukman escaped from a plantation near Morne-Rouge. In order to produce greater unity among the rebels of that region, he conducted an impressive ceremony during the night of August 14, 1791. After an enormous crowd had assembled a violent storm arose, and in the midst of thunder and lightning an old Negro woman appeared, danced wildly, sang, and brandished a huge cutlass over her head. Finally, the silent and fascinated crowd saw her plunge the cutlass into the throat of a black hog. The slaves drank the animal's blood and swore they would execute Boukman's order."[5] Simpson refers to the "petro" (or pethro) rituals that emerged in Haiti and helped bring about the revolution that freed Haitian slaves. The loa associated with these rituals are aggressive and exacting, capable of supporting violent activities. They are "hot." On the other hand, rada loa are "cool" deities and are capable of punishing believers and nonbelievers, but these gods are not associated with the anger that marks petro loa.

It is inaccurate to suggest that rada rituals are geared toward good and petro toward evil. This is far too simplistic. *Serviteurs*—practitioners who on occasion are possessed by the loa—do not make this type of moral distinction, although ritualistic distinctions are made in that petro and rada loa are served in different locations when possible. In fact, most practitioners work "with both hands." Life in Haiti requires the benefits of both "points," or approaches to the gods. The distinction is one of aggression, not one of moral or ethical conduct. In other words, there are some requests that are better handled by petro loa and others that are best handled by rada loa. An example of this involves a general need for good crops involving rada loas, while the Haitian revolution of the nineteenth century required the assistance of aggressive petro manifestations of the loa. Hence, "it was the Petro cult, born in the hills, nurtured in secret, which have both the moral force and the actual organization to the escaped slaves who plotted and trained, swooped down upon the plantations and led the rest of the slaves in the revolt that, by 1804, had made of Haiti the second free colony in the western hemisphere, following the United States. Even today the songs of revolt, of 'Vive la Liberte,' occur in Petro ritual as a dominant theme."[6]

The key relationship in Vodun is between invisible forces (loas, etc.) and humans; all else simply facilitates or harms this connection. Therefore, loa—both petro and rada—are extremely important within Vodun in that they are the guardians of humans, and humans are able to adjust their life situations through proper attention to these deities. According to tradition, the loa were once human and now, as divine forces manifest in physical objects, they have particular areas of interaction. One of the consequences of the slave trade was the blending of various deities and their functions: "in some cases, the deity of the numerically dominant group absorbed the similar deities of the others; or the emphatic character of one tribe, such as the warlike quality of the Nagos, gave their deity of war, Ogoun, preeminence over all other representatives of that principle. And yet, because Voudoun [Vodun] was a collective creation, it did not exact the abandonment of one tribal deity in favor of another."[7] Because there are so many gods, and because financial resources are limited, practitioners of Vodun in Haiti must carefully arrange their responsibilities and work to manage the total number of deities that receive attention. Failure to do this can easily result in one becoming overextended and in danger of failing to adequately meet religious obligations. To be a part of a Vodun community means at a fundamental level to serve the loa. Yet, there is only so much one person, or even one community, can do with regard to service. One way in which to manage one's responsibilities of service involves recognition of the various categories of loa. There are major loa and lesser deities.

The details and full complexities of Vodun practice and cosmology are beyond the scope of this brief survey, but suffice it to say that the former require less attention than the latter, who are more easily influenced through ceremonies. The major deities are as follows.

Bondye is the supreme deity, creator of the universe, and the one who controls human life and destiny. The loa, in a sense, are manifestations of Bondye and are thereby also dependent on Bondye. Many of the most widely recognized deities are associated with particular Catholic saints and songs, and all loas are associated with distinct activities or abilities. Damballah, represented by the snake, is associated with the heavens and dominates the sky. Agwe is the guardian of the sea. Ogoun, who is associated with the machete, is a protector and is often associated with political power and warfare. Erzulie, associated with the Virgin Mary, is connected to wealth and fine items such as jewelry and perfumes, but is also known for her generosity. Legba is the intermediary between the loa and humans. He opens the lines of communication between the two, and as a result he must be addressed first during any ceremony. (Ceremonies always begin with various prayers, some of which have strong Roman Catholic elements such as the naming of particular saints. The non–Roman Catholic prayers, however, tend to be more energetic.) Pictorial representations of Legba show an old man, bent from years of hard farm work.[8] Gede, represented by the cross one finds on a grave, controls death and, as a consequence, cemeteries. Representations of Gede are similar to those of Legba in that both show the signs of poverty, but for Gede this involves the starving beggar. A general grouping of loa[9] in Haitian Vodun would include, but not be limited to, the following:

African Name	Rada/Saint/Petro Name	Functional Identification/ Color
Mawa-Lisa	Bondye	Creator
Legba	Papa Legba/St. Peter/ Kafou Legba	Trickster/Messenger—red
Aziri	Erzulie/Virgin Mary/ Erzulie Je-Rouge	River goddess/Goddess of love—blue/pink
Da Ayido	Damballah/St. Patrick	Primordial serpent—white
Gu	Ogoun/St. James/Ogou Ferary	God of iron and war—red
Agbe	Agwe/St. Ulrich (Ulrique)	Protector of the sea— white/green/pink
Zaka	Cousin Zaka/St. John the Baptist/St. Isidore	God of agriculture— blue/red/green

African Name	Rada/Saint/Petro Name	Functional Identification/ Color
Gede	Gede/St. Gerard or St. Expedit/Baron la Koa	Lord of cemeteries/Death—black
Loko	Papa Loko	God of agriculture—yellow
Hohovi	Marassa	Sacred twins
	Jean Petro	Leader of petro loa
	Simbi	Guardian of ponds—black/grey
	Bosou	Spirit of military might

When loa possess individuals during ceremonies, the possessed person moves in ways that are associated with that particular loa. For example, those possessed by Legba, represented by an old man, will move in ways that express the bent and arthritic joints associated with an old farmer. While the loa are associated with particular natural materials, saints, and particular *vevers*, they are also associated with the trees in the oum'phor yard—*reposoirs*—that are decorated using the colors associated with particular deities. Practitioners of Vodun also recognize the existence of other forces beside the loa. In addition, the dead and ancestral loa must also receive attention in order to maintain life's proper balance. The Vodun cosmology is complex and thick with various spiritual beings that have the potential, in numerous ways, to impinge upon human life. While these categories of cosmic forces are recognized widely, there is no consensus concerning how people within the religion divide their attention. For example, not all within Vodun maintain a distinct set of practices related to the ancestors.[10]

Those who serve the loa are also aware of the presence of *baka*, or evil spirits, that often take the form of various animals. In recognizing the complexity of the cosmos, some attempt to increase their good in their life through manipulation and evil deeds. For instance, a magician, or *bocor*, may work with dangerous spirits in order to achieve desired ends at the expense of others. One of a bocor's tools, the one that is most firmly lodged in popular imagination, is the zombie—the soulless body that follows the orders of the bocor. While the work of the bocor is firmly lodged in popular depictions of Vodun, most involved in the religion serve the loa in order to benefit themselves within the context of the larger community, to increase the good, and not to inflict injury or harm on others. What one gathers, however, from this discussion of good versus evil is an understanding that these terms point to conditions and attitudes that are fluid and transformable. That is, nothing is inherently evil or bad, nor is anything unchangeably good.

Long after the end of the slave trade and the restructuring of socioeconomic relationships and hierarchies, researchers such as Maya Deren argued that middle-class Haitians in the cities often turned away from Vodun and embraced Christianity because of the latter's social acceptability.[11] In some instances in the late twentieth century, political figures manipulated Vodun to maintain control over the population. An example of this involves President Francois Duvalier ("Papa Doc"), who first came to power in Haiti in 1957, using Vodun ceremonies and priests within his special police force and as informants during his po-

A Mam'bo in Cuba.

litical dictatorship. Life remained difficult under the rule of his son, Jean Claude Duvalier ("Baby Doc") because, as some priests of Vodun noted, Damballah had withdrawn from the land because of the political abuses that marked the period of the Duvaliers.[12] Under President Jean-Bertrand Aristide, an effort was made to allow the practice of Vodun, Protestantism, and Roman Catholicism. Nonetheless, a stigma remained attached to Vodun.

Voodoo in the United States

It is important to remember that the spirit of revival that fueled the development of the black churches discussed elsewhere in this volume did not surface until almost the 1700s. Prior to then, attention to the Christianization of enslaved Africans was spotty at best. This did not mean that Africans in the North American colonies were without religious options, however. To the contrary, it is safe to assume that Africans in North America maintained some of their African religious beliefs. African retentions would have been a somewhat common occurrence, whether or not whites recognized and wrote about them. As was the case in the Caribbean and in South America, Africans from various cultural groups were placed together on North American plantations, and this resulted in a blending of religious practices and beliefs, most of which clearly differed from traditional Protestant or Catholic activities. One of the traditions that developed early within this context of religious diversity was Voodoo, a tradition that may have developed in the North American colonies as early as the 1600s.

When most envision Voodoo, thoughts turn to the southeastern corner of the country, with a particularly strong focus on Louisiana, where the signs of Voodoo were scattered early across the religious landscape. Some argue that Louisiana, with its slaves brought directly from the French West Indies, was the birthplace of Voodoo within North America, although the nature of plantation life in areas of Georgia and South Carolina would have also allowed for the growth of such African-based traditions. In other words, "the coastal plantations that absorbed the slave traffic were remote from one another. The jungle swamps of the low country and the wide expanses of water separating the coastal islands made communication difficult among the plantation laborers of this section. With the continued arrival of Africans to these isolated plantation communities native ceremonies and customs were renewed or exchanged."[13]

The Haitian Revolution in 1791 only intensified the practice of this tradition in North America as colonizers fled the island with slaves in tow.[14] It should be noted that after 1860 most enslaved Africans in North America were born in North America. This would not mean an end to Voodoo practices; it simply meant a greatly reduced influx of new information by which to maintain the full integrity of knowledge about and the practice of Voodoo ceremonies. Therefore, few of the loa associated with Vodun in Haiti survived in North America, and in Louisiana the religion was dominated by attention to Damballa, or Damballa Wedo, or Li Grand Zombi. Others included Legba (St. Peter), as well as new loa that emerged within the North American context: St. Marron, the patron of runaway slaves, gains the attention of Voodoo practitioners, as did St. Expedite whose status as a Catholic saint is open to speculation. St. John the Baptist also played an important role in early North American Voodoo, as did St. Raymond, who is sought out for favors, as well as St. Rita, who is associated with children.[15] In addition, St. Michael is recognized as Daniel Blanc, and St. Anthony as Ogou.

Our best guess is that, as was the case in Haiti, authorities and slave owners attempted to suppress the practice, but this was done with limited success because their actions only served to reinforce the secretive nature of the rituals and to push practices "underground." While efforts to suppress the tradition failed, the great caution with which believers had to operate did make spotty the transition of the oral-based tradition. This resulted, in some cases, in the mutation of Voodoo into less refined and more magic-centered practices such as Hoodoo. By way of a brief distinction between the two, Voodoo involves complex religious traditions with a full cosmology, rituals performed in the context of community, and an elaborate array of ceremonial positions and religious leaders. Hoodoo, on the other hand, does not contain the same attention to community, but rather involves manipulation of forces for the benefit of particular individuals. Furthermore, Hoodoo does not entail the same complex cosmology.

In spite of this blurring of the line between Voodoo and Hoodoo, Voodoo practices not only survived but thrived, based on interests from both blacks and whites. One of the prime examples of Voodoo thriving involves the popularity of the early Voodoo queen Marie Laveau, who reigned for forty years. She replaced the first Voodoo queen in New Orleans, Sanite Dede, in 1830.

When ceremonies were held publicly in New Orleans' Congo Square—and we have little to substantiate assumptions concerning what occurred—many of the components of Voodoo such as the use of drums were forbidden and replaced by clapping and movement of the legs.[16]

Most ceremonies that were deeply tied to Voodoo as opposed to being a mere manipulation of its more magical aspects, as in the case of "root work" or Hoodoo, took place secretly, and as a result we have very little information regarding their content and form. However, Lyle Saxon provides an interesting possibility with respect to how information concerning such ceremonies might spread to those who serve the loa. He writes:

> A message could be conveyed from one end of the city to another in a single day without one white person's being aware of it. It is said that a Negro cook in a kitchen would sing some creole song while she rattled her pots and pans, a song which sounded innocuous enough to any white listener, but at the end of the verse she would sing a few words intended as a message. Another Negro working nearby would listen intently and at the end of the second verse would hear the message repeated. This second servant would then go outside to attend to her duties. She would sing the same song and her voice would be heard by servants in the house next door. In this way, by means of song, news of the meeting of a Voodoo society would be carried from one end of the city to another and upon the appointed night Negro men and women would slip from their beds before midnight and would assemble for their ceremonies.[17]

One cannot be certain that word of secret ceremonies was actually spread this way, but there is little reason to believe it impossible when one considers that figures such as Frederick Douglass spoke of slaves using songs as a way of spreading messages. More to the point, Nat Turner's revolt made use of spirituals as a way of spreading word concerning upcoming events. Why not, then, think in terms of the logistics for Voodoo ceremonies spreading in like manner? Whether through songs or some other means, word concerning the exploits of particular religious leaders did spread.

With time, Voodoo in New Orleans changed and lost some of its connection to the tradition as practiced in Haiti. In recent years much of what is known about Voodoo in New Orleans, Louisiana actually revolves around Hoodoo, items, tours, and information peddled to tourists. One need only consider the various shops lining the French Quarter that sell "Voodoo dolls" and other items for tourists. Or, one can actually move further back in history and mark this shift through earlier advertisements by a "witch doctor": "Emile Laile P. H.; Meaning Professor of Hoodoo; All manner of Hants and Hoodoos removed; with neatness and dispatch. No witch doctor is too strong for My Power. . . . Special attention to Emergency calls."[18] Such advertisements were known as early as the 1890s.[19]

While in some circles the tradition was reduced to trinkets, superstition, and superficial activities, others maintained service to a central group of loa. This devotion did not completely mirror the tradition as practiced in portions of Haiti, although there is no standard mode of service to the loa and no standard doctrine even in Haiti. Nonetheless, Voodoo gained a visibility that led to recognition as a vital and vibrant tradition. In 1945, Voodoo was recognized by the World Order of Congregational Churches as a religion practiced within some one thousand Voodoo communities in Louisiana alone.[20] Nonetheless, participation in Voodoo remains difficult for believers in that a stigma attached to the practice of nonmainstream forms of religion such as Voodoo persists in the United States. Voodoo has gained numerous African American converts, however, for a variety of reasons. Some who are Afrocentric prefer Voodoo because they believe it brings them closer to African-based religion and allows them to move beyond European-based religious orientations. Others begin serving the loa because Christian churches, from their perspective, do not offer useful approaches to dealing with life issues. Still others appreciate the manner in which Voodoo manifests a stronger appreciation for the earth and for the human's relationship to the other—entailing a sense of communion with, as opposed to stewardship over, the earth.

A layer of secrecy remains that makes it hard to know exactly how many, as writer Zora Neale Hurston put it, are "warmed by the fires of Voodoo." In part this stems from the way in which some within the tradition blur the line between Christian commitments and service to the loa. For example, Mother Doris, who became known in Louisiana after World War I, downplayed the Voodoo origins of her work, instead labeling herself a Christian while maintaining attention to healing associated with the roots of Voodoo in the southern United States. In fairness it was not uncommon for practitioners of Vodun in Haiti to also consider themselves Christian (Roman Catholic), but this was based on an understanding of Christian and Vodun being compatible. For Mother Doris, the label *Christian* is meant to point out the uneasiness with which Voodoo is met in most social circles.

Nonetheless, Voodoo has spread across the United States, often practiced with a great deal of secrecy because of continuing suspicion (and often hostility) toward alternative forms of religious practice. In part this spread is the result of the influx of Haitians into the United States. Cities such as New Orleans and New York house complex and strong communities of those loyal to the loa of Voodoo. Figures such as Ava Kay Jones, one of the more visible Voodoo priestesses in the United States, have gained positive attention in academic and more popular circles. Concerning her practice of Voodoo, Jones says: "So you see I walked away from a possible teaching career and a legal career [she has a law degree] to help keep alive the traditions I value from Africa. A tradition that was never completely lost. . . . I don't want to turn my back on my heritage. . . . I now see my role in life as working with the spirits."[21] Another priestess that has received attention in recent years is "Mama Lola" (Alourdes Margaux), a Voodoo mam'bo who served as the subject for one of the most important contemporary investigations of Voodoo in the United States, written by anthropologist Karen McCarthy Brown.[22]

According to Brown, Mama Lola's reputation extends beyond New York, resulting in trips to various cities in the United States as well as the Caribbean and South America to provide services based on her religious knowledge.[23] Service to the loa changes with movement from Haiti to the United States in that networks that were once assumed as sources of assistance with ceremonies and other practices are not necessarily in place because immediate family is not present. Hence, the content of religious community—or spiritual family—changes. Mama Lola is Haitian, but those under her guidance, who are a part of her "house," represent the diversity of New York City including African Americans. As Brown notes, "Alourdes moves in two directions at once. Through her service to the spirits, she retraces the pathways back home in order to shore up weakening bonds of blood and friendship. But at the same time she reaches out to new people such as myself. She uses her spiritual skills to pull us into the family, into the network of gifts and obligations that constitute her survival strategy."[24]

Mama Lola is the central figure in an urban Vodun or Voodoo community composed of those initiated—"children of the house"—and more casual clients who come to address particular issues and concerns. While casual clients provide some income, children of the house are obligated to provide money and time for the maintenance of the house or temple.[25] The priestess, Mama Lola, is responsible for assistance with issues of daily living as well as larger issues confronting her "children." To give this assistance, Mama Lola taps into the energy and insight only the loa can provide. The loa provide this guidance in exchange for offerings. In this sense the loa and humans are mutually dependent, the loa wanting attention vis-à-vis ceremonies and humans wanting assistance and insight.

The loa must receive proper attention, and this includes recognition of birthday celebrations. One such celebration for Kouzen Zaka (Cousin Zaka) began with preparation of the foods to be served during the event and the placement of the food at the deity's altar. Other loa will also receive songs during the celebration, but the arrangement of food points to the centrality of Kouzen Zaka.

Those invited to the celebration arrived long before the initial prayers were offered; they brought with them food and other items needed for the birthday, and they moved around Mama Lola's house greeting each other and awaiting the start of the celebration. When the time arrived, Mama Lola began the prayers and songs marking the start of the ceremony. These initial prayers are Catholic prayers, and they are used at virtually all celebrations regardless of which loa is being honored. Those who are new servants of the loa learn the songs and positioning of the body—when to kneel, when to stand, and so forth—from those with greater knowledge.

Once the Catholic prayers are completed, creole songs begin and at this point the most significant moments of the ceremony start. (When available, drums are used to increase the energy of the ceremony in preparation for the coming of the loa. Drums, however, are not always available, and in these cases clapping replaces the beat of the drums.) As mentioned earlier, Legba is the first loa to receive attention through song. This is because without Legba's intervention the other loa cannot be contacted; Legba alone can open the "gate" to interaction between humans and deities. Alourdes holds in one hand her sacred rattle (*ason*) and in the other a cup. The ceremony continues:

> on either side of her were ritual assistants, one holding a candle and a bottle of gin, the other a bottle of molasses. These elements were lifted up to each of the cardinal directions in turn. Alourdes shook the *ason* sharply each time the group dipped at the knees and changed direction. Then, facing the larger of the altar tables, all three stepped to the right, bent their knees in a quick movement like a curtsey, stepped to the left, and turned all the way around, then repeated the same gestures in reverse, with an initial step to the left. A third time, again starting with a step to the right, the small band of ritualizers dipped and twirled. Then they headed out the door and down the narrow hallway to the Legba shrine. Throughout the salutation, all the people present sang.[26]

Using movements similar to those for Legba, but at times omitting certain items such as alcohol for loa who do not drink it, the other loa are greeted until time to greet the major loa for this celebration. Songs are sung with increasing energy to Kouzen Zaka, enticing him to come to this ceremony being held in his honor.

Those gathered at such ceremonies anxiously await the arrival of loa. Through possession—the loa "riding" its "horse," as possession is

> ### Outline of Mama Lola's Ceremony for Kouzen Zaka
>
> * Catholic prayers and songs
> * Creole songs—(with drums when available or clapping)
>   * Alourdes—holding ason and cup
>   * Ritual Assistant—one candle and a bottle of gin
>   * Ritual Assistant—bottle of molasses
> * Elements lifted up in each of the cardinal directions (in turn) while Alourdes shakes the ason and group bends knees and changes direction
> * Alourdes and assistants perform "dance"
> * Exit to the Legba shrine

often called—the servant loses control of his or her being. The portion of the person's being referred to as the "big guardian angel" (*gwo bo-nanj*) is displaced by the loa, and the horse, the servant of the loa, takes on the characteristics and personality of the loa. When the loa is in control, the person possessed is dressed in the clothing associated with the loa. There is an exchange between loa and the servants gathered. The god speaks—helping the servant possessed and/or the others gathered through words and deeds that heal and guide—and this process can last for many hours, as various loa manifest. After the last releases the possessed servant, those gathered begin to leave. In due time, the remaining food, in keeping with the loa's wishes, is distributed among members of the religious community.[27]

Basic Beliefs in Voodoo

Because this religion is primarily an oral tradition, the work of priests and priestesses in maintaining proper ritual conduct is important with regard to the preservation of the religion. These religious leaders are those who have a special relationship with the gods in that they have been selected by a particular god (loa) for service and have undergone initiation into the secrets of the tradition. They have the most detailed understanding of rituals and ceremonies, and people will select (and move between) Vodun communities based on the level of demonstrated knowledge held by a particular houn'gan or mam'bo. One of the central functions of the religious leader is to address physical illness that is both a result of environment and the result of psychological destruction caused by oppression. This is done by discovering the invisible cause of the physically manifested problem. Although the religious leader addresses the holistic healing of clients in a way that modern medicine does not, clients will be referred to doctors for treatment when necessary.

Voodoo was molded into an important religion that helps to make sense of life. Attention is not given to a "heaven" as in the case of Christian churches, and there is no sense of a transhistorical paradise as in Islam. Voodoo works to transform the here and now—to connect the visible and invisible forces in the world for the improvement of life on earth. This push for a better life is the basic purpose of Voodoo: On some level serving the loa involves an arrangement by which both the loa and the human(s) benefit. The loa receives sacrifice and attention, and the human(s) receives requested guidance and good fortune. Both parties are expected to follow through on their obligations, and when humans fail misfortune can result. If events are not in keeping with reasonably expected results based on proper service, humans are entitled to question the loa and complain. This certainly differs from the process in Christian churches in which undesirable events do not call God into question. Rather, Christians question themselves and assume the event—although far from desirable—must still be a part of God's will.

Concluding Thoughts

Devotion to the loa, Voodoo, is most widely associated with Haiti, but this tradition also gained ground in places such as Louisiana during the period of slavery. The power of the loa and the charisma of Voodoo's religious leaders such as Marie LaVeau increased the tradition's appeal over the years. With time, Voodoo spread beyond its initial locations in North America.

Voodoo is a vital and vibrant religious system, one that serves the needs of an undetermined number of people living in the United States. The cosmological structure of Voodoo gives those who serve the loa a way of engaging the world, of understanding the "ups and downs" that make up life, and to do so within the context of community. What is interesting is the manner in which, for Voodoo as well as the other traditions in this volume, such wonders are worked using rather mundane and ordinary items that, within the context of religious engagement, gain great authority and produce wonders because they are in contact with the loa, ancestors, and other cosmic forces.

Today, in neighborhoods across the country, in the houses of religious leaders such as Mama Lola and Ava Kay Jones, African Americans gather to give service to the loa, African deities who were brought to the Americas during the period of slavery. Through ceremonies marked by elaborate outfits, energetic songs and dances, sacrifices, and spirit possession, all meant to enliven and protect the community, practitioners of Voodoo make sense of the world.

Notes

1. Within the religion's African context I use the term *Vodu* or *Voudoun*; within the Haitian context I refer to it as *Vodun*; and, in the context of the United States, I refer to the tradition as *Voodoo*.

2. Joseph M. Murphy, "Haitian Vodou," in *Working the Spirit: Ceremonies of the African Diaspora* (Boston: Beacon Press, 1994), 10.

3. Milo Rigaud, *Secrets of Voodoo*, trans. Robert B. Cross (San Francisco: City Lights Books, 1969), 9.

4. Karen McCarthy Brown, *Mama Lola: A Vodou Priestess in Brooklyn* (Berkeley: University of California Press, 1991), 220–21.

5. George Eaton Simpson, *Religious Cults of the Caribbean: Trinidad, Jamaica, and Haiti* (Rio Piedras, Puerto Rico: Institute of Caribbean Studies, University of Puerto Rico, 1980), 236.

6. Maya Deren, *Divine Horsemen: The Living Gods of Haiti* (Kingston, NY: McPherson & Company, 1953), 62.

7. Ibid., 59.

8. Ibid., 99.

9. Adapted from Robert Farris Thompson's *Flash of the Spirit* (New York: Vintage Books, 1983), Milo Rigaud's *Secrets of Voodoo*, and Laennec Hurbon's *Voodoo: Search for the Spirit* (New York: Harry N. Abrams, 1995). Names in bold indicate that the loa is either strictly petro or is manifest almost strictly as petro. The arrangement of the loa carries no connotations of importance or ranking.

10. Simpson, *Religious Cults of the Caribbean*, 250.

11. Deren, *Divine Horsemen*, 15.

12. Hurbon, *Voodoo: Search for the Spirit*, 118–19; Brown, *Mama Lola*, 309.

13. Savannah Unit, Georgia Writers' Project, Works Project Administration, *Drums and Shadows: Survival Studies Among the Georgia Coastal Negroes* (Garden City, NY: Anchor Books, 1972), xxii.

14. Jessie Gaston Mulira, "The Case of Voodoo in New Orleans," in Joseph E. Holloway, ed., *Africanisms in American Culture* (Bloomington: Indiana University Press, 1990), 35.

15. Jim Haskins, *Voodoo & Hoodoo: Their Tradition and Craft as Revealed by Actual Practitioners* (New York: Stein and Day, 1978), 61.

16. Mulira, "The Case of Voodoo in New Orleans," 44.

17. Quoted in Robert Tallant, *Voodoo in New Orleans* (New York: Collier Books, 1946; Macmillan, 1971), 74.

18. Quoted in Tallant, *Voodoo in New Orleans*, 214.

19. Jim Haskins, *Voodoo & Hoodoo*, 95.

20. Mulira, "The Case of Voodoo in New Orleans," 63.

21. Ron Bodin, *Voodoo: Past and Present*, Louisiana Life Series (Lafayette, LA: Center for Louisiana Studies, University of Southwestern Louisiana, 1990), 80.

22. Brown, *Mama Lola*.

23. Ibid., 4.

24. Ibid., 47–48.

25. Ibid., 37.

26. Ibid., 54.

27. This account of Zaka's celebration is drawn from Brown, *Mama Lola*, 38–68.

Timeline

1536	First African baptized in Roman Catholic Church
1619	Enslaved Africans arrive in Virginia
1623	Africans enter the Episcopal Church
1641	Earliest recorded account of an African Church member (Massachusetts)
1669	Africans first baptized into Lutheran Church
1702	Society for the Propagation of the Gospel in Foreign Parts attempts to convert slaves
1773	First black church (Baptist) formed—Silver Bluff Church
1780–1830	Second Great Awakening
1787	Free African Society formed in Philadelphia
1796	Black Methodists form a church in New York
1807	First African Presbyterian Church founded
1816	African Methodist Episcopal (AME) Church formed
1828	Oblate Sisters of Providence is founded in Baltimore, Maryland
1830	Marie Laveau becomes Voodoo Queen
1831	Maria Stewart becomes first woman to lecture publicly on religio-political issues
1831	Work of Oblate Sisters of Providence recognized by the Pope
1832	African Lutheran Church founded by Jehu Jones
1834	Black Baptist associations begin to form
1844	First African parish (Chapel of Nativity in Pittsburgh) formed

1848	"Zion" added to African Methodist Episcopal Church in America
1850	John Payne elected the first bishop for Africa for Episcopal Church
1852	Sisters of Holy Family take canonical vows
1854	James Healy ordained as African American priest
1863	Emancipation Proclamation issued and Great Migration begins
1864	St. Francis Xavier Catholic Church becomes first parish for African Americans
1864	AME and AMEZ (African Methodist Episcopal Zion) churches consider merger
1866	First statewide Baptist convention forms
1866	Prophet Cherry organizes the Church of the Living God, Pillar of Truth for All Nations; during the 1940s, the organization moves to Philadelphia
1867	Patrick Francis Healy becomes first African American Jesuit priest
1869	Colored Cumberland Presbyterian Church organized
1870	Colored Methodist Episcopal Church formed
1874	Patrick Healy becomes the first African American president of a Catholic university (Georgetown University)
1875	James A. Healy becomes the first African American Catholic bishop (Portland, Oregon)
1878	Mathilda Beasley organizes the Third Order of St. Francis Catholic order for African American nuns
1884	Samuel David Ferguson becomes first African American bishop of the Episcopal Church
1886	Augustus Tolton ordained a Roman Catholic priest
1889	Daniel Rudd sparks conversation in Catholic Church on status of African Americans
1889	Rabbi Leon Richelieu organizes Moorish Zionist Temple in New York
1889	Epiphany Apostolic College founded to train African American priests
1893	William Saunders Crowdy begins having visions that result in the formation of the Church of God and Saints of Christ

1894	Julia A. Foote ordained in the AMEZ Church
1895	National Baptist Convention, USA formed
1895	National Federation of Afro-American Women founded
1896	National Association of Colored Women formed
1896	Crowdy establishes his first organization devoted to his teachings
1897	Charles Mason forms the Church of God
1897	Episcopal priest Alexander Crummell founds the American Negro Academy for scholarship and the arts
1897	Afro-American Presbyterian Synod formed
1898	Crowdy's organization grows to more than twenty congregations
1899	Crowdy's congregations take the form of a church
1900	Reverdy C. Ransom organizes the Institutional Church and Social Settlement House in Chicago which is dedicated to the Social Gospel, an understanding of Christianity as having importance for the correction of social ills
1903	W.E.B. DuBois publishes *Souls of Black Folk*
1903	Eliza Healy becomes first African American superior of a Roman Catholic convent
1906	Asusa Street Pentecostal revival begins
1906	Mason's Church of God renamed Church of God in Christ
1906	Roman Catholic Church organizes the Catholic Board for Mission Work among Colored People
1908	Crowdy dies
1909	Knights of Peter Claver Roman Catholic fraternity formed
1913	Noble Drew Ali establishes Canaanite Temple
1913	Mother Leafy Anderson develops Eternal Life Christian Spiritualist Church in Chicago
1915	National Baptist Convention of America formed
1917	Headquarters for Crowdy's organization established in Belleville, Virginia
1918	Edward T. Demby becomes first African American bishop in Episcopal Church
1919	Wentworth Arthur Matthew organizes the Commandment Keepers Congregation

1920	Mother Leafy Anderson founds Eternal Life Spiritualist Church in the Crescent City (New Orleans)
1923	Father Hurley starts Universal Hagar's Spiritual Church
1924	Islamic Mission of America founded
1930	Master Fard Muhammad appears in Detroit
1930	Wentworth Arthur Matthew's Commandment Keepers Congregation of the Living God is incorporated
1932	"Golden Age of Gospel Music" begins when Thomas Dorsey writes "Take My Hand, Precious Lord"
1941	Joseph Oliver Brown becomes first African American Roman Catholic bishop in the twentieth century
1944	Prophet Jones founds Universal Triumph, the Dominion of God, Inc.
1944	*LIFE* magazine article on Prophet Jones
1944	Baptist minister Adam Clayton Powell Jr. becomes first African American elected to Congress from New York
1946	Francisco Mora becomes first Santería priest in the United States
1946	Prophet Cherry dies
1947	Lewis A. McGee founds Free Religious Fellowship
1948	AME Church ordains Rebecca M. Glover
1951	Afro-American Presbyterian Synod disbands
1954	CME Church ordains a woman
1955	Civil Rights Movement begins
1956	Colored Methodist Episcopal Church becomes Christian Methodist Episcopal Church
1957	Interdenominational Theological Center founded
1957	Southern Christian Leadership Conference formed
1959	Walter King becomes first African American initiated into Santería priesthood (in Cuba)
1961	Progressive Baptist Convention formed
1961	First African American Santería priestess initiated
1962	John Burgess elected first African American bishop over white diocese
1962–1965	Vatican II takes place
1963	Baptist minister Martin Luther King Jr. issues the "Letter from a Birmingham Jail"

1964	Malcolm X leaves Nation of Islam
1964	First Santería drum dance in the United States is held
1964	Martin Luther King Jr. receives Nobel Peace Prize
1964	Edler G. Hawkins becomes first African American moderator of the United Presbyterian Church (part of Presbyterian Church, USA)
1965	Malcolm X killed
1966	National Committee of Black Churchmen formed
1966	Ben Carter has a vision and begins plans to move his community to Liberia
1967	Wallace Muhammad goes on hajj
1968	Civil Rights Movement under King ends with his assassination
1968	Ben Carter visits Liberia to prepare for relocation of his community
1969	Ben Carter's community moves to Liberia
1969	Members of Ben Carter's community begin to move from Liberia to Israel
1972	Ben Carter becomes Rabbey and Adonia Rabbey
1973	Rabbi Matthew dies
1974	Katie Geneva Cannon becomes first African American woman ordained in the Presbyterian Church
1974	Lawrence W. Bottoms becomes first African American moderator of the Presbyterian Church in the United States (part of the Presbyterian Church, USA)
1975	The Honorable Elijah Muhammad dies and is replaced by Wallace Muhammad
1975	Wallace Muhammad begins to reenvision the Nation of Islam
1976	Thelma Cornelia Adair becomes first African American woman moderator of the United Presbyterian Church in the United States (part of the Presbyterian Church, USA)
1977	Pauli Murray ordained as the first African American woman Episcopal priest
1977	Joseph L. Howze becomes first African American Roman Catholic diocesan bishop

1978	Ben Carter explores the possibility of relocating the Abeta Hebrew Israel Culture Center to Liberia
1978	Members of Abeta Hebrew Israel Culture Center begin moving to Liberia
1978	Sandra Wilson ordained and becomes first African American woman to pastor a congregation
1978	Congress of National Black Churches formed
1978	Louis Farrakhan reestablishes the Nation of Islam under the teachings of Elijah Muhammad
1980	Wallace Muhammad changes name to Warith Deen Muhammad
1980s–1990s	Church burnings gain media headlines
1985	Louis Farrakhan goes on hajj
1987	National Black Catholic Congress convenes
1988	National Missionary Baptist Convention of America splits from the National Baptist Convention of America
1988	Eugene Marino elected first African American archbishop
1989	National Baptist Convention, USA completes construction of the first "World Center" built by a black denomination
1989	Barbara Harris elected first African American woman bishop in Episcopal Church
1989	Joan Salmon Campbell becomes first African American woman moderator of the Presbyterian Church, USA
1990	African American Humanist Declaration developed
1990	George Stallings's Imani Temple declares independence from Rome
1990s	General movement of the black middle class back into black churches occurs
1990s	Number of Megachurches (churches with more than 3,000 members) grows, many marked by a "Gospel of Prosperity"
1991	George Stallings ordains an African American priest in Imani Temple
1991	Schism develops in Nichiren Shoshu of America which leads to development of Soka Gakkai International, USA
1995	First woman ordained a bishop in the Lutheran Church

1995	Nation of Islam Million Man March is held
1996	Nation of Islam World Day of Atonement is held
1997	Sheilah Edwards elected vice-general director for Soka Gakkai
1998	Ronnie Smith elected vice-general director for Soka Gakkai
2000	Vashti Murphy McKenzie elected first woman bishop in the AME Church

Glossary

Aleyo: Person who attends Santería ceremonies, but has not been initiated.

Ashé: Cosmic energy in Santería.

Babalawo: A priest in Santería who can perform divination.

Babalocha: A priest in Santería who takes on responsibility for training other priests or priestesses.

Bhikkhus: Buddhist monks.

Bhikkunis: Buddhist nuns.

Bocor: A magician.

Bodhisattva: One who vows to assist others to become liberated from suffering.

Buddha: The enlightened one.

Cabbalistic sciences (Kabbalah): This term, used by figures like Crowdy, refers to Jewish mysticism.

Cabildo: A social club in Cuba used during the period of slavery to teach the Catholic faith and also used by enslaved Africans to preserve their African practices.

Cantor: The person who leads prayers in the Jewish synagogue.

Collares: Necklace received in Santería.

Conjure: The manipulation of natural materials for spiritual benefit, associated with magic.

Connectional church: The various local congregations that make up the denomination.

Convention: A gathering of like-minded congregations.

Daimoku: The information contained in the Gohonzon that embodies the Dharma.

Dharma: Doctrine provided by the Buddha.

Dhyana: Deep meditation.

Diocese: Geographic area overseen by a bishop.

Divination: The process of securing information concerning one's destiny.

Dukka: Suffering.

Egun: Ancestors in Santería.

Eleke: A beaded necklace received as the first step one takes in becoming a priest in Santería.

Emigrationism: The nineteenth-century movement to take African Americans back to Africa.

Fundamentos: Elements that represent the characteristics and functions of a particular orisha.

Glossolalia: Speaking in tongues, a language the person has not studied, as a sign of being filled with the Holy Spirit.

Gohonzon: A small scroll containing the diamoku and embodying the dharma that is the primary object of devotion for Buddhists who follow the teachings of Nichiren.

Great Awakening: Period of energetic worship and revivals prior to the twentieth century during which many people converted and joined churches.

Hajj: The pilgrimage to Mecca required of all able Muslims.

Hoodoo: A popularized version of Voodoo that is associated with magical practices and lacks the detailed cosmology and ritual structures of Voodoo.

Hounfor (also Oum'phor): The place of worship in Vodou.

Houn'gan: A priest in Vodou.

Houn'guenicon: The person in charge of the chorus during Vodou ceremonies.

Houn'sih cuisiniere: The person responsible for cooking animals that have been sacrificed during Vodou ceremonies.

Houn'sih ventailleur: The person who secures animals used in ceremonies.

Houn'torguiers: Drummers used in Vodou ceremonies.

Imam: A religious leader in Islam.

Invisible institution: The informal and secret meetings of slaves thought to represent the beginnings of more formal religious practices.

Itinerant ministry: The concept of ministers moving between congregations.

Iyalocha: A priestess in Santería who takes responsibility for training other priests or priestesses.

Ka'ba: Small stone building in the Great Mosque at Mecca containing the Black Stone said to have been given to the patriarch Abraham by the angel Gabriel.

Kaidan: The sanctuary of Buddhism often associated with the temple Taisekiji, founded by Nikko Shonin.

Karma: The effects of one's actions.

Kosenrufu: The push toward world peace.

La place: One who prepares animals for sacrifice in Vodou.

Loa: A deity in the Vodou tradition.

Lucumi: The term used to name Yoruba slaves in Cuba.

Mam'bo: A Vodou priestess.

Mam'bo caille: Apprentice learning to be a priest of the loa.

Merindilogun: A form of divination using sixteen cowrie shells that are tossed on a mat.

Middle Passage: The movement of enslaved Africans across the Atlantic Ocean, to the Americas.

Myohorenge-kyo: The chant done by members of Soka Gakkai.

Mystere: Another term for a Vodou deity.

Nirvana: Liberation.

Oba: A king in Yoruba.

Obi: A form of divination using coconut cut into four pieces.

Odu: Story that provides information used during divination.

Omoricha: Persons who have been initiated as priests or priestesses in Santería.

Ori: Destiny in Santería.

Orisha: A god in Santería.

Parish: A local congregation.

Passover: Jewish holiday celebrating God's safeguarding the Children of Israel from the killing of the firstborn in Egypt (Exodus 12:23–27), and God's freeing of them from bondage in Egypt.

Peculiar institution: A reference to the system of slavery.

Peristyle: The central area of a Vodou ceremonial place of worship.

Petro loa: Aggressive manifestations of Vodou deities.

Presbyter: A church elder.

Presbytery: A grouping of ministers and elders from various congregations within a district of the church.

Rabbi: One trained for professional ministry, for leading a synagogue congregation; a teacher who can explain Jewish law.

Rada loa: Calm manifestations of Vodou deities.

Ramadan: Ninth month of Muslim calendar, during which the Prophet Muhammad received his first revelation. It is a month of fasting in Islam.

Reglas: A term used for the social clubs in Cuba.

Reine silence: Person responsible for keeping Vodou ceremonies orderly.

Rosh Hashanah: The Jewish New Year.

Samaara: This world.

Spirit guides: Figures who aid and protect humans.

Spiritualism: The religious movement revolving around rituals meant to bring the living and the dead into contact.

Spiritualists: Persons who seek contact with the deceased in order to improve temporal existence.

Synagogue: House of worship for a Jewish congregation.

Synod: A district of the church.

Talmud: Jewish tradition represented by the Mishnah (Jewish traditions composed of the laws that supplement the laws given in the Bible) and the Gemara (commentary on the Mishnah).

Tanha: Desire that causes suffering.

Tantras: Esoteric Buddhist scriptures.

Torah: The five books of the Bible credited to Moses, representing the Pentateuch (the first five books of the Bible).

Ummah: The world community of Islam.

Vever: The design associated with the various Vodou gods.

Vinaya: Discipline utilized by the followers of the Budda.

Yom Kippur: The "Day of Atonement," during which Jews fast and pray.

Biographies

Oba Efuntola Oseijeman Adelabu Adefunmi I (1928–2005)

Born Walter King, Oseijeman Adefunmi was the first African initiated into the priesthood of Santería. The ceremony took place in Cuba in 1959. Before that date, he had spent time with the Kathrine Dunham dance troupe exploring African-based cultural practices. After his initiation, he founded the Shango Temple in Harlem. With time, he began the process of removing the Catholic masking that covered the gods of the religion. To aid in this process, he and two others formed the African Theological Archministry, Inc., in 1960. This resulted in friction with the Santería community in New York. He eventually made a break with that community and began the process of constructing a community of practice that he considered more in line with traditional Yorùbá beliefs and rituals. Oyotunji African Village was founded in 1970. Two years later he was initiated into the priesthood of Ifa while in Nigeria. This was followed, in 1982, with permission to speak on behalf of the Ooni of Ife (in Nigeria). He was the first African American to receive this privilege.

Richard Allen (1760–1831)

Allen was born in Philadelphia, Pennsylvania, as a slave on the estate of Benjamin Chew. At seventeen, Allen converted and began preaching. After the Revolutionary War, he traveled as a preacher. He was eventually invited to preach in Philadelphia. Recognizing the plight of the blacks at St. George's Methodist Episcopal Church, he helped to found the Free African Society and eventually took the lead in developing the African Methodist Episcopal Church. He served as the denomination's first bishop.

Ben Ammi (Date of Birth Unavailable)

The Hebrew Israelites recognized their leader, Ben Ammi (born Ben Carter), as being the "Messianic Leader of the Kingdom of God." Little information is available concerning his early life, but it is known that he was a foundry worker in Chicago when he became a part of the Abeta Hebrew Cultural Center in the 1960s. After having a vision from God, Ben Ammi moved members of his organization to Liberia in the late 1960s, prior to relocating to Israel in 1969. The transition was not smooth, but by 1990, the Hebrew Israelites achieved status within Israel that allowed for some sense of security and access to resources.

Richard Henry Boyd (1843–1922)

Boyd was born into slavery, in Mississippi. He held various jobs before entering ministry. Once involved in the church, he played a significant role in the formation of a Baptist association in Texas. His abilities were recognized, and when the National Baptist Convention formed he was named its first secretary for Home Missions. In 1897, two years after the convention was founded, he developed its Publishing Board as well as other business ventures. His control over the Publishing Board was a factor in the split resulting in the National Baptist Convention, USA and National Baptist Convention of America.

Nannie Helen Burroughs (1878–1961)

Burroughs was born in Virginia and spent her early years in Washington, DC. After attending the M Street High School, she became the secretary for the Foreign Mission Board of the National Baptist Convention. She played an active role in developments beyond this job in that she was one of the founding figures of the Woman's Convention in 1900, through which women in the church increased their influence.

Addie Butler (1946–)

Butler received her education at Howard University and Pennsylvania State University and the doctorate from Teachers College at Columbia University. She has held numerous positions including assistant dean at the Community College of Philadelphia. She has also been a member of the Board of Trustees for the Lutheran Theological Seminary in Philadelphia. After years of working in the Lutheran Church, Butler became the first African American woman to serve as vice-president of the Evangelical Lutheran Church in America in 1997.

Katie Geneva Cannon (1950–)

In 1974, Cannon became the first African American woman ordained in the Presbyterian Church (USA). Nine years later she became the first African American woman to receive the Ph.D. from Union Theological Seminary (New York City). After receiving her degree, Cannon held several positions and is currently the Annie Scales Rogers Professor of Christian Ethics at Union Theological Seminary (Richmond, Virginia). Cannon's early writings served to frame what is currently known as Womanist Thought.

Nathaniel Carter (1875–1904)

Carter, having moved from Virginia, was trained by local ministers in Maryland and ordained into the ministry in 1896. He was one of the first African Americans ordained into Lutheran ministry. In order to support work with African American Lutherans in Maryland, Carter traveled through the Midwest raising money. His efforts were successful, and in 1897 St. Philip's Evangelical Lutheran Church was built. He pastored the church until his death.

Miriam Chamani (Date of Birth Unavailable)

Priestess Miriam, the head of the Voodoo Spiritual Temple in New Orleans, is one of the city's most widely recognized and called upon mam'-bos. She began ministry within the black Spiritual churches of Chicago, being ordained a bishop at Angel All Nations Spiritual Church. In 1990 she and her husband, priest Oswan Chamani, founded the Voodoo Spiritual Temple in New Orleans, Louisiana.

Frank Cherry (?–1965)

Documentation concerning the location of his birth and his years prior to his adult years is unavailable. However, it is known that as an adult he held various jobs as a day laborer, and as a sailor he traveled outside the United States. It was while abroad that Cherry says he was spoken to by God and instructed to work with African Americans in the United States. In the vision, God called him a prophet and told him to provide African Americans with proper information concerning their true religion—Judaism. In 1866 he organized the Church of the Living God, Pillar of Truth for All Nations. In the 1940s, the organization moved to Philadelphia. He led this congregation until his death in 1965.

George Clements (1932–)

Clements earned two degrees from St. Mary of the Lake Seminary. After completing his education in 1957, he began work in the pastorate. During his time in Chicago, Clements was very involved in the civil rights struggle, including serving as chaplain for the local Black Panthers. In 1969 he was made pastor of Holy Angels Church in Chicago. Clements, in addition to civil rights activism, took a great interest in the adoption of children in need, founding the One Church–One Child, One Church–One Addict, and One Church–One Inmate initiatives. In 1981, he became the first priest to adopt a child.

James Hal Cone (1938–)

Perhaps the best known black theologian in the country, Cone is often referred to as the "father" of academic black liberation theology. In 1965, he received the Ph.D. from Garrett Theological Seminary/Northwestern University. He spent the first several years of his teaching career at Philander Smith College and Adrian College. Cone eventually moved to Union Theological Seminary, where he is currently the Charles A. Briggs Professor of Systematic Theology.

Suzan Johnson Cook (Date of Birth Unavailable)

Johnson Cook received her education at Emerson College, Teachers College of Columbia University, and Union Theological Seminary, and she received the Doctor of Ministry degree from United Theological Seminary (Dayton, Ohio). She is the founder and pastor of Bronx Christian Fellowship. Prior to that she served in various capacities, including as the first female pastor of Mariner's Temple Baptist Church in Manhattan. Johnson Cook also served in 2002 as the first woman president of the Hampton (Virginia) University Ministries' Conference. She also served on President Clinton's National Advisory on Race.

William Saunders Crowdy (1847–1908)

Crowdy was born during slavery, in Charlotte Hall, St. Mary's County, Maryland. In 1863, he ran away and joined the Union Army.

After the Civil War, he moved to Guthrie, Oklahoma, and started a farm. After some years at this endeavor, he moved to Kansas City, Missouri, and married Lovey Yates Higgins. He and his wife eventually moved back to Guthrie, and while there he had visions that encouraged him to leave the Baptist Church and start a new church, one in keeping with the scriptures. After preaching to family and friends, Crowdy preached in Texas and Illinois. He formalized his following into a church in Chicago, in 1896. In 1900 he moved the organization to Philadelphia. Seven years later, Crowdy had a stroke and died in 1908.

Louis Farrakhan (1933–)

Before entering the Nation of Islam, Farrakhan trained as a musician and had a career as an entertainer. A service during which the Honorable Elijah Muhammad spoke to him inspired him to join the Nation of Islam and to train under Malcolm X. Over the course of the years, Farrakhan's stature in the movement increased. He received prestigious appointments, including a position as the National Spokesperson for the organization. A few years after the Honorable Elijah Muhammad's death, Farrakhan became disillusioned with the changes made to the organization by Wallace Muhammad. In 1978, Farrakhan formed The Nation of Islam based on the original teachings of the Honorable Elijah Muhammad.

Arnold Josiah Ford (1890–1935)

Ford, a member of Marcus Garvey's Universal Negro Improvement Association (UNIA), was a rabbi and is credited for much of the initial work in establishing Judaism within Harlem's African American community. He was born in Barbados and taught music for some time before moving to the United States in 1912. From that date until 1920, he was involved in music as the bandmaster of the New Amsterdam Musical Association of New York. During this period he embraced Judaism and began calling himself an Ethiopian Jew. Unable to convince Garvey to embrace Judaism, Ford founded the Beth B'nai Abraham Congregation in New York, in 1924. He preached that African Americans were Hebrews. When he became aware of the Jews in Ethiopia, he decided to bring together his love for Judaism and things African by moving to Ethiopia. He arrived in Ethiopia in 1930, and died five years after his arrival.

Robert Franklin (1954–)

Franklin is an ordained minister in the Church of God in Christ. Before receiving the Ph.D. from the University of Chicago, Franklin completed studies at Morehouse College. After completing his training, Franklin held several positions, including Director of Black Church Studies at Emory University and a faculty post at Colgate-Rochester Divinity School. He also served as president of the Interdenominational Theological Center, and he is currently on the faculty at Emory University.

Henry Highland Garnet (1815–1882)

Garnet was born in New Market, Kent County, Maryland. In 1824, Garnet's father, mother, and their children were able to move to Pennsylvania because of the death of their owner, Col. William Spencer. The family, now having the name Garnet, moved to New York City after two years in Pennsylvania. Garnet attended school and traveled as a cabin boy on a ship to Cuba. In 1831 he started school at the Episcopal Collegiate School in New York City. Two years later, he became a part of the Presbyterian Church. He continued his schooling, eventually studying for the ministry at Oneida Theological Institute, completing his studies in 1839. After the completion of his education and his ordination in 1843, he worked as a pastor. He is best known for his efforts as an abolitionist. In this capacity he gave speeches in the United States and Europe. In 1865, he became the first African American to speak before the House of Representatives.

William H. Gray III (1941–)

Gray has distinguished himself as a Baptist minister, as a congressman, and most recently as the president of the United Negro College Fund. Gray earned a Master of Divinity degree from Drew Theological Seminary in 1966. After graduation, Gray was called to serve as the pastor of Union Baptist Church, where he developed community service programs that brought attention to his ministry and the church. In 1972, with his father's passing, he became pastor of Bright Hope Baptist Church, where he continued his interest in community activism. In 1978 he was elected to Congress and was elected chair of the House Budget Committee in 1985. A few years later, Gray became the highest ranking black member of Congress when he was named majority whip. Gray combined this political career with continued church ministry at Bright

Hope. In 1991, Gray left political office in order to head the United Negro College Fund.

Herbie Hancock (1940–)

Hancock, the internationally known musician, has been a Buddhist for almost thirty years (see Appendix 2). His musical skills were noticed early, and over the course of his career he has worked with figures such as Miles Davis, and he has also led his own groups. Hancock has recorded numerous albums, and many of his compositions have become jazz standards. Among his many awards is an Oscar for his work on the film "Round Midnight." Buddhism has played an important role in his personal and professional development.

Barbara Clementine Harris (1930–)

After receiving education training at Metropolitan Collegiate Center and Villanova University, Harris was ordained a deacon in 1979 and a priest in the Episcopal Church in 1980. She held several positions in the church, including service as the executive director of the denomination's publishing company. Her outspoken stance on various issues received attention, and in 1988 she was made an assistant bishop in Massachusetts. This made her the first woman to be elected a bishop in the Episcopal Church.

James Augustine Healy (1830–1900)

Healy was born near Macon, Georgia. He was educated at a Quaker school in New Jersey. He and his brothers were also given an opportunity to study at Holy Cross College in Massachusetts. Healy was baptized into the Roman Catholic Church in 1844. He became the first African American priest in 1854. After pastoring, he was made the first African American bishop in 1875. In 1900, he was appointed Assistant to the Papal Throne, only one step below the office of cardinal.

James Theodore Holly (1829–1911)

Holly was born in Washington, DC. His family moved north, living in a variety of cities including New York. He maximized whatever educational opportunities were presented to him while working as a shoemaker. He held various jobs including ownership of a bootmaking shop that he and his brother opened in Vermont. In 1851, Holly left the

Roman Catholic Church and became a member of the Episcopal Church. He was ordained a deacon in 1855 and a priest one year later. While serving as the pastor of a church in New Haven, Connecticut, he maintained an interest in the feasibility of emigration. In 1861, he and several members of his church relocated to Haiti and founded the Holy Trinity Episcopal Church in Port-au-Prince. This work was a struggle, but his work was eventually recognized by the Episcopal Church and he was made, in 1874, Episcopal Missionary Bishop of Haiti. He labored to build the Episcopal Church until his death.

Thomas L. Hoyt Jr.   (1941–)

A bishop in the Christian Methodist Episcopal (CME) Church, Thomas Hoyt Jr. is also one of the leading black scholars of the New Testament in the United States, having received his Ph.D. from Duke University in 1975. He also received degrees from Lane College and the Interdenominational Theological Center (ITC). Prior to his election to the bishopric in 1994, Hoyt held numerous teaching posts, including positions at the ITC, Howard, and Hartford Seminary. His numerous writings have influenced seminarians and churches across the country. He has held numerous interdenominational posts, including with the Faith and Order Commission of the World Council of Churches and the National Council of Churches.

George William Hurley   (1884–1943)

"Father" Hurley was the founder of one of the most significant black Spiritual churches in the country—the Universal Hagar's Spiritual Association, later changed to the Universal Hagar's Spiritual Church. He was involved with various churches, only to be disappointed by the teachings. He eventually founded his own congregation, which grew into a network of congregations. In order to provide training for those interested in a deeper understanding of the workings of the Spirit, Hurley founded the Hagar's School of Mediumship and Psychology in 1924. After his death, several new leaders emerged within the church, but none with the success that marked Hurley's ministry.

Ozro Thurston Jones Sr.   (1891–1972)

Born in Arkansas, Jones began preaching at the age of twenty-one. After working as an evangelist, he became an administrator in the Church of God in Christ. He served as the first president of the denomination's

Youth Department. He moved through the ranks of the denomination, eventually becoming one of its first bishops. With the death of the denomination's founder in 1961, he became the new senior bishop. He held this position until 1968.

William R. Jones (1938–)

Jones received his education at Howard University and Harvard University and then received his Ph.D. from Brown University. He is a minister within the Unitarian Universalist Association, having also served on its Board. In addition, he has held various academic posts, including at Florida State University, from where he recently retired. In 1992 he was recognized as the American Humanist Association Humanist Pioneer of the Year. His writings and ministry provide much of the groundwork for African American Humanism, and his book *Is God a White Racist?: A Preamble to Black Theology* (1973) was one of the first treatments of humanist principles in black religion.

Jarena Lee (1783– ?)

Lee was born in New Jersey. Early in her life she experienced a deep desire to convert to Christianity. After moving to Philadelphia, she encountered Richard Allen and was converted. Lee felt a call to preach and worked to secure permission from the male leadership of the church to exercise this calling. Richard Allen recognized that she was gifted but refused to allow her to preach, although she was given permission to work as an exhorter, without ordination. She spent the remainder of her life as an evangelist.

Eugene Marino (1934–2000)

After attending a seminary, Marino was ordained a Catholic priest in 1962. After serving in various capacities, he was made an auxiliary bishop in 1974. He was only the third African American to gain this position. He became the first African American archbishop in 1988, in Atlanta, Georgia.

Wentworth Arthur Matthew (1892–1973)

Rabbi Matthew was born in Lagos, Nigeria, and raised in the West Indies by his mother. He moved to New York City in 1913 and worked a variety of jobs. His religious life revolved around Pentecostalism, and his sociopolitical life revolved around Marcus Garvey and the UNIA (Universal Negro Improvement Association). It was in the context of the UNIA that Matthew met Arnold Ford and became interested in Judaism. After studying with Ford, Matthew established his own organization in 1919. He called it the Commandment Keepers, Holy Church of the Living God. Rabbi Matthew ordained many African Americans who then established other Jewish congregations. He led the Commandment Keepers until his death in 1973.

Ava Muhammad (1950–)

Muhammad received her law degree from Georgetown University in 1975. After some time in the Nation of Islam, she became the first woman to serve as the leader of a mosque—Mosque #15 in Atlanta, Georgia. She was also appointed the Southern Regional Minister. Both events took place in 1998. She has also served as the national spokesperson for Minister Louis Farrakhan. Many of her writings are primary materials in the Nation of Islam's articulation of its doctrine and activities.

Warith Deen Muhammad (1933–)

The son of the Honorable Elijah Muhammad, Warith Deen Muhammad held control of the Nation of Islam after his father's death in 1975. Determined to bring the organization into line with the world community of Islam, he began rethinking its theology, aesthetics, and practices. Those who did not leave with Louis Farrakhan during the split in the late 1970s remained under Warith Deen Muhammad's new organizational structure. He changed his name to Warith Deen Muhammad, from Wallace Muhammad, during this period. The name of his organization was changed to the Muslim American Mission, with a membership open to all believers. His religious leadership has been recognized in a variety of ways, including his being the first Imam to offer prayer in the United States Senate. He leads the largest group of African American Muslims in the country.

Anna Pauline Murray (Pauli) (1910–1985)

Murray received her Bachelor of Arts degree from Hunter College in 1933. For some time after graduation, Murray worked as a teacher through the Works Progress Administration (WPA). Murray eventually enrolled in Howard University's Law School and completed her studies in 1944 as the only woman in her class. She also received the LL.M. degree in 1945 from the University of California, Berkeley, after being denied admission to Harvard University although she had won a Rosenwald Fellowship for study at the university. In 1965 she became the first African American to earn the Doctor of Juridical Science degree from Yale Law School. Murray held numerous prestigious positions. In 1946 she became the first African American to hold the position of deputy attorney general of California. Murray eventually accepted a position (1956) as the only female associate at the law firm of Paul, Weiss, Rifkind, Wharton, and Garrison in New York City. Leaving her tenured position at Brandeis University in 1973, Murray began studies at General Theological Seminary in New York City in preparation for a life in church ministry. Murray became the first African American woman to be ordained an Episcopal priest in 1977. Murray ministered in the Episcopal Church of the Atonement (Washington, DC) and the Church of the Holy Nativity (Baltimore, Maryland) before retiring in 1984.

William Sinkfold (1946–)

Sinkfold was born in San Francisco, California, and was educated at Harvard University and Starr King School for Ministry. After college, Sinkfold held a variety of positions in marketing before opening his own business called Sinkford Restorations, Inc. With time, his commitment to community activism sparked an interest in ministry. Having spent years as a member of the Unitarian Universalist Association (UUA), he trained for ministry and took a position within the UUA. He served in a variety of capacities, including as an officer of the African American Unitarian Universalist Ministry and in the Unitarian Universalist Urban Concerns and Ministry Committee. In 2001, Sinkfold became the first African American president of the UUA.

Mary Jane Small (1850–?)

Small was born in Tennessee. Little is known about her early years. At the age of twenty-three she had a conversion experience. In 1890 she expressed a desire to preach, and five years later she was ordained a deacon. She worked in various capacities in the African Methodist Episcopal Zion Church, eventually serving as the president of the Woman's Home and Foreign Missionary Society.

Gardner Calvin Taylor   (1918–   )

Born in Louisiana, Taylor was ordained in 1938. He completed his academic training at Oberlin School of Theology. Taylor pastored several churches before moving to New York City and Concord Baptist Church in Brooklyn, New York. His preaching abilities have been widely recognized. In fact, he is often called the "dean of black preachers." He served as one of the first presidents of the Progressive Baptist Convention.

James Varick   (1750–1827)

Varick was born in Orange County, New York. He joined John Street Methodist Church in 1766 and became very active. He, like Richard Allen, objected to the discriminatory practices of the church, and he played a role in developing the African Methodist Episcopal Zion Church. In fact, he was one of the first deacons ordained in the new denomination, and he became its first bishop. He worked to solidify the denomination's structure. In addition, he worked with *Freedom's Journal*, the first black newspaper in the United States.

Williams Jacob Walls   (1885–1975)

Walls served as a bishop and historiographer within the African Methodist Episcopal Zion Church. He received his academic training at Livingstone College and Hood Theological Seminary. He pastored several churches before becoming the editor of the *Star of Zion*, the African Methodist Episcopal Zion Church's journal. After serving in this capacity, he was elected a bishop of the church in 1924. He wrote *The African Methodist Episcopal Zion Church*, which is one of the more significant treatments of his denomination.

Gayraud Stephen Wilmore Jr.   (1921–   )

Wilmore, one of the premier historians of African American religion and minister in the Presbyterian Church, received his education at Lincoln University and Lincoln University Theological Seminary. He held various positions such as the Martin Luther King Jr., Professor of Social Ethics at Boston University and Martin Luther King Jr., Memorial Professor of Black Church Studies at Colgate Rochester Divinity School. Wilmore was also a founding member of the National Conference of Black Churchmen that provided the first reflections on black theology.

In addition, he has held various church-related positions, including associate secretary of the Social Education and Action Section of the United Presbyterian Church Board of Christian Education.

Yaweh Ben Yaweh (1935–)

Born Hulon C. Mitchell Jr., Yaweh Ben Yaweh grew up in Enid, Oklahoma. After attending junior college, he enlisted in the Air Force. After completing his time in the service, he enrolled in Philips University, after which he completed additional training at Atlanta University. While in Atlanta, he became a member of the Nation of Islam. His affiliation with the Nation of Islam was followed by a short period of time with the Modern Christian Church. Shortly after leaving this church, he took the name Yaweh Ben Yaweh. He moved to Miami and developed a following based on his eclectic doctrine. The Nation of Yaweh believes that the Bible (and the teachings of Yaweh Ben Yaweh) provides the blueprint for life. Yaweh Ben Yaweh's organization faced legal difficulties, and as a result he and several other members of the organization served prison sentences.

Appendix One

Responsibilities for the Christianization of Enslaved Africans

In this document, Charles Colcock Jones outlines the responsibilities of the Presbyterian Church for the Christianization of enslaved Africans. Charles Colcock Jones, *The Religious Instruction of the Negroes in the United States: Electronic Edition*, 1804–1863 (pages 155–75, 206–17). Funding from the Library of Congress/Ameritech National Digital Library Competition supported the electronic publication of this title. Documenting the American South (http://docsouth.unc.edu), The University of North Carolina at Chapel Hill Libraries, Rare Book Collection. Used by permission.

The Religious Instruction of the Negroes

CHAPTER I

The Obligations of the Church to afford the Gospel to the Negroes

There are one or two positions upon which the argument under this head is based, and as preliminary thereto demand attention.

The Gospel is the gift of God to our lost and ruined race. Our Divine Lord "was made flesh"—John 1: 1–14. He took upon himself our nature:—Heb. 2: 11–18; for our benefit. That benefit is eternal life. "In him was life, and the life was the light of men.["]—John 1: 4, 17, 3. "For God so loved the world that he gave his only begotten Son, that whosoever believeth in him should not perish, but have everlasting life."—3: 16. "Thanks be unto God for his unspeakable gift."—2 Cor. 9: 15.

It hath pleased the Almighty, in his sovereignty, to bestow the Gospel upon but a portion of the human race. He has, however, chosen to employ human agency in extending the knowledge, and the consequent blessings of this glorious gift, to all mankind, in fulfilment of his expressed designs, and his own most precious promises. He has made it the duty under the most solemn commands, of all who possess the Gospel to impart it to those who are destitute of it. The possession of the gift implies the obligation to impart it. No man may question this position who allows himself to be guided by the conviction, or reason, the dictates of conscience, or the declarations of the word of God.

In attempting to fulfil this day, the general and the just rule of action is, that we impart the Gospel to those of our fellow-men who are most dependent upon us for it—who are most needy and most accessible.

These three peculiarities meet in the case of the Negroes; and consequently they stand first in their claims upon our benevolent attention. And our remarks in confirmation shall be directed,

1. *To the Negroes in the Slave States.*

They are the most dependent of all people upon us for the word of life.

A glance at the civil condition and connection of this people with us, will demonstrate the point. They are, in the eye of the law, property; over which there is an absolute control as such, excepting in so far as they are human beings, and by law are protected in life and limb. The law, however, makes no provision for their religious training, and all the privileges of religion are regulated by the customs of society and the will of owners; nor is it in the power of any one to interfere between the master and the servant, and dictate what privileges his servant ought and must enjoy, any more than he may interfere between parent and child.

Throw these facts together. By law or custom, they are excluded from the advantages of education; and by consequence, from the reading of the word of God: and this immense mass of immortal beings is thrown for religious instruction upon oral communications entirely. And upon whom? Upon their owners. And their owners, especially of late years, claim to be the exclusive guardians of their religious instruction, and the almoners of divine mercy towards them, thus assuming the responsibility of their entire christianization!

All approaches to them from abroad are rigidly guarded against, and no ministers are allowed to break to them the bread of life, except such as have commended themselves to the affection and confidence of owners. I do not condemn this course of self-preservation on the part of our citizens. I mention it only to show more fully the point in hand; the entire dependence of the Negroes upon ourselves for the Gospel.

While this step is taken, another has already been taken, and that of a long time; namely, Negro preachers are discouraged, if not suppressed, on the ground of incompetency and liability to abuse their office and influence to the injury of the morals of the people and the infringement of the laws and peace of the country. I would not go all the lengths of many on this point, for from my own observation, Negro preachers may be employed and confided in, and so regulated as to do their own color great good, and community no harm: nor do I see, if we take the word of God for our guide, how we can consistently exclude an entire people from access to the Gospel ministry, as it may please Almighty God from time to time, as he unquestionably does, to call some of them to it "as Aaron was." The discouragement of this class of preachers, throws the body of the people still more in their dependence upon ourselves, who indeed cannot secure ministers in sufficient numbers to supply our own wants.

Nor have the Negroes any church organizations different from or independent of our own. Such independent organizations are, indeed, not on the whole advisable. But the fact binds them to us with still stronger dependence. And, to add no more, we may, according to the power lodged in our hands, forbid religious meetings, and religious instruction on our own plantations; we may forbid our servants going to church at all, or only to such churches as we may select for them; we may literally shut up the kingdom of heaven against men, and suffer not them that are entering to go in!

It is not too much, therefore to say that the Negroes are in a state of almost absolute dependence upon their owners for the words of eternal life.

They are the most needy of any people in our country. This is very evident, from the exposition which we have given of their dependence; as well as of their moral and religious character. They have no education, no immediate access to the word of God, no competent teachers of their own color, no competent number of white teachers, and are in a state of great ignorance and moral degradation.

And lastly, they are the most accessible. They speak the same language with ourselves; dwell in the same land, at our own doors; and are members of our households. No law forbids the religious instruction of the Negroes, orally, by proper instructors, either during the week or on the Sabbath day; and any minister of the Gospel, or any owner, may undertake the good work, and prosecute it as largely and as long as he pleases.

We are prepared now to take up the obligation of the church of Christ in the slave-holding States to impart the Gospel of Salvation to the Negroes within those States.

1. That obligation is imposed upon us in the first instance by the providence of God.

This follows undeniably from all our previous statements, in the history of their religious instruction, and in the sketch of their moral and religious condition. But it may be of some service to be particular under this head. It was by the permission of Almighty God, in his inscrutable providence over the affairs of men, that the Negroes were taken from Africa and transported to these shores. The inhabitants of the Colonies at their first introduction had nothing to do with the infamous traffic, and were, we may say, universally opposed to it. The iniquity of the traffic and of their first introduction, rests upon the Mother Country.

Being brought here they were brought as slaves; in the providence of God we were constituted masters; superiors; and constituted their guardians. And all the laws in relation to them, civilly, socially, and religiously considered, were framed by ourselves. They thus were placed under our control, and not exclusively for our benefit but for theirs also.

We could not overlook the fact that they were men; holding the same relations to God as ourselves—whose religious interests were certainly their highest and best, and that our first and fundamental duty was to provide to the extent of our ability, for the perpetual security of those interests. Our relations to them and their relations to us, continue the same to the present hour, and the providence of God still binds upon us the great duty of imparting to them the Gospel of eternal life.

2. The obligation is imposed upon us by the word of God.

As already evinced from general principles and commands; the sum of all is, that the Gospel is the gift of God to men, and those who possess it are bound to bestow it upon those who do not.

A few passages of a general character may be advanced, bearing strongly on the point in hand.

"Go ye into all the world and preach the Gospel to every creature." Our Lord in this command recognizes men, not as of a particular nation or color, but collectively, as the intelligent and accountable creatures of God. "God hath made of one blood all the nations of men." It is therefore necessary that the Gospel be preached to the Negroes as well as to the other varieties of the race, and seeing that they have not put it from them, nor judged themselves unworthy of everlasting life, we cannot, we dare not, neglect them and turn to others.

"Thou shalt love thy neighbor as thyself." And, who are our neighbors if the Negroes are not? They are members of the same great family of men; and members of our own communities and parts of our very households; and spend their days in our service. If we see them stripped of necessary religious privileges, and lying in their depravity, helpless, and exposed to eternal death, shall we be neighbors unto them if we look upon them and see their misery and pass by without affording them what relief may be in our power?

"All things whatsoever ye would that men should do to you, do you even so to them." Were we in the condition of the Negro and he in our own; able to read and to appreciate the word of God, and to impart it to us, would we not think it his duty to do it? Yes. And if he neglected that duty we should consider him deficient both in humanity and religion.

But we advance a step further. The word of God recognizes the relation of master and servant, and addresses express commands to us as masters.

In the constitution of his visible church on earth Almighty God included the servants of families; commanded the sign of his everlasting and gracious covenant to be made in their flesh, and thereby secured to them, as well as to children the privileges and blessings of the same. He would have them trained up in the knowledge of his most holy name and for his service: nor must they be neglected, nor excluded. Gen. 17: 12–13. "And he that is eight days old shall be circumcised among you, every man child in your generations, he that is born in the house or bought with money of any stranger, which is not of thy seed;" and the command is repeated, to show his tender regard for the poor, and that his covenant embraces them. "He that is born in thy house and he that is bought with thy money must needs be circumcised; and my covenant shall be in your flesh for an everlasting covenant." In obedience to this command Abraham "in the self-same day circumcised his son Ishmael and all that were born in his house, and all that were bought with his money." v. 23. He apprehended the will of God as expressed in the covenant, and received the divine approbation: "for I know him that he will command his children and his household after him, and they shall keep the way of the Lord to do justice and judgment, that the Lord may bring upon Abraham that which he hath spoken of him." Gen. 18: 19.

The rest of the Sabbath was secured to servants in the Decalogue: "in it thou shalt not do any work, thou nor thy son, nor thy daughter, thy man-servant nor thy maid-servant."—Exod. 20: 8–11. The sacred festivals were opened to them, and along with their masters they were to rejoice before the Lord: they were also to present sacrifices and offerings to the Lord, in the appointed place and eat of them "before the Lord," with their masters. "Thou mayest not eat, within thy gates, the tithe of thy corn, or of thy wine, or of thy oil, or the firstlings of thy herds, or of thy flocks, nor any of thy vows which thou vowest, nor thy free will offerings, or heave offering of thine hand: but thou must eat them before the Lord, in the place which the Lord thy God shall choose, thou and thy son and thy daughter, and thy man-servant and thy maid-servant."—Deut. 12: 17, 18. "And thou shalt keep the feast of weeks: and thou shalt rejoice before the Lord thy God, thou, and thy son, and thy daughter, and thy man-servant, and thy maid-servant." So also "the feast of tabernacles."—Deut. 16: 1–16.

Thus in the Old Testament, the law of God, and the Sanctuary and all its privileges, were opened to servants and secured to them by the declared will of God: and it was the duty of masters to command their households after them, that they should keep the way of the Lord to do justice and judgment: otherwise the Lord would not bring upon them the promised blessings.

The New Testament is, if possible more explicit. In several epistles, the relation of master and servant is recognized, and the mutual duties of each arising out of that relation mutually insisted upon. Masters and servants are addressed as belonging to the same churches and heirs of the same grace of life: 1 Tim. 6: 1–5. Eph. Col.

What kind of servants are intended? Slaves: the original teaches us so, while the very duties enjoined upon servants and the observations made upon their condition, (1 Cor. 7: [sic]) confirms the fact that they were literally Slaves. And the kind of slavery that existed among the Jews was that allowed in the Old Testament; which may be considered identical with that which prevails amongst us at the present time; and no one will deny that the slavery which existed among the Greeks and Romans and Gentile nations, was identical with our own. All authentic history, and the codification of the Roman laws made in the reign of Justinian, prove it. The slaves were more heterogenous in their national origin, than ours. Among them however existed Negroes: and in no small numbers. Indeed a traffic in Negro slaves had been carried on for centuries before Isabella gave permission for their transportation to these western shores; and they were sold, and scattered over all the east.

When therefore the New Testament addresses commands to Masters, we are the identical persons intended. We are Masters in the New Testament sense. We are addressed as directly and as identically, as when we are Fathers, and it is said "Fathers provoke not your children to wrath."

And what are these commands? "And ye Masters, do the same things unto them, forbearing threatening: knowing that your Master also is in Heaven: neither is there respect of persons with him." Eph. 6: 9.

As servants are exhorted to fulfill their duties to their masters, "as the servants of Christ, doing the will of God from the heart:" having respect to their accountability to God; so also masters are exhorted to do the same things, to fulfill their duties to their servants, from the same principle of obedience to God and respect to future accountability.

"Masters give unto your servants that which is just and equal: knowing that ye also have a Master in Heaven." Col. 4: 1. Masters are here required to treat their servants justly and equitably, in respect, of course, to all their interests, both for time and eternity; for they shall account to God for the same.

Thus doth God put his finger upon us as Masters. He holds up before our faces our servants and our duties to them. He commands us to fulfil those duties under the pain of his displeasure. He tells us that in the performance of duty he does not respect us more than he respects them.

Can any one doubt that among the duties of Masters, is that of imparting, and causing to be imparted to them the Gospel of Salvation? Supposing Masters gave unto their servants that which was just and equal for this present life—and gave no more:—would that come up to the spirit and power of the command? Would it be just and equal for masters to suffer them to remain in ignorance of the way of salvation, to die and be eternally lost? Surely not. Says Job. "If I did despise the cause of my man-servant or of my maid-servant, when they contended with me: what shall I do when God riseth up? And when he visiteth what shall I answer him? Did not he that made me in the womb, make him? And did not one fashion us in the womb?" If we neglect to evangelize our servants, they may justly have a controversy with us; and if we continue to despise their cause, in the day when God riseth up for judgement, we shall be speechless.

Thus by the providence and word of God are we under obligations to impart the Gospel to our servants.

It may be added, that we cannot disregard this obligation thus divinely imposed, without forfeiting our humanity, our gratitude, our consistency, and our claim to the spirit of christianity itself.

Our Humanity

Humanity is that kindness and good will towards our fellow creatures which prompts us to sympathize with them in their necessities and sufferings, and to exert ourselves for their relief.

The Lord Jesus has furnished us with the most beautiful and striking illustrations of this virtue. "What man shall there be among you, that shall have one sheep, and if it fall into a pit: will he not lay hold on it and lift it out?" "Doth not each one of you, loose his ox or his ass from the stall and lead him away to watering? And ought not this woman being a daughter of Abraham, whom Satan hath bound, lo these eighteen years, be loosed from this bond?" Matt. 12: 10–13 Luke 13: 14–16, 14: 2–6. Apply the reasoning: "How much then is a man better than a sheep or an ox?" When our servants are sick and diseased, we do not suffer them to want; we physic and nurse them. But are not their souls more precious than their bodies? Much more then should we lift our servants from the pit of ignorance, moral pollution and death into which they have fallen. Much more should we strive to loose them (bound for so many years!) from the bonds of sin and satan and lead away their famishing souls to the water of life.

Our Gratitude

They nurse us in infancy, contribute to our pleasures and pastimes in youth; and furnish us with the means of education. They constitute our wealth, and yield us all the comforts and conveniences of life; they may in a degree adopt towards us, the language of Jacob to Laban, "thus I was: in the day the drought consumed me, and the frost by night and my sleep departed from mine eyes:" they watch around our languishing beds in sickness; share in our misfortunes, weep over us when we die; prepare us for the burial and carry us to the house appointed for all the living.

The obligations, the sacrifice and service are not to be all on one side, in the relation of master and servant. If we have been made partakers of their carnal things, our duty is also to minister unto them in spiritual things, Rom. 15: 27. 1 Cor. 9: 11. And shall we consider it "a great thing" to fulfil this duty? The kindest and the most grateful return which we can make them, is to put them in possession of the richest gift of God to men, the Gospel of our Lord and Saviour Jesus Christ.

If we neglect to do this, we shall forfeit also our consistency.

Consistency is the correspondence of our conduct or practice with our professed principles. Ezra 8: 22. And it is an exceedingly rare virtue.

As philanthropists and christians, we are contributing of our substance; and offering up our prayers, that Christ's kingdom may come, and that his Gospel may be preached to every people under heaven. We have indeed assisted in sending missionaries to the heathen, thousands of miles from us; and to multitudes of destitute white settlements in our own country; in founding Theological Seminaries and filling them with students, that the demand for laborers in the great harvest might be supplied. We have assisted in having the gospel preached in our public prisons; in the harbors of our sea-port cities, and along the lines of our canals and the shores of our lakes and rivers, to those who do business on the great waters. We have assisted in gathering the children of parents of every condition into Sabbath Schools; and in efforts to stay the swellings of the fiery waves of intemperance. We have been printing Bibles and tracts and religious works, with which to supply every family and every individual in our land, and also to meet the urgent demands for the same from other lands. This is all as it should be. But what have we done publicly, systematically and perseveringly for the Negroes, in order that they also might enjoy the gospel of Christ? Why are they as a class overlooked by us in our benevolent regards and efforts? What blindness hath happened to us in part, that we cannot see their spiritual necessities and feel the claims which they undeniably have upon us? Our Lord in view of our works, will say to us, "these ought ye to have done and not to leave the other undone."

We cannot cry out against the Papists for withholding the Scriptures from the common people and keeping them in ignorance of the way of life, for our inconsistency is as great as theirs, if we withhold the Bible from our servants, and keep them in ignorance of its saving truths, which we certainly do while we will not provide ways and means of having it read and explained to them.

The celebrated John Randolph, on a visit to a female friend, found her surrounded with her seamstresses, making up a quantity of clothing. "What work have you in hand?" "O sir, I am preparing this clothing to send to the poor Greeks." On taking leave at the steps of the mansion, he saw some of her servants in need of the very clothing which their tender-hearted mistress was sending abroad. He exclaimed, "Madam, madam, the Greeks are at your door!"

If we neglect to impart the Gospel to the Negroes, our inconsistency will be most glaring and shameful.

And furthermore, we shall forfeit our claim to the spirit of Christianity itself.

The remarks under the head of consistency evidenced this position, but nevertheless it will allow of a distinct consideration.

This spirit is love. "Thou shalt love the Lord thy God with all thy heart, with all thy mind, and with all thy strength; and thy neighbor as thyself." Love is of God. "He that loveth is born of God, for God is love." "In this was manifested the love of God towards us, because that God sent his only begotten Son into the world, that we might live through him."—1 John 4: 7–11. His love has respect to the immortal souls of men; their everlasting salvation. For this our Lord Jesus Christ came into the world and labored, suffered and died on the cross. The same spirit is wrought in the hearts of all who are truly his disciples. Their chief joy is the glory of God in the salvation of men; the increase of the church upon the earth. The cherished and ever-living desire of their soul is that men may be converted to God. To effect this conversion they willingly labor and submit to sacrifices, even, if need be, unto death. This is the spirit which burns and glows in all the word of God; unquenchable—invincible in its progress, because originated and sustained by the grace and power of the Almighty.

"I am a debtor both to the Greeks and to the Barbarians, both to the wise and to the unwise. So, as much as in me is, I am ready to preach the Gospel to you that are at Rome also. For I am not ashamed of the Gospel of Christ; for it is the power of God unto salvation, to every one that believeth; to the Jew first and also to the Greek." "I say the truth in Christ, I lie not, my conscience also bearing me witness in the Holy Ghost; that I have great heaviness and continual sorrow of heart. For I could wish that myself were accursed from Christ for my brethren, my kinsmen according to the flesh."—Rom. 1: 14–16, and 9: 1–3. "For the love of Christ constraineth us because we thus judge that if one died for all, then were all dead: and he died for all that they which live, should not henceforth live unto themselves, but unto him which died for them, and rose again."—2 Cor. 5: 14–15. "I will very gladly spend and be spent for you (for your souls,")—12: 15. "Yea, and if I be offered (i.e. my strength and life offered up,) upon the sacrifice and service of your faith, I joy and rejoice with you all."—Phil. 2: 17.

Where then this spirit is wanting, there is wanting the very spirit of Christianity itself. "The salt has lost his savor; wherewith shall it be salted? It is thenceforth good for nothing, but to be cast out, and to be trodden under foot of men!"—Mat. 5: 13–16.

The idea that we possess the spirit of Christianity in its perfection, while we constantly and directly neglect the evangelization of the Negroes, when it lies within our power, is preposterous in the extreme. We are neither "the light of the world:" nor "the salt of the earth."

Reverse the order of Providence. Let us recur to the illustration already adduced. Were we in the condition of the Negro, and he in our condition, able to read and to appreciate the Gospel: experimentally acquainted with it: a partaker of its privileges and of its eternal hopes; would we consider it his duty, (a duty which he was well able to perform,) to make us partakers with himself in the Gospel: that Gospel to which we have a right as the gift of God to all men; and which we could claim at his hands as the divinely appointed almoner of God's mercy to us: that Gospel which is every thing to perishing sinners and which alone could yield us happiness in our humble lot? Certainly we should. Suppose he would or he did not? Could we believe that he sincerely felt all the amazing and soul-stirring truths which the Gospel contains? Could we believe that he possessed the spirit of the Gospel? No, no! We could not!

"There is that scattereth and yet increaseth; and there is that withholdeth more than is meet, and it tendeth to poverty. The liberal soul shall be made fat, and he that watereth shall be watered also himself. He that withholdeth corn, the people shall curse him; but blessing shall be upon the head of him that selleth it."—Prov. 11: 24–6. "Now if any man have not the spirit of Christ, he is none of his."—Rom. 8: 9.

"Whoso hath this world's goods and seeth his brother have need and shutteth up his bowels of compassion from him, how dwelleth the love of God in him?"—1 John 3: 16–20. With more tremendous emphasis let it be asked "Whoso hath the word of eternal life and seeth his brother have need, and shutteth up his bowels of compassion from him, how dwelleth the love of God in him? Let this question be answered to that God who without respect of persons judgeth according to every man's work!["]

Such are the considerations which we must address to ourselves, who reside in the Southern States, in order that we may be awakened to the great duty of imparting the Gospel to the Negroes.

2. *We now turn to the Negroes in the free States.*

And our remarks on the duty of affording them the Gospel, need not be protracted after what has been said.

It is the duty of the white churches in the free States to afford the Gospel to the Negroes, for the following plain reasons among others.

1. *Because of their general poverty.*

They are, as a class, a poor people; among, if not, "the poor of the land." And consequently are not able to give suitable encouragement to the institutions of religion; not able to build churches, support ministers, or buy books and maintain Sabbath schools. The means must come from purses other than their own. Such has been the fact in the majority of instances where the Gospel has received an adequate support among them. More than the majority have little or nothing to give; they barely make out to obtain the necessaries of life.

2. Because of their moral degradation.

This has been in a measure demonstrated. The statements already made need not be repeated. They are a proper field for missionary effort; and have been to a great extent, very strangely overlooked. Such a mass of ignorance and vice can in no way be desirable in any community, whether we view them in a civil or religious light. Their corrupting influence in cities, where they chiefly congregate, has never been inquired into, nor duly appreciated.

3. Because of their entire dependence upon the whites for their every improvement.

They have almost no spirit of moral improvement among themselves; it is not to be expected from them considering their character and circumstances. They have no men of influence, no leaders of their own color, who are able to sway the people; to project and execute plans for their general religious improvement. Nor have they societies of their own for the purpose. The truth is, they do not look to themselves; they do not depend upon themselves. They look up to and depend upon the whites. The feeling of subjection and dependence which they had in a state of slavery, is hereditary and is kept alive by the frequent accession of Negroes, escaped from servitude or set free. Then the vast superiority of the whites in point of numbers, intelligence, morality, and station, cherish it. Hence the efforts of the whites for their benefit are received with special favor and relied upon. At least it was so in times past. They have of late years been taught to distinguish between friendly and hostile whites; and they have been inflated with high notions of their perfect equality with the whites in wisdom, standing, rights, and importance. The effect has been, and it should not be deemed extraordinary, that they have become rather heady and high-minded; some of their friends have not been able to do them the good that they wished; and others disgusted, have ceased to feel and to act for them. Whether they will be ultimately benefitted by this increase of knowledge and sense of importance, remains to be seen.

4. Because of consistency.

The efforts for the moral and religious improvement of the Negroes in the free States, do not correspond with the profession of interest in them, as a class of people.

With some, the bestowment of freedom is the sum of all duty. And freedom is the grand catholicon for all the evils which harrass and oppress the colored man. It has not proved exactly so, in the free States.

There are districts in Rhode Island, in New Jersey, New York, and Delaware, once peopled with Negroes. They were emancipated on the soil, and now there is scarcely one to be seen. They have been scattered and driven off, and have melted away before the whites. Their few descendants are "making out to live" in cities, and in country situations, here and there. At the present day the Negroes are not reached as a class by education and religion. They are not a desirable population— so confessed on all hands; and their intelligence, morality and thrift in the free States, give but poor encouragement to the doctrine of emancipation in those parts of the Union where they are held to service.

The overwhelming majority in the free States are whites. They possess all the intelligence, wealth, and power; and move on without disturbance from the few Negroes among them. The weight of the Negroes upon the wheels of society is scarcely felt. But what would be the state of things if the whites were in the minority and they the majority? I shall not undertake to furnish an answer to the question which every man of ordinary consideration can do for himself the moment after it is put to him. The great duty of the churches and friends of the Negroes in the free States, is to attempt, more systematically and efficiently, their moral and religious improvement. . . .

CHAPTER IV. BENEFITS

LET us proceed to the more agreeable employment of showing the Benefits, which would flow from the religious instruction of the Negroes. . . . Religion will tell the master that he is a master "according to the flesh," only; that his servants are fellow-creatures, and he has a master in heaven to whom he shall finally account for his treatment of them. Religion will tell the servant "to be obedient to masters according to the flesh, with fear and trembling, in singleness of heart as unto Christ; knowing that whatsoever good thing any man doeth, the same shall he receive of the Lord whether he be bond or free." The master will be led to inquiries of this sort. In what kind of houses do I permit them to live; what clothes do I give them to wear; what food to eat; what privileges to enjoy? In what temper and manner, and in what proportion to their crimes do I allow them to be punished? What care do I take of their family relations? What am I doing for their souls' salvation? In fine, what does God require me to do to, and for them and their children, in view of their happiness here and hereafter? Light will insensibly break into his mind. Conscience will be quickened, and before he is aware perhaps, his servants will be greatly elevated in his regards, and he will feel himself bound and willing to do more and more for them. The government of his plantation will not be so purely selfish as formerly. His interest will not be the sole object of pursuit, nor offences against that visited with sorer punishment than offences against God himself. He will have an eye to the comfort, the interest of his people, and endeavor to identify their interest with his, and also to make them see and feel it to be so. It will be a delight to him to see them enjoy the blessings of the providence and the grace of God.

Such an attempt at a discharge of duty on religious grounds, will produce favorable influences, upon the feelings and conduct of servants. Religion will cause them to understand their duties better, and to perform them more perfectly and cheerfully.

The pecuniary interests of masters will be advanced as a necessary consequence.

I do not mean that the introduction of the Gospel upon a plantation in and of itself puts new life and vigor into the laborers and the soil which they cultivate, and necessarily makes them more profitable to owners, than plantations where the Gospel is not introduced at all. By no means. Such a statement would be unfounded in fact. For there are owners who take no pains whatever to have their Negroes instructed; but who feed and clothe and lodge them well, and are humane and take the best care of them, and by careful, skilful and pushing management, go far beyond their religious neighbors in their incomes. But I mean, that religious instruction is no detriment, but rather a benefit: that, other things being equal, the plantation which enjoys religious instruction will do better for the interests of its owner, than it did before it enjoyed such instruction. Virtue is more profitable than vice; while this is allowed to be no discovery, no man will question its truth.

Increased attention to the temporal comfort of servants would improve their health; and the expense of lost labor by sickness, and of physicians' bills would be saved. Their wants being more liberally supplied and sharing more largely in the fruit of their labors, many temptations to theft, to which they are exposed, would be removed; and they would become more industrious and saving. Crime would be diminished. For teachers in order to reformation, would charge upon the Negroes the sins to which they are most addicted and expose their enormity and consequent punishment in the world to come. They are sometimes found guilty of notorious sins and scarcely know that they are sins at all. Religious instruction would lead them to respect each other more, to pay greater regard to mutual character and rights; the strong would not so much oppress the weak; family relations would be less liable to rupture; in short, all the social virtues would be more honored and cultivated. Their work would be more faithfully done; their obedience more universal and more cheerfully rendered. The genuine effects of religion upon them would be, "with good will doing service, as to the Lord and not unto men."

And who can tell the pleasurable feelings of a humane and Christian master, in view of a moral reformation of his servants? He will thank God that he is, if not wholly, yet measurably relieved from perpetual watching, from fault-finding and threatening and heart-sickening severity; and that he can begin at least to govern somewhat by the law of love. The good character of his people render them more valuable as property, and even should he not make as much as formerly, the loss is more than balanced by what he sees his people enjoy and by the comfort and satisfaction which he possesses himself. The religious instruction of the Negroes will contribute to safety.

"The thing that hath been it is that which may be;" and although, as a slave-holding country, we are so situated, that, so far as man can see, the hope of success on the part of our laboring class, in any attempt at revolution is forlorn, yet no enemy (if there be an enemy) should be despised, however weak, and no danger unprovided for, however apparently remote. Success may not indeed crown any attempt, but much suffering may be the consequence both on the one part and on the other. It is then but a prudent foresight, a dictate of benevolence and of wisdom, to originate and set in operation means that may act as a check upon, if not a perfect preventive of evil.

I am a firm believer in the efficacy of sound religious instruction, as a means to the end desired. And reasons may be given for that belief. They are to be discovered in the very nature and tendency of the Gospel. Its nature is peace, in the broadest and fullest extent of the word. Its tendency, even when its transforming influence upon character is not realized, is to soften down and curb the passions of man; to make him more respectful of another's interests, and more solicitous of his favor; more obedient under authority, and patient under injuries; and to enhance infinitely in his estimation the value of human life. His conscience is enlightened and his soul is awed. He knows God reigns to execute judgment, and it will require greater effort to excite him to unhallowed deeds. But when character is transformed by the Gospel, its nature and tendency are perfected. The servant recognizes a superintending Providence, who disposes of men and things according to his pleasure; that his Gospel comes not with reckless efforts to wrench apart society and break governments into pieces, but to define clearly the relations and duties of men, and to lay down and render authoritative, those general principles of moral conduct which will result in the happiness of the whole, and in the peaceable removal of every kind of evil and injustice.—To God, therefore, he commits the ordering of his lot, and in his station renders to all their dues, obedience to whom obedience, and honor to whom honor. He dares not wrest from the hand of God his own care and protection. While he sees a preference in the various conditions of men he remembers the words of the Apostle:— "Art thou called being a servant? Care not for it; but if thou mayest be free, use it rather. For he that is called in the Lord, being a servant, is the Lord's freeman: likewise, also, he that is called being free, is Christ's servant. Ye are bought with a price, be not ye the servants of men. Brethren, let every man wherein he is called, therein abide with God."

Besides the general and special influences of the Gospel now adverted to, safety will be connected with the very dispensation of it, in two particulars, which I would not omit to mention. The first is:—The very effort of masters to instruct their people, creates a strong bond of union and draws out their kindly feelings to their masters: kindness produces kindness: love begets its own likeness. The presence also of white instructors, settled ministers or missionaries, in their private as well as public religious assemblies and free intercourse with the people and with their influential men and leaders, exert a restraining influence upon any spirit of insubordination that may exist, and at the same time give opportunities for its detection. The Negroes are as capable of strong personal attachments to their religious instructors as are any other people; and of their own will are inclined to make confidential communications.

The second particular is, that the Gospel being dispensed in its purity, the Negroes will be disabused of their ignorance and superstition, and thus be placed beyond the reach of designing men. The direct way of exposing them to acts of insubordination is to leave them in ignorance and superstition, to the care of their own religion. Then may the blind lead the blind, and both shall fall into the ditch: then may they be made the easy and willing instruments of avarice, of lust, of power or of revenge. Ignorance—religious ignorance—so far from being any safety, is the very marrow of our sin against this people, and the very rock of our danger. Religion and religious teachers they must and will have, and if they are not furnished with the true they will embrace the false. . . . That the Negroes are intellectually and morally, in a degraded state, I trust will not be denied; and of course no man acquainted with human nature, will deny that constant connection and intercourse with a degraded people, will exert a deleterious influence upon persons of more elevated character, if there be not some peculiar causes in existence, or some special effort made, to counteract it. I do not hesitate to say that the influence of the Negroes on the general intelligence and morality of the whites is not good. There are those who deny it. I differ with them, and am happy in believing that the majority of my fellow citizens are with me. We are so accustomed to sin in the Negroes (which in them appears a matter of course,) that our sensibilities are blunted.

When we cease to "abhor that which is evil," we shall not long "cleave to that which is good." "First endure—then embrace"; is as true in sober prose as in flippant poetry. Planters will generally confess that the management of Negroes is not only attended with trouble and vexation from time to time, but with provocations to sin. Masters and mistresses of families have their trials. And the kind of influence which Negroes exert over our children and youth, when permitted to associate with them, is well known to all careful and observing parents.

Now we shall defend ourselves from the injuries to our moral and religious character, received through our colored population, by their religious instruction, at least in very large measure. And on the principle or promise of the word of God, "he that waters shall be watered also himself." God bestows his blessing immediately upon those who do their duty. There is also a rebound for good, in benevolent action. The effort to do good, strengthens the principle from which it proceeds. The way to strengthen and increase holiness in the soul is to abound in works of holiness. It is by giving our talents to the exchangers that we gain other talents.

By taking in hand the religious instruction of the Negroes, an ample field will be opened for the most vigorous exercise of the piety and zeal and talents of the church; a great proportion of which is now rusting for want of use. And when it pleases God to give success to our labors, and we see them assuming a higher standard of morals; the current of their opinions turning against ignorance and vice, their appearance and deportment becoming more respectable, we shall be favorably affected ourselves. As the one class rises so will the other; the two are so intimately associated they are apt to rise or fall together; to benefit servants, evangelize the masters; to benefit masters, evangelize the servants. Much unpleasant discipline will be saved to the churches.

Appendix Two

Herbie Hancock's Approach

This interview outlines aspects of Herbie Hancock's approach to life and sheds light on his perception of Buddhism and its value. It is taken from "Feature: Creativity, Music and the Human Spirit," *SGI Quarterly* No. 24 (April 2001). Used by permission.

The Art of Life: Interview with Herbie Hancock
Herbie Hancock

Can you talk about what it means to live a creative life?

At this point in my life, my primary focus is not on the art form that my career has been built around to date. What I focus on primarily is the real source—or the purpose—that my art form, music, is about. That is, life itself.

At the foundation of artistic expression is the very core of life. So what I'm finding is that the more I attempt to expand and develop my life, the greater the impact is on my music. Music becomes a tool for that expression. My focus is to practice this particular art form with the hope that ultimately it will be a catalyst in the listeners' appreciation of their own lives. My hope is not particularly that the audience will be inspired by my music and put me on a pedestal. That's not what it's about. I hope that somehow it triggers something within themselves where they feel that their life has more meaning, substance and inspiration. That they become more aware of something that is already in them.

That's the hope. And I think that where one is "coming from" is extremely important. Your vision for that pathway, your intention, is very important.

There seems to be a big distance between what you are saying and the general understanding of creative talent, or genius.

There is a tendency for people to be very forgiving about the attitude of the artist, as long as the artistic expression pleases them. They almost expect an artist to be a little weird and a little egotistical, rude. But I'm very much against that. One very strong realization that I have at this point is that the most important art is one everyone is involved in, the art of living. And that is the most difficult one, the most important one to master and develop. And so everyone is an artist in that sense. This really helps me in my own appreciation of the lives of others.

What did you learn working with great masters like Miles Davis?

I've been speaking pretty generally, but to be specific, there are certain characteristics that I strive to be aware of as being very important, and one of them is risk-taking. But, I have to add, with a sense of responsibility. Without a sense of responsibility you can get yourself in a lot of trouble taking risks. Miles very much supported the idea of taking risks with the music. That's what he wanted us to do. He wanted us to constantly try to work on things, and constantly try to find new ways of expressing ourselves. So he very much encouraged risk-taking. As a matter of fact, he wasn't concerned at all about our mistakes. He was much more concerned about the courage that it takes to make mistakes. When you're on the edge, then you will make "mistakes"; if you're reaching for something, there will be "mistakes"—it's not going to sound so perfect. But it's the search and the honesty and the integrity that people can feel. They can hear it and they can feel it in their hearts. And that is what touches and moves them.

It is my Buddhist practice that is at the core of these realizations that I've had. It has really opened my eyes to things that I have observed and heard from my musical mentors. And I've been able to see how the things I have learned about creating music can be applied to life.

I've learned that any situation can be viewed from an infinite number of vantage points. With Miles I got that through music. I learned that a composition, a tune, a piece of music written by someone, is one example, one expression, of an idea. A jazz musician can take that song and, through the realization that it is an example, can create other examples by looking for other ways to view the piece of music.

That concept can also be applied to daily life. There is a natural tendency for us as human beings to see the situations that happen to us from one vantage point. But what Buddhism teaches us, and what life teaches us, is that a situation can be looked at in many, many different ways. And the way we look at that situation, and how we deal with it as a result of seeing it from other vantage points, can determine whether that life situation is going to have a negative or a positive effect on our future.

There are many things we get exposed to that at the outset appear to be negative, appear to be an obstacle or a problem. "Why did this happen to me?" That kind of reaction. But it is through those challenges that one can develop a strong foundation, deeper roots and an appreciation of one's own ability to overcome obstacles and to grow from them. This gives one a sense of self-worth. We can actually come to appreciate the obstacles themselves, and we can develop a deeper appreciation for our own life. So challenges are really an opportunity to get us closer to freedom. Real freedom is when you're not afraid of any situation that might happen to you in the future.

Can you talk about the relationship between creativity and suffering?

There is a tendency for people to feel that an artist has to suffer, or pay his dues, in order to have a message that can translate as feeling through his art form. I don't deny the importance of having things to deal with in one's life, or how these can be instrumental in stimulating the creative juices. But what I realize at this point is that if you're striving hard to challenge yourself, whether it is through your art form, or whatever kind of job you may have, or with your family, or just the daily life that you live, there is no way you can avoid experiencing suffering to some degree. And it is through these sufferings and challenges that you can not only stimulate the creative juices but also develop a sense of self-sufficiency or autonomy. If you are not confronting such situations, it means either that you're not challenging your life or your art or that you're asleep, sleeping on the job, so to speak.

There is no one who can escape from suffering. Because materialism is so rampant and out of balance today, there's a tendency to think that if you're rich and you have the "right car," the "right job," a spouse or a mate, all those trappings, then you can be happy. When in fact it doesn't work that way. The most valuable qualities of life are priceless; they cannot be bought or sold. And they have more to do with recognizing that you can overcome situations in your life, recognizing that obstacles are the means for growth in your life, with developing compassion and appreciation for the people in your life, for the environment that we live in. Developing courage. There are so many important qualities that give life meaning and beauty and that dwarf that kind of materialistic viewpoint. Of course we all do need to be able to survive in life, but I think things have gone just too far in the materialistic direction.

Technology is often seen as a dehumanizing force in society. Do you think it also has creative possibilities to offer?

As far as I can tell, there haven't been any real attempts to start a movement to explore the possible uses of technology to address the real issues of everyday life, the real problems. Like problems with peer pressure, man's inhumanity toward man, social problems, problems with sexism, problems with drugs, situations to do with sexual identity. All of the real things that people have to deal with in everyday life. I haven't seen anybody really attempt to explore the use of technology for those things. People in the world of technology have a tendency to be dazzled by it. And they think it is really helping the world—"Look how fast things are moving!" But look at the newspapers. Look at the front page, look at the first five pages. How many situations do you see in those first five pages where technology is being used? Generally, the answer is "none" because those possibilities haven't really been explored.

The most important art is one everyone is involved in, the art of living. And that is the most difficult one, the most important one to master and develop.

I've been noticing that quite often today you see the word "knowledge" or the word "information," especially in this new technological age. The word that seems to have disappeared from the vocabulary is the word "wisdom." You never see that anymore.

What most concerns me is that the human being is no longer the fulcrum, or the focus of life. It's somewhere low down on the list of priorities. If human happiness is not at the top of our concerns, then none of the other elements will have any meaning. What purpose is there for technology unless it somehow serves the human spirit and our relationship to the environment in which we live?

One of the initiatives that I've started is to explore the use of technology to address these human issues and concerns. I've started a foundation called the Rhythm of Life Foundation that will collect money for individuals and organizations that are doing this. I started to realize, once I embarked on that project, that I needed a means to develop some examples. So we formed the Rhythm of Life Organization (ROLO). Our first project is one we are conducting in the San Francisco Bay Area with the acronym BAYCAT, Bay View-Hunter's Point Center for the Arts and Technology. The idea for this school that we want to build is not only to be able to give young people access to high-end computers but also to teach them programming with the hope of encouraging them to develop software that deals with the issues that they face in everyday life. We want to encourage them to come up with new visions for the use of technology.

If you think about it, the people who built the technological age are now in the process of adapting to the age that they themselves built, whereas people who were born into it don't have to adapt. It comes naturally to them.

Why do you think it is important to work with young people?

In the 1960s, a lot of major changes were instigated by people in their early teens. What they did really changed the world in many ways. I think that in the not-too-distant future, if we are lucky, a very similar kind of revolution can happen globally through the efforts of people in their teens. I am afraid that if something like this does not happen, not only is the future going to be rocky, but it will become more and more dangerous.

One of the things that I have realized is that so many of the problems that people have to face day-to-day are not problems created by the "have-nots." They've been primarily created by the "haves." Because, unlike the have-nots, the haves have been in the position to have that kind of global impact.

What we need is to create a table of life where everyone is encouraged to bring whatever it is that they may have to offer.

To be honest, I consider myself one of the haves. I'm one of the fortunate ones in life, on the planet. But there is a tendency for people who might be considered the haves to think that the have-nots have nothing to bring to the table of life. The haves, with all of their philanthropic intentions, are often coming from a position of arrogance, thinking that they are the only ones who have the capacity to bring anything to the table. There is a tendency for the haves to feel inherently superior to the have-nots, thinking that the have-nots are stupid, not bright enough. But what they don't realize is that it is not the have-nots who have created the problems for the world.

What we need is to create a table of life where everyone is encouraged to bring whatever it is that they may have to offer. You can never tell where the next great concepts can come from. It may be from any place on the planet, including those places that are ignored, forgotten or even looked down upon. Unless we provide a means so that everyone may come to the table of life to bring what they have to offer, we can never experience the advantage of their impact in helping move life forward.

Very often the have-nots, in order to survive and overcome, have had to learn certain lessons in life. The haves may need that kind of creativity, wisdom and vision. Part of the undercurrent of ideas for the Rhythm of Life Organization comes from this kind of realization. The fact that on this planet we all need each other. And we need to help put each other in the position to provide the things we all need to move forward together.

Appendix Three

The Benefits of the End of Slavery

In this essay, Nathaniel Paul explores the religious and political benefits of the end of slavery. Nathaniel Paul, *An Address Delivered on the Celebration of the Abolition of Slavery in the State of New York* (July 5, 1827) [Albany: John D. Van Steenbergh, 1827]. This is the complete manuscript of the address. For an adapted version see: Milton C. Sernett, ed., *Afro-American Religious History: A Documentary Witness* (Durham, NC: Duke University Press, 1985), 180–87.

The Celebration of the Abolition of Slavery

Through THE LONG LAPSE of ages, it has been common for nations to record whatever was peculiar or interesting in the course of their history. Thus when Heaven, provoked by the iniquities of man, has visited the earth with the pestilence which moves in darkness or destruction, that wasteth at noonday, and has swept from existence, by thousands, its numerous inhabitants; or when the milder terms of mercy have been dispensed in rich abundance, and the goodness of God has crowned the efforts of any people with peace and prosperity; they have been placed upon their annals, and handed down to future ages, both for their amusement and profit. And as the nations which have already passed away, have been careful to select the most important events, peculiar to themselves, and have recorded them for the good of the people that should succeed them, so will we place it upon our history; and we will tell the good story to our children and to our children's children, down to the latest posterity, that on the fourth day of July, in the year of our Lord 1827, slavery was abolished in the State of New York.

Seldom, if ever, was there an occasion which required a public acknowledgment, or that deserved to be retained with gratitude of heart to the all-wise disposer of events, more than the present on which we have assembled.

It is not the mere gratification of the pride of the heart, or any vain ambitious notion, that has influenced us to make our appearance in the public streets of our city, or to assemble in the sanctuary of the Most High this morning; but we have met to offer our tribute of thanksgiving and praise to almighty God for his goodness; to retrace the acts and express our gratitude to our public benefactors, and to stimulate each other to the performance of every good and virtuous act, which now does, or hereafter may devolve as a duty upon us, as freemen and citizens, in common with the rest of the community.

And if ever it were necessary for me to offer an apology to an audience for my absolute inability to perform a task assigned to me, I feel that the present is the period. However, relying, for support on the hand of Him who said, "I will never leave nor forsake"; and confiding in your charity for every necessary allowance, I venture to engage in the arduous undertaking.

In contemplating the subject before us, in connection with the means by which so glorious an event has been accomplished, we find much which requires our deep humiliation and our most exalted praises. We are permitted to behold one of the most pernicious and abominable of all enterprises, in which the depravity of human nature ever led man to engage, entirely eradicated. The power of the tyrant is subdued, the heart of the oppressed is cheered, liberty is proclaimed to the captive, and the opening of the prison to those who were bound, and he who had long been the miserable victim of cruelty and degradation, is elevated to the common rank in which our benevolent Creator first designed, that man should move—all of which have been effected by means the most simple, yet perfectly efficient: Not by those fearful judgements of the almighty, which have so often fell upon the different parts of the earth; which have, overturned nations and kingdoms; scattered thrones and sceptres; nor is the glory of the achievement, tarnished with the horrors of the field of battle. We hear not the cries of the widow and the fatherless; nor are our hands affected with the sight of garments rolled in blood; but all has been done by the diffusion and influence of the pure, yet powerful principles of benevolence, before which the pitiful impotency of tyranny and oppression, is scattered and dispersed, like the chaff before the rage of the whirlwind.

I will not, on this occasion, attempt fully to detail the abominations of the traffic to which we have already alluded. Slavery, with its concomitants and consequences, in the best attire in which it can possibly be presented, is but a hateful monster, the very demon of avarice and oppression, from its first introduction to the present time; it has been among all nations the scourge of heaven, and the curse of the earth. It is so contrary to the laws which the God of nature has laid down as the rule of action by which the conduct of man is to be regulated towards his fellow man, which binds him to love his neighbor as himself, that it ever has, and ever will meet the decided disapprobation of heaven.

In whatever form we behold it, its visage is satanic, its origin the very offspring of hell, and in all cases its effects are grievous.

On the shore of Africa, the horror of the scene commences; here, merciless tyrant, divested of everything human, except form, begins the action. The laws of God and the tears of the oppressed are alike disregarded; and with more than savage barbarity, husbands and wives, parents and children, are parted to meet no more: and, if not doomed to an untimely death, while on the passage, yet are they for life consigned to a captivity still more terrible; a captivity, at the very thought of which, every heart, not already biased with unhallowed prejudices, or callous to every tender impression, pauses and revolts; exposed to the caprice of those whose tender mercies are cruel; unprotected by the laws of the land, and doomed to drag out miserable existence, without the remotest shadow of a hope of deliverance, until the king of terrors shall have executed his office, and consigned them to the kinder slumbers of death. But its pernicious tendency may be traced still farther: not only are its effects of the most disastrous character, in relation to the slave, but it extends its influence to the slave holder; and in many instances it is hard to say which is most wretched, the slave or the master.

After the fall of man, it would seem that God, forseeing that pride and arrogance would be the necessary consequences of the apostasy, and that man would seek to usurp undue authority over his fellow, wisely ordained that he should obtain his bread by the sweat of his brow; but contrary to this sacred mandate of heaven, slavery has been introduced, supporting the one in all the absurd luxuries of life, at the expense of the liberty and independence of the other. Point me to any section of the earth where slavery, to any considerable extent exists, and I will point you to a people whose morals are corrupted; and when pride, vanity and profusion are permitted to range unrestrained in all their desolating effects, and thereby idleness and luxury are promoted, under the influence of which, man, becoming insensible of his duty to his God and his fellow creature; and indulging in all pride and vanity of his own heart, says to his soul, thou hast much goods laid up for many years. But while thus sporting, can it be done with impunity? Has conscious ceased to be active? Are there forebodings of a future day of punishment, and of meeting the merited avenger? Can he retire after the business of the day and repose in safety? Let the guards around his mansion, the barred doors of his sleeping room, the loaded instruments of death beneath his pillow, answer the question. And if this were all, it would become us, perhaps, to cease to murmur, and bow in silent submission to that providence which had ordained this present state of existence, to be but a life of degradation and suffering.

Since affliction is but the common lot of men, this life, at best, is but a vapor that ariseth and soon passeth away. Man, said the inspired sage, that is born of a woman, is of few days and full of trouble; and in a certain sense, it is not material what our present situation may be, for short is the period that humbles all to dust, and places the monarch and the beggar, the slave and the master, upon equal thrones. But although this life is short, and attended with one entire scene of anxious perplexity, and few and evil are the days of our pilgrimage; yet man is advancing to another state of existence, bounded only by the vast duration of eternity! In which happiness or misery await us all. The author of our existence has marked out the way that leads to the glories of the upper world, and through the redemption which is in Christ Jesus, salvation is offered to all. But slavery forbids even the approach of mercy; it stands as a barrier in the way to ward off the influence of divine grace; it shuts up the avenues of the soul, and prevents its receiving divine instruction; and scarce does it permit its miserable captives to know that there is a God, a Heaven or a Hell.

Its more than detestable picture has been attempted to be portrayed by the learned, and the wise, but all have fallen short, and acknowledged their inadequacy to the task, and have been compelled to submit, by merely giving an imperfect shadow of its reality. Even the immortal Wilberforce, a name that can never die while Africa lives, after exerting his ingenuity, and exhausting the strength of his masterly mind, resigns the effort, and calmly submits by saying, "never was there, indeed, a system so replete with wickedness and cruelty to whatever part of it we turn our eyes; we could find no comfort, no satisfaction, no relief. It was the gracious ordinance of providence, both in the natural and moral world, that good should often arise out of evil. Hurricanes clean the air; and the propagation of truth was promoted by persecution, pride, vanity, and profusion contributed often, in their remoter consequences, to the happiness of mankind. In common, what was in itself evil and vicious, was permitted to carry along with it some circumstances of palliation. The Arab was hospitable, the robber brave; we did not necessarily find cruelty associated with fraud or meanness with injustice. But here the case was far otherwise. It was the prerogative of this detestable traffic, to separate from evil its concomitant good, and to reconcile discordant mischief. It robbed war of its generosity, it deprived peace of its security. We saw in it the vices of polished society, without its knowledge or its comforts, and the evils of barbarism without its simplicity; no age, no sex, no rank, no condition, was exempt from the fatal influence of this wide wasting calamity. Thus it attained to the fullest measure pure, unmixed, unsophisticated wickedness; and scorning all competition or comparison, it stood without rival in the secure and undisputed possession of its detestable pre-eminence." Such were the views of this truly great and good man, together with his fellow philanthropists, took of this subject, and such are the strong terms in which he has seen fit to express his utter abhorrence of its origin and effects. Thus have we hinted at some of the miseries connected with slavery. And while I turn my thoughts back and survey what is past, I see our forefathers seized by the hand of the rude ruffian, and torn from their native homes and all that they held dear or sacred. I follow them down the lonesome way, until I see each safely placed on board the gloomy slave ship; I hear the passive groan, and the clanking of the chains which bind them. I see the tears which follow each other in quick succession adown the dusky cheek.

I view them casting the last and longing look towards the land which gave them birth, until at length the ponderous anchor is weighed, and the canvas spread to catch the favored breeze; I view them wafted onward until they arrive at the destined port; I behold those who have been so unfortunate as to survive the passage, emerging from their loathsome prison, and landing amidst the noisy rattling of the massy fetters which confine them; I see the crowd of traffickers in human flesh gathering, each anxious to seize the favored opportunity of enriching himself with their toils, their tears and their blood. I view them doomed to the most abject state of degraded misery, and exposed to suffer all that unrestrained tyranny can inflict, or that human nature is capable of sustaining.

Tell me, ye mighty waters, why did ye sustain the ponderous load of misery? Or speak, ye winds, and say why it was that ye executed your office to waft them onward to the still more dismal state; and ye proud waves, why did you refuse to lend your aid and to overwhelm them with your billows? Then should they have slept sweetly in the bosom of the great deep, and so have been hid from sorrow. And, oh thou immaculate God, be not angry with us, while we come into this thy sanctuary, and make the bold inquiry in this thy holy temple, why it was that thou didst look on with the calm indifference of an unconcerned spectator, when thy holy law was violated, thy divine authority despised and a portion of thine own creatures reduced to a state of mere vassalage and misery? Hark! While he answers from on high: hear him proclaiming from the skies—Be still, and know that I am God! Clouds and darkness are round about me; yet righteousness and judgement are the habitation of my throne. I do my will and pleasure in the heavens above, and in the earth beneath; it is my sovereign prerogative to bring good out of evil, and cause the wrath of man to praise me, and the remainder of that wrath I will restrain.

Strange, indeed, is the idea, that such a system, fraught with such consummate wickedness, should ever have found a place in this the otherwise happiest of all countries, a country, the very soil of which is said to be consecrated to liberty, and its fruits the equal rights of man. But strange as the idea may seem, or paradoxical as it may appear to those acquainted with the constitution of the government, or who have read the bold declaration of this nation's independence; yet it is a fact that can neither be denied or controverted, that in the United States of America, at the expiration of fifty years after becoming a free and independent nation, there are no less than fifteen hundred thousand human beings still in a state of unconditional vassalage.

Yet America is first in the profession of the love of liberty, and loudest in proclaiming liberal sentiments towards all other nations, and feels herself insulted, to be branded with any thing bearing the appearance of tyranny or oppression. Such are the palpable inconsistencies that abound among us and such is the medley of contradictions which stain the national character, and renders the American republic a by-word, even among despotic nations. But while we pause and wonder at the contradictory sentiments held forth by the nation, and contrast its profession and practice, we are happy to have it in our power to render an apology for the existence of the evil, and to offer an excuse for the framers of the constitution. It was before the sons of Columbia felt the yoke of their oppressors, and rose in their strength to put it off that this land became contaminated with slavery. Had this not been the case, led by the spirit of pure republicanism, that then possessed the souls of those patriots who were struggling for liberty, this soil would have been sufficiently guarded against its intrusion, and the people of these United

States to this day, would have been strangers to so great a curse. It was by the permission of the British parliament, that the human species first became an article of merchandize among them, as they were accessary to its introduction, it well becomes them to be first, as a nation, in arresting its progress and effecting its expulsion. It was the immortal Clarkson, a name that will be associated with all that is sublime in mercy, until the final consummation of all things, who first looking abroad, beheld the sufferings of Africa, and looking at home, he saw his country stained with her blood. He threw aside the vestments of the priesthood, and consecrated himself to the holy purpose of rescuing a continent from rapine and murder, and of erasing this one sin from the book of his nation's iniquities. Many were the difficulties to be encountered, many were the hardships to be endured, many were the persecutions to be met with; formidable, indeed, was the opposing party. The sensibility of the slave merchants and planters was raised to the highest pitch of resentment. Influenced by the love of money, every scheme was devised, every measure was adopted, every plan was executed, that might throw the least barrier in the way of the holy cause of the abolition of this traffic. The consequences of such a measure were placed in the most appalling light that ingenious falsehood could invent; the destruction of commerce, the ruin of the merchants, the rebellion of the slaves, the massacre of the planters, were all artfully and fancifully pictured, and reduced to a certainty in the minds of many members of parliament, and a large proportion of the community. But the cause of justice and humanity were not to be deserted by him and his fellow philanthropists, on account of difficulties. We have seen them for twenty years persevering against all opposition, and surmounting every obstacle they found in their way. Nor did they relax aught of their exertions, until the cries of the oppressed having roused the sensibility of the nation, the island empress rose in her strength, and said to this foul traffic, "thus far hast thou gone, but thou shalt go no farther." Happy for us, my brethren, that the principles of benevolence were not exclusively confined to the isle of Great Britain. There have lived, and there still do live, men in this country, who are patriots and philanthropists, not merely in name, but in heart and practice; men whose compassions have long since led them to pity the poor and despised sons of Africa. They have heard their groans, and have seen their blood, and have looked with an holy indignation upon the oppressor: nor was there any thing wanting except the power to have crushed the tyrant and liberated the captive. Through their instrumentality, the blessings of freedom have long since been enjoyed by all classes of people throughout New England, and through their influence, under the

Almighty, we are enabled to recognize the fourth day of the present month, as the day in which the cause of justice and humanity have triumphed over tyranny and oppression, and slavery is forever banished from the State of New York.

Among the many who have vindicated the cause of the oppressed, within the limits of this state, we are proud to mention the names of Eddy and Murray, of Jay and Tompkins, who, together with their fellow philanthropists embarked in the holy cause of emancipation, with a zeal which well expressed the sentiments of their hearts. They proved themselves to be inflexible against scorn, persecution, and contempt; and although all did not live to see the conflict ended, yet their survivors never relaxed their exertions until the glorious year of 1817, when, by the wise and patriotic legislature of this state, a law was passed for its final extirpation. We will mourn for those who are gone, we will honour those who survive, until time extinguishes the lamp of their existence. When dead, they shall still live in our memory; we will follow them to their tombs, we will wet their graves with our tears; and upon the heart of every descendant of Africa, their deeds shall be written, and their names shall vibrate sweetly from ear to ear, down to the latest posterity. From what has already taken place, we are encouraged to expect still greater things. We look forward with pleasing anticipation to that period, when it shall no longer be said that in a land of freemen there are men in bondage, but when this foul stain will be entirely erased, and this, worst of evils, will be forever done away. The progress of emancipation, though slow, is nevertheless certain: It is certain, because that God who has made of one blood all nations of men, and who is said to be no respecter of persons, has so decreed; I therefore have no hesitation in declaring from this sacred place, that not only throughout the United States of America, but throughout every part of the habitable world where slavery exists, it will be abolished. However great may be the opposition of those who are supported by the traffic, yet slavery will cease. The lordly planter who has his thousands in bondage, may stretch himself upon his couch of ivory, and sneer at the exertions which are made by the humane and benevolent, or he may take his stand upon the floor of Congress, and mock the pitiful generosity of the east or west for daring to meddle with the subject, and attempting to expose its injustice: he may threaten to resist all efforts for a general or a partial emancipation even to a dissolution of the union. But still I declare that slavery will be extinct; a universal and not a partial emancipation must take place; nor is the period far distant. The indefatigable exertions of the philanthropists in England to have it abolished in their West India Islands, the recent revolutions in South

America, the catastrophe and exchange of power in the Isle of Hayti, the restless disposition of both master and slave in the southern states, the constitution of our government, the effects of literary and moral instruction, the generous feelings of the pious and benevolent, the influence and spread of the holy religion of the cross of Christ, and the irrevocable decrees of Almighty God, all combine their efforts, and with united voice declare, that the power of tyranny must be subdued, the captive must be liberated, the oppressed go free, and slavery must revert back to its original chaos of darkness, and be forever annihilated from the earth. Did I believe that it would always continue, and that man to the end of time would be permitted with impunity to usurp the same undue authority over his fellow, I would disallow any allegiance or obligation I was under to my fellow creatures, or any submission that I owed to the laws of my country; I would deny the superintending power of divine providence in the affairs of this life; I would ridicule the religion of the Saviour of the world, and treat as the worst of men the ministers of the everlasting gospel; I would consider my Bible as a book of false and delusive fables, and commit it to the flames; nay, I would still go farther; I would at once confess myself an atheist, and deny the existence of a holy God.

But slavery will cease, and the equal rights of man will be universally acknowledged. Nor is its tardy progress any argument against its final accomplishment. But do I hear it loudly responded,—this is but a mere wild fanaticism, or at best but the misguided conjecture of an untutored descendant of Africa. Be it so. I confess my ignorance, and bow with due deference to my superiors in understanding; but if in this case I err, the error is not peculiar to myself; if I wander, I wander in a region of light from whose political hemisphere the sun of liberty pours forth his refulgent rays, around which dazzle the star like countenances of Clarkson, Wilberforce, Pitt, Fox and Grenville, Washington, Adams, Jefferson, Hancock and Franklin; if I err, it is their sentiments that have caused me to stray. For these are the doctrines which they taught while with us; nor can we reasonably expect that since they have entered the unbounded space of eternity, and have learned more familiarly the perfections of that God who governs all things that their sentiments have altered. Could they now come forth among us, they would tell that what they have learned in the world of spirits, has served only to confirm what they taught while here; they would tell us, that all things are rolling on according to the sovereign appointment of the eternal Jehovah, who will overturn and overturn until he whose right it is to reign, shall come and the period will be ushered in; when the inhabitants of

the earth will learn by experience what they are now low to believe—
that our God is a God of justice, and no respecter of persons. But while,
on the one hand, we look back and rejoice at what has already taken
place, and on the other, we look forward with pleasure to that period
when men will be respected according to their characters, and not according to their complexion, and when their vices alone will render
them contemptible; while we rejoice at the thought of this land's becoming a land of freemen, we pause, we reflect. What, we would ask,
is liberty without virtue? It tends to lasciviousness; and what is freedom
but a curse, and even destruction, to the profligate? Not more desolating in its effects is the mountain torrent, breaking from its lofty confines and rushing with vast impetuosity upon the plains beneath,
marring as it advances all that is lovely in the works of nature and of
art, then the votaries of vice and immorality, when permitted to range
unrestrained.

Brethren, we have been called into liberty; only let us use that liberty
as not abusing it. This day commences a new era in our history; new
scenes, new prospects, open before us, and it follows as a necessary consequence, that new duties devolve upon us; duties, which if properly attended to, cannot fail to improve our moral condition, and elevate us
to a rank of respectable standing with the community; or if neglected,
we fall at once into the abyss of contemptible wretchedness: It is righteousness alone that exalteth a nation, and sin is a reproach to any
people. Our liberties, says Mr. Jefferson, are the gift of God, and they
are not to be violated but with his wrath. Nations and individuals have
been blest of the Almighty in proportion to the manner in which they
have appreciated the mercies conferred upon them: an abuse of his
goodness has always incurred his righteous frown while a right improvement of his beneficence has secured and perpetuated his gracious
smiles: an abuse of his goodness has caused those fearful judgments
which have destroyed cities, demolished thrones, overturned empires,
and humbled to the dust, the proudest and most exalted of nations. As
a confirmation of which, the ruinous heaps of Egypt, Tyre, Babylon,
and Jerusalem, stand as everlasting monuments. If we would then answer the great design of our creation, and glorify the God who has
made us; if we would avert the judgment of Heaven; if we would honor
our public benefactors; if we would counteract the designs of our enemies; if we would have our own blessings perpetuated, and secure the
happiness of our children and our children's children, let each come forward and act well his part, in whatever circle he may move, or in whatever station he may fill; let the fear of God and the good of our fellow

men, be the governing principles of the heart. We do well to remember, that every act of ours is more or less connected with the general cause of the people of colour, and with the general cause of emancipation. Our conduct has an important bearing, not only on those who are yet in bondage in this country, but its influence is extended to the isles of India, and to every part of the world where the abomination of slavery is known. Let us then relieve ourselves from the odious stigma which some have long since cast upon us, that we were incapacitated by the God of nature, for the enjoyment of the rights of freemen, and convince them and the world that although our complexion may differ, yet we have hearts susceptible of feeling; judgment capable of discerning, and prudence sufficient to manage our affairs with discretion, and by example prove ourselves worthy of the blessings we enjoy. That it is the duty of all rational creatures to consult the interest of their species, is a fact against which there can be no reasonable objection. It is recorded to the honour of Titus, who perhaps was the most benevolent of all the Roman emperors: on recollecting one evening that he had done nothing the day preceding, beneficial to mankind, the monarch exclaimed, "I have lost a day." The wide field of usefulness is now open before us, and we are called upon by every consideration of duty which we owe to our God, to ourselves, to our children, and to our fellow-creatures generally, to enter with a fixed determination to act well our part, and labour to promote the happiness and welfare of all.

There remains much to be done, and there is much to encourage us to action. The foundation for literary, moral and religious improvement, we trust, is already laid in the formation of the public and private schools, for the instruction of our children, together with the churches of different denominations already established. From these institutions we are encouraged to expect the happiest results; and while many of us are passing down the declivity of life, and fast hastening to the grave, how animating the thought, that the rising generation is advancing under more favourable auspices than we were permitted to enjoy, soon to fill the places we now occupy; and in relation to them vast is the new responsibility that rests upon us; much of their future use fullness depends upon the discharge of the duties we owe them. They are advancing, not to fill the place of slaves, but of freemen: and in order to fill such a station with honor to themselves, and with good to the public, how necessary their education, how important the moral and religious cultivation of their minds! Blessed be God, we live in a day that our fathers desired to see, but died without the sight: a day in which science, like the sun of the firmament, rising, darting as he advances his beams to every quarter of the globe. The mists and darkness scatter at his approach, and all nations and people are blessed with his rays; so the glorious light of science is spreading from east to west, and Afric's sons are catching the glance of its beams as it passes; its enlightening rays scatter the mists of moral darkness and ignorance which have but too long overshadowed their minds; it enlightens the understanding, directs the thoughts of the heart, and is calculated to influence the soul to the performance of every good and virtuous act. The God of Nature has endowed our children with intellectual powers surpassed by none; nor is there anything wanting but their careful cultivation, in order to fit them for stations the most honorable, sacred, or useful. And may we not, without becoming vain in our imaginations, indulge the pleasing anticipation, that within the little circle of those connected with our families, there may hereafter be found the scholar, the statesman, or the herald of the cross of Christ: Is it too much to say, that among that little number there shall yet be one found like to the wise legislator of Israel, who shall take his brethren by the hand, and lead them forth from worse than Egyptian bondage, to the happy Canaan of civil and religious liberty; or one whose devotedness towards the cause of God, and whose zeal for the salvation of Africa, shall cause him to leave the land which gave him birth, and cross the Atlantic, eager to plant the standard of the cross upon every hill of that vast continent, that has hitherto ignobly submitted to the baleful crescent, or crouched under the iron bondage of the vilest superstition. Our prospects brighten as we pursue the subject, and we are encouraged to look forward to that period when the moral desert of Africa shall submit to cultivation, and verdant groves and fertile valleys, watered by the streams of Siloia, shall meet the eye that has long surveyed only the wide spread desolations of slavery, despotism, and death. How changed shall then be the aspect of the moral and political world! Africa, elevated to more than her original dignity, and redressed for the many aggravated and complicated wrongs she has sustained, with her emancipated sons, shall take her place among the other nations of the earth. The iron manacles of slavery shall give place to the still stronger bonds of brotherly love and affection, and justice and equity shall be the governing principles that shall regulate the conduct of men of every nation. Influenced by such motives, encouraged by such prospects, let us enter the field with a fixed determination to live and to die in the holy cause.

Appendix Four

The Role of Women in the Episcopal Church

This document outlines the struggles of the Episcopal Church to address the role of women in the life of the church. It was presented in October of 1966. Published by www.womenpriests.org! Appendix B, part 2. In *Women Priests: Yes or No?*, Emily C. Hewitt & Suzanne R. Hiatt (New York: Seabury Press, New York, 1973), 109–14. Reprinted with permission of the Domestic and Foreign Missionary Society of the Protestant Episcopal Church in the United States of America.

Progress Report to the House of Bishops from The Committee to Study the Proper Place of Women in the Ministry of the Church

The creation of the Committee to Study the Proper Place of Women in the Ministry of the Church was authorized by the House of Bishops in September, 1965, and its members were subsequently appointed by the Presiding Bishop. The Committee consists of: The Bishop of Rochester, Chairman; Mrs. Irvin Bussing of California, Secretary; The Bishop of New Hampshire; The Bishop of Oklahoma; Mrs. Charles M. Hawes III of the Virgin Islands; Rev. Dr. Alden D. Kelley of Bexley Hall; Mrs. Theodore O. Wedel of New York.

Of the women serving on the Committee, one has been an executive in public relations and advertising, another has been engaged in professional Church work for many years, both in this Church and on an ecumenical level, and the third has recently received a Bachelor of Divinity degree.

The Committee presents this preliminary Report, indicating the direction of its thinking, and making some initial recommendations to the House of Bishops.

SCOPE AND URGENCY

The Committee presents this preliminary Report, indicating the place of women in the Church's ministry demands the facing of the question of whether or not women should be considered eligible for ordination to any and all Orders of that Ministry. No one would deny that women are part of the lay ministry of the Church, and the Committee does not think that another examination of the status of Deaconesses alone would do justice to the matter.

The Committee is convinced that a number of factors give the question a new urgency, require a fresh and unprejudiced look at the whole issue, and warn against uncritical acceptance of beliefs, attitudes, and assumptions that have been inherited from the past and strongly persist at the present time. Three such factors seem especially important:

a. The growing place of women in professional, business, and public life, in medicine, in teaching, in politics and government, in the Armed Forces, even in high executive positions within this Church.

b. The development of new forms of ministry that permit greater flexibility and call for many more specialized skills than is the case when the ministry is limited largely to one priest in charge of one parish, a generalist rather than a specialist. As one member of the Committee put it, "We need to stop talking or thinking of the ministry as though it were a single unitary vocation. Rather, we need to think of the many functions of ministry which are needed today—the sacramental ministry, preaching, theological and Biblical research, teaching, pastoral work and counseling, social service, etc. In an age of specialization and of a tremendous explosion of knowledge we must face the fact that no one person can possibly be adequate in all these areas. . . . We need to encourage specialization according to a person's gifts and interests and organize our corporate life to use specialists." This fact requires consideration of how women may be used in a changing and increasingly specialized ministry.

c. The growing importance of the issue in ecumenical relationships. The question is being discussed in many parts of the Anglican Communion. . . . The initiation of a study of the experiences of ordained women was urged by the World Conference on Church and Society, meeting at Geneva in the summer of 1966. In this country, the Consultation on Church Union has reached the point of considering the drafting of a plan of union, involving this Church and a number of others that now admit women to the ordained ministry, and the question of the ordination of women in such a united Church obviously must be faced as the negotiations proceed.

Nor does it seem that the question of the ordination of women in the Orthodox and Roman Churches can be regarded as finally and forever decided in the negative, particularly in view of other changes that have occurred, especially in the Roman Church.

There is a sentence in one of the official documents of Vatican II that reads, "Since in our times women have an ever more active share in the whole life of society, it is very important that they participate more widely also in the various fields of the Church's apostolate" [*The Documents of Vatican II*, Walter M. Abbott, S.J., General Editor (New York: Guild Press, 1966), 500]. The Archbishop of Durban, South Africa, Dr. Dennis Hurley, recently predicted that "there are going to be some fantastic developments in the role of women in the Church." (See Christian Century, September 15, 1966.) And in an interview with the Secretary of this Committee, given on October 11, 1966, the Rev. Dr. Hans Küng, Professor in the University of Tubingen (Germany) stated, "There are two factors to consider regarding the ordination of women to the Sacred Ministry of the Church. The first is that there are no dogmatic or biblical reasons against it. The second is that there are psychological and sociological factors to be considered. The solution to the problem depends on the sociological conditions of the time and place. It is entirely a matter of cultural circumstances."

BURDEN OF PROOF

The Committee has become increasingly convinced that the burden of proof is on the negative in this matter.

For, to oppose the ordination of women is either to hold that the whole trend of modern culture is wrong in its attitude toward the place of women in society, or to maintain that the unique character of the ordained ministry makes that ministry a special case and justifies the exclusion of women from it.

REASONS GIVEN AGAINST THE ORDINATION OF WOMEN

Mental and Emotional: The alleged mental and emotional characteristics of women are said to make them unsuitable to serve as clergymen. Such arguments are never very clear, consistent, or precise.

Sometimes, the weakness of women is stressed, despite the fact that women are healthier and live longer than men. Or, it is claimed that women think emotionally rather than rationally and that they overpersonalize problems or decisions.

The same sort of arguments could be used to show that women are unfit for almost any business, professional, or public responsibility. They were used against the admission of women to higher education, to the practice of medicine and law, and against women suffrage. They are still being used against the admission of women to the House of Deputies of the General Convention.

None of these negative arguments has been borne out in any other walk of life. Women have proved to be capable, often brilliant, lawyers, statesmen, scientists, and teachers. They have enriched the practice of medicine, and politics have neither been redeemed nor debased by their participation.

As experience has demonstrated, only experience can show the extent to which women might fulfill a useful role in the ordained ministry, as well as ways in which their role might be different from the role of men. Here, as in other callings, women would need to be better than men in order to compete with them.

Emil Brunner states, "It is absolutely impossible to put down in black and white, as a universal rule, which spheres of activity 'belong' to women and which do not. This can only become clear through experience; and for this experience, first of all the field must be thrown open."

Because the field has not been thrown open, any judgment based on the Church's experience with professional women workers is limited and inadequate. With the highest respect for the contributions these women are now making, the Committee is convinced that an absolute bar at the level of ordination has a deterring effect upon the number of women of high quality who enter professional Church work or undertake theological study, and that the same bar places theologically trained women in a highly uncomfortable and anomalous position.

Marriage Versus Ministry: There is alleged the impossibility or impracticality of combining the vocation of a clergyman with domestic responsibilities, with marriage, as well as the bearing and care of children. Would it be possible for a wife and mother of a family to bring to the priesthood the required degree of commitment, concentration, and availability?

First, it must be said that many women choose careers and never marry, others combine marriage and careers. The Church recognizes that the latter is an entirely legitimate vocation, both in the secular world and in the Church itself.

Secondly, the question of married women is partly answered by the fact that married men are permitted to serve as bishops, priests and deacons in the Anglican Communion. Such permission implies an acknowledgment of the strong claims that the wife and family of a married clergyman rightfully have upon his time, his money, and the conduct of his vocation. All would grant that a clergyman has a duty, as well as a right, to take into account his wife's health, or his children's education, in considering a call, in negotiating about his salary, in determining his standard of living and the amount of money he will give away.

While other, and perhaps more serious, problems might exist for a woman who wished to combine ordination with marriage, the Commission is by no means convinced that such a combination would not prove practical in many instances. Even such demanding professions as teaching and medicine are finding ways of using skilled and trained married women with children, both on a part-time and a full-time basis. Many intelligent women find that they are better wives and mothers by combining an outside calling with the care of a family. Many also can look forward to years of full-time professional work after their children are grown.

The Commission would ask whether the leadership of the Church does not possess resourcefulness and imagination similar to that displayed by other institutions in using married women, if not often as ministers in charge of parishes, yet as assistants, or for the specialized types of ministry that are sure to develop much more rapidly in the future. It is thought unlikely that any great number of women would seek ordination, considering the very real difficulties involved. But difficulty is not impossibility, and at the least there need be no fear that women will "take over" the Church.

Theological Arguments: Then there are certain theological objections which seem to the Committee to present a strange mixture of tradition and superstition.

Biblical: Some of the objections rest on a rather literal approach to the Bible and fail to take into account the degree to which the Bible is conditioned by the circumstances of its time. It is not necessary to dwell upon the Creation Story, in which woman is created after man and taken from him, nor be influenced by the fact that women were excluded from the covenant-relation of God with Israel, any more than one would support polygamy or slavery because both have clear sanction in the Old Testament. Nor is one moved by the familiar argument that our Lord chose only men to be his apostles. Any sound doctrine of the Incarnation must take full account of the extent to which Jesus lived and thought within the circumstances and environment of his own time. To deny such facts is to deny the full humanity of Jesus and to subscribe to a grotesque Docetism. Our Lord did choose women as close associates, even if he did choose men as the transitional leaders of the new Israel. The Committee also believes that St. Paul, as well as the authors of Ephesians and the Pastoral Epistles, were sharing in the passing assumptions of their own time, as well as advising wise strategy for the First Century Church, in recommending that women keep silent at services, cover their heads, and be subordinate to their husbands; just as St. Paul thought it wise to send a run-away slave back to his master. Much more permanent and basic are St. Paul's words, "There is neither Jew nor Greek . . . slave nor free . . . male nor female; for you all are one in Christ Jesus."

Image of God: Then, there is a cluster of theological objections based on the assumption that the female is a less true or complete image of God than the male; and that, therefore, woman is less capable, or is quite incapable, of representing God to man and man to God in the priesthood, and of receiving the indelible grace of Holy Orders.

This line of reasoning has a number of curious sources. In the Bible, God is thought and spoken of as "he," for the most part, as would be entirely natural in a culture first militant and warlike, always patriarchal, and with a developing monotheism. Even so, God can be compared with a mother who comforts her child.

Jesus Christ was born a man. Obviously, God's unique child would need to be born either a man or woman; and, again, in a patriarchal culture, only a man could fulfill the role of Messiah, Lord, or Son of God. When one calls God personal, one can mean no more than that human personality is the best clue we have to the nature of God. Perhaps male personality is a better clue than female personality in a masculine-dominated society, but who would presume to project such sexual differentiation upon the very nature of God? The first of the Anglican Articles of Religion states that God is "without body, parts, or passions." To call God "he," implies no more than to call the entire human race "man" or "mankind."

The view that the female is a less true or complete image of God than the male is sometimes still supported by a tradition coming from Aristotle and St. Thomas Aquinas, which holds that woman is an incomplete human being, "a defective and/or misbegotten male." This tradition was based upon the prescientific biology which held that woman was an entirely passive partner in reproduction. On this subject, the

Rev. Dr. Leonard Hodgson has commented, "We should be unwise to base our theological conclusions on notions of a prescientific biology which has never heard of genes or chromosomes."

Emotional and Psychological Pressures: The Commission is also aware that all the intellectual arguments against the ordination of women are connected with and reflect strong emotional and psychological pressures. These pressures may point to profound truth about men and women and their relationship to each other. Or, they may reflect magical notions of priesthood and Sacraments that linger on in the most sophisticated minds.

Or, they may reflect the fact that our deepest emotional experiences in the life of the Church, experiences often associated with the birth and baptism of children, maturity and Confirmation, worship and Sacraments, the pastoral ministry in times of crisis, joy and sorrow, are all closely associated with an episcopate and a priesthood that is exclusively male. Or, they may illustrate the sad fact that historical and psychological circumstances frequently make the Church the last refuge of the fearful and the timid in a changing world and that, the more rapidly the world changes, the stronger become the pressures to keep the Church safe and unchanged. Or, they may represent a threat to the present ordained ministers, to their wives, to lay men or lay women. The Commission is disturbed by the scorn, the indifference, the humorless levity, that is occasioned by the question of seating women in the House of Deputies, let alone their admission to ordination.

Finally, one cannot place much weight upon the common opinion that women themselves do not wish to be ordained. Who knows? Most women obviously do not, just as most men do not wish to become clergymen. But some women do. Kathleen Bliss has written, "This is not a woman's question, it is a Church question." The Church's answer must be determined, not primarily by what is good for woman, but what is good for the Church.

Appendix Five

Racial Problems of the Catholic Church

This document discusses the racial problems plaguing the Catholic Church during the mid-twentieth century. It was presented on April 18, 1968. Excerpts from "A Statement of the Black Catholic Clergy Caucus," first published by the National Office of Black Catholics in its magazine of black liturgy, *Freeing the Spirit* Vol. 1, No. 3 (Summer 1972), reprinted with permission. James H. Cone and Gayraud S. Wilmore, editors. *Black Theology: A Documentary History*, 1966–1979 (Maryknoll, NY: Orbis Books, 1979), 322–24.

A Statement of the Black Catholic Clergy Caucus

The Catholic Church in the United States, primarily a white racist institution, has addressed itself primarily to white society and is definitely a part of that society. On the contrary, we feel that her primary, though not exclusive work, should be in the area of institutional, attitudinal and societal change. Within the ghetto, the role of the Church is no longer that of spokesman and leader. Apart from a more direct spiritual role, the Church's part must now be that of supporter and learner. This is a role that white priests in the black community have not been accustomed to playing and are not psychologically prepared to play.

The Catholic Church apparently is not cognizant of changing attitudes in the black community and is not making the necessary, realistic adjustments. The present attitude of the black community demands that black people control their own affairs and make decisions for themselves. This does not mean, however, that black leadership is to be exercised only in the black community, but must function throughout the entire gamut of ecclesial society.

It is imperative that the Church recognize this change. White persons working in the black community must be educated to these changing attitudes, and must be prepared to accept and function in conjunction with the prevailing attitudes of the black community.

One of these changes must be a re-evaluation of present attitudes towards black militancy. The violence occurring in the black communities has been *categorically* condemned and has called forth a wide variety of response, from "shoot to kill" to the recommendation of the Kerner Report.[1] Such violence has been specified as "Negro violence," as though there were a substantial or significant difference between violence in the black community and that which has occurred consistently throughout the history of the United States and of the World. Black people are fully aware that violence has been consciously and purposely used by America from its fight for independence to its maintenance of white supremacy. Since the black man is encouraged to fight abroad for white America's freedom and liberty, we are now asking why it is not moral for him to fight for his liberty at home. We go on record as recognizing:

1. the reality of militant protest;
2. that non-violence in the sense of black non-violence hoping for concessions after white brutality is dead;
3. that the same principles on which we justify legitimate self-defense and just warfare must be applied to violence when it represents black response to white violence;
4. the appropriateness of responsible, positive militancy against racism is the only Christian attitude against this or any other social evil.

Because of its past complicity with and active support of prevailing attitudes and institutions of America, the Church is now in an extremely weak position in the black community. In fact, the Catholic Church is rapidly dying in the black community. In many areas, there is a serious defection especially on the part of black Catholic youth. The black community no longer looks to the Catholic Church with hope. And unless the Church, by an immediate, effective and total reversing of its present practices, rejects and denounces *all* forms of racism within its ranks and institutions and in the society of which she is a part, she will become unacceptable in the black community.

We, *The Black Catholic Clergy Caucus*, strongly and deeply believe that there are few choices left to the Catholic Church, and unless it is to remain an enclave speaking to itself, it must begin to consult the black members of the Church, clerical, religious and lay. It must also

begin to utilize the personnel resources of black Catholics in leadership
and advisory positions in the whole Church and allow them to direct,
for the most part, the mission of the Church in the black community.
It is especially important that the financial resources channeled into the
work of the Church in the black community be allocated and admin-
istered by black Catholic leadership. To this end, in charity, we demand:

1. That there be black priests in decision-making positions on the
   diocesan level, and above all in the black community.
2. That a more effective utilization of black priests be made. That
   the situation where the majority of black priests are in institutions be changed; that black priests be given a choice of assign-
   ment on the basis of inclination and talent.
3. That where no black priests belong to the diocese, efforts be
   made to get them in, or at least consultation with black priests
   or black-thinking white priests be made.
4. That special efforts be made to recruit black men for the priesthood. Black priests themselves are better qualified for this recruitment at a time when the Catholic Church is almost irrelevant
   to the young black men.
5. That dioceses provide centers of training for white priests in-
   tending to survive in black communities.
6. That within the framework of the United States Catholic Conference, a black-directed department be set up to deal with the
   Church's role in the struggle of black people for freedom.
7. That in all of these areas black religious be utilized as much as
   possible.
8. That black men, married as well as single, be ordained permanent deacons to aid in this work of the Church.
9. That each diocese allocate a substantial fund to be used in establishing and supporting permanent programs for black leadership training.

Note

1. This was the report issued by the federal government's 1968 commission charged with exploring race riots during the 1960s. It was named after
the chair of the commission, Otto Kerner, governor of Illinois.

Appendix Six

Funds for African Americans

This statement generated by the National Black Economic Development Conference and presented by James Foreman (May 4, 1969) called for religious organizations in the United States to provide African Americans with funds based on the monetary advances they gained through slavery. "The Black Manifesto," April 26, 1969. James H. Cone and Gayraud S. Wilmore, eds., *Black Theology: A Documentary History, 1966–1979* (Maryknoll, NY: Orbis Books, 1979), 80–89, and vol. 1 (1993), 27–36.

The Black Manifesto

INTRODUCTION: TOTAL CONTROL AS THE ONLY SOLUTION TO THE ECONOMIC PROBLEMS OF BLACK PEOPLE

Brothers and Sisters:

We have come from all over the country burning with anger and despair not only with the miserable economic plight of our people but fully aware that the racism on which the Western World was built dominates our lives. There can be no separation of the problems of racism from the problems of our economic, political, and cultural degradation. To any black man, this is clear.

But there are still some of our people who are clinging to the rhetoric of the Negro, and we must separate ourselves from these Negroes who go around the country promoting all types of schemes for black capitalism.

Ironically, some of the most militant Black Nationalists, as they call themselves, have been the first to jump on the bandwagon of black capitalism. They are pimps, black power pimps and fraudulent leaders, and the people must be educated to understand that any black man or Negro who is advocating a perpetuation of capitalism inside the United States is in fact seeking not only his ultimate destruction and death but is contributing to the continuous exploitation of black people all around the world. For it is the power of the United States Government, this racist, imperialist government, that is choking the life of all people around the world.

We are an African people. We sit back and watch the Jews in this country make Israel a powerful conservative state in the Middle East, but we are concerned actively about the plight of our brothers in Africa. We are the most advanced technological group of black people in the world, and there are many skills that could be offered to Africa. At the same time, it must be publicly stated that many African leaders are in disarray themselves, having been duped into following the lines as laid out by the western imperialist governments. Africans themselves succumbed to and are victims of the power of the United States. For instance, during the summer of 1967, as the representatives of SNCC, Howard Moore and I [James Forman] traveled extensively in Tanzania and Zambia. We talked to high, very high, government officials. We told them there were many black people in the United States who were willing to come and work in Africa. All these government officials, who were part of the leadership in their respective governments, said they wanted us to send as many skilled people as we could contact. But this program never came into fruition, and we do not know the exact reasons, for I assure you that we talked and were committed to making this a successful program. It is our guess that the United States put the squeeze on these countries, for such a program directed by SNCC [Student Nonviolent Coordinating Committee] would have been too dangerous to the international prestige of the United States. It is also possible that some of the wild statements by some black leaders frightened the Africans.

In Africa today there is a great suspicion of black people in this country. This is a correct suspicion since most of the Negroes who have left the States for work in Africa usually work for the Central Intelligence Agency (CIA) or the State Department. But the respect for us as a people continues to mount, and the day will come when we can return to our homeland as brothers and sisters. But we should not think of going back to Africa today, for we are located in a strategic position. We live inside the United States, which is the most barbaric country in the world, and we have a chance to help bring this government down.

Time is short, and we do not have much time and it is time we stop mincing words. Caution is fine, but no oppressed people ever gained their liberation until they were ready to fight, to use whatever means necessary, including the use of force and power of the gun to bring down the colonizer.

We have heard the rhetoric, but we have not heard the rhetoric which says that black people in this country must understand that we are the vanguard force. We shall liberate all the people in the United States, and we will be instrumental in the liberation of colored people the world around. We must understand this point very clearly so that we are not trapped into diversionary and reactionary movements. Any class analysis of the United States shows very clearly that black people are the most oppressed group of people inside the United States. We have suffered the most from racism and exploitation, cultural degradation and lack of political power. It follows from the laws of revolution that the most oppressed will make the revolution, but we are not talking about just making the revolution. All the parties on the left who consider themselves revolutionary will say that blacks are the vanguard, but we are saying that not only are we the vanguard, but we must assume leadership, total control, and we must exercise the humanity which is inherent in us. We are the most humane people within the United States. We have suffered and we understand suffering. Our hearts go out to the Vietnamese, for we know what it is to suffer under the domination of racist America. Our hearts, our soul and all the compassion we can mount go out to our brothers in Africa, Santo Domingo, Latin America and Asia who are being tricked by the power structure of the United States which is dominating the world today. These ruthless, barbaric men have systematically tried to kill all people and organizations opposed to its imperialism. We no longer can just get by with the use of the word "capitalism" to describe the United States, for it is an imperial power sending money, missionaries and the army throughout the world to protect this government and the few rich whites who control it. General Motors and all the major auto industries are operating in South Africa, yet the white dominated leadership of the United Auto Workers sees no relationship to the exploitation of the black people in South Africa and the exploitation of black people in the United States. If they understand it, they certainly do not put it into practice, which is the actual test. We as black people must be concerned with the total conditions of all black people in the world.

But while we talk of revolution, which will be an armed confrontation and long years of sustained guerrilla warfare inside this country, we must also talk of the type of world we want to live in. We must commit ourselves to a society where the total means of production are taken from the rich and placed into the hands of the state for the welfare of all the people. This is what we mean when we say total control. And we mean that black people who have suffered the most from exploitation and racism must move to protect their black interest by assuming leadership inside of the United States of everything that exists. The time has ceased when we are second in command and the white boy stands on top. This is especially true of the welfare agencies in this country, but it is not enough to say that a black man is on top. He must be committed to building the new society, to taking the wealth away from the rich people, such as General Motors, Ford, Chrysler, the DuPonts, the Rockefellers, the Mellons, and all the other rich white exploiters and racists who run this world.

Where do we begin? We have already started. We started the moment we were brought to this country. In fact, we started on the shores of Africa, for we have always resisted attempts to make us slaves, and now we must resist the attempts to make us capitalists. It is in the financial interest of the United States to make us capitalist, for this will be the same line as that of integration into the mainstream of American life. Therefore, brothers and sisters, there is no need to fall into the trap that we have to get an ideology. We HAVE an ideology. Our fight is against racism, capitalism and imperialism, and we are dedicated to building a socialist society inside the United States where the total means of production and distribution are in the hands of the State, and that must be led by black people, by revolutionary blacks who are concerned about the total humanity of this world. And, therefore, we obviously are different from some of those who seek a black nation in the United States, for there is no way for that nation to be viable if in fact the United States remains in the hands of white racists. Then too, let us deal with some arguments that we should share power with whites. We say that there must be a revolutionary black vanguard, and that white people in this country must be willing to accept black leadership, for that is the only protection that black people have to protect ourselves from racism rising again in this country.

Racism in the United States is so pervasive in the mentality of whites that only an armed, well-disciplined, black-controlled government can insure the stamping out of racism in this country. And that is why we plead with black people not to be talking about a few crumbs, a few thousand dollars for this cooperative, or a thousand dollars which splits black people into fighting over the dollar. That is the intention of the government. We say . . . think in terms of total control of the United States. Prepare ourselves to seize state power. Do not hedge, for time is short, and all around the world the forces of liberation are directing their attacks against the United States. It is a powerful country, but that power is not greater than that of black people. We work the chief industries in this country, and could cripple the economy while the brothers fought guerrilla warfare in the streets. This will take some long range planning, but whether it happens in a thousand years is of no consequence. It cannot happen unless we start. How then is all of this related to this conference?

First of all, this conference is called by a set of religious people, Christians, who have been involved in the exploitation and rape of black people since the country was founded. The missionary goes hand in hand with the power of the states. We must begin seizing power wherever we are, and we must say to the planners of this conference that you are no longer in charge. We the people who have assembled here thank you for getting us here, but we are going to assume power over the conference and determine from this moment on the direction which we want it to go. We are not saying that the conference was planned badly. The staff of the conference has worked hard and has done a magnificent job in bringing all of us together, and we must include them in the new membership which must surface from this point on. The conference is now the property of the people who are assembled here. This we proclaim as fact and not rhetoric, and there are demands that we are going to make and we insist that the planners of this conference help us implement them.

We maintain we have the revolutionary rights to do this. We have the same rights, if you will, as the Christians had in going into Africa and raping our Motherland and bringing us away from our continent of peace and into this hostile and alien environment where we have been living in perpetual warfare since 1619.

Our seizure of power at this conference is based on a program, and our program is contained in the following Manifesto:

We the black people assembled in Detroit, Michigan, for the National Black Economic Development Conference are fully aware that we have been forced to come together because racist white America has exploited our resources, our minds, our bodies, our labor. For centuries we have been forced to live as colonized people inside the United States, victimized by the most vicious, racist system in the world. We have helped to build the most industrial country in the world.

We are therefore demanding of the white Christian churches and Jewish synagogues, which are part and parcel of the system of capitalism, that they begin to pay reparations to black people in this country. We are demanding $500,000,000 from the Christian white churches and the Jewish synagogues. This total comes to 15 dollars per nigger. This is a low estimate for we maintain there are probably more than 30,000,000 black people in this country. $15 a nigger is not a large sum of money and we know that the churches and synagogues have a tremendous wealth, and its membership, white America, has profited and still exploits black people. We are also not unaware that the exploitation of colored peoples around the world is aided and abetted by the white Christian churches and synagogues. This demand for $500,000,000 is not an idle resolution or empty words. Fifteen dollars for every black brother and sister in the United States is only a beginning of the reparations due us as people who have been exploited and degraded, brutalized, killed and persecuted. Underneath all of this exploitation, the racism of this country has produced a psychological effect upon us that we are beginning to shake off. We are no longer afraid to demand our full rights as a people in this decadent society.

We are demanding $500,000,000 to be spent in the following way:

1. We call for the establishment of a Southern land bank to help our brothers and sisters who have to leave their land because of racist pressure on people who want to establish cooperative farms, but who have no funds. We have seen too many farmers evicted from their homes because they have dared to defy the white racism of this country. We need money for land. We must fight for massive sums of money for this Southern Land Bank. We call for $200,000,000 to implement this program.

2. We call for the establishment of four major publishing and printing industries in the United States to be funded with ten million dollars each. These publishing houses are to be located in Detroit, Atlanta, Los Angeles, and New York. They will help to generate capital for further cooperative investments in the black community, provide jobs and alternatives to the white-dominated and controlled printing field.

3. We call for the establishment of four of the most advanced scientific and futuristic audio-visual networks to be located in Detroit, Chicago, Cleveland, and Washington, D.C. These TV networks will provide an alternative to the racist propaganda that fills the current television networks. Each of these TV networks will be funded by ten million dollars each.

4. We call for a research skills center which will provide research on the problems of black people. This center must be funded with no less than 30 million dollars.

5. We call for the establishment of a training center for the teaching of skills in community organization, photography, movie making, television making and repair, radio building and repair and all other skills needed in communication. This training center shall be funded with no less than ten million dollars.

6. We recognize the role of the National Welfare Rights Organization and we intend to work with them. We call for ten million dollars to assist in the organization of welfare recipients. We want to organize the welfare workers in this country so that they may demand more money from the government and better administration of the welfare system of this country.

7. We call for $20,000,000 to establish a National Black Labor Strike and Defense Fund. This is necessary for the protection of black workers and their families who are fighting racist working conditions in this country.

8. [Revised and approved by Steering Committee] We call for the establishment of the International Black Appeal (IBA). This International Black Appeal will be funded with no less than $20,000,000. The IBA is charged with producing more capital for the establishment of cooperative businesses in the United States and in Africa, our Motherland. The International Black Appeal is one of the most important demands that we are making for we know that it can generate and raise funds throughout the United States and help our African brothers. The IBA is charged with three functions and shall be headed by James Forman:
    (a) Raising money for the program of the National Black Economic Development Conference.
    (b) The development of cooperatives in African countries and support of African Liberation movements.
    (c) Establishment of a Black Anti-Defamation League which will protect our African image.

9. We call for the establishment of a Black University to be funded with $130,000,000 to be located in the South. Negotiations are presently under way with a Southern University.

10. We demand that IFCO allocate all unused funds in the planning budget to implement the demands of this conference.

In order to win our demands we are aware that we will have to have massive support, therefore:

(1) We call upon all black people throughout the United Sates to consider themselves as members of the National Black Economic De-

velopment Conference and to act in unity to help force the racist white Christian churches and Jewish synagogues to implement these demands.

(2) We call upon all the concerned black people across the country to contact black workers, black women, black students and the black unemployed, community groups, welfare organizations, teacher organizations, church leaders and organizations explaining how these demands are vital to the black community of the U.S.

Pressure by whatever means necessary should be applied to the white power structure of the racist white Christian churches and Jewish synagogues. All black people should act boldly in confronting our white oppressors and demanding this modest reparation of 15 dollars per black man.

(3) Delegates and members of the National Black Economic Development Conference are urged to call press conferences in the cities and to attempt to get as many black organizations as possible to support the demands of the conference. The quick use of the press in the local areas will heighten the tension and these demands must be attempted to be won in a short period of time, although we are prepared for protracted and long-range struggle.

(4) We call for the total disruption of selected church-sponsored agencies operating anywhere in the U.S. and the world. Black workers, black women, black students, and the black unemployed are encouraged to seize the offices, telephones, and printing apparatus of all church-sponsored agencies and to hold these in trusteeship until our demands are met.

(5) We call upon all delegates and members of the National Black Economic Development Conference to stage sit-in demonstrations at selected black and white churches. This is not to be interpreted as a continuation of the sit-in movement of the early sixties but we know that active confrontation inside white churches is possible and will strengthen the possibility of meeting our demands. Such confrontation can take the form of reading the Black Manifesto instead of a sermon or passing it out to church members. The principle of self-defense should be applied if attacked.

(6) On May 4, 1969, or a date thereafter, depending upon local conditions, we call upon black people to commence the disruption of the racist churches and synagogues throughout the United States.

(7) We call upon IFCO to serve as a central staff to coordinate the mandate of the conference and to reproduce and distribute en masse literature, leaflets, news items, press releases, and other material.

(8) We call upon all delegates to find within the white community those forces which will work under the leadership of blacks to imple-

ment these demands by whatever means necessary. By taking such actions, white Americans will demonstrate concretely that they are willing to fight the white skin privilege and the white supremacy and racism which has forced us as black people to make these demands.

(9) We call upon all white Christians and Jews to practice patience, tolerance, understanding, and nonviolence as they have encouraged, advised, and demanded that we as black people should do throughout our entire enforced slavery in the United States. The true test of their faith and belief in the Cross and the words of the prophets will certainly be put to a test as we seek legitimate and extremely modest reparations for our role in developing the industrial base of the Western world through our slave labor. But we are no longer slaves, we are men and women, proud of our African heritage, determined to have our dignity.

(10) We are so proud of our African heritage and realize concretely that our struggle is not only to make revolution in the United States, but to protect our brothers and sisters in Africa and to help them rid themselves of racism, capitalism, and imperialism by whatever means necessary, including armed struggle. We are and must be willing to fight the defamation of our African image wherever it rears its ugly head. We are therefore charging the Steering Committee to create a Black Anti-Defamation League to be funded by money raised from the International Black Appeal.

(11) We fully recognize that revolution in the United States and Africa, our Motherland, is more than a one-dimensional operation. It will require the total integration of the political, economic, and military components and therefore, we call upon all our brothers and sisters who have acquired training and expertise in the fields of engineering, electronics, research, community organization, physics, biology, chemistry, mathematics, medicine, military science, and warfare to assist the National Black Economic Development Conference in the implementation of its program.

(12) To implement these demands we must have a fearless leadership. We must have a leadership which is willing to battle the church establishment to implement these demands. To win our demands we will have to declare war on the white Christian churches and synagogues and this means we may have to fight the total government structure of this country. Let no one here think that these demands will be met by our mere stating of them. For the sake of the churches and synagogues, we hope that they have the wisdom to understand that these demands are modest and reasonable. But if the white Christians and Jews are not willing to meet our demands through peace and good will, then we declare war and we are prepared to fight by whatever means

necessary. . . . Brothers and sisters, we no longer are shuffling our feet and scratching our heads. We are tall, black and proud.

And we say to the white Christian churches and Jewish synagogues, to the government of this country, and to all the white racist imperialists who compose it, there is only one thing left that you can do to further degrade black people and that is to kill us. But we have been dying too long for this country. We have died in every war. We are dying in Vietnam today fighting the wrong enemy.

The new black man wants to live and to live means that we must not become static or merely believe in self-defense. We must boldly go out and attack the white Western world at its power centers. The white Christian churches are another form of government in this country and they are used by the government of this country to exploit the people of Latin America, Asia, and Africa, but the day is soon coming to an end. Therefore, brothers and sisters, the demands we make upon the white Christian churches and the Jewish synagogues are small demands. They represent 15 dollars per black person in these United States. We can legitimately demand this from the church power structure. We must demand more from the United States Government.

But to win our demands from the church which is linked up with the United States Government, we must not forget that it will ultimately be by force and power that we will win.

We are not threatening the churches. We are saying that we know the churches came with the military might of the colonizers and have been sustained by the military might of the colonizers. Hence, if the churches in colonial territories were established by military might, we know deep within our hearts that we must be prepared to use force to get our demands. We are not saying that this is the road we want to take. It is not, but let us be very clear that we are not opposed to force and we are not opposed to violence. We were captured in Africa by violence. We were kept in bondage and political servitude and forced to work as slaves by the military machinery and the Christian church working hand in hand.

We recognize that in issuing this manifesto we must prepare for a long-range educational campaign in all communities of this country, but we know that the Christian churches have contributed to our oppression in white America. We do not intend to abuse our black brothers and sisters in black churches who have uncritically accepted Christianity. We want them to understand how the racist white Christian church with its hypocritical declarations and doctrines of brotherhood has abused our trust and faith. An attack on the religious beliefs on black people is not our major objective, even though we know that we were not Christians when we were brought to this country, but that Christianity was used to help enslave us. Our objective in issuing this Manifesto is to force the racist white Christian church to begin the payment of reparations which are due to all black people, not only by the Church but also by private business and the U.S. government. We see this focus on the Christian church as an effort around which all black people can unite.

Our demands are negotiable, but they cannot be minimized; they can only be increased and the Church is asked to come up with larger sums of money than we are asking. Our slogans are:

ALL ROADS MUST LEAD TO REVOLUTION
UNITE WITH WHOMEVER YOU CAN UNITE
NEUTRALIZE WHEREVER POSSIBLE
FIGHT OUR ENEMIES RELENTLESSLY
VICTORY TO THE PEOPLE
LIFE AND GOOD HEALTH TO MANKIND
RESISTANCE TO DOMINATION BY THE WHITE CHRISTIAN
    CHURCHES AND THE JEWISH SYNAGOGUES
REVOLUTIONARY BLACK POWER
WE SHALL WIN WITHOUT A DOUBT

Appendix Seven

Negative Consequences of Slavery on the Christian Faith

Daniel Payne discusses the negative consequences that slavery had on the spread of the Christian faith. Daniel Payne, "Daniel Payne's Protestation of Slavery," *Lutheran Herald and Journal of the Franckean Synod* (Fort Plain, NY: Committee of Publication of the Franckean Synod, 1839): 113–15.

Protestation of Slavery

Speech of Brother Daniel A. Payne, delivered at the last session of the Franckean Synod, June, 1839, in favor of the adoption of the Report on Slavery. Written out by himself.

Mr. President—I move the adoption of the Report, because it is based upon the following propositions:

American Slavery brutalizes man—destroys his moral agency, and subverts the moral government of God.

SIR—I am opposed to slavery, not because it enslaves the black man, but because it enslaves *man*. And were all the slave holders in this land men of color, and the slaves white men, I would be as thorough and uncompromising an abolitionist as I now am; for wherever and whenever I may see a being in the form of a man, enslaved by his fellow man, without respect to his complexion, I shall lift up my voice to plead his cause, against all the claims of his proud oppressor; and I shall do it not merely from the sympathy which man feels towards suffering man, but because God, the living God, whom I dare not disobey, has commanded me to open my mouth for the dumb, and to plead the cause of the oppressed.

Slavery brutalizes man. We know that the word man, in its primitive sense, signifies———. But the intellectual and moral structure of man, and the august relations which he sustains to the Deity, have thrown around the name, and the being designated by it a halo of glory, brightened by all the ideas, that are ennobling on earth, and blessed in eternity. This being God created but a little lower than the angels, and crowned him with glory and honor; but slavery hurls him down from his elevated position, to the level of brutes! Strikes this crown of glory from his head, and fastens upon his neck the galling yoke! And compels him to labor like an ox, through summer's sun and winter's snow, without remuneration. Does a man take the calf from the cow and sell it to the butcher? So slavery tears the child from the arms of the reluctant mother, and barters it to the sou-trader for a young colt, or some other commodity! Does the bird-catcher tear away the dove from his mate? So slavery separates the groaning husband from the embraces of his distracted and weeping wife! And are the beasts of the forest hunted, tortured and slain at the pleasure of the cruel hunter? So are the slaves hunted, tortured and slain at the pleasure of the monster slavery! To treat a man like a brute is to brutalize him. We have seen that slavery treats man like a brute, therefore slavery brutalizes man! But does slavery stop there? Is it content with merely treating the external man like a brute? No, sir, it goes further, and with a heart as brazen as that of Belshazzar, and hands still more sacrilegious, it lays hold of the *immortal mind, seizes the will, and binds that which Jehovah did not bind—fetters that which the Eternal made as free to move and act as the breath of Heaven! It destroys moral agency!* To destroy moral agency is to fetter or obstruct the will of man. Now let us see if slavery is innocent of this. The very moment that a man conceives the diabolic design of enslaving his brother's body, that very moment does he also conceive the still more heinous design of fettering his will, for well does he know that in order to make his dominion supreme over the body, he must fetter the living spring of all its motions. Hence the first lesson the slave is taught is to yield his will unreservedly and exclusively to the dictates of his master. And if a slave desire to educate himself or his children, in obedience to the dictates of reason, or the laws of God, he does not, he cannot do it without the consent of his master. Does reason and circumstances and the Bible command a slave to preach the gospel to his brethren? Slavery arises, and with a frown, and oath and a whip, fetters or obstructs the holy volition of his soul! I knew a pious slave in Charleston, who was a licensed exhorter in the M[ethodist] E[piscopal] C[hurch]; this good man was in the habit of spending his Saturday nights on the surrounding plantations, preaching to the slaves. One night, as usual, he got into a canoe, sailed across the river, and began to preach to the slaves on a certain plantation upon James' Island. While in the very act of preaching the unsearchable riches of Christ to dying men, the patrols seized him and whipped him in the most cruel manner, and compelled him to promise that he would never return to preach again to those slaves. In the year 1834, several colored brethren, who were also exhorters in the M.E.C. commenced preaching to several *destitute white families*, who gained a subsistence by cultivating some poor lands about three or four miles from Charleston. The first Sunday I was present, the house was nearly filled with these poor white farmers. The master of the house was awakened to a sense of his lost condition. During the following week he was converted. On the third Sunday from the day he was convinced of sin he died in the triumphs of faith, and went to heaven. On the fourth Sunday from the time the dear brethren began to preach, the patrols scented their track, and put them on the chase. Thus an end was put to their labors. Their willing souls were fettered, and the poor whites constrained to go without the preaching of the gospel. In a word, it is in view of man's moral agency that God commands him to shun vice, and practice virtue. But what female slave can do this? I lived 24 years in the midst of slavery, and never knew but six female slaves who were reputedly virtuous! What profit is it to the female slave that she is disposed to be virtuous? Her will, like her body, is not her own; they are both at the pleasure of her master; and he brands them at his will. So *it subverts the moral government of God.*

In view of the moral agency of man, God has most wisely and graciously given him a code of laws, and certain positive precepts, to control and regulate moral actions. This code of laws, and these positive precepts, with the divine influence which they are naturally calculated to exert on the mind of man, constitutes his moral government.

Now, to nullify these laws—to weaken or destroy their legitimate influence on the human mind, or to hinder man from yielding universal and entire obedience to them is to subvert the moral government of God.

Now, slavery nullifies these laws and precepts—weakens and destroys their influence over the human mind, and hinders men from yielding universal and entire obedience to them; therefore slavery subverts the moral government of God. This is the climax of the sin of slavery! This is the daring Monster! He stretcheth out his hand against God, and strengtheneth himself against the Almighty—he runneth on him, even on his neck, upon the thick bosses of his buckler. Thus saith the Lord, "Thou shalt not commit adultery." But does the man who owns a hundred females obey the law? Does he not nullify it, and compel the helpless woman to disobey God? Concerning the religious instruction of children, thus saith the Lord, "Bring them up in the nurture and admonition of the Lord." But what saith slavery? "They are my property, and shall be brought up to serve me. They shall not *even learn to read his word*, in order that they may be brought up in his nurture and admonition." If any man doubts this, let him read the slave code of Louisiana, and see if it is not death to teach slaves. Thus saith the Lord, "Remember the Sabbath day, to keep it holy." Does not slavery nullify this law, and compel the slave to work on the Sabbath? Thus saith the Lord, "Obey thy father and thy mother." Can the slave children obey this command of God? Does not slavery command the children to obey the master, and him alone? Thus saith the Son of God, "What God hath joined together let no man put asunder." Does not slavery nullify this law, by breaking the sacred bands of wedlock, and separating the husband and the wife forever? Thus saith the Son of God, "Search the Scriptures." Does not slavery seal up the word of God, and make it criminal for the slave to read? In 1834, the legislature of South Carolina enacted a law prohibiting the instruction of any slave; and Mr. Lawrence, in a pamphlet which he published in 1835, to defend this law, declared, that "if the slaves were permitted to read the Bible, ninety of them would become infidels, like Voltaire, where ten would become christians." "Go ye into all the world, and preach the gospel unto every creature," saith the Son of God. Does slavery permit it? In 1835, a minister of the Episcopal Church, in the city of Charleston, appealed to the civil authority for permission to preach to the free population of an evening, but they would not permit him.

The objector may reply, that at the present moment there are four Methodist missionaries, and one Lutheran, laboring among the slave population of South Carolina. We answer, that this is true, and we are glad of it; but this fact does not overthrow our proposition, not falsify what we have stated, for although a few planters have permitted the gospel to be preached to their slaves, the majority of them prohibit it, and this permission is extraneous to slavery, and is not part of its creed nor code. Slavery never legislates for the religious instruction of slaves, but, on the contrary, legislates to perpetuate their ignorance; and there are laws this very moment in the statute-books of South Carolina and other states, prohibiting the religious instruction of slaves. But this is not all that slavery does to subvert the moral government of God. The slaves are sensible of the oppression exercised by their masters; and they see these masters on the Lord's day worshipping in his holy Sanctuary. They hear their masters professing christianity; they see these masters preaching the gospel; they hear these masters praying in their families, and they know that oppression and slavery are inconsistent with the christian religion; therefore they scoff at religion itself—mock their masters, and distrust both the goodness and justice of God. Yes, I have known them even to question his existence. I speak not of what others have told me, but of what *I have both seen and heard from the slaves themselves*. I have heard the mistress ring the bell for family prayer, and I have seen the servants immediately begin to sneer and laugh; and have heard them declare they would not go in to prayers; adding, if I go in she will only just read, "Servants obey your masters;" but she will not "break every yoke, and let the oppressed go free." I have seen colored men at the church door, *scoffing at the ministers*, while they were preaching, and saying, you had better go home, and set your slaves free. A few nights ago between 10 and 11 o'clock a runaway slave came to the house where I live for safety and succor. I asked him if he was a christian; "no sir," said he, "white men treat us so bad in Mississippi that we can't be christians."

Sir, I taught school in Charleston five years. In 1834 the legislature of our state enacted a law to prohibit colored teachers. My school was filled with children and youth of the most promising talents; and when I looked upon them, and remembered that in a few more weeks this school shall be closed, and I be permitted no more to teach them, notwithstanding I had been a professor—seven years, I began to question the existence of the Almighty, and to say, if indeed there is a God, does he deal justly? Is he a just God? Is he a holy Being? If so, why does he permit a handful of dying men thus to oppress us? Why does he permit them to hinder me from teaching these children, when nature, reason and Revelation command me to teach them? Thus I began to question the Divine government, and to murmur at the administration of his providence. And could I do otherwise, while slavery's cruelties were pressing and grinding my soul in the dust, and robbing me and my people of those privileges which it was hugging to its breast, and giving thousands to perpetuate the blessing which it was tearing away from us? Sir, the very man who made the law alluded to, did that very year, and at that very session of the legislature, give 20,000 dollars to increase the property of South Carolina College.

In a word, slavery tramples the laws of the living God under its unhallowed feet—weakens and destroys the influence which those laws are calculated to exert over the mind of man; and constrains the oppressed to blaspheme the name of the Almighty. For I have often heard them sneeringly say, that *"The Almighty made Charleston on a Saturday night, when he was weary, and in a great hurry." O, Brethren of the Franckean Synod! Awake! AWAKE! To the battle, and hurl the hottest thunders of divine truth at the head of this cruel monster, until he shall fall to rise no more; and the groans of the enslaved are converted into the songs of the free!*

Appendix Eight

The Nature and Purpose of Black Humanism

This document was issued by African Americans for Humanism to outline the nature and purpose of Black Humanism. Excerpts from "An African American Humanist Declaration," published in *Free Inquiry* vol. 10, issue 2 (Spring 1990): 13–15. Reprinted with permission.

An African-American Humanist Declaration

Slavery and racism have taken their toll on the African-American community. It seems as though every possible solution to the problems that have resulted from these twin evils has been advocated or implemented on some level. But the problems have remained, and in some cases have worsened.

Many thinkers maintain that the history of African-Americans is unique. Unlike any other group, African-Americans were kidnapped from their homeland, enslaved, and brutally victimized in every way imaginable by a strict system of segregation. Only during the past three decades has it become popular for mainstream Americans to oppose racism. Segregation was "officially" practiced in the South on a large scale until the 1960s. Thus slavery and segregation have characterized most of the history of African-Americans. (It must also be noted that the enslavement and segregation of a minority by a majority differs greatly from the oppression of a majority by a minority.) Many other factors have been attributed to the unique condition of African-Americans.

Some have boldly stated that unless these factors are properly recognized and understood, the quest for freedom, justice, and equality will be in vain. As Lyndon B. Johnson said in 1965, "Freedom is not enough. You do not wipe away the scars of centuries by saying: Now you are free to go where you want, do as you desire."

But not everyone agrees with this analysis. Some maintain that opportunities for African-Americans have increased dramatically. They believe that the legacy of slavery and rigidly enforced segregation have been grossly exaggerated. They claim that many of the problems attributed to slavery did not arise until a hundred years after it was abolished, and that therefore slavery is irrelevant to today's problems. They believe that racism is a relic of the past or an insignificant factor in the problems plaguing the African-American community. They claim that liberal programs have been great failures, and further maintain that African-Americans could solve their problems if they would only modify their behavior and emulate the good habits of other ethnic groups.

Moderates, liberals, radicals, socialists, conservatives, anarchists, and others who cannot be categorized, have presented many conflicting ideas regarding the past, present, future, and even the identity of African-Americans. Never in the history of the United States has a people been plagued with so many problems and so much confusion.

Many strategies to end the confusion and solve the problems have been tried, with few positive results. But if more critical thought had gone into the planning of these strategies, they either would have been successful, or would never have been tried at all.

There are still many questions that seem almost to defy answers. How much does racism affect American society today? How limited or plentiful are the opportunities for African-Americans? What effects have the distortion, destruction, and suppression of African history had on African-Americans and on the way they are viewed and treated by the rest of society? How committed is white America to equality and the elimination of racism? If racism still exists and cannot be eradicated, is there anything African-Americans can do to solve their problems? Do African-Americans have an identity crisis, and must they pursue an identity other than "American"?

These questions are uncomfortable, and even frightening to some. But they must be answered. And they are by no means the only questions that must be answered. There are arguments from all points of view and from people of all backgrounds. But the best way to determine the proper course of action of society is through the free flow of humane ideas. If an argument or proposed solution is an error, the best way to detect the error is through the use of reason. But humanism will not live up to its full potential if most of its adherents will not open their minds and honestly pursue the truth. Everyone must be willing to reexamine their beliefs and reassess the arguments they have rejected.

And no matter how bleak the present or future looks, one must never despair of the human species. When one struggles for the betterment of humanity, there is glory even in the face of defeat.

Today the world needs a critical, rational, and humane approach to living. This is what humanism is all about.

African-Americans in general might not be familiar with the true humanist outlook—an outlook that is essential to the modern world. Because many scholars have viewed society and history from a biased Eurocentric viewpoint, the significance of African-Americans to the humanist tradition has not been widely known. Racism and racial insensitivity have affected the entire nation, humanists included. But a new initiative has been taken to broaden the humanistic world view by making humanism more attractive to African-Americans.

Humanism incorporates a number of important ethical principles, including:

- A commitment to the application of reason and science to the understanding of the universe and to the solving of human problems.
- A concern with securing justice and fairness in society, and with eliminating discrimination and intolerance.
- A belief in enjoying life here and now and in developing humanity's creative talents to their fullest.
- A belief in the cultivation of moral excellence.
- Skepticism toward untested claims to knowledge.
- Openness toward new ideas.
- A belief in optimism rather than pessimism, hope rather than despair, learning in the place of dogma, truth instead of ignorance, joy rather than guilt or sin, tolerance in the place of fear, love instead of hatred, compassion over selfishness, beauty instead of ugliness, and reason rather than blind faith or irrationality.

Historically, the churches have been the most influential institutions in the African-American community, and African-Americans have been ardent believers. Church leaders have professed to have the solutions to the social, political, and economic ills with which African-Americans must contend. But despite their claims—or perhaps because of them— problems continue to plague the African-American community. Great strides have been made during the past forty years, but many problems have worsened, and new ones have arisen. More attention must be given to the importance of critical thinking in the quest for freedom, justice, and equality for African-Americans.

The African-American community is confronted by moral dilemmas that free thought, reason, good conduct, and proper action can best help solve. Examples include:

1. *Unwanted pregnancy.* Many religious leaders stress abstinence and marital fidelity as panaceas for the social problems resulting from human sexuality. But most humanists believe that all rational and humane solutions must be discussed, including the use of contraceptives and abortion. Attention must also be given to education, family counseling, and self-esteem building.

2. *Alcohol and substance abuse.* Alcoholism and drug abuse are major problems in the African-American community. These problems are of pressing concern, and solutions may require urgent, thorough, and rational measures. African-Americans as a group have been unfairly maligned by the media and targeted by police and government in the War on Drugs. Yet many white drug dealers continue to grow rich and go virtually unmolested. Many controversial solutions have been proposed, including the decriminalization of certain drugs. Humanism can be influential in the search for solutions to these problems and others that may arise from them. Humanism stresses abstinence from dangerous drugs, and moderation in the consumption of alcohol. It promotes self-love, and realizes that abusive and self-destructive behaviors interfere with the pursuit of happiness. It acknowledges the need for Secular Organizations for Sobriety (SOS).

3. *Economic development.* Although many African-American religious institutions have made laudable efforts toward economic development, millions of African-Americans have been attracted to Bible passages that teach that the accumulation of wealth is immoral and a complete waste of time. By thinking freely and challenging long-held beliefs and traditions, African-Americans have always been at an economic disadvantage; many seek comfort in a possible reward in the afterlife. But fatalism is always dangerous, and "wait for the rapture" is questionable advice.

4. *Organ transplants.* The United States has an acute shortage of vital organs. Forty percent of the people awaiting organ transplants are African-Americans. But ironically and sadly, largely because of deep spiritual beliefs, African-Americans are the least likely to donate their organs. Openly discussing and challenging religious beliefs may convince more African-Americans to become voluntary organ donors, thereby helping potential organ recipients from all backgrounds. Further research could also be stimulated to help find out why so many African-Americans are in need

of organs. More attention must also be given to diseases—such as sickle-cell anemia—to which African-Americans are prone. Ways to improve health care and insurance should also be addressed.

5. *Self-reliance.* Too much emphasis has been placed on faith in charismatic African-American leaders, and not enough on individual responsibility, self-confidence, and freedom of thought. Through humanism, African-Americans can learn to have at least as much faith in themselves as they have in their leadership, because ultimately, individual choices become crucial factors in the shaping and modeling of one's life.

6. *Unity.* Humanism can teach African-Americans to unite around goals that are common to humanity. To unite mainly on religious grounds excludes some of the community's greatest minds and impedes progress.

The organizational aims of African-Americans for Humanism are to:

- Fight against racism in every form.
- Incorporate an Afrocentric outlook into a broader world perspective.
- Add depth and breadth to the study of history by acknowledging the great contributions made by people of African descent to the world, with the purpose of building self-esteem among African-Americans and helping to demonstrate the importance of all peoples to the development of world civilization.
- Develop eupraxophy, or "wisdom and good conduct through living" in the African-American community by using the scientific and rational methods of inquiry.
- Solve many of the problems that confront African-Americans through education and self-reliance, thereby affirming that autonomy and freedom of choice are basic human rights.
- Develop self-help groups and engage in any humane and rational activity designed to develop the African-American community.
- Emphasize the central importance of education at all levels, including humanistic moral education, developing a humanistic outlook, and providing the tools for the development of critical reason, self-improvement, and career training.

Never has a large, significant international humanist organization attracted great numbers of people of color. But this objective can be attained if we make a concerted effort to demonstrate how humanism is, has been, and can be relevant to the entire world community.

African-Americans for Humanism Advisory Board

Dave Allen, writer, Washington, DC

James Anders, Professor of Mathematics, Florida State University

Bonnie Bullough, Dean of Nursing, State University of New York at Buffalo

Vern Bullough, Distinguished Professor of History and Sociology, State University of New York College at Buffalo

Leonard Harris, Professor of Philosophy, Morgan State University, Baltimore

Norman Hill, Human Rights Activist, New York City

Ismael Jaffree, Attorney, Youngstown, Ohio

William Jones, Professor of Black Studies, Florida State University

Mike McBryde, Freelance Artist and Writer, Pittsburgh

Emmanuel Kofi Mensah, Andrews University, Lagos, Nigeria

James Moss, Psychiatrist, New York City

Verle Muhrer, Penn Valley Community College, Kansas City, Missouri

Hope N. Tawiah, Chairman, Rational Centre, Accra, Ghana

Charles U. Ufomadu, Bigard Memorial Seminary, Imo State, Nigeria

David M. Washington, Artist, Chicago

Fred Whitehead, Penn Valley Community College, Kansas City, Missouri

Kwasi Wiredu, Professor of Philosophy, University of South Florida

Selected Bibliography

I have made an effort to limit this bibliography to sources dealing explicitly with African American experience within the traditions discussed in this book. What follows is simply a sampling of available resources, limited to books and web sites.

Books

African American Denominations

Booth, William D. *The Progressive Story: New Baptist Roots.* Nashville: Townsend, 1981.

Campbell, James T. *Songs of Zion: The African Methodist Episcopal Church in the United States and South Africa.* New York: Oxford University Press, 1995.

Fitts, Leory. *A History of Black Baptists.* Nashville: Broadman, 1985.

Gregg, Howard D. *History of the African Methodist Episcopal Church: The Black Church in Action.* Nashville: AMEC Sunday School Union, 1980.

Jackson, Joseph H. *A Story of Christian Activism: The History of the National Baptist Convention, U.S.A., Inc.* Nashville: Townsend, 1980.

Lakey, Othal Hawthorne. *The Rise of "Colored Methodism": A Study of the Background and the Beginnings of the Christian Methodist Episcopal Church.* Dallas: Crescendo, 1972.

Montgomery, William E. *Under Their Own Vine and Fig Tree: The African American Church in the South, 1865–1900.* Baton Rouge: Louisiana State University Press, 1993.

Patterson, J. O., et al. *History and Formative Years of the Church of God in Christ with Excerpts from the Life and Work of Its Founder, Bishop C. H. Mason.* Memphis: Church of God in Christ Publishing House, 1969.

Phillips, Charles Henry. *The History of the Colored Methodist Episcopal Church in America.* New York: Arno Press, 1972.

Sanders, Cheryl J. *Saints in Exile: The Holiness-Pentecostal Experience in African American Religion and Culture.* New York: Oxford University Press, 1996.

Walker, Clarence E. *A Rock in a Weary Land: The African Methodist Episcopal Church during the Civil War and Reconstruction.* Baton Rouge: Louisiana State University Press, 1982.

Walls, William J. *The African Methodist Episcopal Zion Church: Reality of the Black Church.* Charlotte, NC: AME Zion Publishing House, 1974.

Washington, James. *Frustrated Fellowship: The Black Baptist Quest for Social Power.* Macon, GA: Mercer, 1986.

African Americans in Historically White Denominations

Balmer, Randall, and Lauren Winner. *Protestantism in America.* New York: Columbia University Press, 2002.

Cimino, Richard. *Lutherans Today: American Lutheran Identity in the Twenty-First Century.* Grand Rapids, MI: W. B. Eerdmans, 2003.

Davis, Cyprian. *The History of Black Catholics in the United States.* New York: Crossroads, 1991.

Lagerquist, L. DeAne. *The Lutherans.* Westport, CT: Greenwood Press, 1999.

McGreevy, John T. *Parish Boundaries: The Catholic Encounter with Race in the Twentieth-Century Urban North.* Chicago: University of Chicago Press, 1996.

Murray, Andrew E. *Presbyterians and the Negro: A History.* Philadelphia: Presbyterian Historical Society, 1966.

Shattuck, Gardiner H., Jr. *Episcopalians and Race: Civil War to Civil Rights.* Lexington: University Press of Kentucky, 2000.

Wilmore, Gayraud S. *Black and Presbyterian: The Heritage and the Hope.* Philadelphia: Geneva Press, 1983.

African American Humanism

Allen, Norm, Jr., ed. *Personal Paths to Humanism.* Amherst, NY: Prometheus Books, 2003.

Morrison-Reed, Mark D. *Black Pioneers in a White Denomination*, 3rd ed. Boston: Skinner House Books, 1994.

Pinn, Anthony B., ed. *By These Hands: A Documentary History of African American Humanism.* New York: New York University Press, 2001.

———. *African American Humanist Principles: Living and Thinking Like the Children of Nimrod.* New York: Palgrave/Macmillan, 2004.

African American Religious Experience

Andrews, William L., ed. *Sisters of the Spirit: Three Black Women's Autobiographies of the Nineteenth Century.* Bloomington: Indiana University Press, 1986.

Collier-Thomas, Bettye. *Daughters of Thunder: Black Women Preachers and Their Sermons, 1850–1979.* San Francisco: Jossey-Bass, 1998.

Higginbotham, Evelyn Brooks. *Righteous Discontent: The Women's Movement in the Black Baptist Church, 1880–1920*. Cambridge, MA: Harvard University Press, 1993.

Lincoln, C. Eric, and Lawrence Mamiya. *The Black Church in the African American Experience*. Durham, NC: Duke University Press, 1990.

Pinn, Anthony B. *The Black Church in the Post–Civil Rights Era*. Maryknoll, NY: Orbis Books, 2002.

Pitts, Walter F. *Old Ship of Zion: The Afro-Baptist Ritual in the African Diaspora*. New York: Oxford University Press, 1993.

Raboteau, Albert. *Slave Religion: The "Invisible Institution" in the Antebellum South*. New York: Oxford University Press, 1978.

Sernett, Milton C. *Bound for the Promised Land: African American Religion and the Great Migration*. Durham, NC: Duke University Press, 1997.

Townsend Gilkes, Cheryl. *If It Wasn't for the Women: Black Women's Experience and Womanist Culture in Church and Community*. Maryknoll, NY: Orbis, 2000.

Weisenfeld, Judith, and Richard Newman. *This Far By Faith: Readings in African-American Women's Religious Biography*. New York: Routledge, 1996.

Wilmore, Gayraud. *Black Religion and Black Radicalism*. Garden City, NY: Doubleday, 1972.

Black Spiritual Churches

Baer, Hans A. *The Black Spiritual Movement: A Religious Response to Racism*. Knoxville: University of Tennessee Press, 1984.

Berry, Jason. *The Spirit of Black Hawk*. Jackson: University Press of Mississippi, 1995.

Jacobs, Claude F., and Andrew J. Kaslow. *The Spiritual Churches of New Orleans: Origins, Beliefs, and Rituals of an African-American Religion*. Knoxville: University of Tennessee Press, 1991.

Buddhism

Prebish, Charles S., and Kenneth K. Tanaka, eds. *The Faces of Buddhism in America*. Berkeley: University of California Press, 1998.

Queen, Christopher S., ed. *Engaged Buddhism in the West*. Boston: Wisdom Publications, 2000.

Williams, Angel Kyodo. *Being Black: Zen and the Art of Living with Fearlessness and Grace*. New York: Penguin Compass, 2000.

Judaism

Brotz, Howard M. *The Black Jews of Harlem: Negro Nationalism and the Dilemmas of Negro Leadership*. New York: Schocken Books, 1970.

Chireau, Yvonne, and Nathaniel Deutsch, eds. *Black Zion: African American*

Religious Encounters with Judaism. New York: Oxford University Press, 2000.

Fauset, Arthur Huff. *Black Gods of the Metropolis: Negro Religious Cults of the Urban North.* Philadelphia: University of Pennsylvania Press, 2002.

Wynia, Elly M. *The Church of God and Saints of Christ: The Rise of Black Jews.* New York: Garland Publishing, 1994.

Nation of Islam

Clegg, Claude Andrew, III. *An Original Man: The Life and Times of Elijah Muhammad.* New York: St. Martin's Press, 1997.

Essien-Udom, E. U. *Black Nationalism: A Search for Identity in America.* Chicago: University of Chicago Press, 1962.

Farrakhan, Louis. *Torchlight for America.* Chicago: FCN Publishing Company, 1993.

Gardell, Mattias. *In the Name of Elijah Muhammad: Louis Farrakhan and the Nation of Islam.* Durham, NC: Duke University Press, 1996.

Lincoln, C. Eric. *The Black Muslims in America,* 3rd ed. Grand Rapids, MI: Wm. B. Eerdmans, 1994.

Muhammad, Elijah. *Message to the Black Man in America.* Philadelphia: Haim's Publications, 1965.

Tate, Sonsyrea. *Little X: Growing Up in the Nation of Islam.* San Francisco: HarperCollins, 1997.

White, Vibert L., Jr. *Inside the Nation of Islam: A Historical and Personal Testimony by a Black Muslim.* Gainesville: University Press of Florida, 2001.

Santería

Brandon, George. *Santeria from Africa to the New World: The Dead Sell Memories.* Bloomington: Indiana University Press, 1993.

Canizares, Raul. *Cuban Santeria.* New York: Destiny Books, 1999.

Curry, Mary Anthrell. *Making the Gods in New York: The Yoruba Religion in the African American Community.* Dissertation, City University of New York, 1991.

Gregory, Steven. *Santería in New York City: A Study in Cultural Resistance.* New York: Garland Publishing, 1999.

Mason, Michael Atwood. *Living Santería: Rituals and Experiences in an Afro-Cuban Religion.* Washington, DC: Smithsonian, 2002.

Murphy, Joseph M. *Santería: An African Religion in America.* Boston: Beacon Press, 1989.

Sunni Islam

Austin, Allan D. *African Muslims in Antebellum America: Transatlantic Stories and Spiritual Struggles.* New York: Routledge, 1997.

Dannin, Robert. *Black Pilgrimage to Islam.* New York: Oxford University Press, 2002.

McCloud, Aminah Beverly. *African American Islam.* New York: Routledge, 1995.

Turner, Richard. *Islam in the African-American Experience.* Bloomington: Indiana University Press, 1997.

Voodoo

Bodin, Ron. *Voodoo: Past and Present.* Louisiana Life Series. Lafayette, LA: Center for Louisiana Studies, University of Southwestern Louisiana, 1990.

Brown, Karen McCarthy. *Mama Lola: A Vodou Priestess in Brooklyn.* Berkeley: University of California Press, 1991.

Haskins, Jim. *Voodoo & Hoodoo: Their Tradition and Craft as Revealed by Actual Practitioners.* New York: Stein and Day, 1978.

Holloway, Joseph E., ed. *Africanisms in American Culture.* Bloomington: Indiana University Press, 1990.

Savannah Unit, Georgia Writers' Project, Works Project Administration. *Drums and Shadows: Survival Studies Among the Georgia Coastal Negroes.* Garden City, NY: Anchor Books, 1972.

Tallant, Robert. *Voodoo in New Orleans.* New York: Collier Books, 1946; Macmillan, 1971.

Web Sites

General African American Church Information

http://www.blackandchristian.com

Provides important information on black churches, including articles, as well as links to other sites. It is one of the more useful and comprehensive Internet resources.

http://www.cnbc.org

This is the site for the Congress of National Black Churches. This organization is a partnership between many of the African American denominations, and it provides information concerning community outreach programs undertaken.

http://divinity.library.vanderbilt.edu/kmsi/default.htm

This link will take readers to the Kelly Miller Smith Institute on black churches at Vanderbilt University. This institute sponsors conferences and research projects related to black churches.

http://www.gospelweb.org

This site is devoted to information concerning gospel music.

http://www.morehouse.edu/leadershipcenter/index.htm

This is the web site for the Leadership Center at Morehouse College. This center sponsors conferences and sociologically based research projects related to church growth and church social activism and political involvement.

African American Churches

http://www.amecnet.org

This is the official web site for the African Methodist Episcopal Church. It provides basic historical and organizational information. In addition, it provides information concerning recent events.

http://www.c-m-e.org

On its official site, the Christian Methodist Episcopal Church provides basic information related to its history and current activities.

http://www.cogic.org/main.htm

This is the official site for the Church of God in Christ. It provides general information concerning this denomination and provides links to related sites.

http://www.nationalbaptist.org

On the National Baptist Convention, USA, Inc., web site, readers will find general information concerning the church's history, development, activities, and beliefs.

http://www.nbcamerica.net

This is the official web site for the National Baptist Convention of America. It contains basic information concerning the work of this denomination as well as its history and beliefs.

http://www.pnbc.org

This is the site for the Progressive National Baptist Convention. It includes information concerning its programs, history, structure, and agenda.

http://www.theamezionchurch.org

On this web site, the official site for the African Methodist Episcopal Zion Church, general information concerning the activities, history, and structure of the church is available.

African Americans in Historical White Denominations

http://www.aala-online.org

This is the official web site for the African American Lutheran Association. It provides general information concerning the African American presence in the Lutheran Church as well as the organization's history and mission.

http://www.elca.org

This web site for the Evangelical Lutheran Church in America provides basic information concerning the history, beliefs, structure, and mission of this denomination.

http://www.episcopalchurch.org

This is the web site for the Episcopal Church discussed in this volume. It provides history, beliefs, and other pieces of general information concerning the denomination.

http://www.nbcongress.org

This is the official web site for the National Black Catholic Congress. It provides information concerning the work of this organization, and general information concerning the impact of African Americans on the Roman Catholic Church.

http://www.pcusa.org

This is the official web site for the Presbyterian Church (USA). It contains general information concerning the makeup of the church, its mission, history, and recent activities.

http://www.pcusa.org/ideas/0405wint/blackpresby.htm

This site provides information concerning African Americans in the Presbyterian Church as well as information for African Americans within this denomination.

http://ube.org

This is the site for the Union of Black Episcopalians. It provides information concerning its membership and history as well as news concerning African American Episcopalians.

http://www.vatican.va/phome_en.htm

This is the official web site for the Vatican and the Pope of the Roman Catholic Church. It provides general information concerning the Vatican (archives, library, museum).

African American Humanism

http://www.iheu.org

Often there is information related to African American humanism on this web site for the International Humanist and Ethical Union.

http://www.secularhumanism.org/aah/

This is the home page for African Americans for Humanism. It provides general information concerning this organization as well as information on the Council for Secular Humanism (its sponsoring organization).

http://www.uua.org

This official web site of the Unitarian Universalist Association often contains information related to its African American membership.

Black Spiritual Churches

http://www.fatherhurley.com
This site provides general information on Father Hurley and his teachings.

http://www.fatherhurley.com/uhsc/
This is the web site for the Universal Hagar's Spiritual Church. It contains basic information concerning the church's beliefs, history, and mission.

Buddhism

http://www.nichirenscoffeehouse.net/directory/Africa.html
This site contains information related to African American Buddhists, including information on the achievements of particular individuals.

http://www.proudblackbuddhist.org/
This is the African American Nichiren Shoshu Cultural Buddhist web site. It contains information related to this form of Buddhism and provides information concerning individuals who practice it.

http://www.sgi-usa.org
This is the web site for Soka Gakkai International-USA. Most African American Buddhists are affiliated with this organization. Also see: www.sgi.org.

Judaism

http://www.bethshalombz.org
This site provides information on the Beth Shalom B'nai Zaken Ethiopian Hebrew Congregation and its relationship with Rabbi Matthew.

http://www.churchofgod1896.org
This site provides information on the Church of God and Saints of Christ, including its history, beliefs, and activities.

http://www.kingdomofyah.com
This is the web site for the Hebrew Israelites. It contains information concerning their beliefs and history.

Nation of Islam

http://www.muhammadspeaks.com
This is the web site for the Nation's paper, *Muhammad Speaks*. Its contents include audio and visual presentations of speeches by Messenger Elijah Muhammad.

http://www.noi.org
This is the official web site for the Nation of Islam. It contains information concerning the Nation of Islam's history, teachings, and objectives.

Santería

http://www.church-of-the-lukumi.org
   This is the web site for the Church of the Lukumi Babalu Aye. It contains basic information on the tradition and about the history, structure, and membership of the church.

http://orisha.net/
   This site provides links to various sites addressing this religion.

http://www.oyez.org/oyez/resource/cas/793/
   This site contains information concerning the Supreme Court case *Church of Lukumi Babalu Aye v. Hialeah* over the issue of animal sacrifice. This case was briefly mentioned in the chapter on this tradition.

Sunni Islam

http://www.calltohumanity.org
   This organization, National Youth Adult Association, is concerned with the creation of community based on Islamic principles. It supports the work of Warith Deen Muhammad.

http://www.masnet.org/
   This site provides information concerning Islam in the United States. Some of its content relates to African American Muslims.

Voodoo

http://www.voodoospiritualtemple.org/
   This is the site for the Voodoo Spiritual Temple in New Orleans. The site offers information concerning the history and activities of the temple.

http://www.yorubapriestess.tripod.com/
   This web site provides information concerning Ava Kay Jones, a Voodoo priestess in New Orleans.

Index

About the Author

ANTHONY B. PINN is the Agnes Cullen Arnold Professor of Humanities and Professor of Religious Studies at Rice University. Pinn is the author/editor of fifteen books, including *Varieties of African American Religious Experience* (1998); *The Black Church in the Post–Civil Rights Era* (2002); and *Terror and Triumph: The Nature of Black Religion* (2003).

CPSIA information can be obtained
at www.ICGtesting.com
Printed in the USA
LVHW011532210719
624771LV00011B/152/P